THE EVOLVING
PHYSIOLOGY OF
GOVERNMENT

CANADIAN PUBLIC
ADMINISTRATION IN TRANSITION

GOVERNANCE SERIES

Governance is the process of effective coordination whereby an organization or a system guides itself when resources, power, and information are widely distributed. Studying governance means probing the pattern of rights and obligations that underpins organizations and social systems, understanding how they coordinate their parallel activities and maintain their coherence, exploring the sources of dysfunction, and suggesting ways to redesign organizations whose governance is in need of repair.

The series welcomes a range of contributions – from conceptual and theoretical reflections, ethnographic and case studies, and proceedings of conferences and symposia, to works of a very practical nature – that deal with problems or issues on the governance front. The series publishes works both in French and in English.

The Governance Series is part of the publications division of the Centre on Governance and of the Graduate School of Public and International Affairs at the University of Ottawa. This is the 21st volume published in the series. The Centre on Governance and the Graduate School of Public and International Affairs also publish a quarterly electronic journal, www.optimumonline.ca.

The published titles in the series are listed at the end of this book.

THE EVOLVING PHYSIOLOGY OF GOVERNMENT

CANADIAN PUBLIC ADMINISTRATION IN TRANSITION

edited by
O. P. Dwivedi,
Tim A. Mau,
and Byron Sheldrick

University of Ottawa Press

Ottawa

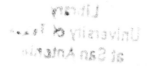

The University of Ottawa Press acknowledges with gratitude the support extended to its publishing list by Heritage Canada through its Book Publishing Industry Development Program, by the Canada Council for the Arts, by the Canadian Federation for the Humanities and Social Sciences through its Aid to Scholarly Publications Program, by the Social Sciences and Humanities Research Council, and by the University of Ottawa.

We also gratefully acknowledge the University of Guelph and the Centre on Governance at the University of Ottawa whose financial support has contributed to the publication of this book.

LIBRARY AND ARCHIVES CANADA CATALOGUING IN PUBLICATION

The evolving physiology of government : Canadian public administration in transition / edited by O.P. Dwivedi, Timothy Mau and Byron Sheldrick.

(Governance series, 1487-3052)
Essays originally presented at a conference honouring professor J.E. Hodgetts on the occasion of his ninetieth birthday, held in Guelph, Ont., in September 2007.
Includes bibliographical references and index.

ISBN 978-0-7766-0706-1

1. Public administration--Canada. 2. Canada--Politics and government. I. Dwivedi, O. P., 1937- II. Sheldrick, Byron M. III. Mau, Timothy, 1969- IV. Series: Governance series (Ottawa, Ont.)

JL75.E86 2009   351.71   C2009-900360-0

Published by the University of Ottawa Press, 2009
542 King Edward Avenue
Ottawa, Ontario K1N 6N5
www.press.uottawa.ca

uOttawa

TABLE OF CONTENTS

FOREWORD

John Meisel

Professor J. E. Hodgetts is the unwitting motivator and fairy godmother of the conference that brought together the papers in this volume. The latter is not exactly a Festschrift, for such a collection in his honour appeared in 1982 (Dwivedi, 1982). And how many such encomia can a modest man endure? So no one breathed the "F-word" when the authors of the papers gathered in these pages met in Guelph, Ontario, in September 2007 to honour Canada's doyen of the study of public administration. He was, nevertheless, the raison d'être of our being there and the inspiration and model of much of the work that nourished the minds of the attendees not only for the two days of the conference but for years and decades before. Whatever name one wishes to bestow on what, by common consent, turned out to have been a quite unusually successful intellectual exercise, it was an elaborate embroidery drawing on diverse strands of Ted Hodgetts's lifelong oeuvre.

The banquet on September 21, 2007, was not only the principal social event of the gathering, but it also provided a rare and precious opportunity to hear the guest of honour reflect on the history and nature of the academic discipline he so greatly nourished and embellished. The preface for this volume contains the notes that underlay his talk. It was my honour and pleasure to introduce Ted, and my notes for this occasion constitute, with some emendations and additions, the backbone of this foreword.

A graduate of the University of Toronto and Chicago, and a one-time denizen of Oxford, Ted taught inspiringly at Queen's, Toronto,

Memorial, and Dalhousie, and was the principal of Victoria College and then president of Victoria University in Toronto. Deeply involved with the Lambert and Glasgow Commissions and with a hand in Gomery II, he likewise contributed to numerous other inquiries in Canada and abroad on a wide range of subjects. The Institute of Public Administration of Canada (IPAC) awarded him its coveted Vanier medal and named a literary prize after him. Several universities have bestowed honorary degrees on him. It says something about the enduring value of his academic and educational contributions that the most recent LL.D. from the University of Toronto was awarded while Ted was enjoying his nineties.

He has made immense and critical contributions to the literature on public administration as an author and editor. Moreover, he has inspired and overseen outstanding work by generations of students, both graduate and undergraduate. Several of them, now stellar performers themselves, have written some of the papers that follow. But his contribution has been prodigious elsewhere as well, ranging from being the co-author of the legendary *Democratic Government and Politics*, to editing the Letters to the Editor of Eugene Forsey and in between clarifying such diverse trifles as education or man's toying with the atom. Countless government studies and reports have benefitted from his expertise and blue pencil. He received a Rhodes Scholarship and was inducted into the Order of Canada and the Royal Society of Canada.

I could go on, and on, and on like this listing Ted's achievements, Brownie points, and honours, but I prefer to identify some aspects of his life and oeuvre I find particularly significant and endearing. First, he has a most amazing way with words. Who else would have the wit to entitle a study of the early Ontario public service, *From Arm's Length to Hands On*? His prose is always crystal clear, colourful, luminous, and mercifully devoid of even a whiff of jargon. Yet, it is laced with allusions to unexpected intellectual and commonplace reference points, thereby imbuing his subject with uncommon vitality and vividness. Being a generous cuss, he shares his mastery of Her Majesty's tongue with others. As an editor he has acted as "midhusband" at the birth of innumerable manuscripts, improving not only their content and style but also their shape. He has been remarkably adroit in subduing immense masses of material into manageable dimensions, both in relation to his own explorations and to those of his students. By coincidence, the last time he and I returned to Kingston by VIA rail from one of O. P. Dwivedi's Guelph comparative public policy and administration conferences, he gave me a pointer respecting the writing of my memoirs. It relieved a paralyzing case of writer's block and sent me galloping into the past.

Only a very few of my acquaintances match his absolutely sure judgment. In matters both academic and personal, he has always resisted seduction by current fads and fashions. His mind unerringly homes in on the essence of things and he is never swayed by the marginal or ephemeral, no matter how trendy they may be. He brings to his life and work an unassailable integrity rooted in his complete personality.

The word "complete" is critical here. He is the complete man in the sense that he has, in his persona, synthesized his life experiences and insights. Although a giant among academics and governance practitioners, he is also a fully realized human being—family man, humane lover and respecter of nature, amateur of the arts and music, builder of model boats, informed observer of sports, warm friend. One of his talents that struck me early on in our friendship was his skill as a carpenter. Later I fell for his carvings of birds. All of these personal interests and talents have made him the fascinating, enjoyable, and stimulating human being he is. But this is not all. Since he is so complete a person, he has drawn quite naturally on all these features to inform his teaching, his writing, and his policy advice. This is one reason why all that he does is so engaging.

I cannot resist now repeating something I said about Ted a while back. This may seem self-indulgent, but who knows better than I how I read him? I had the pleasure and honour of including his magisterial, *The Canadian Public Service 1867–1970*, characteristically subtitled, *A Physiology of Government*, in a series of books I edited for the Social Science Research Council. In the foreword, I characterized Ted's achievement in his book as follows: "Professor Hodgetts' well-known skill in synthesizing and organizing complex data, his vigorous style, and his unerring eye for the colourful phrase and telling illustration have produced a compelling, lively, encyclopaedic, yet easily followed, study of the public service set in the context of Canada's most persistent problems" (Meisel, 1973: viii). These words, written thirty-five years ago, apply not only to one book but equally well to the whole corpus of his work on Canadian public administration.

Yet, he has done even more. In what some fancy thinkers might later have referred to as a paradigm shift, he has grafted a dimension onto his chosen specialty that almost no one saw or bothered with before. While many so-called social scientists, organization theorists, management consultants, and even bureaucrats have fallen into the trap of steering public administration into a soulless, desiccated drudgery, he has been an indefatigable champion of its quintessential human character. And he has maintained that its study can elevate not only the polity but also the scholar.

Here is the piece of timeless advice that he and David Corbett offered their readers over fifty years ago in the foreword to their *Canadian Public Administration: A Book of Readings*: "We hope that by studying public administration the student will develop his capacity for original thought about society. At its best, this subject should be a means of liberal education, leading to knowledge of oneself and others, broadening the sympathies and freeing the mind from prejudices engendered by familiar social circumstances" (Hodgetts and Corbett, 1960).

It is a privilege to celebrate so distinguished and so humane a scholar and practitioner at this conference. And it is not only a privilege but also a pleasure and a rare opportunity to benefit from his reflections—dare I say, *mature* reflections—on his art and craft.

Editors' Note: J. E. Hodgetts's reflections follow next as the preface to this volume.

REFERENCES

Dwivedi, O. P. (1982). *The Administrative State in Canada: Essays in Honour of J. E. Hodgetts*. Toronto: University of Toronto Press.

Hodgetts, J. E., and D. Corbett. (1960). *Canadian Public Administration: A Book of Readings*. Toronto: MacMillan.

Meisel, J. (1973). Foreword to *The Canadian Public Service: A Physiology of Government, 1867–1970*, by J. E. Hodgetts. Toronto: University of Toronto Press.

PREFACE
FROM THERE TO HERE

Colleagues, associates, and friends: Let me begin by offering both commiserations and congratulations to the University of Guelph and to its Department of Political Science for their inability to resist the blandishments of that force of nature otherwise known as Professor O. P. Dwivedi. As usual, he has succeeded in organizing others to his command and, as the chief beneficiary of his initiatives, I must express my appreciation to him and to those he has rallied to his cause for arranging and hosting this splendid conference in my honour. I am much moved to see so many old friends, colleagues, and former students and do appreciate the effort all of you have made to be present and to participate in these proceedings.

As a newly minted nonagenarian, you should not be surprised to find that my preference is to ruminate on selective certitudes of my past association with the subject of this conference rather than engage in a feisty projection into its uncertain future—a task that I am happy to see has already enlisted the intellectual attention of the participants in this seminar.

Some of you know that in recent years I have been desultorily engaged in the pursuit of what Marshall McLuhan called "probes," whereby following a process of free association, I have been exploring various facets of my life. Iain Gow, who is in the habit of sending tasty quotations to me, may perhaps have sensed my intentions for this evening: In a recent submission quoting Paul Theroux he warns that "fogeydom is the last bastion of the bore and reminiscence is its anthem." Despite this subtle hint, I intend to draw this evening on a probe entitled "How Did I Get from There to Here?" It begins with a confession: Noting that it has famously been said that the unexamined life is not worth living, I admit that I should long ago have committed suicide, in that self-examination has not been an exercise I have pursued with much vigor, preferring a more fatalistic stand. Indulge me, therefore, as I seek for a few minutes to rectify my sins of omission.

I'm a small-town boy, brought up in the shadow of a charismatic older brother who influenced my choices in so many ways, including my decision to embark on the honours course in the political economy department at the University of Toronto rather than pursue what I thought was a natural bent for biological sciences. Seventy years ago the departmental organization and the offerings of its faculty were typical of what existed elsewhere in this particular field of academe. Specialization, with its infinite regressions, grinding exceeding small, had not yet arrived. The economist lay down with the political scientist, indeed one often doubled for the other. Schools of business had not routed commerce and finance and, in turn, its faculty consorted happily with those in political economy. History was so much a part of the curriculum that with the resurrection of the Political Science Association in 1935, it happily shared the annual joint session where the respective presidents gave their addresses. Nor was it deemed odd that economists dominated the affairs of a political science association. So slender were the resources that the department could not meet all the requirements for a degree without collaboration from history and philosophy, and the "pass subjects" of English, French, and "religious studies" provided by the colleges.

Nor was there much choice from the main menu: Both in politics and economics the stress was on theory and the history of thought, institutions coming in a poor third and getting their prime exponent in 1937 with the arrival of MacGregor Dawson, when I was halfway through my undergraduate course. His seminal textbook on Canadian government did not arrive until ten years later, close on the heels of Alex Corry's comparative study, *Democratic Government and Politics*, both timed to coincide with my first ventures in teaching. The pickings, in short, were exceedingly slim: Stephen Leacock's *Elements of Political Science*; Dawson's doctoral dissertation for the London School of Economic's Graham Wallis, *The Principle of Official Independence*, and his collection of readings; R. A. Mackay's *Unreformed Senate of Canada*; a few constitutional documents; and no backlog of articles from journals to draw on because most of them had yet to be born.

Equally slim was the number of practitioners in the field. At the outset of the 1950s, Dawson's survey of the teachers in the field revealed a sturdy band of about a dozen and a half spread throughout the English-speaking universities, and many of these doubled in history, economics, or sociology. (I pause to note here the total silence about the situation in the Province of Quebec, a reflection of the two solitudes that we all then took for granted. I am, of course, the poorer for my upbringing as an unreconstructed monophone and envy my younger colleagues' efforts to bridge the gap!) I count myself a member of the next generation, succeeding Alexander Brady, MacGregor Dawson, and Brough Macpherson at Toronto; R. A. Mackay at Dalhousie; Stephen Leacock and Eugene Forsey at McGill; Norman McLeod Rogers and Alexander Corry at Queen's; and Henry Angus at UBC, where he presided over a department of economics, political science, and sociology.

The succeeding generation of which I consider myself a part was not much larger in number and included in descending order of age, Jim Aicheson, Murray Beck, Henry Mayo, Jim Mallory, myself, Frank MacKinnon, Murray Donnelly, and the youngest and the first to die, Norman Ward. All but one of those, Henry Mayo, had received either their M.A.s or Ph.D.s from Toronto, influenced by that small staff with the limited menu I have identified. All of you present this evening are to be located in successor generations, many of you having been exposed either to the persona or writings of this modest band. (I pause once again to note the virtual total absence of women in the generation of teachers to which I belonged, an absence that has begun to be rectified only in recent years.)

What did I carry away from this experience at Toronto as I moved on to the University of Chicago for doctoral work? A great respect for tracing the statutory or constitutional base for an institution (though it took me a long time to forget the constant tirades against the decentralizing decisions of the absentee Judicial Committee of the Privy Council); a concomitant respect for the history of the evolution of institutions and their response to their environments; and, from my somewhat relaxed M.A. program, a love of working independently in the stacks on original documents and crumbling newspapers. Alexander Brady, my thesis supervisor, taught me respect for the written word that, later as an editor, I sought to imbue in others—although I know we are all suffering now from the easy come and go of the word processor.

Political science doctoral programs in the 1940s were in their infancy at Canadian universities. Apart from the Rhodes Scholarships at Oxford and a couple of Commonwealth Fellowships, there were no Canada Council or Social Science Research Council fellowships and no provincial graduate support, a situation forcing reliance on graduate schools in the United States. At Chicago, for example, five of the six fellowships available in economics and political science were held by Canadians, and I am sure my successful application was attributable to Harold Innis, himself a distinguished doctoral student.

Chicago introduced me to several new fields that I had not encountered at Toronto and, so far as I recall, were not elsewhere available in Canada. Harold Gosnell was introducing his electoral studies program that was to blossom into psephology and was soon to engage the early interest of my colleague John Meisel in Canada. Closely related was the pioneer work of Harold Lasswell and Nathan Leites in the field of the psychology of politics, also to be picked up by academics like Paul Fox in their studies of political leadership. Quincy Wright led me into international law and diplomacy, a subject that during my undergraduate time at Toronto was totally absent—a universal deficiency that I believe a Committee of the House of Commons had commented on in the late 1920s. Things had not changed when I returned as a lecturer to Toronto. When Harold Innis called upon me to teach a course listed as local government and I responded by offering to teach a course on international affairs, *à la* Quincy Wright, Innis gave his blessing provided we left the title of the course unchanged; otherwise, Senate approval would have been required. You may recall this was the great period when the United Nations was created and had there been any encouragement from the powers that be, I am certain I would have pioneered in a field that is now so admirably covered by all universities.

In the event, while interested and even somewhat bemused by these other offerings at Chicago, it was the subject of public administration that caught and retained my interest and became the field in which my dissertation was written. Leonard White, the chairman of the department, introduced me to the subject, which seemed to me to have originated entirely in America, although side references to the United Kingdom and to France and Germany tended to modify that first impression and induced me, when I came to teach the subject, to use comparative material. With the help of graduate students, White was producing histories of the US Civil Service to add to his pioneering textbook on public administration.

As a former chairman of the Civil Service Commission, White exemplified a pattern of combining practical service with academe that was new to me. I had come from a department headed by Innis, who deliberately eschewed the "contamination" from such associations (though even he succumbed to taking on a royal commission, and war work temporarily drew into government service many of his colleagues). Even so, the practice in the United States seemed to be much more part of the landscape, particularly in Chicago, where Public Administration Clearing House was just down the street from the university and filled with academics on secondment. Charles Merriam, a previous head of the department, was another example of the close ties between the doers and the thinkers. He had been a leading member of President Roosevelt's Committee on Administrative Management, whose Report of 1936 was, along with White's textbook, my introduction to public administration. To this day, I do not believe governments in Canada have taken the same advantage from academe—the closest they came in our field of public administration was the recent commissioning of studies by the Gomery Commission, mostly from academics—a far cry, say, from the Glassco Commission, with its reliance on study teams largely taken from the emerging field of management consultants.

In retrospect, I suppose my own "in-and-out involvement" with government as an academic was modelled on this early perception of how to bring what was termed "ivory power" to the service of public power. At a very early stage I did indeed face a choice: a lectureship at Toronto versus an entry into the public service to engage in organization and methods studies. I have never regretted the choice I made and always welcomed the role of participant-observer that frequently presented itself to me. In later life, as weary senior officials would quiz me on the prospects of finding "safe haven" in academe, I realized I had made the right choice. Moreover, as my flock of students from public administration found their way into the senior ranks of the public service, I found I had a ready-made army of informants to conduct free research for me. I think one of the warmest endorsements I ever received as a lecturer in public administration was the reaction I received from former students reporting their surprise that what they had learned from the course was not far off "real life" in the public service.

You can see now what sidelines this free-association probe can pursue, but let me return to Chicago. White's interest in administrative history appealed to me and suited my natural leaning to tracing historical roots. It was thus that I was induced to undertake a history of the unification of the British Civil Service, a magnum opus I carried like an albatross back with me to Toronto three years later as I took up a teaching position there. Its revision and refinement were undertaken in the context of breaking in my teaching eye teeth—an experience I suspect shared by many here. In my case it was considerably exacerbated by the fact that two books on the same subject came out before I had completed my thesis, one of them carrying an introduction by my supervisor Leonard White! I was able to forgive him because, as with Brady, White had a fine eye for literary finesse and managed to mute the rotundity of the somewhat Churchillian style I had contracted by being so absorbed in the nineteenth-century works of people like John Stuart Mill and T. B. Macaulay. Along with the good old King James Version, writers such as these have left a lasting impression on my own style.

Edging into the new field of public administration via the historical route has greatly influenced my subsequent research and writing in this field, beginning with an administrative history of the United Canadas in which I found something new to say about the coming of responsible government. Other histories followed, and when, during the meetings of the Institute of Public Administration in the founding city of Charlottetown in 1964, I proposed the creation of a "confederation series," the twenty-five volumes subsequently appearing under my editorship were essentially crafted as administrative histories. Very "old fashioned," I know, but I look with great pride on that row of volumes that I believe will provide the essential institutional memories that are being neglected by the "how-to" variety of publications so popular with business schools.

Chicago also introduced me to two side elements that were essential components of the "public administration" I was to research and teach. One of these came from Herman Pritchett's course on the public corporation, a natural outgrowth from his work with the recently created Tennessee Valley Authority. The paper I did for him on the Canadian Broadcasting Corporation provided the basis for my very first lecture to the class. Subsequently, when I was called upon to give a "sample lecture" to a Saturday morning class while preaching for a job at Queen's, I dusted off my piece on the CBC. It also became the basis for my first presentation to an annual meeting of the Canadian Political Science Association a little later on.

During a hot summer in 1949 I laboured in Ottawa collecting for the first time all known examples of Canadian Crown corporations. The purpose of the task I was told, typically much later, was to provide the appendix to the Financial Administration Act, where special regimes were established for various categories of these nondepartmental forms. The analysis and sortation of these "structural heretics" continued to engage me for many years, involving me in special sessions at two of the triennial conventions of the International Political Science Association, the one in Rome being especially notable for my inability to deliver my paper because an Italian professor wanted to showcase his own students. My offering subsequently appeared in Spanish and Russian. It was at that same session that I had the pleasure of attending a second-rate performance of *La Bohème* with the renowned student of public administration, James Fesler, who instructed me in the fine art of shouting "*bis, bis*" to encourage the portly diva to die and die yet again. I consider my most important contribution as a member of the Lambert Commission (1976–1979) is the section where we tackled the matter of establishing accountability regimes for the welter of nondepartmental entities.

Apart from introducing me to the related side subject of public corporations, Chicago also brought to my attention the subject of administrative law and administrative discretion. While this area loomed large in the arena of American public administration, I was originally inclined to think it had no application in Canada, so little reference to it had appeared in my undergraduate courses. Indeed, even the University of Toronto law school, from what I recall, offered no courses in the subject until after World War II, when Professor Al Abel brought the subject to Canada from the United States, where he had been yet another of those academics who had become a "doer" in one of the great regulatory agencies, the Office of Price Administration. In this he was abetted by people like my chief, Alexander Corry, whose background training was in law and who was offering a course in public administration carrying that emphasis when I arrived at Queen's to take over that course among others.

The state as regulator and entrepreneur continued to be a mainstay of my offerings in public administration over the years, raising as it did the issue of the discretionary authority of public servants to interpret the law and the meaning of "the public interest." I suppose it was this interest in administrative law that induced me to explore the term "accountability" when it arrived on the scene in the late 1970s, the special statutory role assigned to deputy ministers. I am certain that tomorrow's sessions will present the latest developments arising out of this long-held interest of mine and reference to it seems a most appropriate point at which to call these reminiscences to a halt.

One of the great pleasures of having been associated with the teaching life is that, good health prevailing, one need never be out of the loop, particularly with such encouragement as your personal contacts and occasions such as this provide. It has been a long and satisfactory run, and I am duly grateful to all of you for making my cup runneth over this evening.

J. E. Hodgetts

These reflections were rendered as a dinner speech on September 21, 2007, at the University of Guelph as part of the public administration conference organized in his honour.

ACKNOWLEDGMENTS

This book would not have been possible without the help of our colleagues who joined in this enterprise so willingly when the idea of a conference on the evolution of Canadian public administration was first proposed. They all gave selflessly of their time to present their work at a conference held at the University of Guelph in September 2007 and were extremely cooperative in revising their essays in a timely fashion once we had a commitment to publish this book. We would like to express our heartfelt gratitude to each and every one of Ted Hodgetts's friends and former students who helped make this initiative such a huge success. A special note of thanks must be extended to John Meisel, a friend and colleague of Ted Hodgetts for over fifty years, who was kind enough to write the preface for this tome—and indeed to Ted himself for agreeing to lend his good name to our initiative! His willingness to allow the organization of a conference in his honour provided us with instant credibility and a level of scholarly engagement that is rarely seen.

In addition to the contributors to this edited volume, we would like to acknowledge the intellectual contributions of two colleagues who attended the conference but whose work is not represented here in this anthology. The first is Alan Cairns, who set the context by opening up the conference with an examination of Canadian government and politics—then and now—and the other is Jacques Bourgault, who discussed the global challenges confronting Canadian public administration and governance. Furthermore, several our colleagues supported the venture by chairing sessions and acting as discussants for the various papers: Barbara Carroll, Steve Dupre, John Meisel, Richard W. Phidd, Troy Riddell, Donald Savoie, David Siegel, Julie Simmons, Ronald Watts, and Vince Wilson.

As is evident from the list of contributors to this volume and the chairs and discussants noted above, the conference attracted a veritable who's who of Canadian political scientists and scholars of public administration and public policy. However, there were a number of other colleagues from across the country, including Agar Adamson, Ivo Krupka, and Lloyd Stanford, as well as the Department of Political Science at the University of Guelph (Henry Wiseman, Judith McKenzie, Ken Woodside, Pat Kyba, Craig Johnson, Brian Woodrow, William Christian, Dennis Baker, Nanita Mohan, and Radha Persaud), who graciously made the effort to participate in this event. The conference was infinitely richer as a result of their involvement; for that we are grateful.

Furthermore, we are most appreciative of the efforts of Kirsten Craven for her excellent copy-editing of our manuscript; her thoughtful editorial suggestions brought additional tightness and clarity to the prose in the various contributions in this book, resulting in a vastly improved end product. We are particularly indebted to Professor Gilles Paquet, chair of the governing body at the University of Ottawa Press, who endorsed the idea of this book project from the outset. His immediate and enthusiastic commitment to publishing these essays represents yet another example of the widespread affection and respect concomitant with the Hodgetts name.

Finally, we would be remiss if we did not acknowledge the support of Maureen Mancuso, provost and vice-president academic at the University of Guelph, and Alun Joseph, dean of the College of Social and Applied Human Sciences and the Department of Political Science. Without the generous financial assistance provided by the provost, college, and department, this conference (which served as the progenitor for this book) simply would not have been possible. Likewise, we are indebted to Cathie Hosker, Gerie McCauley, and Shelagh Daly for the administrative support they provided for this endeavour. Their hard work and dedication to the cause ensured that we were able to provide a fitting and most memorable tribute to Ted Hodgetts, a towering icon of Canadian public administration.

O. P. Dwivedi, Tim A. Mau, and Byron Sheldrick
University of Guelph, Guelph, Ontario
July 2008

CANADIAN PUBLIC ADMINISTRATION IN TRANSITION

An Introduction

*O. P. Dwivedi, Tim A. Mau,
and Byron Sheldrick*

—

Forty years ago McGregor Dawson, in tones that rocked the rabbit warrens that posed for offices in the old McMaster Building at the University of Toronto, said to a neophyte lecturer: "Hodgetts, I envy you; you are at the threshold of the coming discipline of public administration—the academic world is your oyster". Now, lumbered with the label "father of the academic study of public administration in Canada", you will appreciate the reason for the pleasure I take in seeing so many of my presumptive offspring present here tonight. And, that there are so many of you able to come together in a workshop like this reinforces my recollection of the loneliness of the enterprise just a few short years ago. (Hodgetts, 1984: 115)

PUBLIC ADMINISTRATION IN CANADA: A MAPPING EXPEDITION

How things have changed over the past sixty years! While it may have been a lonely enterprise to study Canadian public administration in the early post-war period, by the 1980s, when Hodgetts made this observation—and certainly in the two decades that have followed—there has been a small but robust community of scholars, some of whom have even developed a global reputation for their intellectual contributions, who have researched and written about a wide range issues and topics germane to Canadian public administration.

The first Canadian scholar who embarked on a scholarly study of the issue of responsibility in government and administration was

McGregor Dawson (1922), whose research was originally produced as a doctoral thesis for the London School of Economics and Political Science. This was followed by his other seminal work, *The Civil Service of Canada* (1929). However, it was not until the end of World War II when he published a third book, *The Government of Canada* (Dawson, 1970 [1947]), that a serious study of the Canadian government and its institutions became available for students in Canadian universities. Dawson admitted while writing the preface to his third book that "it is a disturbing fact that . . . no comprehensive book on the government of Canada had ever been written" (1970 [1947]: v).

Coincidently, a year earlier, in 1946, J. E. Hodgetts went from the University of Toronto to Queen's University to teach the first course on public administration for the returning war veterans. The scholarly work on administration started by Dawson was then continued on by Hodgetts (1955) when he published his book *Pioneer Public Service: An Administrative History of the United Canadas, 1841–1867.* But the administrative history of the federal government remained incomplete until Hodgetts (1973) published another epic, *The Canadian Public Service: A Physiology of Government 1867–1970,* which completed the story from 1841 to 1970. Complementing this work on the federal public service was the book *Provincial Governments as Employers: A Survey of Public Personnel Administration in Canada's Provinces,* which examined administrative systems prevailing at the provincial level (Hodgetts and Dwivedi, 1974). As a result of these publications, basic information about the federal and provincial civil services was finally made available to researchers and practitioners of public administration.

The Canadian system of merit appointments in the public service, unlike its counterparts in the United Kingdom and United States, was slower to evolve. Although the Act of Parliament that established the federal public service in 1868 included a provision to create a board of examiners to consider and appoint the nominees of ministers, this regulation was ignored by successive governments. The patronage system spread rapidly throughout the public service, and it was not until the end of the World War I that the entire Canadian federal public service was brought under the merit system. For a long time patronage remained one of the worst things that could exist in the government; for Dawson (1929: 252), patronage was the dominant fact of life in the Canadian public service.

In 1918 sweeping administrative reforms patterned after the American experience were implemented. A new Civil Service Act placed the entire civil service under the Civil Service Commission, stripping the Treasury Board and departments of any formal power to control the selection, organization, remuneration, grading, or career development of their staff members. Whereas Canada had, until 1918, followed the British tradition of broad classifications based on rank rather than on task, the reinforced Civil Service Commission of 1918 found in the American system a way to overcome patronage. When the qualifications for a job are very precisely defined, it is much easier to determine which candidate is best qualified. It was the beginning of an emerging trend, because the system was eagerly adopted by various Canadian provinces and later by many municipalities. In one stroke, the human resources management system of the Canadian government adopted an emerging American style.

However, the merit system had to be changed to accommodate the soldiers who returned from Europe at the conclusion of World War I, because they demanded recognition of their sacrifice. The government's fear (or gratitude) sparked it into offering special privileges to the veterans. Thus, a special provision was introduced into the Civil Service Act to provide "absolute preference" to war veterans.[1] Hodgetts et al. (1972: 470) reported that from 1945 to 1954, 66 percent of men appointed in the Canadian civil service were veterans. In terms of the overall number of veterans in the public service, however, the figure was more modest. Reporting in the early 1960s, the Royal Commission on Government Organization (Canada, 1962: 346) found that about 40 percent of the entire federal public service consisted of war veterans.

The 1960s and 1970s were marked with some tinkering in the management of human resources, including the introduction of collective bargaining, language training, and the enhanced integration of French-speaking Canadians into the public service. Representativeness, which emerged as a traditional public service value in response to the historic discrimination against Francophone Canadians, eventually expanded to address other disadvantaged groups, such as women, Aboriginal peoples, visible minorities, and the disabled.

Perhaps the most significant reform to the merit system in Canada materialized with the adoption of the Public Service Modernization Act in 2003. With the introduction of this legislation, the merit principle was now defined in law. Significantly, since then, those selected in recruitment competitions no longer have to be the "best" candidate, but rather the preferred hire needs only to meet the essential qualifications that have been identified for the position in question. This change has afforded the deputy minister greater flexibility when making hiring decisions, allowing for other qualifications that may be deemed advantageous in fulfilling the requirements of the job to be considered. This was but one of many reforms that swept the country beginning in the 1980s with the widespread adoption of the new public management (NPM) paradigm. However, prior to reflecting on the changes engendered by the advent of NPM, a brief mention about the nature of the Canadian administrative culture should be made.

THE CULTURE OF CANADIAN PUBLIC ADMINISTRATION

Four civilizations have left their mark on Canada: the French and English civilizations, with their lasting influence on Canadian institutions and culture, followed by the hegemonic American civilization, and the ancient yet continuing culture of the Indigenous people. In addition, during the past few decades, immigrants from Asia, Eastern Europe, Africa, and Latin America and West Indies have enriched the composite culture of Canada. Thus, the culture of Canada can be seen as something that is not only transcendent or sacred but also as a set of sustainable development strategies to help citizens lead their lives with freedom and dignity—it is here where the administrative techniques adapted to deliver public services come into play. In addition, there are also two kinds of sources of Canadian administrative culture: the external (the physical, social, economic, and political environment, as well as foreign influences) and internal workplace sources, which influence the expected behaviour of public servants in the form of controls exercised through various rules and regulations, codes of conduct, and related constraints. These sources penetrate the administration via their contacts with the political, economic, and social systems, and because public servants do not leave their perceptions and their values at the door when they enter their offices to work. Briefly, then, what has been the influence of these sources on the nature and functioning of public administration in Canada?

Writing about the pan-Canadian culture and nationality, Underhill (1966: xvii) stated, "It was to be that of a composite, heterogeneous, plural society, transcending differences of ethnic origin and religion among its citizens. It was also to be an open society, recruiting its population through large-scale immigration." This concept of a nation possessing a composite and heterogeneous culture, which draws upon its different cultural and spiritual traditions, has been further strengthened as Canada matured into a more multicultural and multireligious society in the 1970s and beyond. As such, the cultural inheritance of Canada at the beginning of the twenty-first century includes a wealth of tangible and intangible cultural resources emanating not only from the cultural traditions and beliefs of its "two founding nations" but also from its Indigenous people, as well as from those groups such as Ukrainians, Germans, and the later groups of people coming to live in Canada from West Indies, Latin America, Asia, Africa, and the Middle East. Each cultural group has contributed its distinctive cultural resources.

It should be noted that the cultural heritage of Canada is found not only in tangible assets in museums, archaeological sites, and so on but also includes living practices such as myths, spiritual values, beliefs and behaviours, and most importantly, visions of Canada. Nonphysical aspects are as important a part of our collective cultural heritage as are the historic monuments and works of art and craft. Thus, the resources of cultural heritage consist of its history, languages, values and mores, spiritual traditions, political and social institutions, and the like. Of course, there is no doubt that within these political and social institutions, the Canadian public administration has created its own culture of administration as summed up by Hodgetts (1982: 472) in the following way: "Canada's administrative culture consists of the British heritage of institutions and conventions mingled with American ideas and practices, with adaptations of both to meet indigenous features of a federal state, overlaid by regional and cultural factors." Public administration, as a handmaiden of the governing process, then connects people with each other, as well as with their physical and socio-economic world. In addition, the field strengthens the core Canadian values as a cornerstone of our democratic pluralism. This belief is based on such major ideals as fundamental freedoms for all, equality of all, and universal participation in the governing process. That process requires those who govern to have a vision to protect and enhance democratic ideals—an essential purpose of serving the public by working within the parameters of those values that were identified by the federal Task Force on Public Service Values and Ethics: (1) democratic values: helping ministers, under the law, to serve the public interest; (2) professional values: serving Canadians with competence, efficiency, impartiality, and nonpartisanship; (3) ethical values: acting at all times in such a way as to hold the public trust; and (4) people values: demonstrating respect, fairness, and courtesy in their dealings with both citizens and fellow employees (Canada, Task Force on Public Service Values and Ethics, 2000). These values, in turn, have shaped the administrative culture in Canada. Together, this administrative culture and liberal democratic pluralism have become the foundations of governance in Canada (Dwivedi and Gow, 1999).

NPM, Governance, and Beyond: The Journey from the Mid-1980s Onward

The advent of the NPM movement is typically traced back to the late 1970s, when Prime Minister Margaret Thatcher pursued an administrative reform agenda in the United Kingdom that included privatization, deregulation, and a reconceptualization of the appropriate role of the state in the economy and society. Driven by the globalization agenda, declining levels of public trust in the government and bureaucracy, and financial crisis, a number of Western countries, including New Zealand, Australia, and Canada, gradually followed suit with the NPM agenda, albeit to varying degrees. Yet, clearly there has been a paradigm shift. There has been a palpable move away from the traditional bureaucratic model, firmly rooted in hierarchy and control through rules and regulations, to the so-called post-bureaucratic organization or paradigm (Kernaghan, Marson, and Borins, 2000; Barzelay, 1992: 115–133). As Aucoin (1995: 3) noted, "The new public management that emerged during the 1980s in the four Westminster systems of Australia, Canada, New Zealand and the United Kingdom clearly has entailed the acceptance of new paradigms for the administration of public affairs."

Some scholars have questioned the relevance and importance of NPM, dismissing it as merely the latest public administration fad, but it has been around for far too long and has had far too great an impact on the design and organization of government for that to be the case. Although Pollitt (2003: 26) thinks that it may be a bit "over-the-top" to call NPM a revolution, the reality is that while its heartland may be Australasia, North America, and the United Kingdom, very few countries have been completely immune from NPM reform initiatives. Privatization, deregulation, contracting out, public-private partnerships, an emphasis on results and performance, and a focus on service quality and consumer orientation are administrative reform buzzwords for developed and developing nations alike. Canada has certainly been no exception in that regard, and much has been written about public administration reforms in this country that have been inspired by the tenets of NPM.

Although it is difficult to provide a precise definition for NPM because it encompasses a broad spectrum of administrative reforms that have been adopted more or less vigorously in a variety of political jurisdictions, there have nonetheless been a number of discernable elements that can be highlighted. NPM began with the following major characteristics: (1) accent on results, both in planning and in evaluation of programs and people; (2) service to the public, with a special concern for quality, citizen as client; (3) delegation of authority as close as possible to the level of action, and empowerment of employees; (4) greater attention to cost through comprehensive auditing, contracting out, and introduction of competition; and (5) private sector techniques for motivating employees, such as merit pay, mission statements, and quality circles (Dwivedi and Gow, 1999; Charih and Rouillard, 1997; Osborne and Gaebler, 1992).

In addition, NPM has also introduced notions like corporate management, corporate culture, and bottom-line management, an essentially market-driven rhetoric. This paradigm is based on the premise that by reducing the opportunities for incompetence and corruption through the narrowing down of the scope of government activities, efficient, transparent, effective, and accountable governance would appear. The rationale appears to be that with less bureaucratic structures the problems associated with bureaucracy could be eradicated. Once more, heavy emphasis is being placed on the objective criteria of responsibility and accountability with a blind faith on structures, processes, and procedures, with a total disregard for the moral (or subjective) dimension. In a broader sense, these adjustments meant the end of Keynesianism and the welfare state. Envisioned in economic-monetarist terms, designed by economists and managed by business administration experts, the role of the NPM administrator appears to be to preside over his or her own diminution.

Public management also appears to neglect the importance of law in public administration. This can be seen at two levels. At the top, in introducing notions like corporate management, corporate culture, and even that of management itself, it tends to obscure the fact that relations between senior officials and ministers are constitutional in nature. As we have seen, when Canadian officials answer questions from members of Parliament, they do so in the name of their minister. Faced with the complexities of day-to-day administration and the conflicting values that the system has thrust upon them, they need some fundamental reference point to which they may turn in case of doubt. At lower levels of administration, the law is a guarantor of democratic government: "Government by law is the most bureaucratic of all institutions because to a greater extent than other institutions it feels bound by its own rules" (Dimock, 1952: 399). In this respect, a public manager must differ from a private one, since while the latter may regard the law as a constraint, something he or she must obey, the public manager must also uphold it.

Much of the public management movement evolved as a response to the rigidities and excessive entitlements that came from the excesses of bureaucracy that were introduced in Canada during the period of growth of government services from 1945 to 1975. To be sure, public management proponents usually say that they are aware that the state is not a business, but we saw above that the classic values of accountability and respect for the law tend to be eclipsed by it. In practice, very few public servants actually believe that government should be thought of as a corporation. Gow (1994: 56), for example, found that only 2 percent of the respondents to his survey of Institute of Public Administration of Canada members favoured the corporation as the most appropriate metaphor for public administration. In what is to us quite a realistic fashion, they overwhelmingly chose either a complex system (43 percent) or a living organism (28 percent).

One of the profound debates of our time is that between public and private values. Part of the promise of NPM has been to propose ways to get around traditional constraints, for example, by considerable decentralization. However, a great debate is required about the place the citizens of our societies wish to reserve to public values, which cannot always be reduced to commercial transactions. At the same time, it must be noted that high taxes and complicated bureaucratic systems have created sympathy within the wider political culture for NPM-type changes.

The fact that NPM has produced significant and real changes to the public sector has led to a search for new analytical frameworks. Rhodes (1994), in a groundbreaking article, noted the trend towards the "hollowing out of the state," by which he meant that a variety of what previously had been understood as core state functions could no longer be considered as such. Rather, they had been devolved in a range of public and private partnerships and networks, which ultimately are thought to dominate public policy (Peters and Pierre, 1998). This constituted a new "governance framework" and marked what Rhodes (1996) described as a shift to governing without government. While governance is a concept that is subject to a wide number of interpretative possibilities, it nevertheless marks a more developed analytical conceptualization of the shift that NPM brought about. By understanding administration as rooted in a wide variety of self-sustaining networks in which state and nonstate actors shared power and administrative responsibility, it went beyond a simplistic adoption of market values to contemplate the possibility of nonmarket-based policy networks. Moreover, the structuring of these networks had the possibility of opening up the state, allowing us to revisit the relationship between administration, politics, and democracy and explore new possibilities for thinking about accountability.

CANADIAN PUBLIC ADMINISTRATION FACING THE TWENTY-FIRST CENTURY

The Canadian public service has served us well. It has given dependability and reliability to the institutions of governance, and it has answered the challenge by shifting its orientation from a homogeneous administrative system to a multifaceted administrative culture. Its performance is superior when compared to many nations and it is accommodating demands for change. Admittedly, the accommodation for change may be more readily acceptable at the senior management level than at lower levels. However, for the majority of public servants, these reforms and the NPM movement pose a direct threat to their job security; thus, they engender survival strategies that may not be conducive to a productive and responsible administration. The administrative culture of Canada exhibits a different and sometimes contradictory administrative ethos: different because it is no longer wedded only to the traditional (inherited) bureaucratic values but must accommodate the new management (business-based) values; and contradictory in the sense that senior management and other employees envision their role and status differently. But one thing is clear: For the orderly functioning of

Canadian democratic society, the Canadian administrative culture will have to act as the custodian of traditional public administration values and ideals while accommodating a number of the NPM values. That accommodation is needed if we do not wish to keep on considering Canadian bureaucracy as a barrier to sustainable development in Canada.

There is no doubt that the twenty-first century requires a different kind of public service compared to what has been the case of the traditional civil service until the 1980s. However, the public is now asking for more, to provide not only high-quality service but also a politically correct public service that exhibits the following characteristics: consumer-driven; technologically sophisticated and accessible; continuously available, even on weekends and holidays; providing one-window integrated service delivery (the federal government has already taken some steps towards this, while provincial and municipal governments are trying to follow its lead), so that citizens do not have to go from one office to another in order to get their problems addressed and resolved; efficient; and flexible but transparent and accountable, as well as equitable and participatory, so that it is open to public complaints and yet fast enough to respond to citizens' demands and needs.

It should also be mentioned that Canada has undertaken (and partly thrust upon it as an honest broker between the United States and especially the developing nations) a leadership role in public administration, which in turn has required the Canadian and provincial governments not only to appreciate the nature of comparative administration but also to develop a new concern about the management practices in many countries. It all started during the 1950s, when Canada took important steps to assist many newly decolonized nations, especially within the British Commonwealth, by initiating development assistance programs such as the Colombo Plan. Unlike the Americans, who perceived public administration as an institution contributing mainly to stability and *systems maintenance* and bureaucratization as a functional condition for stability and legitimacy in political development, Canadians had a gentler approach to abrupt reforms and changes. For them, the executive and legislative organs of a government had to work in tandem. In this way, the public administration in developing nations (called "development administration") was to develop slowly into a formidable institution with such ingrained values as democratic pluralism, rule of law, accountability, and responsibility. However, the Canadian influence was more pronounced in former British colonies than in other regions. In addition, as Canadian scholars kept their interest trained on the European and US political systems, comparative administration remained a field of action (especially with the emergence of NPM and governance as fields of study). Thus, both comparative and development administration continue to pose challenges to Canadian public administration scholars (as discussed in chapter 12 by Dwivedi and Mau).

Finally, given the fact that the first tangible manifestations of public sector reforms classified as NPM were first introduced in the late 1970s, it is somewhat of an oxymoron to refer to the NPM paradigm as being "new" in any way. Nonetheless, it does continue to hold much sway among academics and practitioners. As Pollitt (2003: 49) has argued, NPM is certainly far from over: "It may be beginning to seem like 'old hat' in some of the pioneer countries such as New Zealand and the UK, but elsewhere it is still regarded as a central plank in modernization."

Nonetheless, there are those who recognize that the time has come to move beyond NPM. After all, one of the recurring themes in public administration is the need for reform. Although he was writing in the early 1990s, the words of Johnson (1992: 7), a former high-level Canadian public servant and political scientist, continue to resonate:

> One of the interesting paradoxes of government in Ottawa is the apparently recurring need, over the past 30 years, to prescribe new reforms for public administration. Always the goals are the same: to achieve greater effectiveness, efficiency and economy in the administration of public affairs, and to manage the public's resources with probity and prudence.

NPM has resulted in some positive outcomes for public administration to be sure, particularly with respect to enabling many governments to regain control over the public purse. Even with its modest NPM reform effort, Canada has managed to usher in a new era of fiscal surplus since the 1997-1998 fiscal year and has been able to gradually reduce the public debt. But at the same time, as we have stated previously, this paradigm shift has resulted in the emergence of new "problems" that require resolution. For example, there continues to be a debate as to whether the shift to the NPM value of accountability for results has come at too high a price; rules and procedure, after all, do have an important role to play when it comes to satisfying the public interest. Even the United Kingdom and New Zealand, the two countries that pursued NPM most aggressively and the furthest, have started to rethink the merits of the model.

In response to the perceived inadequacy of NPM, which has become the conventional approach to public administration, Janet and Robert Denhardt (2002) have written a book about a new movement they see emerging, namely the "New Public Service." They contrast "old public administration" and the "new public management" with an alternative view of public administration—the New Public Service— which is "a movement grounded in the public interest, in the ideals of democratic governance, and in a renewed civic engagement" (Denhardt and Denhardt, 2002: 4). It remains to be seen what the next major public sector reform initiative in Canada will be. Whatever the new fad or fashion, it is certain that at the very least one will emerge, and there is a strong probability that we will eventually see another paradigm shift in public administration occur. In the meantime, however, NPM has left an indelible mark on public administration, not only in this country but globally. One manifestation of its impact has been the critical importance of a variety of nonstate actors in providing programs and services to citizens. Public administration, therefore, is not merely about government. Rather, it is now a question of governance, or how the state and civil society have come together to share in the responsibility of serving the public interest.

GENESIS OF THE BOOK

The origin of this venture can be traced to a meeting between O. P. Dwivedi, J. E. Hodgetts, and John Meisel in October 2006. After dinner one evening, the three of them started talking about the legacy of some prominent public administration scholars like Donald C. Stone and Dwight Waldo. Dwivedi mentioned that he had known these two personalities and how he had taken part in celebrating their contributions. He then suggested that the time had come to celebrate our own Canadian icon, who would at the time be about to celebrate his ninetieth birthday. Encouraged by Meisel, Hodgetts agreed to let the event unfold. Upon his return from Kingston, Dwivedi broached the matter of organizing a symposium at the University of Guelph in honour of Hodgetts to celebrate his birthday, as well as sixty years of teaching public administration in Canada. Soon, a committee of three—Dwivedi, Tim Mau, and Byron Sheldrick—was struck to organize the event, although it was Mau who shouldered the main organizational responsibility. Consultative meetings took place between Dwivedi, V. Seymour Wilson, James Iain Gow, and Lloyd Stanford to plan the event and seek their support at the initial planning. This resulted in a two-day gathering of a galaxy of Canadian public policy and administration scholars from all over Canada in September 2007 to share their admiration and respect for this intellectual giant.

These distinguished scholars and former practitioners came to Guelph not only to honour Hodgetts as he completed his ninetieth year of full life but also to witness and appreciate how during the past sixty years or more, the study of public policy and administration in this country has matured. To a large extent it can be traced back to Hodgetts, who is now known as the "father of the study of Canadian public administration." Hodgetts, who completed his doctoral work with the world-renowned public administration expert L. D. White at the University of Chicago (who asked him to write a thesis on the British Civil Service), initially came to the University of Toronto in 1944 to teach political science. But within a year, an emissary came from Queen's University to ask him to teach in that institution's Department of Economics and Political Science. It was there in the fall of 1946 that Hodgetts began the first undergraduate course in public administration. With that fateful event, the seeds were sown for the evolution of Canadian public administration.

This volume ultimately commemorates the transformation that has occurred in Canadian public administration over more than the past six decades. The maturation of public administration in this country was indelibly influenced by people like Hodgetts and the work of Royal Commissions examining specific issues, such as management accountability, governance, and ethics. Canada has established its credentials in the field of public management theory and practice, as we are well known worldwide for the PS 2000 initiative and reforms in public service laws and institutions. It is also clear that the impact of globalization, advances in information technology, and cross-cultural exchanges have made our world a lot smaller. Nevertheless, a lot more research and scholarly publication still remain to be done, not only pertaining to the Canadian condition but also about appreciating and understanding non-Western cultures and traditions. Public administration is mature enough now to navigate the unpredictable challenges that globalization has thrust upon us. Therefore, it is incumbent on us to help others beyond the borders of our continent.

ORGANIZATION OF THE BOOK

Conceptually, the book is divided into three parts. Part I of the book contains two chapters that examine theoretical perspectives on the evolution of Canadian public administration. The first chapter, by Iain Gow, explores the various disciplinary approaches and paradigms used to study public administration in Canada since 1960. In his view, three major paradigms can be identified—pragmatic institutionalism, NPM, and governance—with the former being the predominant Canadian public administration paradigm, although he concedes there is no consensus on that point. In the next chapter, Evert Lindquist provides a detailed examination of the relationship between organizational theory and public administration. Lindquist reminds us of the theoretical importance of organizational theory to the study of public administration and of the need to revisit this rich theoretical ground.

Part II of the book contains seven chapters that have been grouped thematically as contemporary issues and challenges for public administration. The range of issues covered here is quite diverse. In chapter 3, Ken Rasmussen and Luc Juillet examine the origins of the merit system in Canada. In chapter 4, Peter Aucoin and Donald Savoie revisit the significance of the politics-administration dichotomy. While it has become commonplace to recognize that "administration is political," it is important to consider the implications of this observation and the relationship between democracy and bureaucracy. Aucoin and Savoie provide a careful examination of the current balance between administrative and political authority and remind us of the need to think carefully about the contours of the politics-administration divide. In chapter 5, C. E. S. Franks continues the examination of the relationship between democracy and bureaucracy with an analysis of the current state of responsible government in Canada and the difficulties involved in ensuring a role for Parliament in overseeing and holding bureaucracy to account.

The remaining papers in part II examine the significance of various dimensions of innovation and change in administrative practices. In chapter 6, Paul Pross examines the changing nature of the regulation of lobbyists, a thorny issue that has always raised the issue of how regulation and administration straddle the very real world of pressure politics. In chapter 7, Caroline Dufour provides a case study of public sector education in Quebec, and how changing values and trends have been incorporated into educational practices for civil servants. Paul Thomas provides an examination of trust and leadership in administration in chapter 8. The question of trust in our public institutions has become an important issue for all public bureaucracies, and public sector reform has increasingly been guided by a perceived need to re-establish trust. An aspect of this pertains to service delivery. In chapter 9, Ken Kernaghan looks at this question and examines the trend towards integrated governance models.

Part III of the book, "The State of the Discipline: Future Challenges in Administration and Governance," comprises four chapters. We begin by drawing together two internationally recognized public administration scholars to reflect on the broader contributions of and influences on Canadian public administration. The reality is that we have much to be proud of in this regard. After all, a compelling case has been made that a Canadian model of public administration exists (Gow, 2002) and that Canada is actually well positioned to "catch the next wave" of public management reform (Aucoin, 2002: 50). Moreover, in his sweeping assessment of the evolution of the Canadian public service, Lindquist (2006: vi) has suggested that the scholars and practitioners of Canadian public administration comprise "a small and remarkably productive community that has accomplished much over the years."

That being said, in chapter 10, Keith Henderson documents some of the reciprocal influences on the study and practice of public administration in Canada and the United States. While Canadian public administration has borrowed much from its southern neighbour regarding public sector reforms, including Planning Programming Budgeting System, zero-based budgeting, and affirmative action and freedom of information legislation, the United States has been looking to Canadian models of health care and welfare policies, as well as proposals for national pharmacare and daycare programs. Henderson highlights the close relationship between the academic and practitioner communities in Canada and muses whether our national school of public administration, the Canada School of Public Service, with its classroom courses, leadership development programs, and topical publications on public administration, might be worthy of emulation in the United States. For his part, in chapter 11, John Halligan addresses issues of Anglophone public administration and notes that, despite some critical differences, there is a great deal of convergence in terms of public management reforms in Canada, New Zealand, Australia, and the United Kingdom. Canada is unique in that it has been more directly impacted by US influences and was slower than some of its Anglophone counterparts to introduce and institutionalize management reforms. However, Halligan asserts that "Canada has been regarded as a major contributor to intellectual development and application of ideas and practice internationally."

In the penultimate chapter of this book, Dwivedi and Mau reflect on the state of comparative and development administration in Canada. While much progress has been made in terms of the evolution of our understanding of the fields of comparative and development administration, they argue that Canadian scholars, like their American and British counterparts, have been much too ethnocentric in their examination of public administration issues. In their view, a much more outward vision of public administration is required to meet the challenges of the twenty-first century. As such, they admonish Canadian public administration scholars to develop research agendas that are more inclusive of development and comparative public administration and, similarly, to champion a more pronounced integration of these fields in the public administration curriculum of their respective post-secondary institutions. While their message is blunt and may lead to discomfiture within the Canadian public administration community, it is one that needs to be heard. Finally, the book concludes with a chapter by Sheldrick, who argues that principles of administrative law and the role of boards and tribunals constitute an overlooked aspect of the study of public administration. With the growing emphasis on judicial processes, litigation, and human rights discourses, this is an area of public administration that warrants greater study. Sheldrick argues that principles of judicial review have generally followed traditional models of administration. The shift to NPM and governance as analytical frameworks for state restructuring, however, has left the courts ill-equipped to play their traditional role of overseeing administrative decisions.

NOTES

[1]   Absolute preference meant that a candidate belonging to this category would be moved to the top of the list when appointment letters were issued, even though the individual may have been at the bottom of the eligibility list. This federal provision was also incorporated into various provincial public services in Canada.

REFERENCES

Aucoin, P. (1995). *The New Public Management: Canada in Comparative Perspective*. Montreal: Institute for Research on Public Policy.

———. (2002). "Beyond the 'New' in Public Management Reform in Canada: Catching the Next Wave?" In *The Handbook of Canadian Public Administration*, edited by C. Dunn, 37–52. Toronto: Oxford University Press.

Barzelay, M. (1992). *Breaking Through Bureaucracy: A New Vision for Managing in Government*. Berkeley: University of California Press.

Canada. (1962). *Royal Commission on Government Organization*. Ottawa: Queen's Printer, volume 1.

Canada, Task Force on Public Service Values and Ethics. (2000 [1996]). *A Strong Foundation: Report of the Task Force on Public Service Values and Ethics*. Ottawa: Canadian Centre for Management Development.

Charih, M., and L. Rouillard. (1997). "The New Public Management." In *New Public Management and Public Administration in Canada*, edited by M. Charih and A. Daniels, 27–45. Toronto: Institute of Public Administration of Canada.

Dawson, R. MacGregor. (1922). *The Principle of Official Independence*. London: P. S. King and Son Ltd.

———. (1929). *The Civil Service of Canada*. Oxford: Oxford University Press.

———. (1970 [1947]). *The Government of Canada*. Toronto: University of Toronto Press.

Denhardt, J. V., and R. Denhardt. (2002). *The New Public Service: Serving, Not Steering*. New York: M. E. Sharpe.

Dimock, M. E. (1952). "Bureaucracy Self-Examined" In *Reader in Bureaucracy*, edited by Robert K. Merton et al. New York: The Free Press.

Dwivedi, O. P., and J. I. Gow. (1999). *From Bureaucracy to Public Management: The Administrative Culture of the Government of Canada*. Peterborough, ON: Broadview Press.

Gow, J. I. (1994). *Learning from Others: Administrative Innovations among Canadian Governments*. Toronto: Institute of Public Administration of Canada.

———. (2002). *A Canadian Model of Public Administration?* Ottawa: Canada School of Public Service.

Hodgetts, J. E. (1955). *Pioneer Public Service: An Administrative History of the United Canadas, 1841–1867*. Toronto: University of Toronto Press.

———. (1973). *The Canadian Public Service: A Physiology of Government 1867–1970*. Toronto: University of Toronto Press.

———. (1984). "Administrative Values and Accountability." In *Public Policy and Administrative Studies: Proceedings of a Workshop Held on 13-14 April*

1984, edited by O. P. Dwivedi, vol. 1, 115–121. Guelph: University of Guelph.

Hodgetts, J. E., and O. P. Dwivedi. (1974). *Provincial Governments as Employers: A Survey of Public Personnel Administration in Canada's Provinces*. Montreal: McGill-Queen's University Press.

Hodgetts, J. E., W. McCloskey, R. Whitaker, and V. S. Wilson. (1972). *Biography of an Institution: The Civil Service Commission of Canada, 1908–1967*. Montreal, McGill-Queen's University Press.

Johnson, A. W. (1992). *Reflections on Administrative Reform in the Government of Canada, 1962–1991*. Ottawa: Office of the Auditor General.

Kernaghan, K., B. Marson, and S. Borins. (2000). *The New Public Organization*. Toronto: Institute of Public Administration of Canada.

Lindquist, E. (2006). *A Critical Moment: Capturing and Conveying the Evolution of the Canadian Public Service*. Ottawa: Canada School of Public Service.

Osborne, D., and T. Gaebler. (1992). *Reinventing Government: How the Entrepreneurial Spirit Is Transforming the Public Sector*. Reading, UK: Addison Wesley.

Peters, B. G., and J. Pierre. (1998). "Governance without Government? Rethinking Public Administration." *Journal of Public Administration Research and Theory*. 8: 2: 223–243.

Pollitt, Christopher. (2003). *The Essential Public Manager*. Maidenhead, UK: Open University Press.

Rhodes, R. A. W. (1994). "The Hollowing Out of the State: The Changing Nature of the Public Service in Britain." *Political Quarterly*. 65: 2: 138–151.

———. (1996). "The New Governance, Governing without Government." *Political Studies*. 44: 4: 652–667.

Underhill, Frank. (1966). "Foreword" In *Nationalism in Canada*, edited by Peter Russell. Toronto: McGraw-Hill.

PART I

THEORETICAL PERSPECTIVES

1 EVOLUTION OF DISCIPLINARY APPROACHES AND PARADIGMS IN THE STUDY OF PUBLIC ADMINISTRATION IN CANADA

Iain Gow

In his article "The Intellectual Odyssey of Canadian Public Administration," J. E. Hodgetts (1997) recalls that at the outset of his career in the mid-1940s, the then grand old man of Canadian public administration, MacGregor Dawson, told him that the discipline was poised for an intellectual takeoff. This remark could be taken as a hypothesis or a question for an overview of the field in Canada. How has it evolved and what does this tell us about knowledge in our subject?

This chapter looks at the evolution of general paradigms in public administration in Canada since 1960, using content analysis of textbooks and the journal *Canadian Public Administration* (*CPA*). Three major paradigms emerge: pragmatic institutionalism, new public management (NPM), and governance. The weak status of these paradigms is linked to the practical or applied nature of public administration. Governance looks like a political science reaction to NPM.

The overview provided here deals with the different approaches, disciplinary and paradigmatic, that have taken the stage during the intervening years. It covers research and publications in public administration in English Canada, with some references to public administration education. Having done a similar study for French Canada (Gow, 1993), this chapter will be limited to some comparisons between findings for English Canada and those for French Canada. Also, although there is close proximity between public administration and public policy, they are different in their purposes and their subject matter, so the chapter will only make a brief comparison of the two.

The most interesting aspect of this subject is what it reveals about the kinds of knowledge we have about public administration. So, after trying to identify disciplinary approaches and paradigms, the chapter will offer some reflections on what they imply. It will be argued that public administration is necessarily rooted in practical considerations and that one satisfactory synthesis will always escape us, but that academics play a useful role in offering analyses, critical comment, and comparisons that can help to alleviate the harmful effects of the fads that sweep the field regularly.

DISCIPLINARY APPROACHES

Table 1.1 lists what I think are the six most important disciplines relevant to public administration in Canada. Public administration in Canada, as an academic discipline, began in the 1920s with two books by MacGregor Dawson (1922; 1929). There is a lot of important material from the eighty preceding years, in the form of government documents and royal commission reports, but these did not reflect any particular disciplinary or even less any paradigmatic approach. Dawson, however, was the sole academic performer of note until after World War II.

Table 1.1 below reminds us that different disciplines are looking for different objects of study when they address public administration; that they may be analytical, normative, or critical; and that what they consider important and desirable varies accordingly. For a number of reasons, disciplinary approaches are not enough to divide people into significant groups of researchers. For one thing, for many it is an interdisciplinary field; the main schools and programs of public administration, public policy, and public management are deliberately so. Some consider that generic management is also interdisciplinary—as Vincent Lemieux put it, management is the least disciplinary of the six.[1] For another, people trained in one contributing discipline may be influenced by or take up another: Marxists keep alive the old Canadian tradition of political economy, many political scientists adopted economic thinking with public choice, an economist may find himself doing management studies or political scientists doing sociological analysis of the public service.

Before turning to the paradigms that have been important in Canadian public administration, it should be noted that two disciplines will be abandoned here without further inquiry. The first is history. Only a few of those publishing in the field, like Granatstein and Heintzman, are professional historians; the others are political scientists, economists, or public servants. So, we will pick them up in trawling for paradigms. The law also seems to be a world apart. In Canada, administrative law emerged late. Under the effects of the doctrine of the rule of law, until 1960 about the only public administration subject that retained the attention of legal researchers was judicial control of the administration (as in the work of Corry, Willis, or Humphrey). Since that time, a substantial body of administrative law has developed (with the help of the Law Reform Commission), but while the legal approach has informed many debates (like those over the ombudsman, freedom of information, or the Charter of Rights and Freedoms), it does not claim to have a general theory of public administration.

This decision to abandon history and law is not undertaken because they are unimportant. They are both essential, but a paradigm is, among other things, a general theory of its subject, and neither history nor law has a serious claim to offering a general theory of public administration, except for Weber's theory of bureaucracy, which is included here.

PARADIGMS

This word was introduced to the social sciences in the 1940s by Merton (1951), for whom it meant a simplified logical model of a social phenomenon, like bureaucracy or political patronage. Then, Kuhn (1970) used it in *The Structure of Scientific Revolutions* to explain the sociology of scientific change. The notion caught on in public administration as in other social sciences; it is used to describe new theories or models or concepts. Unfortunately, it is not always used in the same sense.

Henry (1975) found five paradigms in the evolution of public administration in the United States based on alternating predominance

Table 1.1 Principal disciplinary approaches in Anglo-Canadian public administration, 1950–2005

Discipline	Object of study	Intention	Values retained	Examples

Political science	- role of the state
	- institutions
	- power relations
	- bureaucracy
	- decision-making
	- accountability
	- public finance
		- analytical/
		  descriptive
		- often
		  normative
			- democracy
			- legality
			- effectiveness
			- efficiency
			- equality
			- representation
			- transparency
				Hodgetts
				Rowat
				Kernaghan
				Aucoin
				Thomas
				Savoie
				Sutherland

Law	- powers
	- rights and duties
	- legality
	- judicial control
		-analytical/
		  descriptive
		- often
		  normative
			- rule of law
			- judicial
			  control
			- democracy
			- equity/justice
				Corry
				Russell
				Trebilcock
				Salter

Management	- optimal use of resources - decisions - systems - controls - innovation	- normative	- efficiency - effectiveness - economy - control - flexibility - adaptation - competition	Mintzberg French Borins Marson Charih Daniels

Economics	- optimal use of
	  resources
	- public finance
	- rational choice
	- public goods
	- political market
		- positive/
		  analytical
		- normative
			- efficiency
			- effectiveness
			- economy
			- adaptation
			- competition
				Mackintosh
				Hartle
				Breton
				Migué
				Maslove

Sociology	- ideologies - social systems - organizations - bureaucracy - social classes	- analytical - critical	- domination - democracy - effectiveness - control - equity	Porter Sherif Sigleman Olsen Panitch Bourgault Dion

History	- institutions
	- policies
	- practices
		- analytical-
		  descriptive
			- nation-
			  building
			- democracy
			- effectiveness
				Hodgetts
				Granatstein
				Nelles
				Hilliker
				Whitaker
				Heintzman
				Maclaren
				Wilson

of political science or administrative science. Organization theory seems to lend itself to the identification of succeeding paradigms. However, the definition of the word may lead to very different regroupings: In two French-language Quebec textbooks on organization theory, one of them has a dozen, while another has only two, the functionalist and the critical (including Marxism) (Bélanger and Mercier, 2006; Séguin and Chanlat, 1983). More to our purpose, Candler (2008) identified the following paradigms for purposes of a comparative content analysis of three journals: the politics/administration dichotomy; principles of public administration; planning, organizing, staffing, directing, coordinating, reporting, and budgeting (POSDCORB); public policy; new public administration (NPA); NPM; critical analysis; and network theory.

For the purpose of this chapter, it is better to stick to Kuhn's criteria and categories (Gow and Dufour, 2000). In his definition of a paradigm there were three levels. At the highest level, a paradigm is a metaphysics or an epistemology, a set of beliefs, a standard or a new way of seeing. At the second level, it is a recognized scientific achievement, including theory, beliefs, values, and abstract generalizations. At the third level, paradigms are exemplars or artifacts, problems or solutions familiar to all students. Kuhn thought that paradigms evolved within disciplinary matrixes, but were more specific in these three areas. They were more groups of practitioners than subject matter. He felt that applied sciences demonstrated a somewhat murky version of the paradigm, because the audience was not restricted to fellow academics but included as well the practitioners in the field in question.

With these distinctions in mind, table 1.2 attempts to identify the paradigms that might be most relevant in Canadian public administration. The result is catastrophic: There are eleven paradigms listed! But all is not lost, for they do not all have the same importance.

WEIGHTING THE PARADIGMS

In order to evaluate the relative importance of these paradigms, I looked at nine textbooks published in Canada from 1960 to 2002. I then

Table 1.2 Most relevant paradigms in Canadian public administration, 1950–2005

	Epistemology	Theory	Values	Exemplars, artifacts
Pragmatic institution-alism	- pragmatism - inductive - often normative	- pluralism - state as arbiter	- democracy - efficiency - effectiveness	- politics-administration dichotomy - POSDCORB - rule of law - muddling through
Bureaucracy	- rationalist - universal - inductive	- hierarchy - specialization	- effectiveness - consistency - obedience	- red tape - professional - deformation
Systemism, functionalism	- scientific ambitions - cross-disciplinary - holistic - deductive	- laws of systems - functional requirements	- equilibrium - survival - effectiveness - democracy	- law of requisite variety - input/output - dysfunctions
Rationalism	- scientific ambitions - rationalist	- root and branch rationality	- maximizing utility - minimizing cost - effectiveness	- Planning Programming Budgeting System (PPBS) - prisoner's dilemma
Marxism	- scientific materialism - political economy - normative, praxis	- modes of production - class struggle - stages of development	- proletariat revolution	- relative autonomy of state - state elite
Public choice	- rationalist - micro-economic analysis of politics	- self-interest - budget-maximizing bureaucrat	- harness egoism	- free rider
NPA	- postrationalist - micro-& macro - normative	- moral imperatives for bureaucrats	- justice - equity	

NPM	- pragmatism
	- micro-&
	  macro
	- normative
		- competition
		- contracts
		- privatization
			- efficiency
			- effectiveness
			- innovation
				- steering v.
				  rowing
				- case studies
				- best practices

Neo-institutionalism	- postrationalist
	- inductive
	- middle-range
	  theory
		- economic or
		  historical
		- autonomy of
		  institutions
		- institutions
		  define identity
			- incrementalism
			- conservatism
				- path
				  dependency
				- bounded
				  rationality

Governance	- postmodernist
	- analytical and
	  normative
		- diffusion of
		  power
		- networks
		- return of
		  politics
			- subsidiarity
			- self-regulation
			- consensus
				- social learning
				- horizontality
				- hollow state

Critical	- postmodernist - postrationalist	- deconstruction	- anarchy - humanism	

compared these findings to the recent content analysis of *CPA* done by Candler and some other books of collected articles or studies.

A. THE TEXTBOOKS AND OTHER COLLECTIVES

The nine textbooks include four collections of texts and five works done by one or two authors. More than half of them have been published in the last ten years. Table 1.3 gives a rough guide to the presence of the various paradigms identified in table 1.2.

The first two textbooks were collections of texts: Hodgetts and Corbett (1960) and Kernaghan and Wilms (1971 [1968]). They were organized mainly around the structures and functions of government, with chapters on organization theory and bureaucracy. Neither book gave much attention to epistemology, although Hodgetts and Corbett (1960: viii) set out in the foreword their guiding intellectual queries: "The burning question in public administration is whether officials have too much power; whether too much or too little leeway is given to experts; whether it is possible for the public to be well-served and at the same time to control its public servants." The questions are still very relevant.

Table 1.3 Presence of identified paradigms in Canadian public administration textbooks, 1960–2002

Paradigm	Hodgetts & Corbett 1960	Kernaghan & Wilms 1968	Wilson 1981	Adie & Thomas 1982	Kernaghan & Siegel 1989	Westmacott & Mellon 1999	Inwood 1999	Dunn 2002	Johnson 2002
Pragmatic institution	STR	STR	SUBST	STR	STR	SUBST	STR	SUBST	
Bureaucracy	CHAP	CHAP	STR	CHAP	CHAP		SUBST	CHAP	SUBST
Systemism					REF				
Rationalism							MINOR		SUBST
Marxism				MINOR	SUBST		SUBST	REF	
Public choice			MINOR		SUBST		MINOR	REF	SUBST
NPA			MINOR	REF					
NPM					CHAP		SUBST	STR	SUBST
Neo-institutionalism									
Governance						MINOR			
Critical						CHAP			

Legend: STR = structuring; CHAP = one or more chapters; SUBST = substantial, more than three pages; MINOR = minor treatment, less than three pages; REF = occasional reference.

A decade later, Wilson (1981) published *Canadian Public Policy and Administration: Theory and Environment*. Like Doern and Phidd's (1983) *Canadian Public Policy: Ideas, Structures, Process*, Wilson dealt openly with theory. He quoted with approval a review article on works on public policy that affirmed "all are concerned with questions of theory, but they do not, either on their own or together, suggest a single compelling theory of institutions and policy processes" (1981: 413). Wilson does both. He gives attention to Marxism, corporatism, public choice, and NPA but opts for Max Weber's theory of bureaucracy as the best way to take into account institutions and their environments.

Almost at the same time, Adie and Thomas (1982) published *Canadian Public Administration: Problematical Perspectives*. Like Wilson, they gave their own synthesis of various schools or paradigms, but unlike him, they did not end up confirming one of them. They thought that each discipline had its bias and that separate interdisciplinary schools or departments were necessary to escape these disciplinary biases. They also saw major obstacles to sticking to demonstrable facts. In their view, ideology informs all of our views of public administration. They thought it important to question the validity of our assumptions about relevant people and institutions: "The problem is, however, that this validity is neither demonstrable nor agreed upon" (1982: 383). Behind this screen of unconscious assumptions was conflict over values. Thus, they held that while we had accumulated a good deal of fact about Canadian public administration, interpretations were bound to differ.

Kernaghan and Seigel's (1999 [1989]) big textbook, *Public Administration in Canada: A Text*, has run to four editions since it first appeared in 1989. Following a trend begun by Hodgetts and Corbett, they argue that public administration should be made up from two basic disciplines: political science and organization theory. While their book is in the institutionalist tradition, like Wilson and Doern and Phidd, they give plenty of weight to ideas that specifically cover the first seven chapters out of a total of twenty-seven. Many of the paradigms that have been retained here are covered, and some schools of thought not present here, like corporatism and libertarianism, but the book gives more weight to Marxism and to public choice theories than to the others. In discussing Marxist analysis of public policy, they conclude, "Not many Canadians accept this Marxist view of the state, but it seems to be a valid explanation of certain actions of the state" (Kernaghan and Siegel, 1991: 128). Public choice gets slightly more attention, about five pages in all, and it seems to be more integrated into the analysis, in particular of bureaucratic budget behaviour, rent seeking, and the choice of governing instruments. In the 1999 edition, NPM receives less than two pages as such, but there is a new chapter on alternative service delivery (ASD), a pillar of NPM.

Westmacott and Mellon's (1999) collection of texts, *Public Administration and Policy: Governing in Challenging Times*, has no guiding or organizing paradigm, but some of the authors use new paradigms. In a chapter on provincial-municipal relations, Katherine Graham and Susan Phillips draw on the work of Siegel to illustrate the impact of the concept of governance on studies of local governments (1999: 75), while a chapter on political ideas in policy analysis by Ronald Manzer (1999: 155–165) takes a basically critical stance, eschewing prescriptive policy advice for understanding the effects of changing education policy.

The last three books testify to the progress of NPM. In 1999, Inwood (2009 [1999]) published *Understanding Canadian Public Administration: An Introduction to Theory and Practice*. This book is interdisciplinary, drawing on six basic disciplines and including chapters on law, public policy, and management. It gives minor attention to Marxism, to rationalism, and to public choice, and more attention (about fifteen pages) to NPM, which it tends to identify with Program Review. The view of NPM is at once positive and critical.

In 2002 there appeared *The Handbook of Canadian Public Administration*, edited by Dunn (2002). It should possibly be included in the group of evaluative works that follows, but its comprehensiveness and its attempt to include the political, managerial, policy, and legal approaches to public administration would make it a candidate for a textbook. It gives pride of place to the NPM paradigm. Sandford Borins opens the volume with a text that speaks of NPM as "a global paradigm" that he interprets as an agreement among the public, elected representatives, and public services to obtain high-quality public services and better performance in return for greater autonomy and the necessary resources. David Zussman elaborates the theme of NPM with a chapter on ASD, while Peter Aucoin writes of looking beyond NPM, Barbara Wake Carroll and David Dewar have a chapter on performance management, and Borins has another on information technology. NPM is present all through the book, but chapters such as those by Aucoin and Carroll are more evaluative than full endorsements.

The final textbook is that of Johnson (2002), *Thinking Government: Public Sector Management in Canada*. The direction of this book is given in the title. It is about management, with a chapter on traditional management (POSDCORB gets six pages) and another on NPM. He agrees with others that there has been no great managerial revolution in Canada. In this treatment, both the theory of bureaucracy and its pathologies and that of public choice receive substantial treatment. The book is relatively detached, as are most textbooks, but clearly normative and pragmatic.

I also looked at other collective works that claimed to take the photograph of public administration in Canada: Dwivedi's (1982) volume of essays in honour of Hodgetts; Kernaghan's (1983) collection celebrating twenty-five years of *CPA*; the three volumes prepared by Peters and Savoie (1995; 1998; 2000) for the Canadian Centre for Management Development (CCMD) on the challenges facing public administration at the end of the twentieth century; the Lindquist (2000) collection on the future of the career public service; the Carroll-Seigel-Sproule-Jones (2005) volume of classic Canadian public administration readings; and the three volumes of research studies prepared under the direction of Savoie for the Gomery Commission (Commission of Inquiry, 2006). There are few references to theory in them and no chapters structured so as to test and advance paradigms or theories.

CONTENTS OF *CPA*

The evolution of the contents of the journal *CPA* has been charted by Candler (2008; 2006) in two articles comparing our journal with the

Australian Journal of Public Administration (*AJPA*) and the Brazilian *Revista de Administraçion Publica* (*RAP*) over the course of their existence. In terms of the authors of these 4,206 articles, in all three countries there has been a decline in the share of practitioners; in the most recent period, 1990–2002, the Canadian figure, at 25 percent, is higher than Brazil but lower than Australia. Academic disciplines of authors sorted out into three blocks: political science, in which Canada led with 38 percent; public administration or management, in which Canada (24 percent) came second to Brazil (32 percent); and commerce and management, where Australia led with 36 percent, followed by Brazil with 32 percent, and Canada with 17 percent. The two foyers of public administration in Canada thus seem to be political science and public management or public administration, but not business administration. Still, in the most recent period, Canada had fewer conceptual or comparative articles than the others, more using qualitative methods (more than half) and descriptive statistics. Canada and Australia were the mirror image of each other concerning the level of analysis, where Australia had clearly more articles on the federal government and Canada had more on the provinces. Candler found that only Canada had articles on the nonprofit sector. Canada was also the leader in articles dealing with diversity (10 percent), twice as many as Australia and about seven times as many as Brazil.

In terms of paradigms, despite our different categories, Candler sheds some light on our concerns. The politics-administration dichotomy has all but disappeared in the three countries, but maybe it has just been sublimated into writings on NPM (27 percent in Australia in recent years, 13 percent in Canada, and 9 percent in Brazil). The other large block of articles, about 15 percent in all three countries, concerned principles of administration. NPA, which was defined as being about ethics and citizenship, was the object of 10 percent of articles in *AJPA* in recent years, 8 percent in *CPA*, and 3 percent in *RAP.* Candler remarks that the two Anglo countries failed to notice the Marxist or postmodern approaches, whereas Brazil has had between 6 percent and 12 percent of its articles in these areas in recent decades.

Combined with our reading of public administration textbooks, these results help to clear up some of our concerns about the number of paradigms that exist. The surprising thing about the critical approaches is not that they were absent here and in Australia, but that they were so important in Brazil. We have had Marxist analyses by the likes of Olsen, Panitch, and Nelles, but they were done by political scientists or sociologists, not by public administration authors.

Next, the textbooks show that some major structuring ideas come along only to be integrated with ease into the existing paradigm. The theory of bureaucracy did not rock any foundations of the existing pragmatic institutionalism, but it did give a coherent explanation of modern administrative history and it in no way challenged existing ideas about parliamentary government (Bourgault and Dion, 1990). Similarly, systems analysis influenced virtually everyone's thinking in the 1960s and 1970s, but it did not lead to the overthrow of the preceding paradigm. Its long-lasting effects can be seen in our automatically seeking to place an organization in its environment and in our thinking in terms of inputs and outputs. Combined with an emphasis on rationality, it gave us the Planning Programming Budgeting System (PPBS), performance evaluation, and management by results. Neo-institutionalism did not have such an impact in public administration as in policy studies, because public administration scholars were already institutionalists. NPA as a movement seems to have been confined to the United States and never to have become a dominant paradigm there. Without reference to the NPA movement, we did have a growth of concern over public service responsibility, but it is a very old strain in public administration (think of the Friedrich-Finer debate), and its reinforcement seems to have occurred in response to concerns over bureaucracy and technocracy in the 1960s and 1970s and the perceived threat to public service values posed by NPM after 1980.

THE MAJORS: PRAGMATIC INSTITUTIONALISM, NPM, AND GOVERNANCE

This means that we are left with three major paradigms in public administration in Canada: pragmatic institutionalism, NPM, and governance.

A. Pragmatic Institutionalism

I consider that pragmatic institutionalism is the default position in public administration in Canada. The reason for this is that institutions are the starting point of most studies. This is certainly true in the political science community that studies public administration. As Smith (2005: 101) writes, "In English-speaking Canada, political institutions have never been out of fashion in the study of Canadian politics." I think that this is why neo-institutionalism had so little impact on the Canadian public administration community.

Pragmatic institutionalism is dominant in five of our textbooks. The exceptions are Wilson, with his vigorous defence of bureaucratic theory; Johnson, who gives similar weight to public choice and NPM theory; and Dunn's handbook, which is structured around NPM. The typical political science response to NPM has been scepticism, guarded approval, and the defence of political values in the face of business values. Three of our best-known political scientists illustrate this. On the strength of his work in administrative history, Hodgetts (1991) foresaw in uncanny fashion the dangers of the drift of public sector managers into the domain of politics. In his many writings on NPM since the late 1980s, Aucoin (1990; 1995; 1997; 2002) has not become a booster but has remained the analyst, revealing the apparent inner contradictions of NPM, checking for international variations in its adoption, recalling the virtues of the old bureaucratic model, and looking ahead to the post-NPM period.

Our other internationally best-known writer and editor, Kernaghan (1993; 1997; 2004), has been writing about responsibility, values, and ethics from a political science point of view for decades. In the manner of his textbook with Siegel, he has analyzed many of the themes promoted by NPM: ASD, partnership, empowerment, and information technology. In association with Borins and Marson (two promoters of NPM), he may have moved closer to promoting a certain kind of organization inspired by NPM. *The New Public Organization* gives summaries of management bestsellers, descriptions of many interesting and positive cases and guidelines for introducing changes leading in the direction of the new public organization. The book reflects on possible pitfalls, whether managerial, ethical, or political, but it comes down on the side of the new managerial forms and practices (Kernaghan, Marson, and Borins, 2000). Of course, almost all writers on public administration take normative stands.

If you want to see examples of pragmatic institutionalism, look at the research studies for the Gomery Commission (Commission of Inquiry, 2006). Institutionalism allows for certain compatibilities with the legal approach, so the appearance among them of a professor of law like Sossin is in no way surprising or jarring among these studies. These are wise able studies by very competent people, but I have not noted any structuring theoretical framework as you would find with a public choice adherent like Hartle or Sproule-Jones, or a Marxist like Olsen or Panitch.

Considering the absence of testable theoretical propositions in pragmatic institutionalism, one wonders if it even qualifies as a paradigm. However, it combines a conviction that institutions are important with a strong desire to keep up with the evolving scene and to "get it right." The preoccupation with institutions is so natural that it is only when we come upon its absence, as in Quebec in the 1960s and early 1970s, that we realize it is there. Coming from political science (Savoie, 2006; Pross, 2006; Hodgetts et al., 1972), it naturally began with the parliamentary system, collective and individual ministerial responsibility, central agencies, autonomous agencies, and the public service as an institution. For a long time, it did not give much attention to interest groups. The exemplars that we noted in table 1.2 are either instruments of analysis, like POSDCORB, principles like the politics-administration dichotomy and the rule of law, or a sceptical approach to organizational rationality, somewhat like the paradigm itself ("muddling through"). They are all still with us, sometimes refined or renamed (the politics-administration dichotomy has resurfaced in NPM). POSDCORB may have been updated by Mintzberg's list of managerial functions, the Charter may have placed a new emphasis on judicial control of administration, but institutionalism's exemplars are still relevant.

B. NPM

In 2000 Caroline Dufour and I devoted an article to the question of whether or not NPM is a paradigm (Gow and Dufour, 2000). We took as a starting point that many people claimed NPM to be a new paradigm. Using Kuhn's categories, we came to the conclusion that if it was a paradigm, as a blend of science and art, NPM was a professional paradigm, not an academic one.

NPM has no precise definition. As Charih and Rouillard (1997: 31) put it, NPM was grounded in two simple ideas: first, separate clearly policy from administration and give priority to management in the latter case; and second, apply much more of business management practices to government. In the hands of Osborne and Gaebler (1992), the package of tools proposed for NPM, managerialism or public management included privatization, contracting out, decentralization, partnerships, merit pay, management by results, and service or customer orientation. However, it is more than a tool kit. It is also a culture of innovation, flexibility, economy, and service.

Like public administration, NPM is both applied and normative. Hood (1991) calls it a doctrine, Pollitt (1990) an ideology. Aucoin (1990) finds it both a doctrine and a field of study. On the metaphysical level, NPM values experience over theory. It thrives on case studies and accounts of "best practices," what Bozeman (1993) calls "wisdom knowledge." I listed these things as artifacts, but while most students in public management will know what they mean, they are not artifacts in the sense that those of physical sciences are (as both a problem and a deductive proof). NPM is also built in part on bestseller books on management, something that no other paradigm encounters.

At the theoretical level, NPM is not a general theory but an eclectic approach.[2] As Borins (1994: 4) put it, it manifests "no obvious hierarchy of ideas, no one key principle from which all others can be deduced." Its main idea is one that I have given as an exemplar: The state should steer, not row. Rainey (1994: 42) wrote that a paradigm is "a consensus about the most important research topics and questions and the best ways of trying to analyze them." In these terms, NPM is a new paradigm but not a scientific one, because it has no central theory that has been proven demonstrably superior. Its adherents, who number many public servants, as well as academics, are agreed that traditional public administration was looking in the wrong places with the wrong instruments.

On the whole, therefore, NPM is a weak paradigm, because of its weakness in theory, but it qualifies as a paradigm in terms of new priority subjects, new priority values, and a preference for experience-based knowledge. Dufour and I found that it is not a perfect paradigm because it is possible to be in favour of parts of it without accepting the whole.

C. GOVERNANCE

It is not easy to determine if "governance" qualifies as a paradigm. The word has several meanings. At the United Nations and the World Bank, and in development studies generally, "good governance" simply means good government plus an openness to the private sector. At the Organization for Economic Cooperation and Development (OECD) (1995), the French translation of governance is "*la gestion publique*," or public management. To the founders of the journal *Governance*, it means the interface between government and the higher civil service. To others it means the end of authoritarian government and the beginning of a self-organizing networked society. Used in a normative manner, it may be used by the Right to promote the idea of a reduced or hollow state, and by the Left to value greater participation of civil society in collective decision-making and "social learning" (Paquet, 1999). For analytical purposes, "Governance can be thought of as the actual 'self-organized' network of both private and public sector actors" Lemieux (2000: 120). Lemieux writes that it is a new word for an old fact; for Peters (2000) and Weiss (2001: 796), it is a word or an idea as old as government itself.

In terms of metaphysics, governance, like NPM, does not like the rationalist world of bureaucracy and representative government. Its adherents prefer the wisdom of consensus and negotiated settlements to rational top-down plans. While Rainey and Ryu (2004) say that governance rests on anecdotal evidence, Paquet (1999: 171) insists that learning has to be grounded in practice and criticizes what he calls "scientism" in the social sciences. The preference for research closely linked to practice has been evident at the Canada School for Public Service and the CCMD before it. It has produced a number of documents by using what it calls "action research" methods. For many studies, this has involved creating a working group composed mostly of experienced public servants with one or two academics, and producing a report based on research studies prepared for the group, testimony of other public servants, and the group's own deliberations. Another variation on this method governed the production by academics of the three volumes edited by Peters and Savoie (1995; 1998; 2000) in the late 1990s. Public servant advisers were assigned to each group and then to each author to determine what subjects and what approaches would be most useful to their public service clients and to comment on drafts. While these volumes were written by outstanding scholars, I did wonder how many public servants had the time and the interest to read these 350 to 400 page volumes.

The broad idea of the theory of governance has been mentioned in the attempt to define the word. Governance bases itself on much the same observations as NPM: the loss of power of the nation-state, public financial difficulties, the rise of multinational corporations, globalization, the information technology revolution, and increasing citizen mistrust of government. As in NPM, the government has the job of setting goals for public policies and it governs through contractual arrangement negotiated with its various partners. Legal concerns come second to attention to the results produced by public policies, their agents, and their partners. The frontier between the public and the private sectors is said to be disappearing. However, unlike NPM, governance is a more political approach, concerned as it is to discover how this networked society guides itself (Minogue, Podano, and Hulme, 1998). Peters and Pierre (1998) propose that the likelihood of governance arrangements being introduced depends on the culture and traditions of political systems; to them, countries with strong state traditions where administrative law is important will more likely resist them.

Depending on one's basic ideology, governance gives priority to getting government out of the way of creative entrepreneurs or it enters into partnership with civil society. It values subsidiarity (or delegating decision-making power as close as possible to those who are affected by it), participation, and self-regulation. A recent study of public corporations in Quebec suggested that their boards of directors were giving more importance to the views of their various partners, including more institutional members. It concludes that the general interest is no longer defined by the state (Simard, Dupuis, and Bernier, 2006).

There are several huge problems with this theory. It does not have any version of how the general interest emerges. In a dozen case studies, Lemieux (2000) found that government played many roles, including that of referee. Chevallier (2003: 217) writes that it presents a "mythical, self-regulated, pacified and consensual society." Peters and Pierre (1998) ask why we should expect that the new hands-off arrangements will work any better than the old hierarchical ones. Moreover, I wonder, what is the bargaining power of the poor and the excluded? Where is the sense of community, where is the necessary trust to come from? Frederickson (1997: 78) says that emphasizing coordination does not produce fairness and equity. He adds that the notion of governance "masks the fundamental issue of the role of non-elected officials in a democracy" (1997: 92), thus taking us right back to the same question posed by Hodgetts and Corbett in 1960.

So, is governance a new paradigm? If so, it is a weak one. The variety of meanings attached to it undermines its claim to be a paradigm. It is more a new "buzz word," to use Thomas's (1996) expression. As Heintzman (1997) points out, we have seen all of these arrangements before Confederation. With respect to the recent past, it does propose new and more political places for study, but it does not bring any sweeping changes in methodology. In many ways, it appears to be an updating of the neo-corporatist and policy community theories of the 1970s and the 1980s. There is a tendency to reject rationalism, but that has been common currency since Simon (1957: xxiv–xxv) qualified his own theory with the ideas of "bounded rationality" and "satisficing." As a theory, governance is unproven. Moreover, like NPM, you can accept parts of it without adopting the whole argument. On the values front, it appeals to people for very different reasons. It leaves unsolved the great dilemmas of accountability, justice, and the public interest.

Perhaps governance represents the revenge of the political science nerds in the face of the intrusion of economic and management thinking via NPM. Peters and Pierre (1998) speak of path dependency in the social sciences as in the political phenomena we study. While the academic version of this case emanates from political scientists, we see enough borrowing of ideas and methods, or recycling of individuals to cast doubt on this idea as a general proposition.

IN THE NEIGHBOURS' COURTYARD: PUBLIC ADMINISTRATION IN FRENCH CANADA AND POLICY ANALYSIS

While they had to remain outside the scope of the preceding comments, the paradigms of use in Quebec and in the policy analysis community are relevant here.

A. QUEBEC AND FRANCOPHONE CANADA

When I arrived in Quebec in the early 1960s, I was a little surprised to find that political science was done differently from what I had learned at Queen's. As Cardinal (2005) points out, with the important exception of Jean-Charles Bonenfant, Quebec political science was in those days more of a political sociology, and political scientists often worked in close proximity with sociologists.[3] Léon Dion, Vincent Lemieux, and Gérard Bergeron all drew on sociology and anthropology. At the same time, following the French tradition, the field of administrative law was just beginning to develop, led by Garant (1974; 1966), Dussault (1969), and Barbe (1969). By the 1970s, Alain Baccigalupo and I were contributing more institutionalist studies in political science, as were some of the first productions of l'École nationale d'administration publique (ÉNAP) by Borgeat, Dussault, and Ouellet (1982), for example.

Perhaps because of their lack of concern with institutions, or because of their studies in France, Quebec writers on public administration were more theory minded than were English Canadians. Bergeron (1965;

1977; 1984; 1990), over thirty years, produced four books developing his theory of the state (see also Gow, 1992). For our purposes the most significant aspect of his functionalist theory was the addition of administration as one of the four essential functions of the state, the others being government, legislation, and adjudication. The theory was a big improvement over the traditional division of government functions into the executive, legislative, and judicial, and it clarified many of the issues of relations among these functions (Gow, 1992).

For his part, Lemieux has been the foremost theoretician of public administration in Quebec and, I daresay, in Canada. In one of the studies done for the famous Bureau d'aménagement de l'Est du Québec (BAEQ) in the early 1960s, he introduced us to the strategic analysis of Michel Crozier, the theory that claimed that administrative agents are not only repositories of physical skills and emotions, but also free actors who adopt strategies to defend their interests (Lemieux, 1965). The framework worked well when applied to the regional agents of Quebec departments in Eastern Quebec. Lemieux (1979) also published *Les Cheminements de l'influence* in which he combined systems theory, Crozerian analysis, and structuralism to produce the "laws" governing organizational arrangements in the public sector. Bergeron and Lemieux influenced my colleagues Michel Barrette, Stéphane Dion, Michel Fortmann, and myself (1991 [1987]) when we produced an introductory textbook in public administration in 1987 organized around systems theory, Crozerian analysis, and Bergeron's functionalism. In my own history of the Quebec administration, I used Weberian theory, systems analysis, and development theory to guide my research (Gow, 1986).

It is interesting to note that Bergeron and Lemieux identified the governance idea in the 1970s; both used the word "*la gouverne*" to include all forms of political life in organizations and in society. So far as I know, the only regular contributor of analyses in public administration based on critical theory in Quebec, or Canada for that matter, is Christian Rouillard (2006; 1999).

One of the causes of the differences between English Canadian and French Canadian literature on public administration comes from the activist role of the Quebec state since the Quiet Revolution. As Dufour

(2002) writes, René Lévesque, minister in the Jean Lesage government, sought in 1961 to have set up a graduate program in management intended for Quebec public servants in the École des Hautes Études Commerciales of the Université de Montréal. Although nothing came of this request, this interest continued until a way was found to create l'ÉNAP as a part of l'Université du Québec in 1969. The school had a big impact on academic writing on pubic administration in Quebec. It was largely because of it that Chandler and Chandler (1983) found that there were more publications on Quebec public administration than there were on all of the other provincial administrations combined. Since that time, the creation of an academic master's program and a doctorate and a determined orientation towards research and publication have increased the dominance exercised by l'ÉNAP in Quebec. The school has produced the most writing on public management in Quebec (Charih and Landry, 1997; Guay, 1997; Éthier et al., 1994; Parenteau, 1994).

Other consequences of the activist role of the Quebec state have been critical comments on technocracy (Renaud, 1984; Archibald, 1984; Simard, 1979). This theme seems to be of greater importance in Quebec than in the rest of Canada. For example, there is only one reference to technocracy in my edition of Kernaghan and Siegel, while there is an entire chapter on the subject by Stéphane Dion in the textbook that the four of us wrote in the mid-1980s. The so-called Quebec model produced studies of the Quebec version of corporatism and the spate of recent attacks on it.

Despite these differences, my study of the evolution of public administration in Quebec found much the same categories as I have put forward here (Gow, 1993). A recent textbook by Mercier (2002) includes almost all of them. Many Quebec analysts move easily from French to English and from Quebec institutions to the Canada School of Public Service and the Institute of Public Administration of Canada (IPAC).

B. POLICY ANALYSIS

Policy analysis, or studies, is a field that has some overlap with public administration but is different in its object and its intention.

Whereas public administration is concerned with the preparation and administration of public policy, policy analysis is about the origins, the contents, and the impacts of such policies. Pal (1987: 23) sees the questions of the determinants and the contents of public policies as academic concerns, while those of the contents of policies and their impacts are questions of applied social science. It is not as simple as that, of course, since anyone studying a public policy will be interested in the impacts of past and present policies, but it is a reminder that here, as in public administration, there are academic and practical branches. In policy studies, however, the academics are more autonomous, a subject to which I will return in the final section of this chapter.

Public policy is not a paradigm of public administration, as Candler would have it, but Geva-May and Maslove (2006) found that public administration programs in Canada include more public policy than do schools in the United States. Public policy uses many of the same paradigms, most notably public choice, network analysis, neo-institutionalism, and policy communities. The political economy paradigm has been quite influential in academic policy studies, but it has had very little influence on the contents of public policies (Dobuzinskis, Howlett, and Laycock, 1996; Pétry, 1996).

I have not the means to document this, but my impression is that policy analysis specialists take methodology more seriously than do those who primarily do public administration. To look at graduate programs of public policy, management, and administration, you would think that research methods were covered by them all (Gow and Sutherland, 2004), but publications on public policy are much more likely than those on public administration to include discussions of methodology, while public management is more interested in techniques of intervention than research. Policy analysis, like public administration, gives more importance to historical studies than public management does, but all three are comparative.

KNOWLEDGE FOR PUBLIC ADMINISTRATION

I have argued here that pragmatic institutionalism has been, and continues to be the predominant paradigm in Canadian public administration. Along the way it has changed considerably, informed by systems analysis and comparative studies, but it did not meet a real challenge until the coming of NPM in the 1990s, and now governance. Pragmatic institutionalism is not merely descriptive but contains an analytical and sceptical component, whereby academics evaluate and criticize the new fashions that regularly sweep the field.

If we have one long-standing but evolving paradigm (pragmatic institutionalism) and two recent challengers, it seems to throw us back to the disciplinary divide, to the political and the managerial approaches. As I said, to some extent governance is the response of politically minded analysts to public management. However, if most political scientists worked with a paradigm that was found deeply unsatisfying by many analysts and practitioners, and if the same political scientists found themselves marginalized in their own departments, what does this tell us about this branch of public administration, and what does it mean about the chance to build a new synthesis?[4]

One thing that should be set straight is that, despite its critics, public administration has a role to play that cannot be covered by either public policy or public management. Public administration studies important questions that one or the other does not cover: Public policy is not concerned with administrative theory, management of the public service and financial management, politics and the public service, accountability, public service ethics, technocracy, administrative doctrine, administrative history, or administrative elites; public management is not concerned with political theory, politics and the public service, the role of the state, administrative history, technocracy, pressure groups, political and administrative history, or administrative elites. At the same time, public administration did not deal adequately with problems of productivity, service, flexibility, creativity, and the bottom line, hence the challenge that arose in the form of NPM.

Henry (1975) wrote that public administration was finally emerging from its fractured state to become "public administration as public administration," thanks particularly to the emergence of autonomous schools of public administration. This trend has also occurred in Canada (Pross and Wilson, 1976). There was a flurry of creation of graduate schools around the turn of the 1970s (ÉNAP, Carleton [reformed], Dalhousie, Victoria, Queen's), followed by a long period of stability until quite recently. These schools certainly influenced academic production and they no doubt each established a fairly unified approach to their field. Even so, I do not believe that they can hope to provide a unified approach that will satisfy all or most researchers. With some exceptions for applied fields like program evaluation, most professors remain true to their disciplinary origins: Political scientists deal with the most political aspects of the field, specialists in management or law likewise, and nothing can stop other social scientists from taking up the subject, as in the case of economists with principal-agent theory, transactional economics, and rational choice. Only a synthesis that was highly abstract, as in some forms of systems or cybernetic theory, could hope to cover them all, and it would probably be rejected by the field just because it is so abstract.

This leads to the second point that emerges from our survey. Public administration, like public management, is heavily influenced by the practitioner audience. Moreover, we want to influence practice (Borins, 2003). This means that public administration and public management have more of the characteristics of an applied social science than does public policy. The fact that the audience belongs in major part to the world of practice means that the community who adopts and uses a paradigm works under very different conditions. Practitioners do not like theory and are hard pressed to name any theoretical principles (Gow, 1994; Minogue, 1983: 64). This is probably the reason that the only paradigms that have caught on (with the exception of Weberian bureaucracy) are the woolly or weak ones. Critical paradigms, like Marxism and postmodernism, are of little or no use to practitioners. More rigorous paradigms like public choice are also suspect for their seeming lack of contact with the real world. The more recent paradigms, NPM and governance, call for a methodology grounded in practice and prefer case studies to rigorous academic studies. Management evaluation studies are more likely to be accepted if done by one researcher than by a team, if they use qualitative rather than quantitative methods, if they are done for a single decision-maker, and if they are overseen by a committee of researchers and sponsors (Oman and Chitwood, 1984). All this while, public policy specialists are doing the opposite, developing methodologies with their academic colleagues in mind.

This intimate connection with those we study is both a blessing and a curse. It is a blessing because it gives us immediate feedback to much of what we do. The interaction of academics and practitioners is an outstanding trait of the field. Experienced practitioners who take an interest in research and teaching are formidable partners for university researchers. Even so, the partnership comes at a cost. Not only is the subject matter highly influenced by what practitioners consider relevant, but their methodological preferences ensure that academics remain in the almost impossible position of trying to keep up with what is happening, even as it emerges. Former IPAC president, Luc Bernier (2000), recently asked if researchers could not find the way to predict what will happen instead of always following events. The answer is no, not with these methods. In my study of fifteen major administrative innovations in Canada between 1960 and 1990, in only one case could an academic be considered the initiator, and that was Milton Friedman and the privatization of public enterprises in Britain (Gow, 1994). Sometimes, someone like Don Rowat will take up the cause of an important innovation that happened elsewhere, like the ombudsman or freedom of information. Most innovations came from political pressure, the needs of the bureaucracy, or the availability of new technologies.

So, the practical nature of public administration as we know it affects the kind of studies that we do. Unlike public policy, public administration and public management do not usually test hypotheses, nor do they produce results that are cumulative. They have not given rise to much "enlightening theory" (Hodgetts, 1997: 177; Adie and Thomas, 1982: 383). We have made considerable progress in using comparative methods, and that raises the scientific value of what we do, but the most complete knowledge of PPBS or the envelope system is of very little interest to the contemporary audience. Similarly, good and detailed knowledge of how Jean Chrétien centralized the management of the federal administration will only have the shelf life that similar practices by Stephen Harper or his successors allow.

This has strong consequences for our studies. You are only as good as you are up to date. In receiving his award as outstanding teacher of the year at Brock University, Kernaghan recalled that his book of readings had run to five editions in twenty years; the monumental text that he and Siegel produced had run to four editions in ten years. Innovation comes to our field far less because of some new intellectual approach than because of changes in practice. In that respect, Minogue (1983: 79) was right when he said "action generates inquiry." So, we are not likely to discover dark matter or the administrative genome this way.

This rather banal observation leads to some important conclusions. The three paradigms that I have identified—pragmatic institutionalism, NPM, and governance—are all practical and grounded in practice, and they all are weak paradigms. This makes good sense and will continue to do so. This does not mean that there have been no improvements since Dawson made his optimistic prediction to Hodgetts. We are stronger methodologically thanks to the development of interview techniques by people like Campbell, Bourgault, Dion, and Savoie, and survey techniques by Jabes and Zussman and the Treasury Board. We have greatly added to the value of our studies by comparisons, both within Canada and with other countries, as in the work of Aucoin, Rowat, Carroll, and Dwivedi. The kind of deconstruction of the work of the Auditor General done by Sutherland (1980) and Saint-Martin (2004) or Sutherland's (1991) careful accounting of ministerial resignations have led us beyond the simple generalizations of those early decades.

The lack of a strong common paradigm and the relatively weak scientific status of public administration are linked. As Frederickson (1997) put it, public administration is not so much a social science as an application of social science. Dwight Waldo (cited in Lovrich, 1985: 311) wrote that no scientific paradigm was attainable, because public administration is a profession: "A profession is characterized by an interlocking set of rules, not by rigid doctrine, certainly by nothing resembling a scientific paradigm; and most professions are receptive to ideas and technologies from many sources." Rutgers (1997: 296) agrees that public administration has not had a paradigmatic model of development and adds that "[c]alls for a new and coherent paradigm to provide the discourse with an identity are unwarranted." In his view, "different approaches are necessary to get a coherent view of parts of public administration."

It may or not be a profession, but several authors claim that it is too important to be left to the practitioners (Hodgetts, 1997; Rutgers, 1997). My own view about basing the study of public administration on practice is that no amount of practical experience allows you to put yourself in historical and comparative perspective.

A further dimension of the practical or professional nature of public administration is brought out by Ventriss (1991: 9):

> It is true that public affairs education is too important to be left to those who are exclusively trained in public administration or public policy; conversely, it is also too important to be left to an amalgamation of scholars whose knowledge of public administration is rudimentary at best. Expressing an interest in the public sector is simply not enough to provide proper educational glue. A public affairs program is not an intellectual reservation for those who want to teach—regardless of their intellectual perspective—something about the public sector independent of any knowledge (or interest) in the field as a whole ... Without a substantive connection to the normative content of the field, an interdisciplinary approach is degraded into a state of babel, confusion, and bewilderment.

Two points are of interest to us here. First, if "contending paradigms" are good for research (Lovrich, 1985), Ventriss (1991) makes the argument that some further "glue" is needed in professional education. Second, this glue is the "normative content of the field." It is not only that education and applied research call for commitment to and advancement of certain values, but it is also that almost all people in the field are engaged in a normative pursuit. We want either to improve public administration or to defend the values of democratic public service. In this respect, there is a dimension of moral philosophy in our concern for ethics and democracy, one which is not present in either public management or public policy. This is the reason for the great concern for accountability, for the endless search for the proper way to see that the administration carries out the will of the duly elected government, without being sidetracked by partisan considerations. As Hodgetts (1997: 180) put it, "If, to qualify as a true science, public administration had to be divorced from politics, thereby depriving it of true life and relevance, then better to dismiss the notion of a science."

Two further comments remain in this discussion. First, while we are almost all normative, one can better serve by being critical than by being a booster. It is our duty to "speak truth to power" and not merely to support today's fashion. This, I think our best people do admirably: The Hodgetts, the Kernaghans, the Aucoins, the Savoies, and the Thomases all keep a critical distance and advise, encourage, debunk, and warn. Second, in the founding disciplines, we can be attentive to the truly classic studies that are not dependent on current events for their enduring relevance: Weber, Hodgetts, Eisenstadt, Simon, Crozier, Merton, Silverman, Bergeron, Lemieux, and others. These are the basic building blocks from whence our applied knowledge is derived.

CONCLUSION

The purpose of this chapter was to explore the evolution of disciplinary approaches and paradigms in the study of public administration in Canada. I wondered if the discipline had known an intellectual takeoff, as Dawson had predicted to Hodgetts in the 1940s. While I found five main disciplines interested in public administration—political science, law, management, economics, and sociology—the main rivalry was, and continues to be, between political science and management, the latter having been given a big boost by the NPM movement. Looking into possible paradigms, by returning to the main Canadian textbooks in the field, various collective works, and the content analysis of *CPA* done by Candler, I concluded that there were only three that really count: pragmatic institutionalism, NPM, and governance. They are all weak paradigms. Rather than having all the attributes of a Kuhnian paradigm, they reflect more the sense of the French word "*problématique*," because they are mainly about which are the important questions to be asked and how we should go about answering them. In addition to putting certain aspects of public administration first, they also present values to be given priority, and preference for some methods over others. None of the three are pure rationalists, although rationalistic methods may turn up in pragmatic institutionalism and NPM. However, they all give importance to the point of view of the practitioner, to the extent that there is not much support for rigorous social science methods and little advancement of theory.

The first question that must be answered here is whether or not Dawson was right. The answer is a qualified yes. We have not made much progress on the theoretical front, but we have learned to do many things better. Many movements have passed through, and each leaves some sediment that enriches our field: Systems analysis, rational choice, Marxism, and neo-institutionalism have all affected the field without leading to major changes of approach. Under the impulse of comparative public administration; development administration; management studies at the United Nations, the World Bank, and the OECD; and the study of administrative elites, our methodology has improved considerably. In political science, our stronger courses in methodology have meant that student interns could take on ever more ambitious projects.

On the other hand, the field has a hard time getting respect from academic colleagues in the social sciences. Even some within the fold are unhappy. McSwite (1997: vii, 50–51) writes that public administration is a "dysfunctional family" that keeps on mulling over old issues, old debates, and unsolved problems. McSwite sees the problem as one of misplaced rationalism, the belief that there is truth out there to be discovered, and would prefer an image of public administration reflecting a different model of society, based on community rather than hierarchy. Maybe it is that given our professional situation, people in public administration often line up with "the optimists," as Adie and Thomas called them, although political science professors do a lot of sceptical questioning of such optimism. As we have seen, critical approaches do not get much attention in public administration.

A second point comes forward here. This is whether it matters that there is a lack of unity around a dominant paradigm in public administration. Candler (2008) poses the problem as one of "epistemic community or tower of Babel." This opposition is false. On the one hand, with the increase of comparative studies, few academics today would be unaware of a common core of ideas and proposals presented by both NPM and governance. Moreover, it is possible to use part of a new approach or paradigm without adopting it whole. In view of the weak methodological credentials of the field, we might think that the differences of opinion among the tenants of our various paradigms allow for healthy debate, instead of not very fruitful consensus, especially as the differences often come from disagreements about values. It would be folly to apply theories blindly without reference to national traditions and cultures, as some proponents of public choice have wanted to do (Johnson and Keehn, 1994). This is also true in the world of practice. Students of diffusion of innovations generally agree that it would be disastrous to introduce a new idea, theory, or "best practice" into an administration without first considering if it is compatible with national, local, and organization culture.

Perhaps it is necessary for institutions of public administration education to have a unified outlook to transmit to their students. For researchers and academics, however, the competition among different schools of thought is more useful than harmful.

NOTES

[1]   Personal correspondence with the author, 19 July 2007.

[2]   As Aucoin pointed out in discussion, the exception to this remark is New Zealand, where reforms were firmly guided by public choice, agency theory, and transaction cost economics. See Boston et al. (1996: 16–41).

[3]   This does not mean that they did not study institutions. Léon Dion did two studies of the adoption of Bill 60, creating the province of Quebec's Department of Education, but the approach started with civil society.

[4]   Minogue (1983) wrote, "Public administration is still used as a terminology, but is now essentially devoid of meaning," adding that no social scientist would accept the idea of a separate discipline, but practitioners and Third-World universities still believe in it! Richard Simeon (cited in Wilson, 1981:

426) wrote in 1976 that public policy must be rescued from the "hole" of public administration (see also Whicker, Strickland, and Olshfski, 1993).

REFERENCES

Adie, R. F., and P. G. Thomas. (1982). *Canadian Public Administration: Problematical Perspectives*. Scarborough: Prentice-Hall.

Archibald, C. (1984). *Un Québec corporatiste?* Hull: Éditions Asticou.

Aucoin, P. (1990). "Administrative Reform in Public Management: Paradigms, Principles, Paradoxes, and Pendulums." *Governance*. 3: 2 : 115–137.

———. (1995). *The New Public Management: Canada in Comparative Perspective*. Montreal: Institute for Research on Public Policy.

———. (1997). "The Design of Public Organizations for the Twenty-first Century; Why Bureaucracy Will Survive in Public Management." *Canadian Public Administration*. 40: 2: 290–306.

———. (2002). "Beyond the 'New' in Public Management Reform in Canada: Catching the Next Wave?" In *The Handbook of Canadian Public Administration*, edited by C. Dunn, 36–52. Don Mills, ON: Oxford University Press.

Barbe, R., ed. (1969). *Droit administratif canadien et québécois*. Ottawa: Éditions de l'Université d'Ottawa.

Bélanger, L., and J. Mercier. (2006). *Auteurs et textes classiques de la théorie des organizations*. Quebec: Les Presses de l'Université Laval.

Bergeron, G. (1965). *Fonctionnement de l'État*. Paris: Armand Colin.

———. (1977). *La gouverne politique*. Paris: Éditions Mouton.

———. (1984). *Pratique de l'État au Québec*. Montreal: Québec/Amérique.

———. (1990). *Petit traité de l'État*. Paris: Presses universitaires de France.

Bernier, L. (2000). «Repenser l'administration en tant que discipline.» *Management du secteur public*. 11: 1: 5–7.

Borgeat, L., R. Dussault, and L. Ouellet. (1982). *L'administration québécoise: organisation et fonctionnement*. Sillery, QC: Presses de l'Université du Québec.

Borins, S. (1994). *Government in Transition: A New Paradigm in Public Administration*. Toronto: Commonwealth Association of Public Administration and Management (CAPAM).

———. (2003). "From Research to Practice: A Survey of Public Administration Scholars in Canada." *Canadian Public Administration*. 46: 2: 243–256.

Boston, J., et al. (1996). *Public Management: The New Zealand Model*. Aukland: Oxford University Press.

Bourgault, J., and S. Dion. (1990). "Canadian Senior Civil Servants and Transitions of Government: the Whitehall Model as Seen From Ottawa." *International Review of Administrative Sciences*. 56: 1: 149–169.

Bozeman, B. (1993). "Theory, 'Wisdom,' and the Character of Knowledge in Public Management: A Critical View of the Theory-Practice Linkage." In *Public Management: the State of the Art*, edited by B. Bozeman. San Francisco: Jossey-Bass.

Candler, G. C. (2006). "The Comparative Evolution of Public Administration in Australia, Brazil and Canada." *Canadian Public Administration*. 49:3, 334–349.

———. (2008). "Epistemic Community or Tower of Babel? Theoretical Diffusion of Public Administration." *Australian Journal of Public Administration*, 63:3, 294–306.

Cardinal, L. (2005). "New Institutionalism and Political Science in Quebec." In *New Institutionalism: Theory and Analysis*, edited by A. Lecours, 128–150. Toronto: University of Toronto Press.

Carroll, B., D. Siegel, and M. Sproule-Jones, eds. *Classic Readings in Canadian Public Administration*. Toronto: Oxford University Press.

Chandler, M., and W. Chandler. (1983). "Public Administration in the Provinces." In *Canadian Public Administration: Discipline and Profession*, edited by K. Kernaghan, 138–160. Toronto: Butterworths.

Charih, M., and R. Landry. (1997). *Politiques et management publics*. Sillery, QC: Les Presses de l'Université du Québec.

Charih, M., and L. Rouillard. "The New Public Management." In *New Public Management and Public Administration in Canada*, edited by M. Charih and A. Daniels. Toronto: Institute of Public Administration of Canada.

Chevallier, J. (2003). "La gouvernance, un nouveau paradigme étatique?" *Revue française d'administration publique*. 105–106, 203–217.

Commission of Inquiry Into the Sponsorship Program and Advertising Activities. (2006). *Restoring Accountability: Research Studies. Vols. 1, 2 ,3.* Ottawa: Pubic Works and Government Services.

Dawson, R. M. (1922). *The Principle of Official Independence*. London: P.S. King and Son.

———. (1929). *The Civil Service of Canada*. London: Oxford University Press.

Dobuzinskis, L., M. Howlett, and D. Laycock, eds. *Policy Studies in Canada: The State of the Art*. Toronto: University of Toronto Press.

Doern, G. B., and R. W. Phidd. (1983). *Canadian Public Policy: Ideas Structure, Process*. Toronto: Methuen.

Dufour, C. (2002). *Émergence, institutionnalisation et identité du Management Public en milieu universitaire au Québec*. Montreal: Dissertation, Université de Montréal.

Dunn, C., ed. (2002). *The Handbook of Canadian Public Administration*. Don Mills, ON: Oxford University Press.

Dussault, R. (1969). *Le contrôle judiciaire de l'administration au Québec*. Sainte-Foy, QC: Les Presses de l'Université Laval.

Dwivedi, O. P., ed. (1982). *The Administrative State in Canada*. Toronto: University of Toronto Press.

Éthier, G., et al. (1994). *L'administration publique: diversité de ses problèmes, complexité de sa gestion*. Sillery, QC: Presses de l'Université du Québec.

Frederickson, G. H. (1997). *The Spirit of Public Administration*. San Francisco: Jossey-Bass.

Garant, P. (1966). *Essai sur le service public*. Quebec: Les Presses de l'Université Laval.

———. (1974). *Traité de droit administratif canadien et québécois*. Sainte-Foy, QC: Les Presses de l'Université Laval.

Geva-May, I., and A. Maslove. (2006). "Canadian Policy Analysis and Public Policy Programs: A Comparative Perspective." *Journal of Public Affairs Education*. 12: 4: 413–438.

Gow, J. I. (1986). *Histoire de l'administration publique québécoise 1867–1970*. Sainte-Foy, QC: Les Presses de l'Université Laval.

———. (1992). "La théorie politique de Gérard Bergeron: une clé de lecture de l'administration publique.» In *Être contemporain. Mélanges en l'honneur de Gérard Bergeron*, edited by J-W. Lapierre, V. Lemieux, and J. Zylberberg, 161–178. Sillery, QC: Les Presses de l'Université du Québec.

———. (1993). «Les problématiques changeantes en administration publique (1965–1992).» *Revue québécoise de science politique*. 23: 59–105.

———. (1994). *Learning From Others: Administrative Innovations among Canadian Governments*. Toronto: Institute of Public Administration.

Gow, J. I., et al. (1991 [1987]). *Introduction à l'administration publique: Une approche politique*. Boucherville, QC: Gaëtan Morin.

Gow, J. I., and C. Dufour. (2000). "Is the New Public Management a Paradigm? Does It Matter?" *International Review of Administrative Sciences*. 66: 4: 573–597.

Gow, J. I., and S. L. Sutherland. (2004). "Comparison of Canadian Master's Programs in Public Administration, Public Management and Public Policy." *Canadian Public Administration*. 47: 3: 379–405.

Guay, M-M., ed. (1997). *Performance et secteur public*. Sillery, QC: Les Presses de l'Université du Québec.

Heintzman, R. (1997). Introduction to *Public Administration and Public Management: Experiences in Canada*, edited by J. Bourgault, M. Demers, and C. Williams, 1–12. Sainte-Foy, QC: Les Publications du Québec.

Henry, N. (1975). "Paradigms of Public Administration." *Public Administration Review*. 35: 4: 378–385.

Hodgetts, J. E. (1991). *Public Management: Emblem of Reform for the Canadian Public Service*. Ottawa: Canadian Centre for Management Development.

———. (1997). "The Intellectual Odyssey of Public Administration in English Canada." *Canadian Public Administration*. 40: 2: 171–185.

Hodgetts, J. E., et al. (1972). *The Biography of an Institution: the Civil Service Commission of Canada, 1908–1967*. Montreal: McGill-Queen's University Press.

Hodgetts, J. E., and D. C. Corbett, eds. (1960). *Canadian Public Administration*. Toronto: Macmillan.

Hood, C. (1991). " A Public Management for All Seasons?" *Public Administration*. 69: 1: 3–19.

Inwood, G. J. (2009 [1999]). *Understanding Canadian Public Administration: An Introduction to Theory and Practice*. Scarborough: Prentice-Hall.

Johnson, C., and E. B. Keehn. (1994). "A Disaster in the Making: Rational Choice and Asian Studies." *The National Interest*. 36: 14–22.

Johnson, D. (2006 [2002]). *Thinking Government: Public Sector Management in Canada*. Peterborough, ON: Broadview Press.

Kernaghan, K. (1993). "Partnership and Public Administration: Conceptual and Practical Considerations." *Canadian Public Administration*. 36: 1: 57–76.

———. (1997). "Shaking the Foundations: Traditional versus New Public Service Values." In *New Public Management and Public Administration in Canada*, edited by M. Charih and A. Daniels, 47–65. Toronto: Institute of Public Administration of Canada.

Kernaghan, K. (with J. Gura). (2004). "Integrating Information Technology Into Public Administration: Conceptual and Practical Considerations." *Canadian Public Administration*. 47: 4: 525–546.

Kernaghan, K., ed. (1983). *Canadian Public Administration: Discipline and Profession*. Toronto: Butterworths.

Kernaghan, K., B. Marson, and S. Borins. (2000). *The New Public Organization*. Toronto: Institute of Public Administration of Canada.

Kernaghan, K., and D. Siegel. (1999 [1989]). *Public Administration in Canada: A Text*. Scarborough: Nelson Canada.

Kernaghan, K., and A. M. Wilms, eds. (1971 [1968]). *Public Administration in Canada: Selected Readings*. Toronto: Methuen.

Kuhn, T. S. (1970). *The Structure of Scientific Revolutions*. Chicago: University of Chicago Press.

Lemieux, V. (1965). "L'analyse stratégique des organisations administratives." *Canadian Public Administration*. 8: 4: 535–547.

———. (1979). *Le cheminement de l'influence: Systèmes, stratégies, structures du politique*. Québec: Les Presses de l'Université Laval.

———. (2000). "Government Roles in Governance Processes." In *Modernizing Government: A Preliminary Exploration*, edited by J. Jenson et al. Ottawa: Canadian Centre for Management Development.

Lovrich, N. (1985). «Contending Paradigms in Public Administration: A Sign of Crisis or Intellectual Vitality?» *Administration and Society.* 17: 3: 307–330.

McSwite, O. C. (1997). *Legitimacy in Public Administration: A Discourse Analysis.* Thousand Oaks, CA: Sage Publications.

Mercier, J. (2002). *L'administration publique: De l'École classique au nouveau management public.* Quebec: Les Presses de l'Université Laval.

Merton, R. K. (1951). *Social Theory and Social Structure.* Glencoe, IL: Free Press.

Minogue, M. (1983). "Theory and Practice in Public Policy and Administration." *Policy and Administration.* 11: 1: 63–85.

Minogue, M., C. Podano, and D. Hulme. (1998). *Beyond the New Public Management: Changing Ideas and Practice in Governance.* Cheltenham, UK: Edward Elgar.

Oman, R. C., and S. R. Chitwood. (1984). "Management Evaluation Studies: Factors Affecting the Acceptance of Recommendations." *Evaluation Review.* 8: 3: 283–305.

Organization for Economic Cooperation and Development. (1995). *Governance in Transition.* Paris: OECD.

Osborne, D., and T. Gaebler. (1992). *Reinventing Government.* Reading, UK: Addison-Wesley.

Pal, L. A. (1987). *Public Policy Analysis: An Introduction.* Toronto: Methuen.

Paquet, G. (1999). *Governance through Social Learning.* Ottawa: University of Ottawa Press.

Parenteau, R., ed. *Management public: comprendre et gérer les institutions de l'État.* Sillery, QC: Les Presses de l'Université du Québec.

Peters, B. G. (2000). "Globalization, Institutions and Governance." In *Revitalizing the Public Service: A Governance Vision for the XXIst Century,* edited by B. G. Peters and D. J. Savoie, 29–57. Montreal: McGill-Queen's University Press.

Peters, B. G., and J. Pierre. (1998). "Governance Without Government? Rethinking Public Administration." *Journal of Public Administration Research and Theory.* 8: 2: 223–243.

Peters, B. G., and D. J. Savoie, eds. (1995). *Governance in a Changing Environment.* Montreal: McGill-Queen's University Press.

———. (1998). *Taking Stock: Assessing Public Service Reforms.* Montreal: McGill-Queen's University Press.

———. (2000). *Revitalizing the Public Service: A Governance Vision for the Twenty-first Century.* Montreal: McGill-Queen's University Press.

Pétry, F. (1997). "'Recension' de Dobuzinskis, Howlett, and Laycock." *Politique et Sociétés.* 16: 1: 175–178.

Pollitt, C. (1990). *Managerialism and the Public Service: The Anglo-American Experience.* Cambridge, UK: Basil Blackwell.

Pross, A. P. (2006). "An Unruly Messenger: Interest Groups and Bureaucracy in Canadian Democracy." A paper given to the annual conference of the Institute for Public Administration in Canada, Charlottetown, PEI.

Pross, A. P., and V. S. Wilson. (1976). "Graduate Education in Canadian Public Administration: Antecedents, Present Trends, and Portents." *Canadian Public Administration*. 9: 4: 515–541.

Rainey, H. G. (1994). "On Paradigms, Progress and Prospects for Public Management." *Journal of Public Administration Research and Theory*. 4: 1: 41–48.

Rainey, H. G., and J. E. Ryu. (2004). "Framing High Performance and Innovativeness in Government." In *The Art of Governance: Analyzing Management and Administration*, edited by P. Ingraham and L. E. Lynn, Jr., 20–45. Washington, DC: Georgetown University Press.

Renaud, G. (1984). *À l'ombre du rationalisme. La société, de sa dépendance à sa quotidienneté*. Montreal: Éditions Saint-Martin.

Rhodes, R. A. W. (1994) "Reinventing Excellence: Or How Best-Sellers Thwart the Search for Lessons to Transform the Public Sector." *Public Administration*. 72: 2: 281-289.

Rouillard, C. (1999). *Le syndrome du survivant dans la fonction publique fédérale du Canada: une étude théorique à la lumière de la théorie critique et de la déconstruction derridéenne*. Ottawa: Dissertation, Carleton University.

———. (2006). "Les partenariats public-privé et la reconfiguration de l'État québécois," In *Le Parti Libéral: Enquête sur les réalisations du gouvernement Charest*, edited by F. Pétry, É. Bélanger, and L. Imbeau, 159–177. Quebec: Les Presses de l'Université Laval.

Rutgers, M. (1997). "Beyond Woodrow Wilson: the Identity of the Study of Public Administration in Historical Perspective." *Administration and Society*. 29: 3: 276–300.

Saint-Martin, D. (2004). "Managerialist Advocate or Control Freak? The Janus-faced Office of the Auditor General." *Canadian Public Administration*. 47: 2: 121–140.

Savoie, D. (2006). "The Canadian Public Service Has a Personality." *Canadian Public Administration*. 49: 3: 261–281.

Séguin, F., and J-F. Chanlat. (1983). *Les theories de l'organisation*. Saint-Jean sur Richelieu, QC: Éditions Préfontaine.

Simard, J-J. (1979). *La longue marche des technocrates*. Montreal: Éditions Saint-Martin.

Simard, L., A. Dupuis, and L. Bernier. (2006). "Entreprises publiques et intérêt general à l'heure de la gouvernance." *Administration publique du Canada*. 49: 3: 308–333.

Simon, H. (1957). *Administrative Behavior*. New York: Free Press.

Smith, M. (2005). "Institutionalism in the Study of Canadian Politics: the English-Canadian Tradition." In *New Institutionalism: Theory and Analysis*, edited by A. Lecours. Toronto: University of Toronto Press.

Sutherland, S. L. (1980). "On the Audit Trail of the Auditor General: Parliament's Servant, 1973–1980." *Canadian Public Administration*. 23: 1: 572–580.

Sutherland, S. L. (1991). "Responsible Government and Ministerial Responsibility: Every Reform Is Its Own Problem." *Canadian Journal of Political Science*. 24: 4: 91–120.

Thomas, P. T. (1996). "Beyond the Buzzwords: Coping with Change in the Public Sector." *International Review of Administrative Science*. 62: 1: 5–36.

Ventriss, C. (1991). "Contemporary Issues in American Public Administration Education: the Search for an Educational Focus." *Public Administration Review*. 51: 1: 4–14.

Weiss, T. G. (2001). "Governance, Good Governance and Global Governance: Conceptual and Actual Challenges." *Third World Quarterly*. 21: 5: 795–814.

Westmacott, M. W., and H. Mellon. (1999). *Public Administration and Policy: Governing in Challenging Times*. Scarborough, ON: Prentice-Hall Canada.

Whicker, M. L., R. A. Strickland, and D. Olshfski. (1993). "The Troublesome Cleft: Public Administration and Political Science." *Public Administration Review*. 53: 6: 531–541.

Wilson, V. S. (1981). *Canadian Public Policy and Administration: Theory and Environment*. Toronto: McGraw-Hill Ryerson.

2 PUBLIC ADMINISTRATION RESEARCH AND ORGANIZATION THEORY:

Recovering Alternative Perspectives on Public Service Institutions

Evert Lindquist

INTRODUCTION

Ted Hodgetts's *The Canadian Public Service: A Physiology of Government 1867–1970* (1972) is rightly regarded as a classic study in the field of Canadian public administration. It provided an assessment of an important national institution; explored its historical evolution and the mandates and interests of line and central agencies; and coined the term "structural heretics." It also identified emerging issues and tensions as the public service was growing quickly in a rapidly changing governance environment, many becoming enduring issues and tensions that three generations of scholars wrestle with to this day. Aside from its elegant and often wry rendering of the state of public administration at the national level, *The Canadian Public Service* is intriguing to this reader because Hodgetts drew on concepts and models from organization theory (among other sources) to analyze a complex evolving institution, and anticipated approaches later elucidated in that literature.

Much has changed in the world of public administration and governance in the last thirty-five years, but this chapter argues that the field of Canadian public administration has not kept up with and taken advantage of the organization theory literature, while recognizing there are many other rapidly expanding fields to monitor, including our own. Indeed, our collective understanding of organization theory seems to have virtually frozen since *The Canadian Public Service* was published.

With some exceptions, we have not kept abreast of the literature on organizations, a diverse interdisciplinary field that has exploded since the early 1970s (often grouped into the broad and overlapping areas of organization theory, organizational behaviour, and organizational change and development). Conversely, public sector organizations have not received the attention they should in organizational studies. This chapter argues that such gaps are worthy of note, deserve some explanation, and have implications for how research and faculty renewal in public administration, along with "network" strategies, might evolve in the years to come.

This chapter has five parts. It begins with a closer look at *The Canadian Public Service*, particularly drawing attention to Hodgetts's references to organization theory and the metaphors he invoked to describe and analyze the institution. The second part attempts to gauge contemporary use of organization theory by surveying some well-known texts on Canadian public administration and what strands of the literature they emphasize, and by considering examples of their selected use in articles and books. The chapter then identifies strands of the more recent organization theories that have not been recognized or utilized, and the kind of research agendas they imply. The fourth part attempts to explain why the gaps mentioned above emerged after the 1960s and the possible implications for the field of Canadian public administration, including the narrowing of our relevance over a broader set of issues that confront governments. The chapter concludes by considering how our field of public administration might address these gaps, particularly since there are many other fields that could equally inform our analyses. I suggest that we need to recover the posture Hodgetts had in the 1960s with respect to organization theory and other fields pertinent to public sector governance, but to do so requires adopting network strategies.

Hodgetts's "Physiology" of Government: Working at Many Levels

For most readers, *The Canadian Public Service* is a seminal and comprehensive account of the state of Canadian public administration at the national level in the early 1970s, exploring the internal dynamics and the state of the institution as a whole. For readers with some background in organization theory, turning the pages of *The Canadian Public Service* is a revelation because of the work it taps into and the later theoretical currents it anticipates. Though the book did not use organization theory for scaffolding, Hodgetts was clearly aware of early and then more recent contributions to the literature. In what follows, we consider Hodgetts' intentions, the authors he cited, and the metaphors and perspectives he invoked or anticipated.

The book is best understood as offering, in part, a dialogue with emerging approaches from organization theory, as well as with others from systems analysis and behavioural traditions. In the preface to the volume, John Meisel wrote,

> Professor Hodgetts, while fully cognizant of—and ever ready to draw on—the insights and benefits provided by organization theory, systems analysis, functionalism-structuralism, and most of the other props which have enriched our studies of society, remains closely attached to the historical and environmental parameters within which the public service performs its tasks. (Hodgetts, 1972: vii)

The book accomplished what the author set out to do: primarily to convey the state of the Canadian public service, as well as the issues and tensions emerging during an era of great growth and new forms of political oversight. Hodgetts sought perspectives to assist in this project, rather than using the opportunity to showcase certain streams of theory.

Hodgetts, however, did see *The Canadian Public Service* as providing an opportunity to broaden horizons and open up new theoretical horizons. He wrote,

> The major part of this book, relying on relatively straightforward techniques of analysis, is directed to an attempt to open up the subject, to dissect and describe the anatomy and physiology of the federal public service. If it provides the incentive for others to launch

> studies to fill the many obvious gaps, using more sophisticated
> research techniques, this volume will have attained the limited
> objectives imposed by the prevailing state of our studies. (1972: xiii)

In this regard, Hodgetts anticipated criticism about whether he was relying too heavily on early insights from the organization and administrative literature, and on a historical-legal perspective as his primary empirical approach.

> The public service, both in the tasks it is required to perform and in
> the ways it is organized to accomplish these tasks, is a reflection of
> the community it exists to serve. The verification of this hypothesis
> is attempted in the first four chapters. While this so-called 'ecological
> approach' to public organizations is in keeping with contemporary
> academic fashions, other portions of this book may be viewed by
> many students as wedded too closely to the classical school of public
> administration theorists who enjoyed their heyday in the 1930s.

> The failure to adopt these exciting contemporary tools of analysis is
> not a mark of disapproval or disagreement: the preference for more
> pedestrian modes of inquiry is simply based on an old-fashioned
> notion that we must first learn to walk before we can fly. In this
> respect, such weaknesses as this study exposes are reflections of the
> comparative neglect of the subject by students of Canadian public
> administration and the retarded stage of development in which it
> languished. (1972: xii)

With this frank assessment of the state of the field, Hodgetts identified priorities for where colleagues should invest their energies. He recommended that they focus on deepening their understanding of decision-making, exchange and transactions with the public and inside the bureaucracy, internal adaptive processes, and bureaucratic accountability. Anticipating some push-back from colleagues, he wrote,

> There is a simple, straightforward defence that can be mustered
> in favour of the procedures used for analyzing the allocation of
> programmes to departments and agencies and for exploring the
> internal division of labour: it has not yet been done and it should be
> done before we fly off to the esoteric realms inhabited by modern-
> day organizational theorists and administrative behaviouralists.
> (1972: xii)

It was interesting ground to choose given that Hodgetts monitored
and invoked many of the early and emerging precepts of organization
theory in analyzing public administration developments in Canada.
Some might argue that this remains a compelling argument to this day;
one this author has been mindful of when crafting this chapter.

While Hodgetts did not see theory-building as a priority for the
field of Canadian public administration, he was aware of currents
in the organization theory literature. In addition to the classical
theorists—Weber, Fayol, Taylor, Gulick, Urwick, and White—he
noted Simon's *Administrative Behavior* and Selznick's *Leadership in
Administration* and was undoubtedly aware of the salvos against
the "proverbs" of administration (Simon, 1945; Dahl, 1947), really
a debate about different notions and standards for "sciences" of
administration. Through his reading, but also through secondary
sources (Pfiffner and Presthus,1967; March, 1965), Hodgetts would
have been aware of the following: emerging concepts of power, goals,
decision-making, leadership, survival, and external environment in the
study of organizations from economics, politics, sociology, psychology,
management, and informatics; theoretical and experimental approaches
to understanding individual and group behaviour, including personality,
motivation, strain (what we now call "stress"), and socialization in
workplaces and organizations; ideas about the importance of size and
complexity of organizations and their implications for structure; and
the effects of new technology, such as computers.

That he did not choose to produce a huge bibliography and adopt
more of a conceptual approach in *The Canadian Public Service* reflects
nothing more than a proper focus on the specific task at hand: providing
perspective on the evolution and rapidly increasing complexity of a large-

scale organization. However, Hodgetts repeatedly invoked metaphors that pointed towards new analytic and methodological approaches, as well as towards ones that emerged later in organization theory. His master metaphor, of course, was that of "physiology" (Hodgetts, 1972: 1, 87), but a closer look—in part with the benefit of hindsight and more supple terminology that has since emerged in the field of organization theory—shows that Hodgetts was pointing to many different aspects of organization in a public sector context. These included the following perspectives:

- **Natural organism:** Hodgetts characterized the public service as an organism that would experience "birth, growth, adaptation, and decay" (1972: 5). Elsewhere in the book, he depicted the Canadian public service as interested in survival and thus adapting goals, structure, or position to perceived threats and competition (1972: 1). This was consistent with Selznick's (1948) framework in the structural-functional tradition, with a focus on co-optation.
- **Cybernetics:** Elements of the excerpts from the *Encyclopaedia Britannica* on "physiology" supplied by Hodgetts pointed to the notion that organizations—like organisms—monitor, anticipate, and adapt to change in their environment. Lifted from the organism proper, however, allows one to variously label such perspectives as cybernetics, information-processing, and learning perspectives.
- **Repertoires:** Hodgetts did not cite Cyert and March's (1963) *A Behavioral Theory of the Firm*, but reserved considerable space to describing the public service as a complex organization with a variety of programs and routines, as well as efforts to introduce new routines and procedures for coordination and control. Later, this would become a central feature of Allison's *Essence of Decision* (1971).
- **Transactions and exchange:** Hodgetts wondered how the Canadian public service engaged in "mutual exchange" with

citizens and other elements in its environment (1972: 17), and presumably among constituent programs, departments, and agencies. This interest not only reflected the work of exchange theorists such as Homans (1958), Levine and White (1961), and Blau (1968) but would later be taken up in a very different way by Williamson (1981) to explain how organizations structure themselves to minimize the costs of transactions.

- Tasks and technology: If there is a foundational concept in organization theory, it is not goals, but tasks (Dill, 1958), which often define not only the immediate task environment but also the culture of those conducting the tasks, as well as the individuals and organizations they deal with. Hodgetts was aware of, but did not delve into, tasks, although tasks are closely related to exchange. Tasks are also closely linked to technology, and while he was interested in and the understood the importance of technological change (1972: 26–30), the approach in the book is more historical (Innis, 1995) and did not utilize emerging ideas from the literature. The nature of tasks and technology would become a pivotal dimension for analysis (Thompson 1967; Tushman and Anderson, 1986).

- Morphology: Hodgetts's notion of physiology was also invoked to consider how the structure of an institution might evolve like an organism (biologists would call this "morphology"), not only as part of a natural stage of growth and maturity but also intentionally, to align workings and structure with new environments or to *alter* its external environments and its own. There is a distinction and a tension between these two drivers of morphological change.

- Ecological perspectives and natural selection: Hodgetts identified competitive processes inside and outside the public service arising from its elements worrying about survival—in this sense, strategy or reflex arises from a threat from either the internal or external environment. Hodgetts, like the literature at the time, did not have a well-developed notion of evolving environments, which would come later, but he put his finger on another core issue: whether institutions have the ability to alter strategy and structures as opposed to get getting compromised or "selected" by their environments, such as new governments or different economic circumstances (Child, 1972; Chandler, 1962; Hannan and Freeman, 1989).

- **Punctuated equilibria:** This was certainly not a concept that was circulating in social science circles in the 1960s, since it was coined by Eldredge and Gould (1972) as a perspective from paleontology on evolutionary dynamics (see also Gould, 2002). However, it is worth noting that Hodgetts's historical-institutional-legal perspective relied heavily on having sufficient time to discern and make sense of change. Hodgetts was very aware that he was observing an institution that was in an era of rapid growth, as well as significant and complex internal and external change, with profound implications for the shape and survival of its structures.

- **Organization design and change:** Hodgetts, of course, was interested in the design of organizational structures, even if this was largely derived from the classical tradition of allocating formal responsibility to central, departmental, regional, and noncore public service forms (1972: 129–37). He was aware of growing interest in the sources of motivation for individuals and groups (Argyris, 1957; Herzberg 1966) and the need for new structures and approaches to coordination, many of which were cascading from the political level. From ecological and physiological vantage points, though, he saw this as a process of adaptation and repositioning.

Hodgetts's *The Canadian Public Service* is remembered for its synoptic view of a key institution, with deft historical brushstrokes to depict and explain its trajectory and challenges as it entered into a period of great change. However, in rendering and analyzing this picture, he brought to bear considerable diversity and nuance in conceptual perspectives, even if social science terminology took a few years to catch up with him. This observation, in my view, is possible only if one understands a range of theoretical concepts and traditions from contemporary organization theory. Hodgetts, of course, did not run all these concepts and forms of analysis through the book, which was not his intention. Many were squarely juxtaposed with concepts and approaches advocated by systems theorists like David Easton and Gabriel Almond, so popular at the time.

Based on his evaluation of the "retarded state of development" of Canadian public administration, Hodgetts identified the research priorities of decision-making, internal processes, dealing with external stakeholders, and accountability. The next two generations of enormously productive scholars effectively took this seriously, rapidly exploring the processes, instruments, actors, and values animating the Canadian public service (namely, Aucoin, Borins, Bourgault, Doern, Dwivedi, Good, Gow, Kernaghan, Langford, Phidd, Prince, Pross, Savoie, Schultz, Sutherland, Tupper, Van Loon, Wilson, and Zussman, as well as their students). With these priorities largely addressed, did the field since "fly off to the esoteric realms inhabited by modern-day organizational theorists and administrative behaviouralists"?

CANADIAN PUBLIC ADMINISTRATION AND ORGANIZATION THEORY: FOSSILIZED INSIGHT?

Where might we go to gauge the extent of understanding and use of organization theory precepts in Canadian public administration? One place to begin is with the best-known textbooks in the field. Several nicely crafted textbooks include Kernaghan and Siegel (1999), Inwood (2004), Johnson (2006), and Barker (2008). Each contains one or more dedicated chapters on organization theory.[1] In varying degrees, they contain references to the following authors and themes:

- Formal organization: Typically, there is reference to the work of Weber, Fayol, Gulick, and Urwick on the bureaucratic form and its underpinnings, including goals, hierarchy, offices, and legal authority. All these books contain sections describing the attack on the "proverbs of administration" by Simon on the early efforts to identify principles for design.

- Informal organization and motivation: Each book reviews the contributions of Barnard, Follett, the Hawthorne experiments (Mayo, Roethlisberger, and Dickson), Maslow, Herzberg, Argyris, and McGregor. The focus here is on the informal and human dimensions of organizations, and different leadership styles with this in mind. Some books, in highly selective idiosyncratic ways, delve into certain models of decision-making and participatory management.

- Scientific management, TQM, and change: The books spend considerable time on Taylor and scientific management, which was equally critical and demanding of workers and managers alike. They all consider Total Quality Management (TQM) and, in varying degrees, the principles and approaches to organizational development.

- Systems and environmental perspectives: Some texts, in less thorough and accurate fashion, describe the arrival of systems theory and cybernetic perspectives and their linkages to Thompson's seminal *Organizations in Action* (1967) and contingency perspectives. One book mentions, in passing, population ecology perspectives.

The reviews found in these textbooks are concise and generally dispassionate. Little effort is made to integrate across these approaches, except to make room for the critics, nor are they linked or adapted for a public administration context. The cited literature on true organizational theory rarely extends beyond the 1960s, unless referring to popular writers or, as we shall discuss shortly, new public management (NPM). There is virtually no reference to contemporary literature on organizational analysis from the 1970s and beyond in any of the categories utilized (i.e., no effort to provide the latest thinking and empirical studies in each tradition). None of these textbooks in any way meaningfully review the literature on organizations, tasks, and environments. There is no evidence that any of the above-mentioned authors have conducted research in any of these areas or are familiar with recent research published in journals associated with them.[2]

Another way to arrive at an assessment of the extent of understanding and use of organization theory precepts in Canadian public administration is to identify scholars who have invoked or relied on concepts from organization theory to focus or illuminate their own work. Some examples come to mind, and they include the following:

- Peter Aucoin and Herman Bakvis published *The Centralization-Decentralization Connundrum* (1988), which, among other works, relied on the concepts of organization differentiation and integration from Lawrence and Lorsch's seminal 1967 article.

- Doug Stevens's *Corporate Autonomy and Institutional Control: The Crown Corporation as a Problem in Organization Design* (1993) tapped into the strategy-structure literature, as well as contingency and transaction-cost economics perspectives to inform his analytic framework on how to balance autonomy and control of Crown corporations by governments.

- Jim Desveaux, in *Designing Bureaucracies: Institutional Capacity and Large-Scale Problem Solving* (1995), provided a detailed examination of how the Department of Energy, Mines, and Resources mobilized the capacity to design and announce the National Energy Program, and then out-negotiate Alberta counterparts.

- Lindquist married concepts from the organizational literature on tasks and task environments with policy network concepts in "New Agendas for Research on Policy Communities" (1996) to develop the beginnings of a more elegant theory of central agency internal interactions.

- Barbara Wake Carroll and David Siegel's *Service in the Field* (1999), which, along with concepts from other fields, tapped into the literature on organizational culture; differentiation and integration; front-line and street-level bureaucrat perspectives; self-correcting organizations; dimensions of bureaucracy; public choice and behavioural perspectives on organizations; and matrix organization.

- Jonathan Malloy's dissertation and book, *Between Colliding Worlds* (2003), used concepts from organization theory, such as boundary-spanning, institutional isomorphism, role conflict, and self-designing organizations, to explore the tensions and dynamics of central secretariats in government designed to respond to social movements advocating for women and Aboriginals.

Undoubtedly there are more examples of the utilization of organization theory concepts by Canadian public administration scholars, but I suspect we would quickly conclude that, even with additional examples, it still constitutes selective use and certainly not the focus of empirical investigations of public administration scholars. It would also serve to underscore a key point: The use of such concepts and perspectives from contemporary organization theory is not recognized in the textbooks that define the field in our country. Moreover, these approaches are not likely taught in any traditional Ph.D.-level core course on public administration in departments of political science, unless with a professor who has a strong interest in the area.[3] We have come a long way from the early days of public administration when there was a substantial overlap in scholarship and lesson-drawing from the field of organization, and vice versa. Arguably, the peak period for such lesson-drawing and influence lasted from the 1930s to the 1970s.

This stands in considerable contrast with US public administration scholarship. My sense is that a higher proportion of public administration scholars south of the border have a strong grounding in organizational analysis—it may not be a majority of scholars, but a sufficient number to keep ideas in circulation, canvass newer insights from organization theory, and share them with colleagues. This is attributable to a far stronger presence of quantitative, behavioural, and rational choice traditions in US departments of political science, and, relatedly, more interdisciplinary public policy and public administration schools and programs of scale. Scale not only means that it will be more likely that one or more colleagues in a program will take interest in organization theory (and such a person could be from business, political science, sociology, economics, law, and even public administration) but that the sheer number of specialists in any subdiscipline or subfield greatly increases the chance that there will be scholars who cross over or mine other disciplines. Several examples of crossover scholars immediately come to mind, and examples include Moe (1984; 1990), La Porte (1970; 1996; with Frederickson, 2002), Chisholm (1989), Kelman (2005), and O'Toole and Meier (2004). Such interest has been fostered by journals that welcome articles using organization theory concepts among other contributions—*Administrative Science Quarterly*, *Public Administration Review*, and *Administration and Society*—as well as journals specializing in making such connections, such as the *Journal of Public Administration Research and Theory* and, more recently, the *International Journal of Public Management*.

These positive perceptions, however, might be overstated. Steven Kelman, as the new editor of *International Journal of Public Management*, has aggressively committed himself to fostering a dialogue between scholars from the worlds of organization theory and public administration. This has been reflected in appointments to the journal's editorial board of scholars with strong credentials in organization theory. So, even if the knowledge and linkages in the US look richer from the vantage point of Canada, the connections may be tenuous. This view is buttressed by a recent review by Pfeffer (2006) of the *Oxford Handbook of Public Management* entitled, "Like Ships Passing in the Night: The Separate Literatures of Organization Theory and Public Management." He sees a disjuncture between the literature and missed opportunities: on the one hand, a lack of theory illuminating public management issues and practice, and on the other, a lack of learning from public organizations for the purposes of theory-building.

RECOVERING PERSPECTIVES FROM CONTEMPORARY ORGANIZATION THEORY

One can imagine that a challenge would soon emerge from public administration scholars: If organization theory is so fantastic, why does it not spill over onto our radar scopes and meet us more than halfway? Perhaps, as Hodgetts suggested many years ago, however intriguing, the literature is simply too esoteric, theoretical, and perhaps normatively unaligned with the field of public administration.

With this reasonable question in mind, what horizons might a fuller appreciation of organization theory literature lead to? Here are some snapshots of the possibilities:

- **Institutionalized environments:** In contrast to the political science institutional literature, this work considers the symbolic and positioning needs of organizations and examines ways in which organizations decouple central administration from the "technical core" of organizations, thereby providing a "buffer" from the broader environment (Meyer and Rowan, 1977; Meyer, Scott, and Deal, 1981; DiMaggio and Powell, 1983; 1991; Weick, 1976). Interestingly, this is inherently a comparative perspective, exploring how classes of organizations align (or appear to align) with broader regimes in their environments.

- **Ecological perspectives:** This literature applies concepts from the fields of biology and ecology that examine the rise and fall of natural species to study narrow classes of organization (Hannan and Freeman, 1977; 1989). It aggressively relies on the concept of natural selection, has interesting models of the nature of environmental change, and presumes organizations find it difficult to adapt their structures and strategies to environmental change. More recent contributions consider how specific organizational forms evolve with other forms (Astley, 1985; DiMaggio, 1994; Rao, 2002). If combined with organizational systematics (below), we could ascertain how public service institutions have been evolving, and what is getting "selected" in and out.

- **Organizational systematics:** This approach (McKelvey, 1982) borrows heavily from the fields of systematics and phylogenetics in biology, which seek to identify different species according to key features reflecting reproductive integrity, and to inform assessments and debates about the ontogeny (the evolving structure and development over a typical life of a species member), as well as the evolutionary trajectories, of the species as a whole. Organizational systematics attempts to adapt this logic and methodology for a different species, and it appears fraught with difficulties (e.g., What should be the unit of analysis: organizational structure, technology, or compools?). However, a potential insight here is that we have precious little data and indicators about how the contours of public service institutions and their constituent elements have been changing, and this could also be a comparative approach within and across institutions.

- Organizational fields and networks: There has been tremendous progress in the fields of political science and policy studies with respect to recognizing and characterizing policy networks and communities (see Pross, 1986; Atkinson and Coleman, 1989; Coleman and Skogstad, 1990), and even how to manipulate and nurture these networks and communities (Kickert, Klijn, and Koppenjan, 1997; Lindquist, 1992). However, arguably, there has been less progress and realization of the original promise (Atkinson and Coleman, 1989) for systematic assessments of the dynamics and learning in these networks (Lindquist, 1992) that carefully examine how individuals, information, and other resources move through these networks, and whether and how they can adapt to deal with the broad challenges confronting sectors. Given that a major preoccupation of public service leaders is how to build and work in more robust and flexible networks at the sector and front-line levels, there seems potential for yields in understanding by linking the original organizational field perspectives (Levine and White, 1961; Evan, 1966; Warren, 1967) with the societal sector approach (Scott, 1991) and finer-grained network theory from sociology and related disciplines, anticipated by Kickert, Klijn, and Koppenjan (1997), who tap into organization theory perspectives.

- **Transaction-cost economics and institutional design:** One key reason for delving into networks and systematics from a public administration perspective is because the core responsibilities in public service institutions have evolved, ostensibly from "rowing" to "steering" roles, such as policy design, network facilitation, and monitoring and evaluating programs and performance. There is little analysis of how alternative service delivery arrangements, such as public-private partnerships, actually work with respect to risks, costs, decisions, errors, and oversights. One analytic approach for exploring such matters is the transaction-cost economics set out by Williamson (1981; 1990), which relies on careful examination of task structure, exchange, and institutional arrangements. The key research question here is: When services are spun "outside" the public service, is this really the case? Such analysis would inform how we typically think about the more formal contours of public service institutions.

- **Real-time decision-making:** For many public administration scholars, the notion of "loose-coupling" as a focus of interest and variable (Weick, 1976; Orton and Weick, 1990) may seem beyond the pale. However, Perrow (1984), Frederickson and La Porte (2002), and Roe et al. (2005)—to name but a few examples—have applied the concepts to analyzing how high-reliability organizations (Lerner, 1986) work under stress when monitoring and guiding critical public infrastructure, and how better to design the system and its coordinating capabilities. Reminiscent, in part, of the Mintzberg (1974) empirical study of executive work, this style of research involves close observation and mastery of the technical, cognitive, and decision-making strategies of "operators." It is hard to overstate its importance and relevance, focusing on specific constellations of tasks and responsibilities.

- **Organizational engagement and culture:** Public sector leaders have indicated that they want to change organizational cultures, instilling leadership and improving the feedback loops to executive teams and institutional leaders. Although there has been much ink spilled in academic and applied journals about organizational development and change strategies, there appears to be relatively little analysis of the extent to which organization cultures change, which in turn requires the capability to measure, characterize, and monitor different organizational cultures. There are many frameworks for doing so (e.g., Cameron and Quinn, 2006), and tremendous potential for joining these frameworks, theories of motivation, and assessments to analyze employee engagement surveys. Some work has been done on workplace dynamics (e.g., Lowe, 2000; Verma and Lonti, 2001; Lonti and Verma, 2003; Lonti, Slinn, and Verma, 2002; Lyons, Duxbury, and Higgins, 2006), but more should be done on this important theme associated with the early days of public administration and organization research.

Similar suggestions for research agendas based on conceptual groundwork could be made with respect to writing on radical organizational change and development (i.e., Tushman and O'Reilly, 1996; Greenwood and Hinings, 1996; Freeman and Cameron, 1993; Gersick, 2003); on learning and information utilization incentives (Feldman and March, 1981; March, 1988; March, 1991); and on the adoption of new technologies by organizations, especially involving discontinuities (Barley, 1990; Benner and Tushman, 2003; Tushman and Nelson, 1990; Tushman and Smith, 2002; Tushman and Anderson, 1986), but there is not the space to delve into these areas here.

Contemporary organization theory can be seen as incredibly intriguing and diverse: It has a bewildering array of different guiding metaphors, different levels of analysis, different conceptual frameworks, and different methodological approaches (Morgan, 1980; March, 1965; Scott, 2003; Baum, 2002). It is also a field where colleagues working in all of its myriad traditions seem to delight and celebrate in this diverse and evolving mix, and spend episodic moments trying to make sense of it (March, 1965; Nystrom and Starbuck, 1981; Perrow, 1986;

Williamson, 1990; Powell and DiMaggio, 1991; Clegg, Hardy, and, Nord, 1996; Tsouksas and Knudsen, 2003). None of this curiousness and ferment makes its way into Canadian public administration textbooks and very little into our research literature. Indeed, as a fan of the literature, one finds it hard not to be disappointed by its limited use in Canadian public administration.

In making these points and heaving audible sighs of regret, I should clarify my position in several important ways. First, I do not want to be construed as saying that the field of Canadian public administration research and teaching should become heavily skewed towards organization theory—there are other disciplinary and professional directions in which it could also grow. Nor am I suggesting that by delving into each strand of the literature, it will necessarily yield a sea change in how we perceive public organizations. Nor do I want to argue that the strands or currents in classic organization theory literature long identified as part of the canon by Canadian scholars be ignored or rejected. That said, Canadian textbooks claiming to impart the state of organization theory to students and colleagues need to re-evaluate their claims, and they should make every effort to showcase more recent empirical studies in the thematic areas they mine.

As Kelman and Pfeffer argue in the US context (see above), an ostensibly multidisciplinary field of Canadian public administration needs to move beyond its reliance on two dominant disciplines. One direction to take should entail reconnecting with the rich literature on organizational theory, behaviour, and change. Together, the contributors to this literature provide concepts and ideas that may clarify or raise the level of discussion when probing complex phenomenon such as the public sector. Taking this literature seriously may lead to new research agendas requiring different levels of analysis, new methodologies, and different collaborations. Immersion into these research directions does not mean devaluing public organization and Canadian perspectives; rather, it would probably strengthen them. Given the ubiquity, scale, and economic and democratic importance of public organizations, we should have far more influence on the research being conducted on organizations more generally, and this simply is not happening.

EXPLANATIONS AND IMPLICATIONS OF THE PA-OT GAPS: ARE WE FALLING BEHIND?

Before considering what directions Canadian public administration might take to recover its trade in ideas with organization theory, it will be useful to consider how we arrived at the current state of affairs.

First, all disciplines have fanned out since the 1960s—it is difficult to keep up with particular disciplines and one's subdisciplines, let alone others expanding at least at an equal rate, if not considerably more. In the case of organization theory, the 1960s and 1970s witnessed a remarkable proliferation of analytic and methodological perspectives, and eventually an increase in the number of journals in the area. Even scholars fully committed to organization theory find it hard to keep abreast of all the field's currents.

Second, Canadian political science has been relatively impervious to American and other literature, particularly when it comes to rational and public choice perspectives, and, aside from election and public opinion studies, the application of empirical methods to other areas of the discipline has not been as aggressive. To the extent that organization theory, in many quarters, relies on sophisticated quantitative methodologies, this may have created barriers to the monitoring and exchange of approaches, insights, and findings.

Third, most programs and schools of public administration in Canada are not genuinely interdisciplinary in the way that departments of geography, agriculture, and business have been for a long while. Public administration programs and schools tend to be dominated by political scientists and economists; few sociologists or business school graduates have been hired sporting comprehensives in organizational analysis. Our programs and schools tend to be "bi-disciplinary" in the main, with each discipline experiencing considerable proliferation in perspectives. The field of Canadian public administration—at least until recently—has been moved forward by a relatively small group of productive scholars, mainly political-science trained. Moreover, there was little hiring done during the 1980s, when the gaps between

Canadian public administration and organization theory were not as large and could have been more easily bridged.

Fourth, one can shift vantage points and ask: To what extent has organization theory literature reached out to public administration? The answer here has to be "very little," even though most contributors to the literature would claim that they are agnostic about the kinds of organizations that get studied. Indeed, public organizations are treated no differently than for-profit and third-sector organizations, but public administration scholars would be less likely to see a welcoming hand as a result. Contributors to this literature would be less likely to use as points of departure the concepts and challenges of democratic legitimacy and responsible government—they would be more likely to focus on tasks, interactions, environments, structures, and culture of organizations, whether public or not.

Aside from which organizations tend to be the focus of attention, it is certainly true that with its amazing conceptual, theoretical, and methodological diversity, the literature on organizations does not seem very coherent and can look like a hodgepodge to outsiders. This is well understood by core contributors, as any review of the major volumes dedicated to reviewing the state of the field will demonstrate: March (1965); the two-volume Nystrom and Starbuck (1981); the two editions of Clegg, Hardy, and Nord (1996); Baum (2002); and other integrating volumes, such as the five editions of Scott (2003), Perrow (1986), Williamson (1990), and Aldrich and Ruff (2006).

Conversely, it is important to recognize that there is much more to public administration than organization theory! One has only to review the many compelling topics captured by the *Handbook of Public Administration* edited by Peters and Pierre (2003) to see this is true, even if the handbook is dominated by scholars with political science backgrounds. Yet, there are many other perspectives and substantive areas that have received insufficient attention, particularly in the eyes of practitioners. These include information technology adoption and its impacts; supply-chain management; motivation and engagement of public servants; marketing and conveying of public service work to outside audiences; better use of information; studies on the nature and organization of work in different program areas (as opposed to the politics and managing networks in those areas); making public organizations environmentally sustainable; creating and managing diversity in public administration; and the day-to-day governance and management of departments and agencies, as opposed to outlining the principles of accountability (which several Canadian scholars have done very well). It should be easy to identify other equally compelling lines of investigation. All of this serves to reinforce the point that although organizations may be ubiquitous, there are many themes to mine from different disciplinary and professional perspectives, and organization theory perspectives constitute only one part of this mix.

This line of argument, even if deemed persuasive, needs to be put in perspective. The disinterest in modern organization theory by public administration scholars in Canada (because this has not been the case in the US and in some European quarters), and the juxtaposition of other equally important topics noted above is certainly not a unique problem for our field. Indeed, perhaps it is best to see it as just one case of a larger challenge confronting our public administration scholarly community. Here is our condition: We are a small band of academics (mostly with backgrounds in political science), with an interest in democratic public organizations who collectively attempt to keep abreast of international, national, provincial, territorial, municipal, and Aboriginal developments at the intersection of political and administrative realms. Our revealed preferences are that we believe it important to keep our eye on the high-level governance ball, because that is where authority and reform often flow (though not always!). Individually, but sometimes in pods, we make forays into more selective areas (the voluntary sector, diversity, specific policy domains, public-private partnerships, service delivery, ethics, etc.). Governments have steadily reached beyond public administration scholar-experts to move goalposts further forward in areas such as service quality, technology, alternative service delivery, engagement, and leadership, and as a group we typically play catch-up in these areas, no matter how good our scholarship. Governments are reaching out, as they should, to experts and scholars in many other disciplines (and they do this far better than we do as an interdisciplinary enterprise).

Sometimes we get pulled into these initiatives, but it is clear where the insight, demands, and energy come from.

The implication is that even as our best scholars continue to contribute and exercise influence in important ways (think of accountability, federalism, voluntary sector initiatives, etc.), and we continue to remind practitioners and the next generation of public servants at all levels of the important values and organizing principles in government, we could fall behind in important ways as a scholarly field.

CONCLUSION: EMULATING HODGETTS IN THE EARLY TWENTY-FIRST CENTURY

I have entered into these larger questions from the vantage point of organization theory, but really, the argument could have been made from many other directions and wound up in more or less the same place. These sorts of issues have been broached at meetings of the Canadian Association of Programs in Public Administration and the Canada School of Public Service, so some of these points are not new. I am not suggesting that all public administration scholars should be trained in organization theory, but I worry that too few of our Ph.D. students are aware of the existence of the field, and that, because of the small numbers problem, the chances are low for the few who might mine certain veins of that literature and marry them to public administration topics (or have to move to other fields or countries to get such a grounding). To this observer, this concern implies a multipart question:

- If scholars (and practitioners) need to keep abreast of the insights produced by other disciplines and professions, and, more dramatically, to work with colleagues from those disciplines and professions, to be on the leading (bleeding edge); and
- if we agree that traditional public administration and political science perspectives are *essential lynchpins* for filtering these perspectives to ensure appropriate levels of context are taken

into account, and thus must retain a robust role for reminding all concerned and interested about the distinctiveness of public organizations and how to apply alternative perspectives in a public sector context; and

- if, even though our community of scholars in public policy and administration schools is growing, the number of public administration scholars remains relatively small and possibly shrinking compared to the governance challenges, knowledge demands, and requisite methodological and disciplinary perspectives;

- then, how do we organize ourselves to operate in this environment?

While one partial solution is to write a compelling book that more fully makes the case outlined in these pages (but this task would require less devotion to administrative duties!), my view is that making significant progress is beyond the scope of any one scholar or program. I suspect, too, that the solution is beyond the capacity of any one school or program. It requires cultivating a posture among a community of scholars, where our networks of colleagues and programs across Canada can together find ways to scan, partner, concert, and exercise leverage in a more systematic and intelligent manner.

The foundations arguably are in place: The Canadian Association of Programs in Public Administration has grown steadily more robust over the years and, as noted above, these sorts of issues have been tabled (however, no real action has been taken). I believe that most of our colleagues would have a genuine interest in fostering, tapping into, and working in an interdisciplinary environment (though this would not be everyone's cup of tea, nor should it), and this requires assiduously cultivating networks of expertise outside the usual public administration beats. Indeed, developing such networks and repertoires would be an excellent way to engage governments, even if the goal would *not* be to align all of this activity with the needs of governments and other sponsors, precisely because individual takes on needs and directions are important sources of innovation and the need for certain kinds of insight cannot be anticipated. This model would entail encouraging individuals or groups to monitor and report on different areas of literature in a variety of fields, including organization theory, behaviour, and change.

As I consider these possibilities and juxtapose them against the capabilities we have in our field and the amount of change in public sector governance, there are interesting parallels to the decisions Hodgetts had to make when writing *The Canadian Public Service*. There was so much going on with respect to institutional and theoretical developments that he decided on a synoptic and suggestive study, rather than a comprehensive one, which meant that he did not delve into various domains as deeply as he could have. Only a master of the field of public administration and political science, with one eye firmly on emerging trends and issues in public sector institutions and the other scanning other fields such as organization and systems theory, could strike such an intriguing and productive balance. This chapter is suggesting that we consider collectively adopting a similar strategy at the network level to move our field forward by levering and anchoring insights from other fields along with our own.

NOTES

[1] Inwood (2004), chapters 2 and 3 are respectively on "Theories of Organization" and "Organization Theory and Canadian Public Administration"; Johnson's (2006) chapter 5 is "Theory of Organizational Design and Management Decision-Making"; and Kernaghan and Siegel (1999) and Barker (2008) have chapters 2, 3, and 4 respectively titled, "Public Administration and Organization Theory: The Structural Foundation"; "Public Administration and Organization Theory: The Humanistic Response"; and "Public Administration and Organization Theory: The New Public Management."

[2] The only modern work that gets explored in these works is the more popular management-guru literature, such as *In Search of Excellence* (Peters and Waterman, 1982) and *Reinventing Government* (Osborne and Gaebler, 1992), and so on. One textbook casts NPM as a theory of organization as opposed to a management and political philosophy. Any reference to NPM as having been inspired by organization theory, of course, is a misrepresentation of the literature. NPM proponents were inspired by the literature on public choice, and while this does constitute a theory of organization, it emanated from practitioners who sought out economics

and political science perspectives, and only later was identified as a tradition by academics. While a public administration Ph.D. course should require students to read such literature (the popular and more academic renderings), such reading would not materialize in a standard organization theory course. NPM has had no influence on the organization theory literature—indeed, many of the limitations and appropriate expectations for the NPM approach could have been anticipated by utilizing well-understood ideas in the modern organization theory literature.

[3]   Many years ago, I taught "Organization Theory and Public Organizations" at the University of Toronto's Department of Political Science. A similar course now constitutes one of the three core fields of the Ph.D. program in public administration at the University of Victoria.

REFERENCES

Aldrich, H. E., and J. Pfeffer. (1976). "Environments of Organizations." *Annual Review of Sociology*. 2: 79–105.

Aldrich, Howard E., and Martin Ruff. (2006). *Organizations Evolving*, 2nd ed. Thousand Oaks, CA: Sage.

Aldrich, H. E., and D. A. Whetton. (1981). "Organization-Sets, Action-Sets, and Networks: Making the Most of Simplicity." In *Handbook of Organizational Design*, vol. 1, edited by P. C. Nystrom and W. H. Starbuck, 385–408. New York: Oxford University Press.

Allison, Graham T. (1971). *Essence of Decision: Explaining the Cuban Missile Crisis*. Boston: Little, Brown.

Argyris, Chris (1957). *Personality and Organization*. New York: Harper.

Astley, W. G. (1985). "The Two Ecologies: Population and Community Perspectives on Organizational Evolution." *Administrative Science Quarterly*. 30: 224–241.

Atkinson, Michael, and William Coleman. (1989). *The State, Business, and Industrial Change in Canada*. Toronto: University of Toronto Press.

Aucoin, Peter, and Herman Bakvis. (1988). *The Centralization-decentralization Conundrum: Organization and Management in the Canadian Government*. Ottawa: Institute for Research on Public Policy.

Barker, Paul. (2008). *Public Administration in Canada*, brief edition. Toronto: Thomson Nelson.

Barley, Stephen. (March 1990). "The Alignment of Technology and Structure through Roles and Networks." *Administrative Science Quarterly*. 35: 1: 61–103.

Baum, Joel A. C., ed. (2002). *Blackwell Companion to Organizations*. Oxford: Blackwell.

Baum, J. A. C., and Tim Rowley. (2002). "Companion to Organizations: An Introduction." In *The Blackwell Companion to Organizations*, edited by Baum, 1–34. Oxford: Blackwell.

Benner, Mary J., and Michael L.Tushman. (2003). "Exploitation, Exploration, and Process Management: The Productivity Dilemma Revisited." *Academy of Management Review*. 28: 2: 238–256.

Blau, P. M. (1974 [1968]). "Social Exchange." In *On the Nature of Organizations*, 204–214. New York: John Wiley.

Cameron, K. S., and Robert E. Quinn. (2006). *Diagnosing and Changing Organizational Culture*, revised edition. San Francisco: Jossey-Bass.

Carroll, Barbara Wake, and David Siegel. (1999). *Service in the Field: The World of Front-Line Public Servants*. Kingston and Montreal: McGill-Queen's University Press.

Chandler, Alfred D., Jr. (1962). *Strategy and Structure: Chapters in the History of the American Industrial Enterprise*. Cambridge, MA: MIT Press.

Child, J. (June 1972). "Organizational Structure, Environment and Performance: The Role of Strategic Choice." *Sociology*. 6: 1–22.

Chisholm, Donald W. (1989). *Coordination without Hierarchy: Information Structures in Multiorganizational Systems*. Berkeley: University of California Press.

Clegg, S. R., C. Hardy, and W. R. Nord, eds. (1996). *Handbook of Organization Studies*. Thousand Oaks, CA: Sage.

Coleman, William D., and Grace Skogstad, eds. (1990). *Policy Communities and Public Policy in Canada: A Structuralist Approach*. Toronto: Copp Clark Pitman.

Cyert, Richard, and James G. March. (1992 [1963]). *A Behavioral Theory of the Firm*, 2nd ed. Massachusetts: Blackwell.

Dahl, R. A. (Winter 1947). "The Science of Public Administration: Three Problems." *Public Administration Review*. 7: 1: 1–11.

Dill, W. R. (1958). "Environment as an Influence on Managerial Activity." *Administrative Science Quarterly*. 2: 409–443.

DiMaggio, Paul. (1994). "The Challenge of Community Evolution." In *Evolutionary Dynamics of Organizations*, edited by Joel Baum and Jitendra Singh, 444–450. New York: Oxford University Press.

DiMaggio, Paul J., and Walter W. Powell. (April 1983). "The Iron Cage Revisited: Institutional Isomorphism and Collective Rationality in Organizational Fields." *American Sociological Review* 48: 2: 147–160.

———. (1991). Introduction to *The New Institutionalism in Organizational Analysis*, edited by Walter W. Powell and Paul J. DiMaggio. Chicago: University of Chicago Press.

Duncan, Robert B. (September 1972). "Characteristics of Organizational Environments and Perceived Environmental Uncertainty." *Administrative Science Quarterly*. 17: 3: 313–327.

Dunn, Christopher, ed. (2002). *The Handbook of Canadian Public Administration*. Don Mills, ON: Oxford University Press Canada.

Eldredge, N., and S. J. Gould. (1972). "Punctuated Equilibria: An Alternative to Phyletic Gradualism." In *Models in Paleobiology*, edited by T. J. M. Schopf, 82–115. San Francisco: Freeman, Cooper.

Emery, F. E., and E. L. Trist. (February 1965). "The Casual Texture of Environments." *Human Relations*. 18: 21–32.

Evan, W. (1966). "The Organization-Set: Toward a Theory of Interorganizational Relations." In *Approaches to Organizational Design*, edited by J. D. Thompson, 173–191. Pittsburgh: University of Pittsburgh.

Feldman, Martha, and James March. (June 1981). "Information in Organizations as Signal and Symbol." *Administrative Science Quarterly*. 26: 2: 171–186.

Frederickson, H. G., and Todd R. La Porte. (September 2002). "Airport Security, High Reliability, and the Problem of Rationality." *Public Administration Review*. 62: Special Issue on Homeland Security: 34–44.

Freeman, S., and Kim Cameron. (1993). "Organizational Downsizing: A Convergence and Reorientation Framework." *Organizational Science*. 4: 1: 10–29.

Gersick, Connie J. G. (2003). "Revolutionary Change Theories: A Multilevel Exploration of the Punctuated Equilibrium Paradigm." *Academy of Management Review*. 16: 10–36.

Gould, Stephen Jay. (2002). *The Structure of Evolutionary Theory*. Cambridge: Belknap of Harvard University Press.

Greenwood, Royston, and C. R. Hinings. (1996). "Understanding Radical Organizational Change: Bringing together the Old and the New Institutionalism." *The Academy of Management Review*. 21: 4: 1022–1054.

Gulick, Luther. (1937). "Notes on the Theory of Organization." In *Papers on the Science of Administration*, edited by Luther Gulick and L. Urwick. New York: Institute of Public Administration.

Hannan, Michael T., and John Freeman. (March 1977). "The Population Ecology of Organizations." *American Journal of Sociology*. 82: 5: 929–964.

———. (1989). *Organizational Ecology*. Cambridge: Harvard University Press.

Herzberg, Frederick. (1966). *Work and the Nature of Man*. Cleveland: World Publishing.

Hodgetts, J. E. H. (1972). *The Canadian Public Service: A Physiology of Government, 1867–1970*. Toronto: University of Toronto Press.

Homans, George C. (May 1958). "Social Behavior as Exchange." *American Journal of Sociology*. 63: 6: 597–606.

Innis, Harold A. (1995). *Staples, Markets, and Cultural Change*. Montreal and Kingston: McGill-Queen's University Press.

Inwood, Gregory. (2004). *Understanding Canadian Public Administration: An Introduction to Theory and Practice*, 2nd ed. Toronto: Pearson Prentice Hall.

Johnson, David. (2006). *Thinking Government: Public Sector Management in Canada*, 2nd ed. Peterborough: Broadview.

Kelman, Steven. (2005). *Unleashing Change: A Study of Organizational Renewal in Government*. Washington, DC: Brookings Institution.

Kernaghan, Kenneth, and David Siegel. (1999 [1989]). *Public Administration in Canada: A Text*, 4th ed. Toronto: Nelson.

Kickert, W. J. M., E. H. Klijn, and J. F. M. Koppenjan, eds. (1997). *Managing Complex Networks*. London: Sage.

La Porte, Todd R. (1970). "The Recovery of Relevance in the Study of Public Organizations." In *Toward a New Public Administration*, edited by F. Marini, chapter 2. San Francisco: Chandler Press.

———. (January 1996). "Shifting Vantage and Conceptual Puzzles in Understanding Public Organization Networks." *Journal of Public Administration Research and Theory*. 6: 1: 49–74.

Landau, Martin. (1969). "Redundancy, Rationality, and the Problem of Duplication and Overlap." *Public Administration Review*. 29: 4: 346–358.

———. (1999). "On Multiorganizational Systems in Public Administration." *Journal of Public Administration Research and Theory*. 1: 1: 5–18.

Lawrence, Paul R., and Jay W. Lorsch. (June 1967). "Differentiation and Integration in Complex Organizations." *Administrative Science Quarterly*. 12: 1: 1–47.

Lerner, A. W. (November 1986). "There is More than One Way to be Redundant: A Comparison of Alternatives for the Design and Use of Redundancy in Organizations." *Administration and Society*. 18: 3: 334–359.

Levine, S., and P. E. White. (1961). "Exchange as a Conceptual Framework for the Study of Interorganizational Relations." *Administrative Science Quarterly*. 5: 583–601.

Lindquist, Evert. (August 1992). "Classification and Relevance: A Strategy for Developing a Data-base and Taxonomy of Public Organizations in Canada." A paper presented to the Annual Meetings of the Institute of Public Administration, Winnipeg, MB..

———. (1992). "Public Managers and Policy Communities: Learning to Meet New Challenges." *Canadian Public Administration*. 5: 2: 127–159.

———. (1996). "New Agendas for Research on Policy Communities: Policy Analysis, Administration, and Governance." In *Policy Studies in Canada: The State of the Art*, edited by L. Dobuzinskis, M. Howlett, and D. Laycock, 219–241. Toronto: University of Toronto Press.

Lonti, Zsuzsanna, Sara Slinn, and Anil Verma. (2002). "Can Government Workplaces Be Made World-Class? Policy Challenges for Labour and

Management." *Canadian Labour & Employment Law Journal*. 9: 3: 335–360.

Lonti, Zsuzsanna, and A. Verma. (2003). "The Determinants of Flexibility and Innovation in the Government Workplace: Recent Evidence from Canada." *Journal of Public Administration Research and Theory*. 13: 3: 283–309.

Lowe, Graham S. (2000). *The Quality of Work: A People-Centred Agenda*. Don Mills, ON: Oxford University Press.

Lyons, Sean T., Linda E. Duxbury, and Christopher A. Higgins. (2006). "A Comparison of the Values and Commitment of Private Sector, Public Sector, and Parapublic Sector Employees." *Public Administration Review*. 66: 4: 605–668.

March, James G. (1988). *Decisions and Organizations*. Oxford: Basil Blackwell.

———. (1991). "Exploration and Exploitation in Organizational Learning." *Organization Science*. 2: 1: 71–87.

———. (1999). *The Pursuit of Organizational Intelligence*. Oxford: Basil Blackwell.

March, James G., ed. (1965). *Handbook of Organizations*. Chicago: Rand McNally.

McKelvey, Bill. (1982). *Organizational Systematics*. Berkeley: University of California Press.

Meyer, J. W., and B. Rowan. (September 1977). "Institutionalized Organizations: Formal Structure as Myth and Ceremony." *American Journal of Sociology*. 83: 340–363.

Meyer, J. W., W. R. Scott, and T. Deal. (1981). "Institutional and Technical Sources of Organizational Structure: Explaining the Structure of Educational Organizations." In *Organization and the Human Services*, edited by H. D. Stein, 151–179. Philadelphia: Temple University Press.

Mintzberg, Henry. (1973). *The Nature of Managerial Work*. New York: Harper & Row.

Moe, Terry M. (November 1984). "The New Economics of Organization." *American Journal of Political Science*. 28: 4: 739–777.

———. (1990). "The Politics of Structural Choice." In *Organization Theory: From Chester Barnard and Beyond*, edited by O. E. Williamson. New York: Oxford University Press.

Morgan, Gareth. (1980). "Paradigms, Metaphors, and Puzzle Solving in Organization Theory." *Administrative Science Quarterly*. 25: 4: 605–622.

———. (1986). *Images of Organization*. Newbury Park, CA: Sage.

Nohria, Nitin, and Robert Eccles, eds. (1992). *Networks and Organizations: Structure, Form and Action*. Boston: Harvard Business School.

Nystrom, Paul C., and William H. Starbuck, eds. (1981). *Handbook of Organizational Design*, vol. 1 and 2. New York: Oxford University Press.

Orton, Douglas, and Karl Weick. (April 1990). "Loosely Coupled Systems: A Reconceptualization." *Academy of Management Review.* 15: 2: 203–223.

Osborne, David, and Ted Gaebler. (1992). *Reinventing Government: How the Entrepreneurial Spirit Is Transforming the Public Sector.* Reading, MA: Addison-Wesley.

O'Toole, Laurence, Jr., and Kenneth J. Meier. (November-December 2004). "Desperately Seeking Selznick: Cooptation and the Dark Side of Public Management in Networks." *Public Administration Review.* 64: 6: 681–693.

Perrow, Charles. (1984). *Normal Accidents: Living with High-Risk Technologies.* New York: Basic Books.

———. (1986). *Complex Organizations: A Critical Essay,* 3rd ed. New York: Random House.

Peters, Guy, and Jon Pierre, eds. (2003). *Handbook of Public Administration.* London: Sage.

Peters, Thomas J., and Robert H. Waterman. (1982). *In Search of Excellence: Lessons from America's Best-Run Companies.* Cambridge: Harper and Row.

Pfeffer, Jeffrey. (2006). "Like Ships Passing in the Night: The Separate Literatures of Organization Theory and Public Management." *International Journal of Public Management.* 9: 4: 457–465.

Pfiffner, John M., and Robert Presthus. (1967). *Public Administration,* 5th ed. New York: Ronald Press.

Powell, Walter. (1990). "Neither Market nor Hierarchy: Network Forms of Organization." In *Research in Organizational Behaviour,* volume 12, 295–336. Greenwich, CT: JAI Press.

Powell, Walter W., and Paul J. DiMaggio, eds. (1991). *The New Institutionalism in Organizational Analysis.* Chicago: Chicago University Press.

Pross, Paul. (1986). *Group Politics and Public Policy.* Toronto: Oxford University Press.

Rao, Hayagreeva. (2002). "Interorganizational Ecology." In *The Blackwell Companion to Organizations,* edited by Joel A. C. Baum, 541–556. London: Blackwell.

Roe, Emery, Paul Schulman, Michel van Eeten, and Mark de Bruijne. (2005). "High-Reliability Bandwidth Management in Large Technical Systems: Findings and Implications of Two Case Studies." *Journal of Public Administration Theory and Research.* 15: 2: 263–280.

Scott, W. Richard. (1995). *Institutions and Organizations.* Thousand Oaks, CA: Sage.

———. (2003). *Organizations: Rational, Natural, and Open Systems,* 5th ed. New Jersey: Prentice-Hall.

Scott, W. Richard, and J. W. Meyer. (1991). "The Organization of Societal Sectors: Propositions and Early Evidence." In *The New Institutionalism* on *Organizational Analysis*, edited by W. W. Powell and P. J. DiMaggio, 108–117. Chicago: University of Chicago Press.

Selznick, Philip. (1948). "Foundations of the Theory of Organization." *American Sociological Review*. 13: 1: 25–35.

———. (1957). *Leadership in Administration: A Sociological Perspective*. New York: Harper & Row.

Simon, Herbert A. (1945). *Administrative Behavior: A Study of Decision-Making Processes in Administrative Organizations*. New York: Free Press.

Simon, Herbert A., Donald W. Smithburg, and Victor A. Thompson. (1962). *Public Administration*. New York: Alfred Knopf.

Stevens, Douglas F. (1993). *Corporate Autonomy and Institutional Control: The Crown Corporation as a Problem in Organization Design*. Kingston and Montreal: McGill-Queen's University Press.

Stinchcombe, A. (1965). "Social Structure and Organizations." In *Handbook of Organizations*, edited by J .G. March, 142–193. Chicago: Rand McNally.

Terreberry, S. (March 1968). "The Evolution of Organizational Environments." *Administrative Science Quarterly*. 12: 590–613.

Thompson, James D. (1967). *Organizations in Action*. New York: McGraw-Hill.

Tsouksas, Haridimos, and Christian Knudsen, eds. (2003). *The Oxford Handbook of Organization Theory*. Oxford: Oxford University Press.

Tushman, Michael L., and Philip Anderson. (1986). "Technological Discontinuities and Organizational Environments." *Administrative Science Quarterly*. 31: 3: 439–465.

Tushman, Michael, and Richard Nelson. (March 1990). "Introduction: Technology, Organizations, and Innovation." *Administrative Science Quarterly*. 35: 1: 1–8.

Tushman, M., and C. O'Reilly. (1996). "Ambidextrous Organizations: Managing Evolutionary and Revolutionary Change." *California Management Review*. 36: 4: 8–30.

Tushman, Michael, and Wendy Smith. (2002). "Organizational Technology." In *The Blackwell Companion to Organizations*, edited by Joel A. C. Baum, 386–414. London: Blackwell.

Verma, Anil, and Zsuzsanna Lonti. (May 2001). "Changing Government Workplaces." CPRN Discussion Paper No. W11. Ottawa: Canadian Policy Research Networks.

Warren, R. (December 1967). "The Interorganizational Field as a Focus for Investigation." *Administrative Science Quarterly*. 12: 396–419.

Weick, Karl. (March 1976). "Educational Organizations as Loosely Coupled Systems." *Administrative Science Quarterly*. 21: 1: 1–19.

———. (1995). *Sensemaking in Organizations*. Thousand Oaks, CA: Sage.

Williamson, Oliver E. (November 1981). "The Economics of Organization: The Transaction Cost Approach." *American Journal of Sociology*. 87: 548–577.

Williamson, Oliver E., ed. (1990). *Organization Theory: From Chester Barnard to the Present and Beyond*. New York: Oxford University Press.

Wilson, James Q. (1989). *Bureaucracy: What Government Agencies Do and Why They Do It*. New York: Basic Books, 1989.

PART **II**

CONTEMPORARY ISSUES AND CHALLENGES

3 THE ORIGINS OF MERIT IN CANADA[1]

Ken Rasmussen and Luc Juillet

Merit has been central to human resource practices in Western democracies for over one hundred years. While many of the public service commissions that traditionally guarded merit have been weakened or dismantled over the past two decades, all governments still retain various forms of merit protection in the form of independent boards that hear appeals and do audits, as well as through legislation that upholds the basic principles of merit appointment (Chapman, 2004; Pfiffner and Brook, 2000). As recently as the passage of the new Public Service Employment Act in 2003, Treasury Board President Lucienne Robillard came to the defence of merit, noting, "Claims that we are watering down merit are clearly unfounded. While we are proposing greater flexibility in staffing, we are balancing them with strong safeguards to uphold the merit principle" (Canada, House of Commons, 14 February 2003).

This durability of merit in all human resource regimes is partly a historic legacy and partly a reflection of the basic needs for independence in the appointment of public servants. In its earlier guise, merit was a rallying cry to defeat patronage. In the nineteenth-century battle against patronage, merit appointment represented a host of important public administration values such as professionalism, neutral competence, independent judgment, and a willingness to resist political interference and inappropriate pressure. Appointment based on merit in the nineteenth century was seen as a reform that would take the corrupt patronage-riddled bureaucracy and transform it into a dedicated professional body mindful of the public interest and capable of both supporting government decision-making and informing ministers about their proper roles and responsibilities within the constitutional system.

However, as soon as patronage was defeated, the definition of merit became contested. Merit proved to be an elusive goal, never defined in legislation until the most recent reforms of 2003 and only vaguely in that act. Merit was constantly redefined to satisfy various political concerns and constituencies. While merit proved to be a central ideal in defeating patronage and creating the image of a modern professional public service, the constant redefinitions and the surrounding processes that established merit quickly resulted in a "merit system" that was seen as an impediment that stood in the way of one or more visions of a more democratic, efficient, or representative public service. Despite being regularly ignored, redefined, and subsumed under other concepts, merit retains a powerful aura. As such, few politicians or governments are willing to challenge its centrality in the human resource regimes of government, even though it is currently little more than a synonym for process.

What most contemporary discussions of merit lack is the earlier notion of merit as an ideal that encompasses not only ability but also behaviours that emerge from individuals appointed by merit through an independent process. The original meaning of merit implied a form of subjective responsibility, loyalty, and conscience for the public good (Mosher, 1968: 10). In this ideal form, merit embodied an ethic of service, duty, and professional responsibility for the public interest. As Ingraham (2006: 487) notes, "Merit is related to values, ideals, and ethics, to the appropriate role of the civil service in a democracy and thus to governance in a democratic society." Reform advocates have used the ideal of merit appointment to promote broader notions of merit as an efficient, effective, and dedicated public service that serves the public interest in opposition to the patronage bureaucracy that was indolent, overstaffed, partisan, and corrupt while serving the interests of political parties. In this early battle, merit had a sanctified halo and carried very large expectations as to what it would accomplish when it was enshrined as the principle used as the basis for public service. Yet, something has happened along the way in which few see merit as necessary to the creation of an entire ethic and set of behaviours associated with the public service as a calling or vocation. When the ideal became a system, it had to contend with multiple and competing values associated with different definitions of merit (Best, 1982). As such, it became progressively weighed down by various definitions to the point where merit and process became synonymous.

This chapter examines the origins of merit in Canada and what these origins might teach us as we continue to redefine the concept and struggle with finding an appropriate way to understand the role of the public service in a democracy. This is particularly important as we see a transition to the new governance paradigm in which the crucial role of the public service in our democracy is seen to require greater clarity and further statutory protections (Savoie, 2008). While merit grew out of a strong desire to reform the highly inefficient practice of patronage, it has undergone a number of transformations that have drained much of what made it so attractive to earlier reformers. If merit is to become more than a process, we must recall its origins as an ideal associated with a professional public service and as an important part of the democratic system of governance. An examination of the origins of merit redresses merit as a process and reveals it as a useful proxy for independence, judgment, and neutral competence—the exact characteristics that help public servants play a meaningful role in the transition from management to governance that is occurring in Canada. In short, examining the origins of merit might help reveal a way for the public service to be seen, once again, as an important part of a well-governed society and not, as seen by many current reformers, as an administrative means to political ends.

THE ORIGINS OF THE MERIT SYSTEM IN CANADA

Merit was a central part of the nineteenth-century reform movement, which wanted to create an independent public service that would improve the quality, efficiency, and overall morality of government by eliminating patronage and associated corruption that plagued the public service since Confederation. (Dawson, 1929). Reformers during the nineteenth century believed the best way to bring about positive reform was through the creation of a merit-based public service as established through a process of competitive examination. Such a reform would enhance efficiency by ensuring that only the competent would be appointed, enhancing equity by making sure all Canadians had fair and reasonable access to public employment, and allowing the public service to play a legitimate constitutional role in providing the Crown with honest, fearless, and confidential advice.

The self-interest of political parties, who did not want to relinquish the power to appoint partisans to the public service, limited merit appointment. Legitimizing this purely partisan argument was the fact that an independent public service commission (PSC) would require the prime minister to abandon prerogative powers that supported patronage appointments. In Canada, since Confederation, there has existed a general understanding and acceptance that upon appointment, public servants should not use their office for directly partisan purposes. However, their method of appointment always raised concerns about their ability or willingness to abide by this standard of behaviour. When coupled with the fact that pensions were not guaranteed but required the support of Cabinet upon retirement, that meant that the neutrality of the public service was always questionable. As though to prove the point, there were numerous scandals in the late nineteenth and early twentieth centuries surrounding public servants. There are many accounts of public servants providing untendered contracts to firms connected with the party in power at the time, purchasing supplies at above-market values, and ensuring that those in the private sector who contributed to election funds would receive favourable treatment. While it had been an established principle (before and after Confederation) that active political partisanship on the part of a civil servant would constitute "official misconduct," which meant dismissal, this was rarely acted upon by the party in power (Dawson, 1922).

As with many other ideas in good standing in Canada in the nineteenth century, concepts of administrative reform were imported from Britain. In particular, the ideas were taken from the renowned Northcote/Trevelyan report of 1854, which was referred to endlessly in Canadian debates over reform and was even appended in its entirety to one nineteenth-century inquiry. The central features of the Northcote/ Trevelyan inquiry were the concepts of open competitive examination and selection and promotion by merit. The language of this report made the document read like a manifesto for a rising middle class. The inquiry included language that could be described as meritocratic, technocratic, flattering to the ethic of self-made urban professionalism and hard work (Gowan 1987: 18). Armed with a body of ideas legitimated in the mother country, a growing group of reformers, both inside and outside government, began to agitate for the establishment of an independent PSC that would conduct examinations to serve as the basis of appointment.

While political parties were obviously self-interested when it came to the issue of patronage appointment, the practice did have some legitimacy that made it more difficult to abandon. During much of this period, appointment to the public service was a legitimate part of the Crown prerogative. From the time of the coming of responsible government in 1848, Canada's political elite and much of the administrative elite had comfortably accepted the idea that staffing the public service through the practice of ministerial nomination was simply part of a comprehensive theory of the sovereignty of the Crown. In fact, anything that would remove this power was seen by many within government as constitutionally illegitimate and a violation of the tenets of responsible government. This practice was described in an 1882 Royal Commission on the civil service in the following manner:

> In the spirit and practice of the English constitution, the Crown is the fountain of all appointments, and among the duties and responsibilities of its advisers stand the proper and responsible selection of servants of the State. If it be, at times, expedient for Constitutional Government to institute Commissions to investigate, it is repugnant to them to devolve on such bodies, the duties of governing and administering, for which appointment and promotions form an essential part. (Canada, 1882: 87)

This simple statement captures the problems confronted by merit appointment advocates. The existing constitutional model justified patronage as another name for the Crown prerogative, which made patronage more than just a synonym of corruption. It was a constitutionally legitimate form of action for the executive to engage in. This interpretation of Crown privilege was used to keep the idea of merit appointment illegitimate. The concept of merit appointment by an independent body would violate the Crown prerogative, as well as the conventions surrounding ministerial responsibility, including the need for ministers to be able to report to Parliament on the conduct of the affairs of their departments, such as the manner in which individuals were appointed. Such a situation "was only possible if the government could freely place its own appointments within the administrative system. In this view, the Minister being responsible for the effectiveness of his department would ensure that the most capable person would be placed in the leading posts" (Hodgetts et al., 1972: 14).

Adding weight to this practice of "ministerial nomination" was the manner in which the leaders of Canada's political parties acquired the power of the colonial governors by claiming that "Canada's monarchical constitution validated their comprehensive exploitation of the public service and manipulation of the electoral system" (Stewart, 1986a: 82). Before the achievement of responsible government, the entire patronage of Upper and Lower Canada was in the hands of the Governor General and his appointed council. In both colonies, powerful networks of local notables increased by patronage distribution (Stewart, 1986b: 22). After responsible government, and then with the achievement of Confederation, the Cabinet, and more particularly the prime minister, began to exercise these Crown prerogatives: "Macdonald took over the powers exercised by the governors since 1791 and appointed only his party's supporters to posts throughout the public service. He even evolved a constitutional justification for such a thoroughgoing deployment of patronage for party purposes. 'By constitutional practice,' he insisted, 'appointments are vested in the Crown and the whole responsibility of appointments rests with the ministry of the day'" (Stewart, 1986b: 41). It should be emphasized that this model regarded the use of the Crown prerogative in this manner as an effective check on democracy and as a means of enhancing executive authority while bringing about political stability (Smith, 1987). Of course, this privilege was predominantly used to help build strong political parties.

Initially, the concerns around efficiency that emerged from a patronage bureaucracy were not substantial because the early bureaucracy had few responsibilities and had little impact on the lives of most Canadians. When organization problems did occur, during the period when Britain was rapidly industrializing in the late nineteenth century, the general response was to subsume a nonpartisan, merit-based public service under the institutions of representative and responsible government. Such a model would be based on a separation between the political party and the public service, neutrality, a separation of policy and administration, and a belief that public servants should loyally execute public policy regardless of personal belief. In short, just as the monarchy moved above the political party, the civil service was to find its new constitutional position below the political party (Rohr, 2002: 36). Just as the Crown has no political positions, the new civil service would have complete neutrality. This development was part of establishing a constitutional monarchy that requires "an unpolitical civil service whose primary connection is with the Crown, and which while subordinated to party government, is unaffected by their changes: the two permanent elements, the Crown and the civil service, which not by chance together left the political arena, supply the framework for the free play of parliamentary politics and governments" (Parris, 1968: 164). In this interpretation, the public service is no longer a part of a unified executive and instead has the independence needed to serve each successive government.

MERIT APPOINTMENT AND PROFESSIONAL PUBLIC SERVICE

Shortly after Confederation, arguments favouring merit appointment began to develop when the first in a series of Royal Commissions was called to investigate the public service (Canada, 1869; Canada, 1870). The first Royal Commission that looked at the problem of the public service was established to "inquire into and report upon the organization of the several branches of the Public Service with a special view to their adaptation to the wants of the new Constitution, and to providing for their efficient and economical performance" (Canada, 1869: 4). This Royal Commission did not talk a lot about patronage but was more concerned with creating an effective administrative organization regardless of the method of appointment. The absence of any discussion of patronage cannot, however, be seen as an endorsement of patronage by the commissioners. Rather, they saw administration as separate from politics, as in the classic politics/administration dichotomy. As such, they wanted to make public administration more efficient by ensuring that the partisans who were appointed were capable of handling the nonpolitical nature of the majority of their tasks. Their concern was, accordingly, directed almost exclusively at eliminating conditions relating to the personnel function that was deterring "young men, who were conscious of energy and ability, from adopting the public service as a profession" (Canada, 1869: 5). In trying to create a strong administrative "cadre," the commissioners felt that steps were necessary to ensure that the best young men were recruited, that they would be justly rewarded, and that they could be assured of a fair system of promotion based on merit.

Early reformers emphasized the very basic desire to improve the personnel function of the public service. Principally, there was a strong belief that "only young men should be appointed to the service, that they should enter it in the lowest grade, and that before being appointed they should undergo the ordeal of a rigid examination, and also at every step they take upwards" (Canada, 1870: 11). They also hoped to avoid corruption by paying decent salaries. Early reformers wanted responsibility rewarded with salary and, of course, they advocated the possibility of an assured pension. If efficiency was to be increased by attracting talented young men and rewarding them fairly, the next logical step would be to disencumber "the service from men, who from age and infirmity are no longer efficient for the performance of their duties" (Canada, 1869: 6) They also advocated for a rational system of promotion based on a combination of ability and seniority.

While patronage was rarely mentioned as being the cause of any of the ills that were afflicting the post-Confederation public service, it seems safe to conclude that this practice was never far from the surface. The central point in many of the commission's suggestions was that efficient civil services require a fair and transparent system for advancement and promotion. Early reformers promoted the rules of sound administrative practice in opposition to the chaotic system created by patronage appointment and promotion.

Directly following Confederation, we can see the idea of merit appointment making inroads on the prevailing practice of patronage using two different arguments. First, patronage should be replaced because it was unfair and contradicted a central liberal belief that a man should have the opportunity to succeed or fail according to his own merit and abilities. The second reason was that it was viewed as wrong and inefficient (Owram, 1986: 46). These early reforms saw the public service as a part of the broader political community and that it should be organized according to principles that reflect and represent the best of the political community. By attempting to make the public service more efficient, by definition early reformers were hoping to make it more independent, autonomous, and representative. Patronage was then both unfair and inefficient.

THE CIVIL SERVICE ACT, 1882: A VICTORY FOR MERIT?

The reform movement gained its first substantial victory in 1882 on the heels of the McInnis Royal Commission (Canada, 1881; Canada, 1882). Most of the membership of this commission was drawn from the senior civil service, with the exception of the chairman who was a senator. The commissioners "traveled over the Dominion, heard a host of witnesses, asked them more than three thousand questions, received delegations from the lower ranks of employees, investigated the British and American civil services and produced a comprehensive study of superannuation" (Dawson, 1929: 44). When it was over, Canada had a new Civil Service Act, and more importantly, an established pattern of administrative reform that, despite interruptions, would continue to accelerate until 1908.

The McInnis Commission began its report by strongly endorsing reforms that had taken place a decade earlier in Britain in 1873 (Chapman, 2004). Although they expressed certain doubts "as to whether the public opinion of the Dominion is even now fully alive to the importance of a thoroughly efficient Civil Service" (Canada, 1881: 12), they felt there was "nevertheless a feeling in the public mind that the interest of the public service had been subordinated to a greater or lesser extent to the purposes of political parties" (Canada, 1881: 13). They were of the opinion that politicians, once they realized "how much the prosperity and welfare of the country depends on a pure and efficient Civil Service will not hesitate to abandon a patronage which is found to be injurious to the best interests of the country" (Canada, 1881: 13). Their optimistic faith in the responsibility of politicians, and the influence of an abstract "public interest," would remain largely unrewarded and the political parties would continue to make no distinction between their partisan interests and the national interest with regard to the civil service.

Rejecting the elitist division of the service into the British two-tier model, the McInnis Commission strongly encouraged the adoption of the other two main components of the British system: open competitive examinations and promotion by merit. The attractiveness of these features was their ability to separate politics from administration, creating a neutral bureaucratic apparatus. As the commissioners suggested, "Men who had obtained their places by merit alone, and as the result of impartial examination could not possibly be open to any imputation of political partisanship in office; nor would they be in any degree influenced in the discharge of their duties by political considerations" (Canada, 1881: 20). From this time forward, merit and impartial competitive examination would become the tools reformers used to purify the administrative apparatus, separating it from political control. In short, merit and examination were enshrined as the first new values of a responsible public service.

The commissioners had great faith in merit as a means of creating an impartial civil service; they even argued for its extension as a means to determine promotions. For the commissioners, this was almost as important as competitive examinations because the efficiency of the Service so largely depends on a good system of promotion, that we have felt it necessary to emphasize the importance of avoiding such injustice as we have mentioned, and which cannot fail to be injurious to the best interests of the Service. Men whose just claims are thus passed over become discouraged, they lose their self-respect and hope for the future. Such injustice destroys all incentive to emulation and all desire to excel. Nor does the mischief end there. It affects the whole Service. It is destructive for discipline, and it impairs the usefulness of those who witness as well as of those who suffer it. (Canada, 1881: 17)

According to this view, all subjective assessments of a candidate's worth should be eliminated from the personnel function. Open competitive exams, promotion by merit, and the resulting conventions of neutrality and nonpartisanship would combine to remedy the problems plaguing the public service by replacing the subjectivity of patronage with the fairness and democratic egalitarianism of merit. These reforms would also aid in the creation of a more dignified civil service by moving the civil service towards professional status. As the commissioners argued,

The public service would, under such a system, be open to the public instead of being, to a large extent, a close corporation in the hands of political parties. An opportunity would be given to all intelligent and educated young men to obtain by their merits alone, a start in a service in which promotion, by a continuance of intelligent self-improvement and well directed official labour, would be certain. (Canada, 1881: 20)

The key element in bringing all of these important innovations to fruition was found in the establishment of a Civil Service Commission (CSC) that would be free from political influence and able to appoint by merit. While the first Civil Service Act (1868) created a Board of Civil Service Examiners, it was easily ignored by ministers, and when it was used it provided an examination so rudimentary that only the completely illiterate failed. The board contemplated by the McInnis inquiry was to be more powerful and was to provide the public service with a system of competitive examination conducted all across the Dominion, which would rigorously test every candidate's character for both intellectual and moral qualities. The establishment of the board of examiners was the first clear victory and the first real institutional innovation towards placing merit at the heart of public service recruitment.

Many of the commission's recommendations were accepted and appeared in Canada's second Civil Service Act (1882). This act created a board of examiners independent of party control; it limited the age of new employees to those between eighteen and thirty-five; it began the slow process of formally recognizing the deputy head as the administrative head of the department; and it authorized appointment to the civil service only after an examination. Unfortunately, this act applied only to the inside service and was regarded by politicians, in the words of John A. Macdonald, as a means "to provide that men should write in a good hand, should know the principles of arithmetic and possess a good common school education" (House of Commons, *Debates*, 15 March 1889: 673). It was not intended to eliminate patronage, at least not from the point of view of the prime minister.

While the act was largely ignored, it did bring about a subtle change in the relationship between the public service and the other institutions of government. The public service was slowly gaining independence from these older institutions at the same time as it was gaining increased responsibilities. The civil service was coming to be regarded by an increasing number of politicians and intellectuals as a crucial administrative means to political ends. Just as importantly, however, it was beginning to be seen as an important institution that would further the development of a national interest, as opposed to the prevailing belief in the rightful dominance of vested interests. In the end, the most concrete result of the passing of the Civil Service Act (1882) was the creation of the Board of Civil Service Examiners to conduct qualifying and limited promotion examinations. Despite several objections, the assault on the strictly political model of civil service appointment was gaining momentum.

Typical of this new belief in merit was the view of the nineteenth-century reformer William Dawson LeSueur, who contended that the duty of a deputy minister "is to furnish his Minister with full and accurate information upon all departmental questions which the Minister may be called upon to decide, and to advise the Minister in the public interest. His function is not to suggest to the Minister ways and means of turning this or that contingency to political account, nor to cover with his recommendation things which are advisable solely in a political sense" (Canada, 1892: 627). In short, the deputy was to be completely neutral, as was the public service as a whole. A classic bureaucrat and a classic bureaucracy were to serve as the norm. "A public servant should not be required to navigate political shallows, or take political soundings: his business one would suppose, should be to steer a simple course in the safe waters of public duty" (Canada, 1892: 630). The desire was for a public service commanded by a deputy minister who would ensure that the civil service promoted the interest of the nation in an impartial and efficient manner.

The result was the articulation of the idea that hiring on the basis of merit means that "doors to appointments and promotions in the service will open only to capacity and honesty, and no man or woman who aspires, as all have a right to aspire, to any such position, will have occasion to seek or use any influence less honorable than his or her own merit and fitness for office" (Canada, 1892: xxviii). The dignity of the civil service would be improved and so would that of those who were in it, knowing that their success or failure was related to their own character, ability, and capacity. By championing increasingly rational methods of selecting and promoting civil servants, reformers reflected a changed relationship between individual effort and subsequent success in the job market. Merit, in this sense, is a classically liberal principle in that it makes people responsible for their own success or failure (Sordik-Aron, 1987: 115). Access to positions in the public service was becoming a right available to Canadians with the necessary qualifications.

SCANDAL AND THE PRESSURE FOR MERIT APPOINTMENT

Beginning in the early 1900s, there was a growing sense of frustration with patronage among many members of Parliament but also from the broader public, including many in the business community. Most of these new reformers sympathized with John Willison, Wilfrid Laurier's first biographer, who observed, "[T]here is surely a crying need for reform of the Civil Service in Canada and the protection of honest and efficient public officers from the spoils element which corrupts and bedevils the administration of public affairs" (Willison, 1907–1908: 128). This was unquestionably the predominant attitude among most reformers by the early 1900s. The public service was being harassed by selfish, ignorant, and short-sighted politicians. The solution was a complete reform of the personnel system, which would strengthen the hand of the public service through an emphasis on utility and meritocracy, thereby protecting the true guardians of the public interest. Most reformers sought a new civil service act that would "take every place from top to bottom out of the hands of the politicians who, both at Ottawa and Toronto, have shown themselves so unworthy of being trusted with the power" (Marshall, 1906: 159). This idea sought to free the bureaucracy from the grasp of rapacious politicians, which made it necessary to strengthen the public service.

A willingness to accept independence for the public service was possible because Canadians were becoming more comfortable with the growth of government activity. There was the recognition that the development of an industrial infrastructure demanded "expert knowledge and technical efficiency of the highest order, with a force trained and organized to handle such intricate questions" (Magrath, 1913: 248). There was a growing consensus that the public service needed to be increasingly independent. Thus, it was not only a sense of moral outrage but also pressure from economic interests in the business community that wanted a reformed public service that would be better able to manage the economy in the interests of business (Whitaker, 1987; Johnson and Libecap, 1994). There was a general belief that Canadian government, at all levels, was incompetent and inefficient and that the public was generally ignorant. Accordingly, the need for a new force that could deal effectively with the various problems that faced the state developed (Owram, 1986: 41).

Major reforms that would finally elevate merit appointment as a statutory requirement would eventually come at the end of a two-year parliamentary session between 1906 and 1908 when the Liberal government of Wilfrid Laurier came under consistent attack from the Conservative Opposition, who hoped to expose the corruption and inefficacy in the ongoing administration of the government at the time in order to move forward. There were new demands for new social and economic policies, but both parties were hesitant, partly due to the inadequacy of the machinery of administration at the time. Nevertheless, Robert Borden decided to put the full weight of his party into a new tactic aimed at discrediting the Laurier government (Brown, 1975: 120) The Conservatives ran a "purity in politics" campaign that continued throughout the remaining session of Parliament until the general election at the end of October 1908. One contemporary observer noted that "it was a stormy Session and filled with angry debate and prolonged discussion and personal charges; it was a scandal Session teeming with Opposition allegations of corruption and maladministration" (Canadian Annual Review, 1908: 28).

This session epitomized what had become clear to most Canadians: The public service was corrupt and ineffective due to patronage appointment and was making it impossible for governments to implement their agendas. The Liberal Party, like the Conservatives before them, had many supporters continually clamouring for jobs and private firms accepting rewards in return for their donations. One of Laurier's early biographers noted that the governing party would not only fill all the postmaster jobs, excise officer jobs, and so on, but would extend well beyond this activity: "Supplies must be bought from firms on the patronage list, subsidy hunters, contracts seekers found the way smoother if they subscribed to campaign funds" (Skelton, 1921: 270). Indeed, the distribution of patronage, broadly defined, had become, arguably, the most important function of government. It was noted at the time that

> Sir Wilfrid frequently repeated the story of Lincoln, asked during a crisis in the Civil War whether it was a change in the army command or complications with foreign powers that wrinkled his forehead, and replying, "No it is that confounded postmastership at Brownsville,

Ohio." No other subject bulked so large in correspondence; no other purpose brought so many visitors to Ottawa. It meant endless bombardment of ministers, ceaseless efforts to secure a work from the friend of a friend of the premier, bitter disappointment for the ninety and nine who were turned away. (Skelton, 1921: 270–271)

The move to end this system began in 1907 after relentless pressures from the Opposition caused by scandals and corruption. The Laurier government began by getting rid of all patronage lists for suppliers. Likewise an order-in-council was passed that required that timber licenses were to be granted only at public auction, and a new Elections Act would forbid companies from contributing campaign funds and set heavy fines for ballot tampering. The presence of an increasing number of reform constituencies; the demands for more public policy; growing industrialization, immigration, and urbanization; and the ongoing presence of scandal did eventually force the government's hand beyond its earlier limited reforms. A Royal Commission, headed by John Courtney, the deputy minister of finance, would investigate the civil service (Canada, 1908). The commission stated what nearly everybody knew—that patronage was alive and well in the civil service and the 1882 act had done little or nothing to limit its influence.

Despite recognizing the importance of the formal institutions of government in the creation of administrative responsibility, the 1908 commission concentrated the majority of its effort on reforming the civil service and not the overhead institutions. The guiding assumption in the other inquiries had been that Parliament was strong enough to withstand a weakening of the convention of ministerial responsibility, especially since this convention had led to the rampant abuse of the civil service for what were strictly party purposes. The major concern of this commission, as was true of all the other inquiries, was the creation of accountable administration, not more parliamentary oversight. It believed that strengthening the civil service and Cabinet control would facilitate an increase in responsible administration.

The passage of civil service reform legislation took place before the October 28, 1908, federal election, which the Liberal Party won again, albeit with a reduced majority. Even though the election was fought on the Liberal Party's substantial record of scandal, Borden's focus on clean government, and a commitment to greater public ownership, the Liberals still prevailed. After the election, not surprisingly, the government went on to other matters and lost interest in reforming the public service. However, merit appointment had been established in legislation. While merit appointment initially only applied to the inside or Ottawa-based public service, the reforms created a strong statutory basis of independence and autonomy that would create a powerful and effective public service in the years to come (Grey and Jenkins, 2005).

Merit appointment had as part of its goal the creation of a modern administrative apparatus. However, while the new public service would be an effective administrative instrument, it was also expected to act in ways that would promote the best interests of the nation. While it would not supplant the legislative role of Parliament, it would have independence so that it could play a more meaningful role in governance. This aspect of the reform agenda saw the public service as a democratic institution with a legitimate constitutional role. This legitimacy was based on the fact that public servants were to be merit appointments made with complete independence of the desires of politicians. This would give public servants the ability and duty to make their voices heard without making their wills prevail (Grant, 1934). Yet, this aspect of the quest for merit was not embraced by governments in Canada. There were always reform advocates who wanted to see merit appointment lead to a stronger role for the public service in guiding the nation, especially in the 1930s and 1940s (Brady, 1935). However, the view of politicians would be loudest and a diminished sense of what merit appointment meant for the nation quickly came to prevail.

CONCLUSION: MERIT APPOINTMENT AND THE CAREER PUBLIC SERVICE IN CANADA

With the reforms of 1908, merit eventually triumphed, eliminating the view of the public servant as a handmaiden of a political party. This created a new vision that the public service should become a neutral instrument, impartially serving the equally impartial interests of the state. In this light, public service based on merit appointment would become the preserve of, if not the virtuous, at least the competent. However, it would be unwise to see the triumph of merit as a mere accident of fate. Rather, it was the result of strenuous efforts of modernizers who saw merit appointment as the precondition for creating a professional public service. In this view, the public service would be of service to the nation while also being a valuable resource to a succession of partisan government leaders. The ideal was to have a public service staffed on democratic principles of fairness, equality, and competence while acquiring new behavioural requirements and obligations. In addition, the fact that the public service was now a statutory body was to give the public service new independent authority.

Yet, despite the long battle, the merit system that was created was quick to find disfavour among many critics and would itself be pilloried by a succession of inquiries during the twentieth century, which wanted to see merit relegated to a secondary value in the face of more pressing issues around both efficiency and representativeness. The view recounted in this chapter, however, suggests that what critics missed and continue to miss is the fact that a stable, career-based personnel system, grounded in the values of neutrality, competence, accountability, and attention to the public interest, represents a tremendous triumph in democratic governance (Kearney and Hays, 1998: 50). Over the past sixty years, reform initiatives have tended to see merit, neutral competence, and professionalism as standing in the way of newer and more important values, such as accountability for results, executive leadership, and responsiveness. The benefits associated with having a professional public service characterized by independent judgment and indifference to political pressures has gradually been disappearing.

This is evident when one considers that the independently recruited public service has been notably absent in recent discussions of administrative reform concerned mostly with matters related to administrative efficiency, new managerial techniques, customer satisfaction, decentralizing decision-making, making managers manage, empowering public employees, accountability for performance, and the use of more disaggregated units and agencies. All of these are important and undeniably praiseworthy reforms, yet they should not displace the idea of the public service as independent and independently appointed, allowing for meaningful neutrality and nonpartisanship. More efficient delivery of public programs and more customer satisfaction are vital reforms and essential to effective public service. However, as Guy Peters has noted: "So too is dispassionate and far-sighted policy advice" (Peters, 1994: 752). These latter virtues come from a public service recruited on the basis of a deep and substantive concept of merit.

Is merit appointment still important? There are a number of reasons to believe it is, because merit appointment is the basis of independence, which is important for the reasons that it has always been important—so that public servants will do the right things for Canadians and for Canada. Without some form of independence, it is unrealistic to expect public servants to put the tasks of their department, or the corporate interests of government for that matter, before their own career security and advancement. The key to improved performance is not some new business method, more accountability for performance, or a better pay-for-performance reward system, but independence as guaranteed by merit appointment. If public servants are to perform better, the first requirement is that they must be made more independent of their job. This does not mean that all public servants will use their independence, and there will be many who will always put their career interests or self-interest first, but some degree of independence for those who act in the public interest is significant and worth preserving (Kingston, 2002).

Public servants in Canada are expected to be responsive to legitimate political authority and at the same time represent traditional values of objectivity and rationality, neutrality, and nonpartisanship. Of course, the public service has always combined technical skills with sensitivity to political issues. What has always been at the basis of this balance is the idea of neutral competence based on merit appointment. The public service becomes less effective when it is not capable of giving its cooperation and its best advice to the issues important to partisan leaders because it must be sufficiently uncommitted to do so for a succession of party leaders and ministers from different political parties.

As Heclo notes, "The independence entailed in neutral competence ... exists precisely in order to serve the aims of partisan leadership" (Heclo, 1975: 84).

Compromising the independence of the public service by reducing the meaning of merit appointment lessens the value of the public service to politicians. By eliminating independence, governments risk corrupting the very tools that can help them achieve their goals, including objective expertise, institutional memory, a strong network of communications among stakeholders, and knowledge of government procedures and informal processes (West, 2005). This is the core of how the effective system of a permanent neutral public service can operate and should serve as the basis of trust between politicians and public servants. In this regard, public servants, like politicians, have unwritten job descriptions that emerge from our constitutional conventions, and indeed parts of those job descriptions mean that they are liable to the criticism by politicians who are by nature conservative. It is their job as public servants to uncover the flaws in government policy, and this is never a popular activity for many government leaders who want quick and effective implementation (Du Gay, 2002: 477).

A public service recruited on a deep and substantive concept of merit would not only be a machine to deliver services to citizens but would also be a source of stability and continuity for the state. The fifty-year battle to bring merit to the centre of personnel policy in the years following Confederation was to be resolved in a way that required the public service to carry a heavy load of moral responsibility because of its greater autonomy. In this sense, the modern public service began as a vocation—there was to be a core to being a public servant that should inform one's point of view, create character, and develop individual ambitions and aspirations. In the classic sense, public servants were expected to be disinterested, and this word implies and inspires a sense of impartiality. Public servants would work tirelessly for ministers, but there were certain things they would not do. Their work was not partisan and their ultimate loyalty was to the public interest. They were committed to fairness and honour among their fellow professionals.

The creation of such a profession of public service, however, never meant that public servants should be literally neutral as between the government and the Opposition. Indeed, they are obliged to serve the government against the interests of the Opposition. What is required is that public servants acquire the ability to abstain from partisanship that would compromise any transition of power in which they are expected to loyally serve an incoming government (Mulgan, 2007: 571). The preservation of an independent public service based on merit is compatible with the notion of identifying with a minister. A public servant who pursues his or her own concept of the public interest is just as suspect as one who is too enthusiastic in their support of a minister. What ministers need is dispassionate advice and judgment, and this can come only from a professional public service recruited on the basis of a broad and substantive meaning of merit.

NOTES

[1]   Part of this chapter was adapted from Juillet, Luc, and Ken Rasmussen. (2008). *Defending a Contested Ideal: Merit and the PSC, 1908–2008*. Ottawa: University of Ottawa Press.

REFERENCES

Best, Robert. (1982). "The Meaning of Merit." In *Canadian Public Administration: Problematical Perspectives*, edited by Robert F. Adie and Paul G. Thomas. Toronto: Prentice Hall.

Brady, A. (5 October 1935). "A Review of Better Government Personnel." *University of Toronto Quarterly* 5: 1: 148.

Brown, Robert Craig. (1975). *Robert Laird Borden: A Biography Volume One, 1854–1914*. Toronto: Macmillan of Canada.

Canada. (1869). "Royal Commission to Inquire into the Present State and Probable Requirements of the Civil Service, First Report, House of Commons." *Sessional Papers*. No. 19.

———. (1870). "Royal Commission to Inquire into the Present State and Probable Requirements of the Civil Service, Second Report, House of Commons." *Sessional Papers*. No. 64.

———. (1881). "Royal Commission to Consider the Needs and Conditions of the Civil Service of the Dominion, First Report, House of Commons." *Sessional Papers*. No. 113.

———. (1882). "Royal Commission to Consider the Needs and Conditions of the Civil Service of the Dominion, Second Report, House of Commons." *Sessional Papers*. No. 32.

———. (1892). "Royal Commission Appointed to Enquire into Certain Matters Relating to the Civil Service of Canada, House of Commons." *Sessional Papers*. No. 16c.

———. (1908). "Report of the Royal Commission to Enquire into and Report upon the Civil Service Act and Kindred Legislation, House of Commons." *Sessional Papers*. No. 29a.

Canada, House of Commons. (15 March 1889). *Debates*, 673.

Canada, House of Commons. (14 February 2003). *Debates*.

Chapman, Richard. (2004). *The Civil Service Commission 1855–1991: A Bureau Biography*. London: Routledge.

Dawson, R. MacGregor. (1922). *The Principle of Official Independence*. London: P. S. King and Son Ltd.

———. (1929). *The Civil Service of Canada*. London: Oxford University Press.

Du Gay, Paul. (3 August 2002). "How Responsible Is 'Responsive' Government?" *Economy and Society*. 31: 461–482.

Gowan, Peter. (March/April 1987). "The Origin of the Administrative Elite." *New Left Review*. 162: 2.

Grant, W. L. (July 1934). "The Civil Service of Canada." *University of Toronto Quarterly*. 428–438.

Grey, Andrew, and Bill Jenkins. (2005). "Government and Administration: Public Service and Public Servants." *Parliamentary Affairs*. 58: 2: 230–247.

Heclo, Hugh. (Winter 1975). "OMB and Neutral Competence." *The Public Interest*. 38: 80–99.

Henry Parris. (1968). "The Origins of the Permanent Civil Service, 1780–1830." *Public Administration*. 46: 143–166.

Hodgetts, J. E., et al. (1972). *The Biography of an Institution*. Montreal: McGill-Queen's Press.

Hopkins, J. C., ed. (1908). *The Canadian Annual Review of Public Affairs, 1908*. Toronto: The Annual Review Publishing Company Ltd.

Ingraham, Patricia. (July/August 2006). "Building Bridges over Troubled Waters: Merit as a Guide." *Public Administration Review*. 486–495.

Johnson, Ronald N., and Gary D. Libecap. (1994). "Patronage to Merit and Control of the Federal Government Labour Force." *Explorations in Economic History*. 31: 91–119.

Kearney, Richard, and Steven Hays. (1998). "Reinventing Government, The New Public Management and the Civil Service Systems in International Perspective: The Danger of Throwing the Baby out with the Bathwater." *Review of Public Personnel Administration*. 38: 4: 38–54.

Kingston, William. (April 2002). "A Running Repair for the Civil Service." *The Political Quarterly*. 73: 198–208.

Magrath, C. A. (12 April 1913). "The Civil Service." *University Magazine*. 247–255.

Marshall, John. (14 October 1906). "Civil Service Reform." *Queen's Quarterly*. 159.

Mosher, Fredrick. (1968). *Democracy and the Public Service*. New York: Oxford University Press.

Mulgan, Richard. (2007). "Truth in Government and the Politicization of Public Service Advice." *Public Administration*. 85: 3: 569–586.

Owram, Doug. (1986). *The Government Generation*. Toronto: University of Toronto Press.

Peters, B. Guy. (1994). "Managing the Hallow State." *International Journal of Public Administration*. 17: 3: 739–756.

Pfiffner, James P., and Douglas A. Brook. (2000). *The Future of Merit: Twenty Years after the Civil Service Reform Act*. Baltimore: Johns Hopkins University Press.

Rohr, John A. (2002). *Civil Servants and Their Constitutions*. Kansas: University of Kansas Press.

Savoie, Donald J. (2008). *Court Government and the Collapse of Accountability in Canada and the United Kingdom*. Toronto: University or Toronto Press.

Skelton, Oscar Douglas. (1921). *The Life and Letters of Sir Wilfrid Laurier, Volume Two*. London: Oxford University Press.

Smith, Peter. (20 March 1987). "The Ideological Origins of Canadian Confederation." *Canadian Journal of Political Science*. 2–29.

Sordik-Aron, Cindy. (1987). *Ladies and Gentlemen of the Civil Service: Middle Class Workers in Victorian America*. New York: Oxford University Press.

Stewart, Gordon. (1986a). *The Origins of the Canadian Politics: A Comparative Approach*. Vancouver: University of British Columbia Press.

———. (1986b). "The Origins of Canadian Politics and John A. Macdonald." In *National Politics and Community in Canada*, edited by K. R. Carty and P. W. Ward, 15–47. Vancouver: University of British Columbia Press.

West, William. (2005). "Neutral Competence and Political Responsiveness: An Uneasy Relationship." *The Policy Studies Journal*. 33: 2: 147–160.

Whitaker, Reg. (Summer 1987). "Between Patronage and Bureaucracy: Democratic Politics in Transition." *Journal of Canadian Studies*. 22: 55–71.

Willison, John S. (1907–1908). "Civil Service Reform in Canada." In *Empire Club Speeches*, edited by J. C. Hopkins, Toronto: Warwick Bros and Rutter Ltd., 1908, 126–131.

4 THE POLITICS–ADMINISTRATION DICHOTOMY

Democracy versus Bureaucracy?

Peter Aucoin and Donald J. Savoie

Despite its legions of critics, the politics-administration dichotomy has stood the test of time. To this day, it haunts both students of public administration and practitioners operating at all levels of the public sector, from international organizations down to the smallest municipality. The dichotomy provides an enduring image to elected politicians, public servants, and students of public administration of how policy and administrative decisions should be struck in government. According to the script, politicians are responsible for setting the policy agenda and deciding on policies, while public servants are responsible for administering programs and delivering public services.

That said, students of public administration have long recognized that the politics-administration dichotomy, first popularized by Woodrow Wilson, American scholar and later president, cannot fully reflect reality. Appleby, as far back as 1949, wrote that "public administration is policy making, and administrators are continually laying down rules for the future, and administrators are continually determining what the law is and what it means in terms of action" (Appleby, 1949: 170). Precious few students of government have been willing to challenge Appleby's thesis. Yet, the politics-administration dichotomy goes to the heart of public administration in democratic government, and it still underpins constitutional theory and practice in Westminster-inspired parliamentary systems. These systems assume that ministers govern through policy as the elected political executive but that, in doing so, they rely on a professional career and merit-based public service bureaucracy to conduct administration according to nonpartisan criteria.

In the 1960s, Mosher wrote that "on the theoretical plane the finding of a viable substitute (to the politics-administration) dichotomy may well be the number one problem of public administration" (Mosher, 1982: 6). No substitute has been found, however, and there are none on the horizon. The dichotomy, accordingly, is still employed to explain or justify many things, including, most recently, the introduction of the new public management initiative, with its depiction of ministers and their public service executives in principal-agent relationships rather than superior-subordinate relationships, with these relationships themselves governed by way of contracts. The dichotomy's application has been sufficiently flexible to accommodate this initiative, as it relates not only to ministers and deputy ministers but also to the empowerment of front-line managers and their employees, without, at the same time, demanding changes in the accountability requirements of the Westminster system of ministerial responsibility.

Further, it has enabled senior public service executives to compare their work and their salaries to their private-sector counterparts. The model here is the organization, with its corporate governance boards of directors overseeing and controlling a corporation that is managed under the direction of its chief executive officer, and where directors do not intervene in day-to-day management. In short, the politics-administration dichotomy has been a theory for all seasons, for all purposes, and for all to turn to whenever political or administrative issues need to be accommodated. It thereby remains the most vivid and well understood image of how things should work in government.

The dichotomy has also helped turn the doctrine of ministerial responsibility in the Westminster-Whitehall parliamentary system into a doctrine for all seasons. The two have in turn contributed to what Hodgetts has described as a process of "mutual deniability" (Franks, 2006: 202). Public servants will point to the doctrine to support the thesis that politics permeates virtually every aspect of their work and politicians should therefore be held accountable for both policy *and* administration. For their part, politicians will point to the doctrine to say they ought not to be held accountable for administrative matters. They will argue that, while they set the policy agenda and establish policies, it is the responsibility of public servants to administer operations and deliver public services and that people should turn to them for answers on these matters.

Although the argument thus plays to the advantage of both elected politicians and public servants, some insist that applying the British accounting officer concept, as the Conservative government of Prime Minister Stephen Harper recently did, as well as other practices based on the politics-administration distinctions, constitute attempts "to draw a clear line of division between the political world and the administrative one" that are fundamentally undemocratic (Kroeger, 2006: A15). Kroeger, for example, provides an example that he would consider undemocratic. In a newspaper article titled, "The Elected Should Have the Last Word," he writes, "A regional director could close local offices and lay off staff at will in areas of unemployment. Any intervention by the responsible minister and local MPs would constitute political interference" (Kroeger, 2006: A15). Public servants, however, will also make the case, very often with success, that elected politicians have no business in administrative matters. The merit principle, the Financial Administration Act, and other statutes in Canada, as well as the turning over of the management of performance pay schemes to public servants assisted by a body of outside advisors, all provide ammunition to public servants to push elected politicians away from their offices and responsibilities.

Surely, it should not be a sin against representative democracy for citizens to be informed that a minister has forced the hand of public servants to keep an office open in a high unemployment region. It is far more democratic to have this done in the open for all to see than to have it hidden behind the doctrine of ministerial responsibility. The prime minister and ministers should have the final say on such issues, but, when they meddle in administrative issues, then it should be a matter for Parliament to debate, or at least be informed of, and for citizens to be told.

The purpose of this chapter is to explore developments in the relationship between politicians and public servants. We have witnessed major developments that are reshaping this relationship, including the introduction of access to information legislation, the role of the media, and a new accountability act. This chapter reviews the forces that have reshaped the relationship and then explores how politicians and public servants have reacted to them.

THE FORCES

Political institutions, politicians, and public servants have all fallen sharply in recent years on the public trust scale. Voter turnout is down, memberships in political parties have dropped significantly, and survey after survey reveals that Canada's public servants suffer from severe morale problems. Nevitte insists that citizens today tend to be far more assertive and less deferential towards authority. He maintains that, in Canada at least, this is part of a larger phenomenon—the decline of deference in society—and he adds that the loss of confidence in the public sector is greater than in nonpolitical institutions (Nevitte, 1996; Nevitte and Kanju, 2002: 71).

Governments have attempted to repair their relationships with citizens in a variety of ways: Public opinion surveys and focus groups are now widely employed, and rarely is a new initiative launched without having some kind of public consultation exercise attached to it. We have also seen virtually every government in the Western world introduce access to information legislation over the past twenty-five years or so. Canada's access to information legislation was proclaimed in 1985. The central purpose of the legislation is to provide a "right of access" for Canadians to information under the control of any government institution. The legislation adds that "exceptions to the right of access" should be both limited and specific and, further, that decisions on disclosure "should be reviewed independently of government" (Canada, 1985: 39).

As senior officials predicted when the act was proclaimed, the impact of the legislation has been profound. For one thing, it has generated a demand for good political "firefighters" in both ministerial offices and the public service. It has made policy people cautious. Giles Gherson, a former policy advisor in the federal Department of Human Resources Development and later a journalist, explains: "To address the access to information issue ... I saw myself that officials are extremely leery of putting things on paper that they wouldn't like to see made public or find its way to the media, several months later, that could be embarrassing to the minister" (Gherson, 1997). Conrad Winn, a pollster and political scientist, argues that access to information has seriously inhibited the ability of government departments to ask the right questions when commissioning a survey: "The bottom line for the average public servant is don't embarrass the minister, that is the surest way to have your career stopped or slowed down. If you have polls that ask all kinds of questions that would reveal the truthful complexity of what people think ... then [the polls] will inevitably show the public doesn't like something the government does" (Gherson, 1997).

Hugh Winsor, a *Globe and Mail* journalist, readily admits that the media often take advantage of access to information to get at a story. Yet, he argues, they do that "not so much to find out what the people dislike about the government ... but to try to get an advance look at what the government's agenda might be ... and at the next budget or the next Speech from the Throne by making an access to information request about a public opinion survey which is being commissioned" (Gherson, 1997). Government officials in both central agencies and line departments also readily admit that access to information legislation has made them reluctant to commit their views and recommendations to paper. The concern is for the exposure of individual public servants and their ability to speak the truth to their ministers under the cover of anonymity.

As is well known to students of public administration, there are three basic components to the doctrine of ministerial responsibility: the collective responsibility of the Cabinet, the individual responsibility of ministers, and the anonymity of public servants (Aucoin, Smith, and Dinsdale, 2004). Most students of public administration believe the doctrine must come as a package; that it is not possible to favour one of the three components and discard the other two to suit a particular circumstance or issue (Franks, 1997). One may ask, what is left in the doctrine of ministerial responsibility when public servants lose their anonymity?

Public servants now fear that their views could well appear in the media and force officials to support or defend them in public. One senior official at the Treasury Board Secretariat observed recently, "We are now all sitting ducks. I cringe when I write an email because I never know whether it will appear on the front page of a newspaper six months down the road. It is possible now for someone to ask for all exchanges, including emails, between senior official X and senior official Y. We can no longer blue sky or have a playful mind. We no longer have the luxury of engaging in a frank and honest debate. It is now very difficult to put down on paper—be careful, minister, there are problems with your ideas and what you want to do" (Savoie, 2003: 50).

The fear is that anyone outside government could discover what public servants have written and make it public. One can assume that this leads to less disciplined thinking as explicitly crafted analyses and recommendations in written memoranda give way to PowerPoint presentations with as little substantive material as possible. One can also assume that there is less room for critical thinking. Ironically, even advice along the lines of "be careful" is no longer committed to paper! In consequence, advice has become less transparent. In addition, officials continually attempt to attenuate the impact of the access to information legislation to protect their ministers and their own policy advisory and administrative roles: hardly what supporters of the politics-administration dichotomy think is important. In a detailed review of the application of the legislation, Robarts, a leading student of freedom of information regimes, reports that "requests that were identified as sensitive, or that came from the media or political parties, were found to have longer processing time, even after other considerations were accounted for" (Robarts, 2002: 175).

The concern over the media use of access to information has reached the point where the government is actually directing public servants not to commit anything to paper. For example, in 2005, the federal Department of Indian Affairs and Northern Development told consultants in a $132,000 contract not to leave "a paper trail in government offices," and insisted they deliver their findings through oral briefings (Geddes, 2005). As well, several months after the Harper Conservative government came to power in January 2006, it launched a program review exercise designed to cut at least $2 billion from the expenditure. Public servants were instructed to do everything "orally," including briefings for their ministers that identified potential spending cuts, and to avoid putting anything down on paper.[1] Public servants did as they were told and the approach worked, at least from Harper's perspective. His government was able to announce $2 billion in spending cuts on September 25, 2006, including cuts in politically sensitive programs, without the media being able to report on leaks beforehand (Chase, 2006: A1).

When access to information legislation was first introduced, it was envisaged that it would be "first and foremost" for citizens. Today, the media are the "major users."[2] It was also envisaged that citizens would only turn to the legislation as a last resort, as government departments were expected to respect the intent of the legislation and thus share accessible information freely. This, too, has not turned out to be the case as predicted.

Winsor claims he has "never met a deputy minister who didn't hate the Access to Information Act." The act, he reports, "chews up resources," and senior government officials are "particularly leery" of "information fishermen" who file requests for thousands of pages of documents in the hope of discovering something "hot" they can shop around to the media. He reports that even members of Parliament are now turning to the legislation to get information, a development he described as "ridiculous and an affront to Parliament."[3]

The access to information legislation has served to promote transparency and make government operations more accessible for citizens and, especially, the media. This development has also played havoc with the politics-administration dichotomy by eroding the anonymity of public servants. Senior public servants have now become public figures and must learn to operate in a highly politicized atmosphere.

They no longer enjoy the same kind of anonymity or private space that their predecessors once did (or, for that matter, that their private-sector counterparts still do). The erosion of the dichotomy, and the doctrine of public service anonymity that assumes an administrative space from which public servants could operate behind the public eye, has led to a convergence of skills between politicians and senior executives in the public service.

The modern media that operate around the clock, in real time, and subject to intense competition for viewers and readers, operate to enhance the constant threat of exposure for the public service, as well as, of course, for their political masters. While a good deal of the media exposure of transactions inside government relies on access to information legislation, the British experience over the past two or three decades, where access to information legislation did not appear until 2005, demonstrates how aggressive, assertive, and intrusive the modern media have become in their own right.

The so-called Fourth Estate has always been a central part of liberal democratic politics, but the modern media have developed the capacity to turn virtually all politics, including bureaucratic politics, into a politics conducted according to standards of transparency and political ethics set by the media themselves. Some media have reverted to partisanship, and are not much more than extensions of the party they support. This is obviously the case with those journalists who function as "commentators," yet it also extends, at least in some media, to what otherwise would be deemed "reporting." The messages they communicate are often little more than partisan propaganda. They do not stand apart from partisan politics but rather insert themselves fully in it.

New forms of media on the Internet exacerbate these developments and take them to new heights. However, even for those media, traditional and new, that do not seek to advance a particular partisan political agenda, the effect is still to expose politicians and public servants to a degree that is every day reaching new levels of transparency, and to subject them to ethical standards that keep evolving in their expansion of what is acceptable and not acceptable. The information technology and communications revolution of the past two decades has had a hugely positive effect on both democratic politics and government, and it has transformed the capacity of citizens to mobilize, both locally and internationally, for political action, to build powerful networks to pressure governments, and to engage with governments in shaping and implementing public policy. E-democracy and e-government are now permanent fixtures. And public servants have had to both adapt quickly and harness these new technologies as public administration instruments.

At the same time, however, these same technological developments have had a huge impact on public administration in ways that have affected the technical capacity of the bureaucracy to control the flow of information across departmental boundaries; up and down departmental hierarchies; and out to the public, interest groups, and the media. The more the modern bureaucracy's information systems become digitalized, the more the system distributes and leaks information in all directions. In some respects, this is good: Bureaucratic boundaries are more porous and public servants are more likely to collaborate. Even superiors are inclined to be more open with their subordinates, as they are less able to control or withhold what once would have been secret or confidential information. In any event, this development has also played havoc with the politics-administration dichotomy, insofar as politicians came to expect that administrators had the technical capacity not only to keep information under wraps but to manage its distribution within the bureaucracy.

Finally, if not exhaustively, there has been the development of what has been described variously as the emergence of "the audit society" and "the audit explosion." The principal agents of this development are the now numerous independent audit or review agencies that, according to some observers, are especially prone to use the politics-administration dichotomy to suit their own purposes. In some cases, they assert the dichotomy in order to pursue administrators separately from their political masters. In other instances, they ignore the dichotomy in order to assign responsibility and blame to whomever appears left holding the bag. Whatever their approach, auditors are clearly on the leading edge of what appears to be an insatiable public and media demand for increased transparency and openness in government, as well as for enhanced public accountability for what government does and what it accomplishes or does not accomplish. So-called results-based reporting by government speaks to this demand, but it is clearly not sufficient. The demand from a less trusting and less deferential society also requires "independent," "objective," and "impartial" scrutiny and assessment of government performance: hence the "performance" or "value-for-money" audits by, for example, the Office of the Auditor General of Canada.

The audits and reviews of government performance that are undertaken by these agencies can only rarely establish the precise causal relationships between the policies of government, the resources committed to programs, the level and quality of outputs delivered by government, and whatever outcomes or results there may be. These audits and reviews are accounting and social science exercises, and the knowledge produced by them, especially in attributing success or failure, is rarely definitive. Nonetheless, the audits and reviews of these agencies are usually viewed by the media, the Opposition, and the public as authoritative in their findings and conclusions. They thus have a major effect on the politics-administration dichotomy. For public servants, they enhance the prospect of an exposure of errors, real or alleged. When public servants do not have sufficient control over the management of their operations and services, there is an increased likelihood that they will hunker down and do as little as possible that might subject themselves to criticism. For politicians, the impact is to make them prone to deflect all criticism of any administrative variety as much as possible to their public servants.

THE CONSEQUENCES

The forces outlined above and the various government responses to them have given rise to several consequences for the politics-administration dichotomy. Speaking the truth to power, on the basis of evidence about proposed and actual policies and programs and impartial administration, has come to matter less, while an ability to deal with the media, as well as with interest groups, and a willingness to be politically responsive to the wishes of the government of the day, as defined almost exclusively by the prime minister and his or her most trusted advisors, are now what matters to ministers and their senior public servants.

The instinct for political survival, when seeking to govern large sprawling bureaucracies that have lost both their capacity to work in relative secrecy and in a clear hierarchical structure, is one reason that explains why prime ministers have sought to control things from the centre. The view at the very top is that problems are less likely to surface if the centre keeps a tight rein on things when dealing with the prime minister's priorities. If the "system" is sufficiently responsive, it can manage the issues that matter less to the centre, so long as the departments and agencies keep running on their assigned tracks. For prime ministers these days, it is easy to conclude that you made it to the top because you, and your personally chosen advisors, have better political skills than those of your subordinate ministers and their advisors, including those ministers who also had a run at your party's leadership against you. As the lyrics of the Australian musical comedy *Keating, the Musical* put it in reference to Paul Keating becoming prime minister, "You are the leader of the land"; "You are the man!" It is not surprising that many first ministers in Westminster systems come to view their ministerial colleagues as "mere assistants" to their own office (d'Ombrain, 2007: 197).

The evidence from Canada and other Westminster systems makes clear that the concentration of power in the office of the prime minister is not unique to any single recent prime minister in Canada nor is it limited to Canada. Prime Minister Harper may be taking this development to a new level of centralized command and control, but he did not initiate the development. And, he has his counterparts in Australia and Britain, as anyone the least familiar with the Tony Blair or John Howard regimes will attest. New Zealand has constituted a partial exception to this development, not because it has not had to cope with the same set of forces outlined above—it has—but rather because it adopted a method of appointing its deputy ministers two decades ago that severely restricts the discretion of the prime minister (essentially reducing it to a veto power), and because it adopted a new electoral system one decade ago that requires the construction and maintenance of coalition governments that also serves to reduce the discretion of the prime minister to act unilaterally on a wide number of fronts: policy, communications, and spending.

The excessive concentration of power at the top with the Canadian (and Australian and British) prime minister and her or his court calls for a different configuration of the politics-administration dichotomy. It explains why prime ministers now look for senior public servants with different skills than they once did. Having an intimate knowledge of a policy sector or a government department and its programs has become less important. Although senior public servants still prefer to work on policy issues than on administration, the policy advisory role of public servants is quite different today than it was forty years ago. Networking with their colleagues in other departments and with stakeholders outside of government in support of horizontal or joined-up and collaborative government has become an important policy-cum-political skill. In addition, political executives, starting with the prime minister, are demanding that public servants be much more responsive to their policy agenda, including the demand that they assist them in managing political issues, especially political crises, and also in dealing with the media.

The policy role of public servants now is less about having an intimate knowledge of a relevant policy sector and being able to offer evidence-based policy options, and more about finding whatever evidence there may be as justification for what their political masters have already decided to do (Travers, 2006). In brief, the political ability to know when to proceed, when to delay, when to be bold, and when to be prudent, and to sense a looming political crisis, to navigate through a multitude of horizontal processes and networks, and then justify what elected politicians have decided—these have come to matter a great deal, and to matter a great deal more than the ability to give sound policy advice (Axworthy, 1988: 252). The political dimensions of governance and public administration have begun to outweigh the policy dimensions by a long shot.

These skills are much more akin to the political world than those found in Weber's bureaucratic model. Indeed, Weber insisted that political skills are vastly different from bureaucratic skills, if not at the opposite end from one another, for the politics-administration relationship to work. This is no longer the case. Political skills, albeit not usually or necessarily in a partisan sense, are in high demand, which may explain in part why deputy ministers are rotated more often than in years past and now as often, if not more often, than ministers are themselves shuffled from department to department. Those deemed best by their political masters stay at the centre of government or are sent to departments or with ministers regarded by the centre as in need of a safe pair of hands by their sides. Thirty years ago, the motto was, "Have policy skills will travel." Today, one needs "political skills" to travel and to make it to the top in the public service.

What is important for prime ministers and their courtiers is to make their government look good to the public as electorate, to manage the media as best as possible, and, to the extent possible, to have error-free government. The chances of good public relations on government policy, media management, and error-free government are thought to be much greater if everything is controlled by the centre of government.

Governing from the centre means quick and unencumbered access to the levers of power to make things happen, to address whatever political policy and administrative issues that either concern the prime minister or that need resolution because the media are demanding immediate responses. Only the prime minister is in a position to provide immediate answers to the media on virtually any issue confronting the government. The prime minister and her or his courtiers will also look to any number of sources for new policy initiatives: the campaign platform, which they will have put together; matters of personal interest to the prime minister, including pet projects (for example, Jean Chrétien's Millennium Scholarship Foundation fund); issues that surface when heads of government meet; issues identified by think-tanks; and even those issues identified by the public service.

Governing from the centre suits prime ministers and their courtiers because, from their perspective, they are able to get things done, to see results, to frame the government's communications, and to manage the news media better than when the processes of Cabinet government are respected. Bypassing these processes means that written documents can be kept to a minimum, minutes of meetings do not have to be prepared, records of decisions are not necessary, and only the most essential interdepartmental consultations have to be undertaken. News management is made easier when only a handful of individuals are involved, rather than the many elements of the government's communications bureaucracy. To be sure, this streamlined approach holds considerable appeal for prime ministers in their efforts to cope with the government overload problem, to navigate their priorities through the new demands of horizontal government, and to involve or exclude policy networks of one kind or another, depending on the circumstances.

Making the centre stronger has significant implications for relations between politicians and public servants. Ambitious politicians and public service executives will want to be members of the prime minister's court or, if not, at least be able to have influence with its members. Prime ministers, like monarchs of yore, will always value and reward loyalty. On the other hand, they will not appreciate inconvenient counsel, particularly when advice runs counter to their pet projects or policy preferences.

There is increasing evidence to suggest that senior public servants have become more responsive to the political wishes of the prime minister's court. Martin writes that Ottawa bureaucrats now have the choice to either "fall in line or fall out of favour." He quotes a deputy minister: "When you live in a world where options aren't necessary, I suppose you don't need much of a bureaucracy," and then he concludes that the "government does not want high level bureaucrats to exercise the challenge function" (Martin, 2006: A1, A6). Travers writes that the view among senior bureaucrats in Ottawa is that "instead of sous-chefs helping the government prepare the national menu, bureaucrats complain that they are being used as short-order cooks" (Travers, 2007). At times, this means deputy ministers and other senior public service executives will not speak the truth to power for fear of falling out of favour. At other times, it means they will serve the government's partisan interests in the conduct of government business in order to stay in favour. More generally, however, it means senior public servants will enthusiastically promote the agenda of the prime minister and the court in order to maintain their position in the court, to gain access to the court, or at least to have influence in the deliberations of the court.

This more general development is the one that constitutes the modern form of politicization of staffing of the public service executive cadre. With only a few exceptions, the politicization does not take the form of partisan appointments. Indeed, in the Canadian federal public service, partisan appointments have been and continue to be rare. Rather, Canadian prime ministers do not need to appoint party partisans. They and their political advisers can accomplish the objective of direction and control over the bureaucracy by appointing deputy ministers at the top, and then counting on them to attend to the prime minister's agenda in the conduct of public administration. The loyalty of these public servants is secured by the power of the prime minister to remove them if they do not attend to the prime minister's agenda. The responsiveness of the senior public service generally to the prime minister's agenda is likewise secured by this power of appointment and dismissal at the deputy minister and associate deputy minister ranks.

The careers of senior public servants are controlled by the prime minister and her or his political staff in ways that have taken politicization to new but rarely explicit levels. Those at the very top now have stays at the top that are so brief that they need not worry much about the career consequences of transitions in government, or even of changes in prime ministers. Currying the favour of a prime minister and her or his political advisers to get into the court, to stay there, or at least to influence its decisions is something encouraged by the increased efforts by the prime minister and their political advisers to ensure that politics trumps administration. The professional responsibilities of the public service to be responsive to the government's agenda while maintaining impartiality to partisan politics runs the risk of being compromised as senior public servants are required to become more politically skilled to serve their political masters.

A further and related consequence is the growth in the number and influence of the so-called political staff who serve ministers, including and especially the prime minister. These are staff who are paid from the public purse but who are not public servants. In Canada they are referred to as "exempt staff," because they are appointed in a manner that makes their appointments exempt from the regulations of the Public Service Employment Act that governs the nonpartisan professional public service that is appointed on the basis of merit. The best-known work for the prime minister in the Prime Minister's Office (PMO); the rest work for individual ministers in an office that is separate from the minister's department. They are the partisan-political arm of government, serving ministers who are themselves elected and appointed to office as party partisans under our constitutional system of responsible government. Ministers, including prime ministers, have long had such personal or private staff. In contemporary Westminster systems, however, they have become more important to the exercise of power, especially, of course, the power of the prime minister. Among the most important courtiers in the prime minister's court, accordingly, are senior staff in the PMO.

Political staff add another dimension to the politics-administration dichotomy by buttressing the capacity of politicians in relation to public servants. A recently published book by Jean Chrétien's former top policy adviser, Eddie Goldenberg, paints a picture of an Ottawa under Chrétien in which the central decision-making process involved the prime minister, Goldenberg, and one or two senior public servants working closely with Goldenberg (Goldenberg, 2006). While Goldenberg's personal power and reach may be exaggerated by his account, there is no doubt about the extent to which political staff have become powerful members of the courts of prime ministers, in Canada and elsewhere. The personalization of partisan politics under party leaders has meant that a prime minister's personal advisers are likely to possess more power than ministers, except for those who lead a major ideological faction in the party, a phenomenon that appears less and less in modern mass parties. In recent years, political leaders come and go with greater frequency than in the past, and this means that party leaders who become prime minister increasingly have fewer checks and balances imposed by their party, even paradoxically when they have a contender for their throne, as Chrétien had with Paul Martin, Tony Blair had with Gordon Brown (now Prime Minister Brown), and John Howard had with Treasurer Peter Costello until the 2007 defeat of Howard's government.

Political staff are not meant to have authority over the public service. They are merely staff to those who do have authority, namely, ministers. Yet, in the real world of modern public administration, many political staff are willing to stretch their influence with their minister to encompass the power to direct public servants, if only by way of "suggestions" and "advice" to public servants, as was most recently illustrated by the accounts given by more than one political staffer as to their conduct in the sponsorship scandal. Political staff have power, of course, only to the extent that ministers, and especially the prime minister, allow it. Today, prime ministers, especially those keen on personal command and control, want their political staff to exercise power on their behalf, since this augments the prime minister's power, extending it as deep into the public service as political staffers have the time and the required expertise to go. In the extreme, senior public servants are likely to be willing spectators, if not altogether squeezed out of the action.

Political staff are especially useful to the prime minister not only because they can be used to do partisan work that public servants should not be seen to be publicly doing but because they can do the heavy lifting in transforming the government's public policy agenda into a strategic political agenda. To the degree that the prime minister is inclined to function in a strategic policy manner, as is clearly the case with Harper and was the case with Blair and Howard, public policy becomes excessively politicized; in the process, the boundaries between politics and administration become blurred, if not eliminated altogether. This shows up most obviously in the area of government communications and relations with the media, where "spin" takes on a partisan life of its own to the detriment of public information, results-based reporting, and transparency on the part of the politically neutral and impartial public service.

LOOKING AHEAD

In future, it may be necessary to look to statutes and formal processes to guide the relationship between politicians and public servants rather than to the politics-administration dichotomy as interpreted through the lens of the doctrine of ministerial responsibility. There is a long-standing precedent, of course, in the laws and procedures governing the independent staffing of the public service on the basis of merit, a process from which ministers and politics are excluded. The scope of independent administrative authority and responsibility, and thus accountability, has also evolved over the past few decades, so that the independent staffing system is not the sole exception to ministerial authority over administration. Most recently, there has been the adoption of the accounting officer scheme for deputy ministers (and other deputy heads), a scheme that clearly posits a politics-administration dichotomy. The creation of the Public Appointments Commission (albeit a commission yet to be established as an operational entity) is also meant to speak to a separation of politics and administration, insofar as Governor-in-Council appointments by the prime minister to various arm's length government boards and commissions have long been subject to political considerations, considerations that the commission is meant to minimize in favour of expertise in administration, broadly defined.

The politics-administration dichotomy reared its head in dramatic fashion in the aftermath of the sponsorship scandal, especially given the Gomery Commission's public hearing into the politics and administration—more accurately, the "political administration"—of the sponsorship program. It arose again, from a different direction, in the even more recent RCMP debacles and the report on the governance of the RCMP. At issue in these and other episodes in the past decade or so is the fundamental governance by politicians of the administrative realm. Ministers must be able to direct and control the administration of public affairs if the constitutional principles of responsible government and ministerial responsibility are to secure our parliamentary system of representative democracy. The public service bureaucracy, however expert and nonpartisan, cannot be allowed to rule. It must be subordinate to ministers and to the law as established by Parliament. That said, we do not accept that democracy rules out a politics-administration dichotomy wherein there is an administrative sphere over which administrators, by themselves and/or working under the authority of public office-holders who are not politicians, discharge their duties and responsibilities separately from ministers.

Democracy has always accepted, even required, a dispersal of authority so that a system of checks and balances will limit the possibility of an absolute possession of power by any office holder. Both responsible government and ministerial responsibility are forms of distributed authority with checks and balances present. As everyone now acknowledges, however, the Canadian system of checks and balances has been diminished in its effectiveness over the past several decades to the point where there is now an excessive concentration of power in the prime minister. This concentration of power, it must be emphasized, is well in excess of that required by a prime minister to function as first minister of the government and in order to secure the requirements of responsible government. Chief among the powers that may not be necessary is the power to staff the deputy minister cadre (a power that has now been extended to associate deputy ministers, a category that has expanded significantly over the past two decades).

The same can be said for the powers assigned to ministers in order to secure the democratic requirements of ministerial responsibility. As we noted, at the outset, ministers need sufficient powers to direct and control the administration of public affairs generally. But that need not mean that certain dimensions of administration could not be better positioned under the authority of administrators or others to advance the public interest in good administration. In some instances, such as staffing the public service, this power might be beyond the reach of ministers altogether, although all such powers are always within the reach of Parliament. In some other instances, the powers might be subject to a ministerial directive that would override the decisions of others, such as the power of ministers to issue policy directives to Crown corporation boards or, even more relevant to this discussion, the power of the Minister of National Revenue to issue a directive to the board of management of the Canada Revenue Agency (CRA) with respect to administrative matters that fall within the board's statutory authority. Indeed, the CRA's board of management, a board of office holders who are neither elected politicians nor federal public servants, and who have statutory "governance" powers with respect to the administration of the CRA, is a uniquely Canadian innovation in regard to the politics-administration dichotomy that might be a model for a more general restructuring of the political-administrative interface.

NOTES

1. Consultations with a deputy minister, Ottawa, 11 June 2006.
2. This point was made by several participants at the Quebec City round table held on September 14, 2005, Canada, Commission of Inquiry into the Sponsorship Program and Advertising Activities.
3. Winsor made these observations at the Toronto round table, held on October 5, 2005, Canada, Commission of Inquiry into the Sponsorship Program and Advertising Activities.

REFERENCES

Appleby, Paul H. (1949). *Policy and Administration*. Tuscaloosser: University of Alabama Press.

Aucoin, Peter, Jennifer Smith, and Geoff Dinsdale. (2004). *Responsible Government*. Ottawa: Canadian Centre for Management Development.

Axworthy, Thomas. (1988). "Of Secretaries to Princes." *Canadian Public Administration*. 31: 2: 252.

Canada. (1985). *Access to Information Act*. R.S.C., c. A-1, 39.

Chase, Steven. (26 September 2006). "Ottawa's $2-billion hit list." *The Globe and Mail*, A1.

D'Ombrain, Nicholas. (2007). "The Machinery of Government." *Canadian Public Administration*. 50: 2: 197.

Franks, C. E. S. (1997). "Not Anonymous: Ministerial Responsibility and the British Accounting Affairs." *Canadian Public Administration*. 40: 4: 626–652.

———. (2006). "The Respective Responsibilities and Accountabilities of Ministers and Public Servants: A Study of the British Accounting Officer System and its Relevance for Canada." Commission of Inquiry into the

Sponsorship Program and Advertising Activities. Ottawa: Public Works and Government Service Canada, 2006 Research Studies, vol. 3, 157–230.

Geddes, John. (10 October 2005). "Contract Specifies That Consultant Leave No Paper Trail in Federal Offices." *Maclean's*. <http://www.macleans.ca>.

Gherson, Giles. (3 December 1997). *This Morning*. CBC.

Goldenberg, Eddie. (2006). *The Way It Works: Inside Ottawa*. Toronto: McClelland and Stewart.

Kroeger, Arthur. (7 February 2006). "The Elected Should Have the Last Word." *The Globe and Mail*, A15.

Martin, Lawrence. (9 August 2006). "The Unwritten Bylaw of Bytown: Fall in Line or Fall Out of Favour." *The Globe and Mail*, A1, A6.

Mosher, Frederick. (1982). *Democracy and the Public Service*, 2nd ed. New York: Oxford University Press.

Nevitte, Neil. (1996). *The Decline of Deference: Canadian Value Change in Cross-National Perspective*. Peterborough: Broadview Press.

Nevitte, Neil, and Mebs Kanju. (2002). "Canadian Political Culture and Value Change." In *Citizen Politics: Research and Theory in Canadian Political Behaviour*, edited by Joanna Everitt and Brenda O'Neill, 56–73. Don Mills: Oxford University Press.

Robarts, Alasdair. (2002). "Administrative Discretion and the Access to Information Act: An Internal Law on Open Government?" *Canadian Public Administration*. 45: 2: 175.

Savoie, Donald J. (2003). *Breaking the Bargain: Public Servants, Ministers, and Parliament*. Toronto: University of Toronto Press.

Travers, Jim. (22 August 2006). "Mandarins Learning to Like Harper." *The Toronto Star*. <http://www.thestar.com>.

———. (6 February 2007). "Branding Team Harper." *The Toronto Star*. <http://www.thestar.com>.

5 THE UNFORTUNATE EXPERIENCE OF THE DUELLING PROTOCOLS:

A Chapter in the Continuing Quest for Responsible Government in Canada

C. E. S. Franks

BACKGROUND

This chapter examines a normally neglected aspect of responsible parliamentary government in Canada: the role of Parliament in the accountability of the public service. In particular, it looks at the accountability of Canada's most senior public servants, the deputy ministers and heads of agencies. These deputy heads are now, under changes to the Financial Administration Act through the Harper government's flagship legislation, the Federal Accountability Act, designated as "accounting officers." The accounting officer system makes the deputy heads of departments and agencies accountable for their management responsibilities before parliamentary committees.

This reform, which was first advocated by the Royal Commission on Financial Management and Accountability in 1979 (Canada, 1979), later endorsed by the McGrath Committee on reform of the House of Commons (House of Commons, 1985), and at one point supported by Prime Minister Jean Chrétien, was strongly recommended by the Public Accounts Committee (PAC) after its investigation into the sponsorship program (Canada, House of Commons, 2005). Subsequently, the Commission of Inquiry into the Sponsorship Program and Advertising Activities made the same recommendation (Canada, Commission of Inquiry into the Sponsorship Program and Advertising Activities (Gomery), 2006). The Conservative Party made the accounting officer proposal a core part of their 2006 election platform, and it was a key part of the new Conservative government's first major piece of legislation, the Federal Accountability Act, which received royal assent on December 12, 2006. In November 2006, even before the bill was passed, the PAC began work on developing a protocol to govern the appearance of deputy heads as accounting officers before the committee.[1]

Though the PAC invited the Treasury Board Secretariat to collaborate in producing a joint protocol governing the attendance of accounting officers before it and kept the secretariat fully informed, cooperation was not forthcoming. A few days before the committee was to vote on its protocol, the Privy Council Office (PCO) rushed its own quite different document onto its website (PCO, 2007). Nevertheless, the PAC adopted its own protocol on division, with all government members opposed save one, a former chair of the committee, who abstained (Canada, House of Commons, March 2007). Most members of the committee were not satisfied that the PCO document accurately reflected the intentions and meaning of the statutory provisions regarding accounting officers, and some were not happy with the way the PCO appeared to instruct the committee on how it should conduct its business. In May 2007, the House of Commons concurred in the PAC's report. All opposition parties supported the motion. All government members opposed. The lead government spokesperson, the parliamentary secretary to the president of the Treasury Board, accomplished the impressive feat of accusing the committee and its protocol of destroying ministerial responsibility and accountability without once mentioning that the new Conservative government's showpiece Federal Accountability Act had committed the new government to an even stronger version of the same reform.

The interested parties on the government side that so far have had their way are the PCO and the deputy minister community. They, despite the recommendations of the PAC and the Gomery Commission, the election commitment of the Conservative Party, and the provisions of the Federal Accountability Act, have proven to be the tail that wags the dog on this issue. The Treasury Board and its secretariat were bystanders in the PCO's formulation of its views on this aspect of management policy. The differences between the two protocols, and the implications and consequences of the troublesome situation that the PCO and Parliament have two quite different views on the responsibilities of accounting officers and their accountability before parliamentary committees form the focus of this chapter. The accounting officer reform, and its current contested existence, form an important but far from finished chapter in the quest for responsible government in Canada.

J. E. Hodgetts showed in his path-breaking *Pioneer Public Service* (1955) that responsible government is as much a matter of administrative as of constitutional reform. That the parliamentary-cabinet structure established in pioneer times would ensure that the government selected from, and accountable to, an elected assembly would behave in a responsible manner was and still is an article of hope if not faith to many admirers of responsible parliamentary government (Birch, 1964). But the fact remains that responsible government is an ideal as well as a mechanism, and a responsible parliamentary government will not necessarily behave responsibly. Quite to the contrary, Canadians by now are well aware that a government in a system of responsible parliamentary government can act irresponsibly: *vide* the sponsorship scandal and the findings of the Gomery Commission that investigated it (2006); the HRDC scandal of a few years ago (Auditor General, 2000; Good, 2003); and the recurring litanies of irresponsible behaviour uncovered by the Auditor General in her reports. The role, identity, responsibility, and accountability of the public service, and in particular the deputy heads of departments and agencies, the most senior public servants, has become the key machinery of government issue in the continuing Canadian struggle for responsible government.

The doctrine espoused by the PCO is that all accountability of the public service is internal, private, and within the public service and its relationship with elected ministers. According to this doctrine, public servants are accountable to ministers, ministers to Parliament. Period. End of discussion. The PCO (the central coordinating agency of the government, cabinet secretariat, and in effect the prime minister's department) has stated many times that all accountability of public servants is to ministers and within government, that all accountability to Parliament is by ministers, and even when the public servants in question possess statutory or delegated authority in their own right, they are accountable to their ministers for the use of these powers, and have no accountability relationship with Parliament (e.g., Treasury Board, 2005; PCO, 1993 [1977]; 2003; 2007).

This claim of the PCO has failed to recognize the fact that there are many exceptions in Canada, as elsewhere, to this *pur et dur* version of the doctrine of ministerial responsibility. Hodgetts's "structural heretics," the crown corporations and other non-departmental agencies that possess statutory power in their own right, are one set of exceptions to the belief that ministers possess all responsibility and are the sole individuals who have an accountability relationship with Parliament. Canada's Financial Administration Act states explicitly that crown corporations are accountable to Parliament through their ministers. There are many others.

Britain has offered a practice more relevant for the accountability of the core public service: since the 1860s, Britain, on whose parliamentary system Canada's is based, has had a major exception to the rule that ministers and ministers alone have an accountability relationship with Parliament. The exception is the British system of accounting officers, the civil service "permanent" heads of departments and agencies (equivalent to Canadian deputy ministers and heads of agencies—deputy heads), who hold extensive management responsibilities in their own right and are directly and personally accountable before the PAC of the House of Commons for the conduct of their duties (Franks, 1997; 2006; UK Treasury, 2005; 2007; UK House of Commons, 2007; Glicksman, 2007). Unfortunately, the Canadian government's thirty-year-old interpretation of the role of British accounting officers (PCO, 1977) has been so inaccurate and skewed as to have distorted discussion of this reform in Canada for many decades (Franks, 1997). As a result, this British practice of accountability of heads of departments and agencies before a parliamentary committee has not, until the sponsorship scandal, received serious attention, even though it was supported by the Royal Commission on Financial Management and Accountability (1979), the Special Committee on Reform of the House of Commons

(1985), the Canadian PAC (2005; 2007), and outside commentators (Franks, 1997).

Neither the PAC nor the Gomery Commission quarrelled with the PCO's definitions of responsibility and accountability. These are quite clear and unambiguous. Responsibility, according to the PCO, "identifies the field within which a public office holder (whether elected or unelected) can act; it is defined by the specific authority given to an office holder (by law or delegation)," while accountability "involves rendering an account of how responsibilities have been carried out and problems corrected and, depending on the circumstances, accepting personal consequences for problems the office holder caused or problems that could have been avoided or corrected if the office holder had acted appropriately" (PCO, 2003). In other words, officials who hold responsibility have the authority and duty to act, and, whether minister or public servant, can only be held accountable for deeds, misdeeds, or deeds left undone in the areas in which they possess the responsibility. They cannot be accountable where they do not possess the responsibility. Officials holding statutory responsibility can delegate authority to act to others, but that does not absolve them from their accountability for the actions taken under their powers and responsibility.

The French version of the terms of reference of the Gomery Commission makes this essential link between responsibility and accountability much clearer than does the English. Here the cumbersome English phrase "the respective responsibilities and accountabilities of ministers and public servants," which the commission was required to examine, is translated tightly and clearly as "*la responsabilité des ministres et des fonctionnaires*," with the one French word "*responsabilité*" doing double duty as meaning both words, responsibility and accountability, in the English version. The French version has the virtue of quite properly showing that there is an indissoluble link between responsibility and accountability. They are two sides of the same coin.

The problems are in how the PCO applies its definitions to the workings of Canada's parliamentary-cabinet system. There is no disagreement over the fundamental structure. Ministers, constitutionally and by statute, have responsibility for the management and direction of their departments. Ministers, by constitutional convention, are accountable to Parliament for their departments. However, the Canadian Parliament has assigned many important powers directly or through delegation to public servants, and in particular deputy ministers and heads of agencies, the deputy heads of departments and agencies. For these statutory and delegated duties of deputy heads ministers cannot be accountable because they do not hold responsibility.

The PCO's claim that only ministers can be accountable to Parliament is incompatible with these statutory provisions. The PCO's attempts to reconcile the conflicts between the principle that officials can be accountable only where they hold responsibility and the reality that senior public servants (and others) hold responsibilities in their own right independent of ministers on the one hand, with its claim on the other hand that only ministers have an accountability relationship with Parliament have engendered contradictions that lead to confusion and avoidance of responsibility.

If the ministers do not have the responsibility, they cannot be accountable; if the ministers are accountable, then they must have the responsibility. The PCO's interpretation of accountability to Parliament has broken the essential link between responsibility and accountability. A former Clerk of the Privy Council (the secretary to the Cabinet, head of the public service, and often referred to as deputy minister to the prime minister) told the Gomery Commission at one of its workshops that he had raised this issue with the Treasury Board and had been told that the ministers' broad responsibilities for the management and direction of departments "trumps" the deputies' specific statutory responsibilities. The commission concluded that this was not legally tenable. One law cannot trump another. Both laws must be read as having equal validity and power.

As a result of these contradictions, the accountability of senior public servants before parliamentary committees in Canada—even when they, not the ministers, hold statutory responsibility—is neither logical, orderly, nor in accord with the governing statutes. This has serious consequences. Neither the PAC nor the Gomery Commission could determine who held the responsibility to ensure that the sponsorship program was properly run. Neither minister nor deputy minister admitted holding responsibility. Both indulged in "plausible deniability." Responsibility was missing. As a result, accountability was missing too. The PAC concluded that

> the current interpretation of the doctrine of ministerial accountability dates from a time when government was small, and ministers knew (or ought to have known) their departments with some intimacy. These circumstances have changed, as both the Lambert Royal Commission [on management and accountability] and the authors of the McGrath Report [on reform of the House of Commons] recognized, and while the doctrine remains as valid as ever, its interpretation and practice no longer correspond with contemporary parliamentary or governmental realities. Ambiguities in the doctrine, perhaps tolerable in the past, are now contributing to a situation in which those with responsibility are able to avoid accountability, as the Sponsorship Program has so clearly and so sadly demonstrated. What is needed, therefore, is not the wholesale abandonment of the doctrine of ministerial accountability. Instead, the doctrine needs to be reaffirmed and its interpretation and practice refined and clarified to assure its continuing relevance and utility to our system of government. (Canada, House of Commons, 2005)

The unwillingness of either minister or deputy minister to accept responsibility for the problems uncovered by the Auditor General, the PAC, and the Gomery Commission in the sponsorship program indicates the severity of the problems in assigning responsibility and holding the responsible officials to account. These contradictions and confusions have engendered fundamental difficulties in both the interpretation of statutes relating to the responsibilities of public servants and in Parliament's ability to hold government accountable. The Financial Administration Act assigns directly to deputy heads the responsibility for ensuring that payments under contracts are not made unless the work has been done and the paperwork is in order. The Treasury Board's contracting policies demand that deputy heads administer contracts in accordance with the requirements of prudence and probity (Treasury Board, 2003). In Britain, as well, these contracting responsibilities clearly belong to the accounting officers. The difference is that British accounting officers are personally accountable before the PAC for these responsibilities, while in Canada the PCO claims that deputy heads appear before parliamentary committees to answer questions on behalf of their ministers, even when they, the deputy heads and not the ministers, hold the statutory and delegated responsibilities.

As a result of these frustrations, confusions, and obfuscations in its investigation into the sponsorship affair, the PAC recommended that deputy ministers be identified as accounting officers, following British practice, and that they be accountable before the committee for their management responsibilities. Subsequently, the Gomery Commission, following its investigation into the sponsorship issue, made similar recommendations (2006). Both proposed that these senior public service managers of departments be accountable in their own right for their statutory and delegated management responsibilities before the PAC. Ministers would not be accountable to Parliament for these management responsibilities unless they had explicitly and in writing overruled their deputy heads.

The Conservative Party committed itself to this reform in its election platform (2006) and to introducing the Federal Accountability Act embodying these reforms when it gained power. After the general election of 2006, the new Conservative government introduced, as their first major legislation, their promised Federal Accountability Act. This act identified the holders of twenty deputy ministerial positions and eighty-eight heads of agencies as accounting officers, accountable before parliamentary committees for their management responsibilities.

THE ACCOUNTING OFFICER PROVISIONS OF THE FEDERAL ACCOUNTABILITY ACT

Once the Federal Accountability Act became law, its accounting officer provisions became part of the Financial Administration Act. Close to one hundred deputy heads—deputy ministers and heads of agencies—are now designated as accounting officers under the act. The responsibilities and accountability of accounting officers in the amended Financial Administration Act are as follows:

16.4(1) Within the framework of the appropriate minister's responsibilities and his or her accountability to Parliament, and subject to the appropriate minister's management and direction of his or her department, the accounting officer of a department ... is accountable before the appropriate committee of Parliament for:

(a) the measures taken to organize the resources of the department to deliver departmental programs in compliance with government policies and procedures;

(b) the measures taken to maintain effective systems of internal control in the department;

(c) the signing of the accounts that are required to be kept for the preparation of the Public Accounts pursuant to section 64; and

(d) the performance of other specific duties assigned to him or her by or under this or any other Act in relation to the administration of the department....

16.4(2) The obligation of an accounting officer under this section is to appear before the appropriate committee of Parliament and answer questions put to him or her by members of the committee in respect of the carrying out of the responsibilities and the performance of [these] duties.

The amendments also provide a mechanism by which disagreements between deputy heads and ministers can be resolved:

16.5 (1) Where the appropriate minister and the accounting officer for a department named in Part I or II of Schedule VI are unable to agree on the interpretation or application of a policy, directive or standard issued by the Treasury Board, the accounting officer shall seek guidance in writing on the matter from the Secretary of the Treasury Board.

(2) Where guidance is provided under subsection (1) and the matter remains unresolved, the appropriate minister shall refer the matter to the Treasury Board for a decision.

(3) A decision by the Treasury Board shall be in writing and a copy shall be provided to the Auditor General of Canada.

(4) The copy of a decision provided to the Auditor General of Canada is a confidence of the Queen's Privy Council for Canada for the purposes of any Act of Parliament.

This procedure is more complicated than the one recommended by the PAC and the Gomery Commission, both of which proposed that Canada adopt the British practice in which an accounting officer who feels that a minister's instruction conflicts with his or her duties informs the minister of this in writing, and the minister may then overrule the accounting officer through formal correspondence, which is then passed on to the Auditor General. Nevertheless, these provisions of the Federal Accountability Act, now paragraphs 16.1 to 16.5 of the Financial Administration Act, incorporate the fundamental principle maintained by British practice: that in matters of dispute between accounting officers and their ministers in areas where accounting officers hold responsibility for upholding the requirements of compliance with laws, rules, and requirements of prudence and probity, the final decision and responsibility rests with ministers, not public servants. The difference is that in Britain the accounting officer's own minister makes this final decision and overruling, while in Canada it will be the ministers of the Treasury Board.

While the provisions of the act watered down some of the recommendations of the PAC, the Gomery Commission, and the Conservative's election platform, they were still recognizably a statutory commitment to identifying the management responsibilities of deputy ministers and heads of agencies, designating them as accounting officers, and making them accountable before parliamentary committees in their own right for these responsibilities.

CONFUSION INSTEAD OF CLARITY: THE PAC's PROTOCOL AND THE PCO's ACCOUNTING OFFICERS

The accounting officer provisions of the amended Financial Administration Act were intended to eliminate the confusion over responsibility and accountability. But the PCO document so attenuates the intentions and even meaning of the statutory provisions for accounting officers that it will arguably leave accountability to Parliament worse off and more confused than it was before. For example, the PCO construes the wording of the amended Financial Administration Act, stating that "the accounting officer of a department is accountable before the appropriate committee of Parliament … for the measures taken to organize the resources of the department to deliver departmental programs in compliance with government policies and procedures," to mean that "accounting officers are expected to be able to answer questions about how their departments ensure compliance with applicable management policies," and that accounting officers appear before parliamentary committees "in support of the Minister's accountability" (PCO, 2007). The PCO denies that accounting officers possess responsibilities for which they are accountable in their own right, and reduces their role to the trivial claim that they appear before the committee not to account for responsibility held, but as though they were public relations officers meeting the press to answer questions on behalf of the minister. There is no support for the PCO's contention in either the provisions of the Federal Accountability Act or any other statute. It is an invention out of thin air, whose only rationale is that it supports the PCO's inaccurate and persisting misperception, which is refuted by over a hundred years of British experience with accounting officers, as well as many aspects of Canadian parliamentary practice, that only ministers can have an accountability relationship with Parliament.

The PCO's interpretation is not what was intended by the PAC (Murphy, 2007), the Gomery Commission, and others who pushed for adoption of the accounting officer initiative. Nor is it what the statutory provisions mean. The statutes governing the responsibility of deputy heads for management, primarily the Financial Administration Act and the Public Service Employment Act, while they respect the essential position of ministerial responsibility, identify spheres of management in which deputy heads hold responsibility in their own right, either directly by statutory provision or through delegation by the Treasury Board and the Public Service Commission. This sphere of responsibility that deputy heads hold in their own right is the focus of the accounting officer initiative.

The PCO's document and the PAC's protocol agree on some fundamental points, but they disagree on many others. The key points of agreement are as follows:

- The advent of the accounting officer system does not alter the fundamental and essential importance of ministerial responsibility. The accountability of accounting officers before parliamentary committees exists within the context of the broad responsibility of the minister for the management and direction of the department or agency. The accounting officer provisions of the Financial Administration Act give the final decision to the Treasury Board—composed of ministers—when minister and accounting officer cannot agree. This affirms the ultimate responsibility and accountability of ministers.

- The accounting officer system does not give deputy heads new powers and authority. It codifies and clarifies existing roles, practices, and statutory and delegated duties and responsibilities.

- Accounting officers appear as witnesses before parliamentary committees to answer questions and to provide information. Of course, so do all witnesses before all parliamentary committees, whether ministers, public servants, or private individuals.

- The PAC, like all other parliamentary committees, cannot discipline or direct accounting officers. Committees can only command the attendance of witnesses, demand the production of papers, hold hearings, and report.

- Accounting officers have a duty to appear and cannot send someone else in their stead. Accounting officers should be properly briefed and prepared.

The key points of disagreement are as follows:

- The role of accounting officers before parliamentary committees: The PCO claims "the accounting officer mechanism does not give accounting officers a sphere of accountability that is independent of that of their Ministers," and that they appear before parliamentary committees "in support of the Minister's accountability" (PCO, 2007). The PAC disagrees with both these contentions. It asserts that, according to the statutory provisions, accounting officers appear as the holders of responsibilities in their own right, and are accountable before the committee in their own right, not in support of the accountability of their ministers.

- The role of previous accounting officers: The PCO claims that because only the current deputy has the departmental support required to prepare properly for appearances and the capacity to take corrective action, only he or she is the appropriate witness to answer questions concerning matters that took place before his or her tenure. The PAC is concerned that, with the brief stay of deputy ministers in office, most of the time the accounting officer before the committee did not hold the office when the issues under investigation occurred. The committee believes that responsibility and accountability mean more than being able to take corrective action and involve accepting responsibility for decisions taken. Only the official who held the office at the time possesses personal responsibility and accountability for decisions he or she took or failed to take.

- The meaning of "accountable before" parliamentary committees: The PCO claims that the legal obligation of an accounting officer under the requirement that they are accountable before parliamentary committees "is to appear before the appropriate committee of Parliament and answer questions—that is, provide information and explanations" (PCO, 2007). The PAC asserts the accountability of accounting officers before the committee means more than simply answering questions. It means accounting for responsibility held.

- Accountability to Parliament: The PCO claims that ministers, and ministers alone, are accountable to Parliament for all actions of the executive, including management. The PAC observes that ministers cannot be accountable for matters for which accounting officers and other officials hold statutory or delegated responsibility in their own right independent of ministers.

- The nature of the responsibility of accounting officers: The PCO claims "the responsibilities of an accounting officer belong to the office and not the individual" and that an accounting officer "is not accounting to the committee for his or her personal performance" (PCO, 2007). The PAC asserts the personal performance of the accounting officers is the key to their responsibility and accountability for management and administration. In fulfilling their statutory duty to answer questions, insofar as these questions refer to the responsibilities that accounting officers hold in their own right, they are also explaining and defending their own personal actions.

- The meaning of the statutory requirement that accounting officers sign the accounts of their department or agency: The PCO claims the statutory requirement that accounting officers sign the accounts of their agency means that the accounting officer will inform the PAC about "the steps taken to prepare the accounts and what the department has done in order to ensure that the accounts fairly portray the financial position of the department" (PCO, 2007). The PAC believes that in signing the accounts, the accounting officer provides his or her assurance that the accounts meet the requirements of compliance, prudence, and probity. The act of signing the accounts means far more than the elementary bookkeeping tasks proposed by the PCO.

- The role of the PAC: The PCO claims it is not appropriate for committee members to criticize the accounting officer. The PAC observes that if any official holding statutory or delegated responsibility, whether minister or accounting officer, has misused or failed to ensure proper usage of his or her powers, the committee is entitled, and has a duty, to report its views on the matter to Parliament.

One issue that the PAC's protocol does not address is the question of how the resolution of disagreements between accounting officers and ministers is to be brought to Parliament's attention. The only mention of this in statute is in the clauses that state that when the Treasury Board makes the final decision, it is to be brought to the attention of the Auditor General and is to be regarded as a confidence of the Queen's Privy Council. The PCO goes further and states, "[D]isagreements between Ministers and officials (including those that may have been the subject of the formal resolution process)" must be regarded by accounting officers as "confidential information" and must not be disclosed to the PAC (PCO, 2007). Since the resolution of these disagreements relates to "interpretation or application of a Treasury Board policy, directive or standard," they are statements of government management and administrative policy. To regard them as confidential and not to be discussed by accounting officers when they appear before the committee on an issue under investigation is to prevent the committee from having access to them, and to prevent the committee from knowing who, accounting officer, secretary to the Treasury Board, or Treasury Board itself, is responsible for the decisions being examined by the committee. It also makes confidential decisions that interpret and articulate the government's administrative policies and affect the work of both the PAC and administrators.

FIVE QUESTIONS

(1) DOES THE ACCOUNTING OFFICER SYSTEM OFFEND THE DOCTRINE OF MINISTERIAL RESPONSIBILITY?

The British Treasury states, "The minister in charge of the department is responsible and answerable to Parliament for the exercise of the powers on which the administration of that department depends. He or she has a duty to Parliament to account, and to be held to account, for all the policies, decisions and actions of the department including its executive agencies," and "Under the minister, the head of the department, as its Accounting Officer, is also personally responsible and accountable to Parliament for the management and organisation of the department, including the use of public money and the stewardship of its assets." Further: "The essence of an Accounting Officer's role is a personal responsibility for the propriety and regularity of the public finances for which he or she is answerable; for the keeping of proper accounts; for prudent and economical administration; for the avoidance of waste and extravagance; and for the efficient and effective use of all the resources available to them" (UK Treasury, 2007; 2005).

In a recent report, the Public Administration Select Committee of the British House of Commons recognizes and affirms the management responsibilities of accounting officers and their accountability before the PAC. It also recognizes that "the civil service is responsible to ministers, but, as the role of Accounting Officer shows, that responsibility is complex, and not limited simply to implementing government policies" (UK Public Administration Select Committee, 2007). These quotations, which reflect the tenor of all official British documents on the subject of accounting officers, show that neither the British Treasury nor Parliament sees any conflict between the principle of ministerial responsibility and the responsibilities that accounting officers hold independent of their ministers and their accountability before the PAC.

Where the British find no problems, the Canadian public service establishment finds grave difficulty, incompatibility, and contradiction. During the debate in the House of Commons on concurrence in the PAC's protocol, Pierre Poilievre, the parliamentary secretary to the president of the Treasury Board, argued against concurrence because it would

> transfer the responsibility of minister, the politician, and put it on the backs of the public servant. We do not believe this is healthy evolution in the history of our democracy.... The accounting officer protocol adopted by the committee runs counter to the Federal Accountability Act and chips away at the underpinning principle [ministerial responsibility] of our democratic system of government.... The accounting officer is legally obligated to appear before committees, but the legislation does not make him or her accountable in political arenas for management in the specific areas set out for in the act.... the accounting officer appears before committees in support of the minister's overall accountability. (House of Commons, *Debates*, 27 April 2007)

Further, he stated the government

> does not agree that accounting officers have a personal accountability relationship with Parliament and committees. This seems to reflect the idea that the accounting officer appears in defence of his or her performance, but in fact the accounting officer appears before the committee to support the minister's accountability and ultimately the government's accountability for the way departments, agencies and other government organizations are managed. (House of Commons, *Debates*, 27 April 2007)

The views of the Canadian PCO and the British Treasury differ so fundamentally on so many points about the meaning of ministerial responsibility and the accounting officer system that it is worthwhile to identify and speculate on reasons for this divergence. First, is the reality that Britain has had more than 130 years experience with the system, while Canada has had less than six months. The Canadian parliamentary system developed in a climate and practice of patronage and ministerial involvement in the details of administration that the sponsorship affair shows is still with us. The accounting officer system is explicitly designed to prevent this kind of abuse, or, if it not prevent it, to identify clearly who is to blame. "Responsibility shared is responsibility shirked" according to the PCO (1977). The sponsorship affair proved this. The accounting officer system should prevent, to use Hodgetts' term, the sort of mutual deniability of responsibility between minister and deputy as found by the PAC and the Gomery Commission in their investigations into the sponsorship affair. The Canadian public no longer tolerates the kind of behaviour exhibited by politicians and senior public servants in the sponsorship affair. So far, the central agencies of government have responded with excessive controls and regulations, which the Gomery Commission did not advocate, and have tried their best to avoid what the commission did advocate—a change in administrative culture.

Second, in both Britain and Canada, ministers, not the accounting officers, have the last word. In Britain this is done through an exchange of letters, beginning with the accounting officer objecting to a line of action proposed by the minister, and the minister, if he or she so decides, then overruling the objection and instructing the accounting officer to proceed as instructed. This correspondence is passed on to the Comptroller and Auditor General, who then informs the chair of the PAC. The procedure established in Canada is more complicated but still leaves the ultimate decision in the hands of the Treasury Board, which is composed of ministers.

Third, the Canadian PCO seriously and unfortunately misunderstood the accounting officer system in its 1977 study on responsibility in the constitution (Franks, 1997). These misunderstandings still persist. That the PCO and a government spokesman in Parliament could claim that a system the British have had for over a hundred years will weaken ministerial responsibility shows that some fundamental aspects of the accounting officer system are still profoundly misunderstood by Canadian officials who should know better. The fact that Poilievre could claim that the legislation does not make accounting officers accountable in political arenas for management in the specific areas set out for in the act and "the accounting officer appears before committees in support of the minister's overall accountability," while the legislation itself states to the contrary that "the accounting officer of a department ... is accountable before the appropriate committee of Parliament," with no mention of the minister, shows that the PCO still has not accepted what the legislation explicitly states and demands.

Fourth, the Gomery Commission demanded a change in administrative culture at the level of deputy heads, now the accounting officers. The commission recommended that these senior public servants recognize their duty towards the law and their delegated and statutory responsibilities, along with their duty to serve their ministers and the government of the day. One set of duties does not trump the other. They must both be read and understood as having equal force and power. Parliament's role, through the PAC, is to ensure that accounting officers observe their duties to the law and their delegated and statutory responsibilities for compliance, prudence, and probity in financial administration.

In a recent article, d'Ombrain, one of the key authors of the PCO's *Responsibility in the Constitution*, makes the claim that "ministerial responsibility continues to be the central principle of [the Westminster] constitution" (d'Ombrain, 2007). This is not correct. The three fundamental principles to the Westminster-style parliamentary system are the Rule of Law, the Supremacy of Parliament, and Ministerial Responsibility. The rule of law and the supremacy of Parliament came first. Ministerial responsibility was established by Parliament, over the objections of the Crown, as a means of controlling and holding accountable the wielders of executive power. It has always had exceptions, including, in Britain, the management responsibilities and accountability to Parliament of the most senior public servants, the accounting officers. Just as Parliament itself created the principle of ministerial responsibility, Parliament is entitled to establish the accountability before its committees of other servants of the Crown to whom it has entrusted powers and responsibilities. This is not the Crown's business. It is Parliament's, and Parliament's alone. The Canadian Privy Council Office appears to have forgotten this.

In Britain a dialogue between Parliament and the executive over the meaning of ministerial responsibility and the role and accountability of the civil service has been going on for decades (e.g., UK House of Commons, 2007). This dialogue has scarcely begun in Canada. The sole official voice in defining ministerial responsibility and the role of Parliament in Canada has been the PCO. The PCO is, in the legal sense, an interested party, and there can be no assurance that what the PCO wants is the same as what Parliament wants. This dialogue of one voice changed with the PAC's investigation into the sponsorship affair. The PAC's tenth report on governance in the public service (Canada, House of Commons, May 2005), which recommended that Canada adopt the accounting officer system, was the first sponsorship-related salvo in a struggle that will continue long past the duelling protocol and *Accounting Officers* document (PCO, 2007). The PCO dismissed this PAC report out of hand (PCO, 2005). The Gomery Commission, the Conservative Party, and the continuing interest of the PAC have maintained the quest. The committee continues to take an active part in the discussion of the accountability of the public service. This is the right way to go. In constitutional terms, Parliament and Crown both, not the PCO alone, own the principle of ministerial responsibility. Parliament, through the PAC, has begun to reclaim its share of ownership.

Perhaps the most troubling aspect of the PCO's *Accounting Officers* document (2007) is not that it trivializes the responsibilities and accountabilities of accounting officers but that it presumes to tell Parliament how it should conduct its business. The document contains numerous statements like the following: "The non-partisanship of officials should be respected [by parliamentary committees] and reflected in the subject matter and tone of questions"; "It is not appropriate [for a committee] to censure the accounting officer"; "It will also be necessary for committee members to have due regard to the fact that accounting officers are not Members of Parliament and do not participate in its constitutional and political processes of accountability"; and "The non-partisanship of officials should be respected and reflected in the subject matter and tone of questions."

While the committee itself can advise its chair and members on how to behave and conduct its business, this is not an appropriate role for the PCO. The PCO speaks for the Crown. Since the Bill of Rights of 1689, and even before, it has been a fundamental constitutional principle that the Crown cannot interfere in the proceedings of Parliament and its committees. Parliament regulates its own affairs. Parliament has the constitutional right to determine the terms and conditions of accountability before its committees of officials to whom it has granted powers. Once accounting officers enter the parliamentary precincts, regardless of what the PCO says, constitutional propriety demands that they come under Parliament's rules, not the PCO's. The PCO's concerns about civility and fairness in committee proceedings could have been addressed in a joint protocol. They cannot be addressed by the Crown alone.

(2) CAN DEPUTY HEADS DO WHAT THE ACCOUNTING OFFICER SYSTEM DEMANDS OF THEM?

In proposing the accounting officer system, the Gomery Commission explicitly stated it intended a change in administrative culture, and that change would primarily be demanded of deputy heads, now the accounting officers. The accounting officer system forces deputy heads to accept responsibility for their statutory and delegated powers. It makes them accountable in their own right before the PAC, a public forum, for the use of their management powers and authority. Responsibility in this sense is something people generally prefer to avoid, as the committee and the Gomery Commission found in their investigations into the sponsorship affair. Issues normally do not come before the committee unless the Auditor General has reported on them, and the Auditor General does not normally report unless something has gone wrong. When accounting officers appear before the PAC, they will usually be explaining and defending actions for which they are responsible and which the Auditor General has criticized. The meetings are not likely to be much fun for the accounting officers. It is not surprising they object to this reform. But accepting responsibility and accountability comes with the turf. It is what the job of deputy head and accounting officer involves.

Deputy ministers and heads of agencies have multiple accountabilities: to their ministers in support of the ministers' general responsibility for the management and direction of the department; to the prime minister and the Clerk of the Privy Council for general support of the government's program and as part of the deputy ministerial community; to the Public Service Commission for responsibilities in human resources management delegated to them by the commission; and to the Treasury Board for the management responsibilities delegated to them by the board. Deputy ministerial accountability for some responsibilities assigned directly to them by statute is not entirely clear (Aucoin and Jarvis, 2005). The de facto accountability of deputy heads to the prime minister and Clerk of the Privy Council, though nowhere appearing in legislation, is an enormously powerful force over deputy ministers (Savoie, 1999; Bourgault, 2006). Their statutory accountability before the PAC under the amended Financial Administration Act adds an additional dimension.

Savoie found that the average deputy minister spends approximately one hour a week in face-to-face meetings with his or her minister, though this is normally buttressed by additional telephone communication (Savoie, 1999). Deputy ministers spend far more time in their roles as part of the deputy ministerial community and with the PCO. Bourgault (2006) used "proprioception," a term borrowed from the behavioural sciences, to explain the behaviour and orientation of deputy ministers. They operate in a complex environment with many competing demands on their attention and commitment. In this environment, the Clerk of the Privy Council and the prime minister appoint and dismiss deputy ministers, establish their pay and merit increases, and demand their loyalty. The demands of adherence to rules and regulations, prudence and probity, the requirements of statutes, and the wishes of Parliament can come second to these dominating demands from the centre.

In 1989 Osbaldeston found that the average deputy minister-minister team stayed together for a little over one year before one or the other moved to a different post. Placed within the context of the many years it takes to progress from a policy idea to policy implementation and a working program, or to effect serious administrative reform, this is more like a one-night stand than a long-lasting relationship. On average, deputy ministers occupy a post for slightly more than three years. In April 2007, half the twenty serving departmental deputy ministers in Ottawa had been appointed in the past twelve months and had been in their office for a year or less. All too often, by the time the Auditor General reports on an issue and it arrives at the PAC to be studied, it is likely that, because of this rapid turnover, the current accounting officer is not the responsible official in the sense of actually having made the decisions being studied. This attenuation of the link between responsibility and accountability has concerned the PAC (2005, 2007), as it did the Gomery Commission.

The problem of short stays in office is not limited to the very top level, the deputy ministers and heads of agencies. The tenure of assistant deputy ministers in office is comparably brief, and all too often directors general, who occupy the third level down, are also birds of passage. As a result, some public organizations have three layers of executives at the top who have very limited knowledge about, and experience of, the department, its history, its policies, and its administration. Institutional memory and an appreciation of the history of programs are located four levels below the minister. The result has been described as "organizational Alzheimer's," where organizations lose their histories, accumulated experience, and expert knowledge and, as one long-time public servant put it, "nobody here knows anything any more" (Marson, 2005).

Whatever else these statistics say about the deputy ministerial community, it is clear that their accountability for financial management to the Treasury Board is not a powerful force or major concern in their day-to-day work, unlike their participation in the deputy ministerial community and their relationship with the Clerk of the Privy Council and accountability to the prime minister. It is doubtful, too, whether accountability to their minister is a major concern on a day-to-day basis for most deputy heads. Personal accountability of deputy ministers as accounting officers before the PAC for their management responsibilities would reinforce and complement these other weaker deputy ministerial accountabilities.

Perhaps it is not surprising that the PCO has resisted so adamantly the PAC's accounting officer initiative, two commissions, and the Conservative Party. The PCO regards its 1977 *Responsibility in the Constitution,* flawed though it is in its discussion of the British accounting officers, to be the authoritative text on the principles and practices of responsible government in Canada. The accounting officer initiative, in asserting that deputy ministers and heads of agencies possess responsibilities in their own right, and that they are personally accountable before parliamentary committees for their management responsibilities, contradicts the PCO's views on the role and accountability of these senior public servants and its views on the role of Parliament in accountability processes. The deputy heads themselves do not relish being held personally accountable in a public forum for their management responsibilities. Most of them have little experience as managers. Their backgrounds lie in the field of policy and service in the PCO. The route to promotion to deputy ministerial level in the Canadian public service does not lie in displaying managerial competence.

(3) Can the PAC Do What the Accounting Officer System Demands?

The PAC, like most other committees of the House of Commons, has a spotty record (Malloy, 2006). At times, members of the committee indulge in attacks on witnesses rather than working towards improving the quality of financial management. The committee sometimes pursues scandals at the expense of focusing on problems and solutions. It has done this for over a hundred years, even though this more than a century of experience has proven that scandal-hunting is not productive (Ward, 1962; Malloy, 2006). It too often yields to the partisan temptation to go after ministers in the hope of gaining partisan advantage.

The PAC's protocol observes that the "non-policy" orientation of the committee fosters a spirit of collegiality within the committee that is further encouraged by the committee's structure. An Opposition member chairs the committee because he or she will be motivated to make thorough and tough inquiries into the government's activities. The government retains a majority (or plurality in a minority Parliament) of members on the committee so they can ensure that the committee is fair and balanced in its work.

The committee's protocol recognizes that responsibility for much of financial administration belongs to the nonpartisan public service and should be treated in a nonpartisan manner by the committee. Appreciating the dangers that partisanship poses, the committee, in its examination of expenditures, traditionally seeks consensus among all of its members, regardless of party affiliation. It is to avoid the risk of excessive partisanship that the PAC prefers to have public servants, rather than the political heads of departments, the ministers, as witnesses. Affirming the responsibilities and accountability of the accounting officers before the committee, in the committee's view, strengthens and confirms the nonpartisan nature and duties of the public service.

The collegiality of the committee can break down when an issue is brought to its attention in the reports of the Auditor General and it appears that ministers have abused their powers and have used funds improperly for partisan purposes, as happened in the sponsorship affair. Then the committee's proceedings can become extremely partisan, to the detriment of effective investigation. One side attacks, the other defends. Still, it must be recognized that if the issue the committee is examining involves the improper use of funds by politicians, then the responsible officials in the nonpartisan public service might well have neglected their own duties, and the responsible officials, the committee, and the ministers then might quite rightly, but unfortunately, be dragged into unpleasant, highly partisan, and most likely unproductive committee hearings. The accounting officer system is intended to avoid such messes by deterring senior officials of the nonpartisan public service from neglecting their duties and indulging in such improper behaviour.

Committees of the Canadian House of Commons, unlike their British counterparts, do not have an impressive history of thorough impartial investigations. The contrast between the Canadian and British PACs is particularly striking. In Britain the Treasury and the PAC recognize they have a common interest and concern in ensuring that the country's finances are properly managed. They have a record of over 140 years of working together. A senior Treasury official sits with the committee during its investigations. The committee is nonpartisan in its proceedings. The committee chair maintains firm control over proceedings and ensures that they focus on the responsibilities and accountability of accounting officers. Its reports are influential. The committee and the Treasury work hand in hand in reforming financial administration and ensuring that the responsible officials, the accounting officers, understand and perform their duties.

The experience of the Canadian PAC during the development of its protocol shows that neither the Canadian Treasury Board Secretariat nor the PCO is prepared to work with the committee. To the contrary, these key central agencies appear to regard the committee as an adversary rather than an ally. However, experience has shown that effective accountability cannot be achieved by the committee on its own. Nor can it be achieved by the Treasury Board without the support of public examination and review by the PAC. Both must work together to achieve the kind of financial administration that Canadians demand and expect.

There is no question that the accounting officer system will demand a sort of professionalism from the PAC that it has not always succeeded in achieving. The committee's working procedures are not, however, helped by such admonishments from the PCO as, for example, its claim that "it is never appropriate [for members of the Public Accounts Committee] to use the appearance of the accounting officer to achieve partisan objectives" (PCO, 2007). This is like telling lions they should stop eating meat. The challenge facing the committee is not to make members of Parliament into political eunuchs but to channel their enthusiasm in directions that strengthen accountability and reinforce Canadians' confidence and trust in government.

(4) Can the Treasury Board Do What the Accounting Officer System Demands?

There are as good grounds for concern that the Treasury Board cannot do what is expected of it under the accounting officer system as there are for the Public Accounts Committee. A crucial missing ingredient in the Canadian accounting officer initiative has been the participation of the Treasury Board. As the central management agency of the Government of Canada, the board has broad responsibilities in both financial and human resources management. In financial administration its role is paramount, while in human resources the independent Public Service Commission serves a role in ensuring merit and non-partisanship. Many of the responsibilities of accounting officers in financial management are delegated to them by the board under provisions of the Financial Administration Act. The Treasury Board and the PAC have a common interest in good financial administration. The board's policies demand that deputy heads manage their departments and agencies in compliance with statutes, rules, and policies, and conduct financial administration with prudence and probity (e.g., Treasury Board, 1991; 2003; 2005). The PAC expects accounting officers to observe these same qualities in their responsibilities for financial administration. The committee and the board have a strong common interest. To the detriment of good administration, the PCO has refused to recognize this common interest.

Nor has the Treasury Board been particularly zealous on its own in ensuring that deputy heads do what statutes and board polices demand of them. In his 1989 study of the accountability of deputy ministers, Osbaldeston found that the Treasury Board was not particularly zealous or effective in holding deputy heads accountable for their management responsibilities. A Treasury Board document acknowledges that this weakness continues.

> The Treasury Board's place in ensuring solid managerial accountability in government is central. However, in his study, Gordon Osbaldeston reported that, according to deputy ministers, "their accountability to the Treasury Board is not as clear as their accountability to the Public Service Commission," and that deputy ministers have mixed views about the nature of their accountability to the Treasury Board. The recent round of consultations confirmed this. The means by which the Treasury Board identifies how deputy ministers have exercised the authority delegated to them are not very precise. (2005: 47)

The Treasury Board's efforts towards management accountability, instead of focusing on the specific powers and responsibilities of deputy heads, have been directed to elaborate and idealistic lists of desirable management qualities. Two very knowledgeable observers describe these as "surreal" management reforms emanating "from utopian management frameworks." These "idealized expectations and requirements," they conclude, "are unlikely to assist in the efficient delivery of the intended services or assist with living up to the basic processes norms and values of the Canadian public service" (Clark and Swain, 2005: 454).

These frameworks, and there have been many of them, including the most recent *Management Accountability Framework*, have nothing to do with what is involved in the accountability of accounting officers before the PAC. At best, they are useful as guides and checklists for managers in thinking about the general principles of management. At worst, they are confusing, time wasting, over elaborate, impossible to achieve, and offer no way of resolving conflicts between the massive enumerations of diverse goals, standards, ideals, and ethical principles listed in them. The road to administrative reform in Canada is littered with dead acronyms.

In contrast to this weak and confused accountability to the Treasury Board, the accountability of deputy heads for their responsibilities in human resources to the Public Service Commission is relatively clear and uncomplicated. The commission regards the responsibilities it delegates to deputy heads as belonging to them in their own right, and, unlike the PCO, considers deputy heads to be accountable to the commission, not to their ministers, for the use of these delegated powers. The Public Service Commission can and does, when needed, withdraw the powers it delegates and take over functions until problems in human resources management are resolved (e.g., Public Service Commission, 2006).

(5) What Comes Next?
Not the least of the consequences of the unfortunate refusal of the Treasury Board and PCO to cooperate with the PAC in establishing the ground rules for the attendance of accounting officers before the committee has been that they are at loggerheads when they should be working together. The fact of two competing sets of rules not only must confuse accounting officers, but it also creates a conflict between the

PAC and the Treasury Board where none should exist. But a spirit of cooperation and recognition of mutual interest cannot be achieved as long as the PCO denies the intent and wording of the governing statutes and maintains its untenable view that accounting officers appear before the committee only to answer questions in support of their ministers' accountability, and not, as the statutes dictate, to explain and defend the use of powers and responsibilities they hold in their own right.

Irresponsible and cavalier handling of public funds by governments of whatever political stripe, as all too often uncovered by the Auditor General, offers Parliament and the PAC the temptation to hunt for scandals. If the PCO and the Treasury Board were to take the accounting officer initiative seriously and support the PAC's efforts to clarify and enforce the responsibilities and accountability of deputy heads as accounting officers, these senior public servants would have more tools with which to resist improper demands from ministers. Ministers themselves would benefit. An effective accounting officer system would not load faults and errors onto the shoulders of ministers when the duty to prevent this sort of abuse is the responsibility of accounting officers. An effective accounting officer system would deter both ministers and public servants from the kind of behaviour that leads to scandal-hunting by the committee. It would strengthen the public's trust in government, which has been sadly diminished because of recurring revelations of abuses in recent years. After all, only a miniscule minority of expenditures is questionable. The vast bulk of financial administration is conducted with prudence and probity in compliance with statutes, policies, and rules. But, it is the questionable expenditures that get attention.

In May 2007, once the House of Commons had concurred in the PAC's protocol and it became the law governing the attendance of accounting officers before the committee as far as Parliament and its proceedings are concerned, Shawn Murphy, MP, chair of the PAC, sent a copy of the committee's protocol to all accounting officers. The covering letter ended by stating, "The Committee wishes to point out that, whereas it is for Parliament and Parliament alone to dictate how it will hold the government to account for its spending of public funds, future appearances of accounting officers before the Public Accounts

Committee will be therefore governed by the enclosed protocol regardless of any other directives." This promises to be an opening salvo in what might become a long-lasting dispute between Parliament and the PCO. It did not need to happen this way. Parliament and the Crown share ownership of the doctrine of ministerial responsibility. It is not owned by one alone.

The current situation is not satisfactory, with the PCO having its own version of a protocol for the attendance of accounting officers before parliamentary committees and the PAC having a different one. Where the accounting officer system was intended to produce clarity and eliminate confusion, the PCO has succeeded in muddying the waters to the extent that there is no clarity and the confusion is arguably greater. Those who will suffer most will be the accounting officers, who have been told one version of their duties by the PCO, another by Parliament. Parliament is entitled to determine the terms and conditions of accountability before its committees of officials to whom it has granted powers. It will take many years for the impact of the introduction of the accounting officer provisions to work their way through the system. Over centuries the struggle for responsible parliamentary-cabinet government has pitted the interests of Parliament against those of the government. Parliament won in the past, and will prevail now. The quest for responsible government is far from over.

NOTES

[1]   The author served as a consultant to the PAC in the preparation of the protocol.

REFERENCES

Armstrong, Sir Robert. (25 February 1985). *The Duties and Responsibilities of Civil Servants in Relation to Ministers, Note by the Head of the Civil Service*. UK, Cabinet Office.

Aucoin, Peter, and Mark D. Jarvis. (2005). *Modernizing Government Accountability: A Framework for Reform*. Ottawa: Canada School for Public Service.

Birch, A. H. (1964). *Representative and Responsible Government: An Essay on the British Constitution*. London: Allen and Unwin.

Bourgault, Jacques. (2006). "The Deputy Minister's Role in the Government of Canada: His Responsibility and His Accountability." In Commission of Inquiry into the Sponsorship Program and Advertising Activities (The Gomery Commission). *Restoring Accountability: Research Studies*. 1: 253–296.

Canada, Auditor General. (October 2000). "Human Resources Development Canada: Grants and Contributions." *Report of the Auditor General of Canada*, chapter 11.

Canada, Commission of Inquiry into the Sponsorship Program and Advertising Activities (The Gomery Commission). (2006). Second Report, *Restoring Accountability: Recommendations*. Ottawa: Department of Public Works.

Canada, House of Commons, Special Committee on Reform of the House of Commons. (June 1985). *Third Report*.

Canada, House of Commons, Standing Committee on Public Accounts (PAC). (May 2005). *Governance in the Public Service of Canada: Ministerial and Deputy Ministerial Accountability*, Report 10.

———. (March 2007). *Protocol for the Appearance of Accounting Officers as Witnesses before the Standing Committee on Public Accounts*, Report 13.

Canada, Privy Council Office (PCO). (1993 [1977]). *Responsibility in the Constitution*.

———. (2003). *Guidance for Deputy Ministers*.

———. (August 2005). *Government Response to the Tenth Report of the Standing Committee on Public Accounts*.

———. (March 2007). *Accounting Officers: Guidance on Roles, Responsibilities, and Appearances Before Parliamentary Committees*.

Canada, Public Service Commission. (2006). *Follow-up Audit of the Military Police Complaints Commission: A Report by the Public Service Commission of Canada*.

Canada, Royal Commission on Financial Management and Accountability (The Lambert Commission). (March 1979). *Final Report*.

Canada, Treasury Board of Canada, Secretariat. (1991). *Financial Management Accountability in Departments and Agencies*.

———. (2003). *Contracting Policy*.

———. (2005). *Meeting the Expectations of Canadians: Review of the Responsibilities and Accountabilities of Ministers and Senior Officials, A Report to Parliament*.

Clark, Ian D., and S. Swain. (Winter 2005). "Distinguishing the Real from the Surreal in Management Reform: Suggestions for Beleaguered Administrators in the Government of Canada." *Canadian Public Administration*. 48: 4: 453–476.

Conservative Party of Canada. (2006). *Stand Up for Canada! Federal Election Platform 2006.*

D'Ombrain, Nicholas. (Summer 2007). "Ministerial Responsibility and the Machinery of Government." *Canadian Public Administration.* 50: 2: 195–217.

Franks, C. E. S. (1987). *The Parliament of Canada.* Toronto: University of Toronto Press.

———. (Winter 1997). "Not Anonymous: Ministerial Responsibility and the British Accounting Officers." *Canadian Public Administration.* 40: 4: 626–652.

———. (2006). "The Respective Responsibilities and Accountabilities of Ministers and Public Servants: A Study of the British Accounting Officer System and its Relevance for Canada." In Commission of Inquiry into the Sponsorship Program and Advertising Activities (The Gomery Commission). *Restoring Accountability: Research Studies.* 3: 157–227.

Glicksman, Brian. (Autumn 2007). "The Role of Accounting Officer: A Perspective from Britain." *Canadian Parliamentary Review.* 30: 3: 2–5.

Good, David E. (2003). *The Politics of Public Management: The HRDC Audit of Grants and Contributions.* Toronto: University of Toronto Press.

Hodgetts, J. E. (1955). *Pioneer Public Service: An Administrative History of the United Canadas, 1841–1867.* Toronto: University of Toronto Press.

Malloy, Jonathan. (2006). "The Standing Committee on Public Accounts." In Commission of Inquiry into the Sponsorship Program and Advertising Activities (The Gomery Commission). *Restoring Accountability: Research Studies.* 1: 63–100.

Marson, Brian. (2005). "Organizational Alzheimer's: A Quiet Crisis?" *Canadian Government Executive.* 11: 4: 16–18. <http://www.networkedgovernment.ca>.

Murphy, Shawn. (Summer 2007). "The Appearance of Accounting Officers before the Public Accounts Committee." *Canadian Parliamentary Review.* 30: 2: 4–6.

Osbaldeston, Gordon. (1989). *Keeping Deputy Ministers Accountable.* Toronto: McGraw-Hill Ryerson.

Savoie, Donald J. (1999). *Governing from the Centre: The Concentration of Power in Canadian Politics.* Toronto: University of Toronto Press.

———. (Fall 2006). "The Canadian Public Service Has a Personality." *Canadian Public Administration.* 49: 3: 261–281.

United Kingdom, Cabinet Office. (2006). *Ministerial Code: A Code of Ethical and Procedural Guidance for Ministers.*

United Kingdom, House of Commons, Public Administration Select Committee. (March 2007). *Politics and Administration: Ministers and Civil Servants.* Third Report of Session 2006-07, vol. 1, HC122-1.

United Kingdom, Treasury. (2000). "Responsibilities of an Accounting Officer." *Government Accounting 2000,* Annex 4.1.

———. (2005). *Corporate Governance in Central Government Departments: Code of good practice.*

———. (2007). *Managing Public Money.*

Ward, Norman. (1962). *The Public Purse: A Study in Canadian Democracy.* Toronto: University of Toronto Press.

6 LAW AND INNOVATION:
The Incremental Development of
Canadian Lobby Regulation

A. Paul Pross

Lobbying attempts to persuade government to adopt courses of action preferred by specific interests. It is the representation of interest to power. In all governments it permeates the institutionalized relationships of accommodation and has done so through time immemorial. What makes lobbying an object of political concern today is the fact that the complexities of modern government have rendered this form of representation essential in policy-making, and, in consequence, lobbyists have attained a degree of influence that many consider inappropriate and even a threat to democratic government.

From the time of Sir John A. Macdonald's cry for "ten thousand more," to the sponsorship scandal, to the murky relationship between Brian Mulroney and Karlheinz Schreiber, Canadians have had ample exposure to the less savoury aspects of lobbying. The public is also aware that lobbying by consultants, corporations, and interest groups of all types is an everyday part of the policy process in this country. Even so, Canadians have evinced little interest in understanding how lobbying affects our democracy and, until the 1980s, almost no concern to regulate it.

In this, we behaved much as others have behaved. Elsewhere, too, in the aftermath of scandal, lobby regulation per se is seldom at the forefront of debate. Rather, legislators and political observers are concerned with eliminating corrupt practices or restoring public trust in political institutions or ensuring that the public interest is not subordinated to those of wealthy and powerful special interests. Almost always the first step towards reform has been to regulate those who are lobbied, rather than lobbyists themselves. Legislators in most jurisdictions have accepted certain prohibitions, some more stringent than others. In many countries, for example, members of legislatures are prohibited from earning income from other sources. In France they are also prohibited from belonging to organizations that require their members to adhere to specific policies. Gradually, in each jurisdiction a complex set of regulations has evolved to govern the behaviour of public officials who might be lobbied. Except in the United States, where lobby regulation dates back to the 1870s, reformers only slowly came to the conclusion that lobbyists should also bear the burden of rectitude, and the first attempts were made to develop lobby regulation.

The Canadian federal government reached this position in the 1980s. In doing so, though it lagged behind the American state and federal governments, Ottawa was ahead of other governments. Furthermore, in developing a regulatory approach suited to our particular institutional structure, Parliament created a pattern of regulation that, in the view of the OECD (Organisation for Economic Co-operation and Development), is among the world's most advanced (OECD, 2007).

This chapter follows that development. It begins by describing what are currently regarded as the key elements of effective lobby regulation. No one jurisdiction has addressed every element in its legislation, but most regulators appear to believe they are pertinent to a general understanding of the regulatory environment affecting lobbying. The chapter then traces the evolution of our current legislation and comments on the forces at work in the process. It concludes by speculating on the direction regulation may take in the future.

CORE ELEMENTS IN LOBBY REGULATION

Lobby regulation does not stand alone. First, it rests on the political culture and constitutional provisions of the jurisdiction. A supportive culture and appropriate constitutional provisions are the *sine qua non* for effective regulation; regulation in turn has to respect and conform to these forces. Second, effective regulation depends on a regulatory regime whose broad embrace encompasses governance in the jurisdiction and interacts with lobby regulation. The regulatory regime's composition will vary from jurisdiction to jurisdiction, but it will generally include penal code provisions against bribery and corruption, election laws, legislative rules, regulation of the public service, laws related to interest groups, and laws and regulations directly aimed at lobbying processes and practices.

Where this constitutional and regulatory regime provides a base, lobby legislation can address the following major aspects of regulation:

- The principle goals of regulation: Historically they have been concerned with policing, transparency, openness, and efficacy.
- The definition of lobbying and who should be required to register as lobbyists: North American regulation generally concerns itself with individuals who, regardless of whether they operate independently or from within an association or corporation, receive compensation for making representations to government on behalf of third parties. This approach has not recommended itself in Europe, where corporatist traditions have led legislators to favour self-identification. Every definition, furthermore, calls forth a string of exclusions.
- Specification of regulatory coverage: Regulation may apply only to the lobbying of the legislature but can cover lobbying of the government at large and even the lobbying of paragovernmental organizations that deliver services on behalf of government, or to local government lobbying.
- Determining what should be disclosed: The obvious disclosure requirements include identifying the interests commissioning lobbyists, the objects of lobbying activity, and the persons lobbied, but this contentious field lends itself to expansive and imaginative demands for detail, ranging from demands

for personal information, to reporting expenditures and identifying lobbying techniques.

- Ensuring the timeliness of registry data and public access to it: Immediate registration and frequent reporting of activities have come to be considered essential. Equally, because officials and the public need to be able to make use of registry information in a timely fashion, most registries have introduced online filing and website accessibility to records.
- Fostering compliance: Initially, legislators depended on sanctions to encourage compliance, but experience has shown that education and registry authority to investigate violations are more significant.
- Codes of conduct: In attempts to create a culture of integrity in the lobbying community, many jurisdictions promote professional codes of conduct.
- Administrative capacity: Lately, it has been recognized that effective lobby regulation depends on creating administrative capacity commensurate with the responsibilities assigned to registry officials and commissioners of ethics.
- Regulatory independence: A few jurisdictions have concluded the effectiveness of lobby regulation also depends on their being supervised by senior officials accountable to the legislature rather than to the government of the day.

This list provides a snapshot of the principal elements of the more advanced systems of lobby regulation. These systems did not reach this stage of development overnight. Most of the systems that currently exist have not achieved even the greater part of this development. The majority of countries are still creating the constitutional and regulatory base that may eventually support the direct regulation of lobbyists. As two prominent students of lobbying, Greenwood and Thomas, observe, "Lobby regulation develops as an incremental process" (2004: 381). In the following discussion we will see just how lengthy and tortuous that process can be.

LEGISLATION: MIDWIFE TO INCREMENTAL INNOVATION

There is no doubt that Canada's development of lobby regulation has been incremental. For many years our political mythology held that lobbying was rarely found in this country, and in fact was an unbecoming political activity imported from the United States (Presthus, 1984: 45). Our myopia can be attributed to the fact that lobbying activity focused at the bureaucratic level, where administrative secrecy and a moribund press combined to ensure it received very little publicity. This is still largely the case, but it was particularly true during the years between the beginning of World War II and the late 1960s, when a cohesive and formidably intelligent "mandarinate" exercised immense influence in Ottawa (Granatstein, 1982; Pross, 1992: 55–65). During those years, it was an article of faith with successful lobbyists that the Canadian parliamentary system rendered it "inevitable that Canadian organizations find it essential to influence policy and legislation before the Parliamentary stage is reached" (Dawson, 1967: 454).

These conditions changed during the late 1960s and the 1970s as the consensus of the 1950s evaporated and public opinion became more turbulent. The mass movements of the sixties led to attempts to create more open government. Administrative reform—particularly the growth of central agencies—disrupted familiar patterns of communication between agencies and their policy communities and forced established client groups to debate rivals in public (Aucoin, 1975; Pross, 1992). Growing government complexity led to a diffusion of power and a decline in the legitimacy of the bureaucracy, so that interests found they had not only to persuade policy-makers of the legitimacy of their position but also to promote the legitimacy of the policy-makers themselves in the eyes of the public. Interests organized themselves at a startling rate (Pross, 1986: 62; Macdonald Commission, 1982: 58–59), forcing more open competition for access to policy-makers. A newer breed of lobbyists was prepared to exert public pressure on officials and politicians. Finally, a significant factor was the reform of Parliament. As early as 1971, Presthus noted that backbenchers were being lobbied more frequently than conventional wisdom suggested (Presthus,

1971; MacNaughton and Gregg, 1977). In the 1970s and 1980s, parliamentary committees became more active and independent, thus attracting the attention of groups interested in securing last-minute changes in legislation, stalling bills, or laying the groundwork for future policies (Franks, 1987; Pross, 1992; Stanbury, 1977).

Proliferation of interest groups and a more open style of lobbying excited discussion. Commentaries on interest group activity and lobbying appeared more frequently in the press and an academic literature developed (Stanbury, 1986; Pross, 1992; Smith, 2005). Newspaper and newsmagazine articles tended to stress the similarities to American-style lobbying—particularly its more spectacularly venal aspects—but also drew attention to the Canadian tendency to lobby the bureaucracy in preference to the legislature. Initially, neither journalists nor academics took a critical view of the growth of lobbying. Many welcomed it as a sign of a more open and dynamic polity (Schwartz, 1981; Delbridge, 1984; Litvak, 1984; Paltiel, 1982). When concern did surface, it focused on four different but related issues: the inequalities among interests (Pross, 1986: 261–271; Mahon, 1977); the problem of the special interest state (Corry, 1981); the attempts of some groups to influence the election of certain members of Parliament (Palda, 1985); and the effects of influence peddling (Sawatsky, 1987).

To the extent that these concerns can be disentangled, it is the last that did the most to arouse interest in the regulation of lobbying. During the 1970s, a series of incidents drew attention to the questionable aspects of lobbying at all levels of government, but at the federal level in particular.[1] These episodes precipitated a discussion of public morality and led to the incremental development of conflict of interest guidelines, but not the regulation of lobbying itself (Task Force on Conflict of Interest, 1984). Rather, attention was focused on persuading public office-holders to accept a code of conduct that, in effect, sanitized them.

In Parliament, however, a number of private members were interested in regulating lobbyists. Between 1969 and 1985, twenty private members' bills were presented to the House of Commons,[2] and from time to time the issue was raised in question period (Pross, 1991).[3] These initiatives originated with a small group of private members on both sides of the House who concerned themselves with issues relating to the advancement of democratic institutions. Although they did not act in concert, they did aid and abet one another in campaigns directed at parliamentary reform, the introduction of freedom of information legislation, and the regulation of lobbyists.[4]

These members argued for "transparency": The public at large ought to know more about who is making representations to government about public decisions and what their interest is. They were also concerned about openness in government, arguing that the dissemination of knowledge about the representations being made to government would encourage related interests to participate in public policy debate. By working towards transparency and openness, they challenged what they saw as a distressing tendency towards the growth of secret behind-the-scenes dealing in public policy. They were also interested in efficacy, though this was of less significance, seeing the registration of lobbyists as a means of facilitating communication between Parliament and special publics, as well as a desire, shared by public servants, to establish the bona fides of those seeking to influence government.

John Rodriguez, the NDP MP for Nickel Belt, expressed the sentiments of this group when he spoke of his "frustration and anger… at seeing power wielded by certain individuals" and watching certain groups "influencing decisions through their connections." Rodriguez felt "outrage at how highly placed party people slip into lobbying firms"(interview, 18 November 1986.) Another veteran MP, Walter Baker, expressed his concern in institutional terms:

> All our instruments are becoming suspect. This Parliament is becoming suspect. Members of Parliament are becoming suspect. The Public Service is becoming suspect. Those who talk and push for a point of view, even legitimately, are becoming suspect. The trust which heretofore existed pretty well throughout the country with respect to all kinds of institutions, is breaking down. People are questioning…. [This] ... bill ... [saying], "Let us recognize the

legitimacy of (lobbying) but let us ensure not only that right is done, or that justice is done, but that it appears to be done." And what better way is there, or has there been since time immemorial, than full disclosure? (House of Commons, *Debates*, 19 January 1983: 22012).[5]

The group of MPs received no encouragement from the Liberal government of Pierre Trudeau, which ensured their bills were talked out. Elsewhere, interest was muted and the issue remained in the backbenches.[6] Even the 1984 election, in which the Conservative leader, Brian Mulroney, made much of the numerous scandals that had tarnished the Trudeau government, did not bring forth any demand for lobby regulation. Consequently, on September 9, 1985, Mulroney, now prime minister, surprised his colleagues, the media, and officials when he moved the registration question to the national public agenda.[7] In an "Open Letter" to MPs and senators, which introduced an expected package of measures dealing with public sector ethics, he undertook to introduce legislation to "monitor lobbying activity and to control the lobbying process by providing a reliable and accurate source of information on the activities of lobbyists." He promised to ensure that paid lobbyists would register and identify their clients. This would "enable persons who are approached by lobbyists for Canadian corporations, associations and unions, and by agents on behalf of foreign governments and other foreign interests, to be clearly aware of who is behind the representations" (Consumer and Corporate Affairs Canada, 1985: 32–33).

The prime minister's announcement set in motion a process that culminated four years later in the implementation of Canada's first Lobbyists Registration Act (LRA). It was a process that canvassed a surprisingly wide range of issues—indeed most of the issues that crop up whenever, and wherever, lobby regulation is debated. It demonstrated an incremental development of concepts and understandings and also drew both positive and negative conclusions from American experience. It began with the preparation of a discussion paper by the Department of Consumer and Corporate Affairs that provided background for hearings conducted by the House of Commons Standing Committee on Elections, Privileges and Procedure (Consumer and Corporate Affairs Canada, 1985; House of Commons, Standing Committee on Elections, Privileges and Procedure, 1985–1986: 1: 33). The committee, which counted among its members several MPs who had supported the private members' bills, heard witnesses—chiefly from the lobbying community—in Ottawa and visited Washington, DC, and Sacremento, California, to talk with officials and lobbyists about the US federal and California registration systems.

These sessions persuaded the committee that some form of lobby registration was desirable because "disclosure of information in this area is vital if we are to have an informed public. An informed public is vital for the survival of democracy" (House of Commons, Standing Committee on Elections, Privileges and Procedure, 1986–1987: 2: 8–9). As well, they persuaded the committee that Canada should follow the American practice of monitoring lobbying activity rather than attempting to regulate it—an approach that was consistent with the emerging neo-conservatism of the day. Neo-conservatism also forced the committee to rebut charges that the new system would create a "bureaucratic monster," and led it to recommend a "simple" system of registration that would define lobbying broadly, require enough information to make registration a meaningful exercise, and be reinforced with adequate administrative support. The committee reported to the House of Commons on January 27, 1987, with a document that was concise, informed, and far sighted, an example of parliamentary committee work at its best.

The Minister of Consumer and Corporate Affairs submitted the government's bill, the LRA, to the House in June (House of Commons, 30 June 1987, Bill C-82). At this stage in the development of regulation, issues of definition become paramount as it is in the process of definition that the extent of regulatory coverage becomes apparent. Although, as is frequently pointed out, the government avoided defining either "lobbying" or "lobbyists," it did establish who would be covered by the bill. During the standing committee hearings, it had become clear that the most telling objection to a registration scheme had to do with the problem of defining lobbying in terms that would not discourage individuals from exercising their rights as citizens.

A response to this had been worked out by Baker during the backbenchers' debate. He had concluded that legislation should regulate "those whose principal function is to lobby on behalf of others ... not those ... who occasionally must defend their interest by contact with politicians or officials" (House of Commons, *Debates*, 28 January 1977: 2516). In his posthumous 1985 bill, this was expressed in a slight, but significant, modification of earlier definitions, so that a "lobbyist" became "any person who, *for payment*, attempts to influence, directly or indirectly" (emphasis added) the passage of legislation or the taking of public policy decisions (House of Commons, Bill C-248, An Act to Regulate Lobbyists, s. 2). This perception of the lobbyist as an individual working for compensation was incorporated in the government bill (House of Commons, Bill C-82, LRA, s. 5 [1]) and has been maintained ever since. The government also followed the backbenchers in defining the bill's coverage broadly to include both legislative and administrative lobbying.[8]

However, instead of the inclusive registry that the committee had recommended, the government proposed a cumbersome system of registration that divided lobbyists into two tiers: one for consultant lobbyists, and the other for corporate and interest group representatives. Furthermore, the government rejected the backbenchers' suggestion that "indirect lobbying" and those who "initiate and those who are paid to organize mass mailings or advertising campaigns to disseminate material designed to influence government through public opinion" (House of Commons, Standing Committee on Elections, Privileges and Procedure, 1987: 2: 14) should be required to register, and it allowed strategists who advised clients on lobby campaigns to avoid registration. These included some of the foremost lobbyists in the capital, individuals whose contacts and knowledge of decision processes would be worth far more to clients than direct representation by less influential lobbyists.

Nor did backbencher dissatisfaction with the bill end there. They considered the administrative regime inadequate and the sanctions inappropriate, but their gravest objections had to do with the disclosure requirements. Although the backbenchers had warned that enough information should be required to make registration a meaningful exercise, the bill demanded too little. Consultant lobbyists, within ten days of undertaking to arrange a meeting or otherwise communicate with a public office-holder on behalf of a client, had to provide the name of the client, the client's business affiliations, and the "proposed subject matter of the meeting or communication," as well as any other information that might be prescribed. Corporation and association lobbyists were required simply to register annually by reporting their own names and that of their employer. Thus, the "two-tier system" assumed that the objectives of corporations and formal interest groups are easily discovered, an assumption that overlooked the fact that many corporations and major interest groups are multifaceted organizations with diverse interests whose purposes and backgrounds are not transparent or easily investigated by the public. Furthermore, under this system an unscrupulous interest could quite easily establish an organizational front that would be immune to the disclosure rules applied to others.

Other inadequacies of the disclosure requirements included the fact that they did not require lobbyists to report the object of campaigns or the categories of officials to be approached. Once registered, the consultant lobbyist was not required to file ongoing reports concerning a campaign.

The backbenchers, government, and lobbyists agreed on one point: The disclosure of lobbying expenditures was a minefield that the system should avoid. The standing committee had not been impressed with the results achieved by the Americans through the provision in their legislation for disclosure of expenditures. The MPs themselves concluded that expenditure disclosure had proven "unmanageable both for the lobbyist and the state" (House of Commons, Standing Committee on Elections, Privileges and Procedure, 1987: 2: 14–15) and advised that meaningful disclosure of expenditures was not feasible. The lobbying community was happy to go along with that advice. The Canadian Medical Association gave a typical illustration of the difficulties many organizations would encounter in providing expenditure information.

The CMA would find it very difficult to accurately report on the amount spent on lobbying unless the term was more specifically defined. We could report on the costs of *CMA only activities* where they have a direct, vested interest for the Association or its members—for example, the Association's lobby activities for increased tax deductible registered retirement saving plan contributions. But, we could not accurately report on the cost of: activities of local branches of the Association's provincial divisions, specialty bodies, CMA Councils and Committees, staff, etc., that have bearing on CMA advice and input to government on a myriad of activities such as the control of the medical manpower supply or the Medical and Health Advisory Committee of the Correctional Service of Canada. (emphasis added) (House of Commons, Standing Committee on Elections, Privileges and Procedure, 1985–1986:12: 4–10; 14: 9)[9]

Expenditure disclosure is still not required in most of Canada's lobby regulations, although Quebec has experimented with requiring consultant lobbyists to disclose which of several broad bands of compensation they expect to receive (Quebec, Lobbying Transparency and Ethics Act, s. 9 [10]).

Bill C-82 was given second reading on March 14, 1988, in a brief debate that noted its shortcomings in comparison to the proposals of the committee but did not dwell on them (House of Commons, *Debates* [Daily Version], 14 March 1988: 13680). The bill was referred to a legislative committee that met twice and heard a handful of invited witnesses. During the hearings, those Opposition members who had participated in the work of the Standing Committee on Elections, Privileges and Procedure, and who were bitterly disappointed in the bill, focused on the inadequacies of the two-tier system, the unsatisfactory administrative arrangements, and the less than compelling sanctions.[10] They sought to expand the reporting requirements of the bill and attempted to introduce a bar to the charging of contingency fees. They were unsuccessful. The chair of the legislative committee—himself an Opposition member—found their amendments inadmissible, and the bill was reported back for third reading with only technical amendments put forward by the House of Commons (House of Commons, Legislative Committee on Bill C-82, 1988: 4: 3–4: 6).

Opposition members felt cheated. Because the report of the standing committee had been a compromise position, they had hoped that "the Government would introduce a Bill which pretty well mirror-imaged the unanimous report of the parliamentary committee" (House of Commons, *Debates* [Daily Version], 25 July 1988: 17923). Instead, a very much weaker proposal had been put forward and pushed through the legislative committee. It required lobbyists to do little more than register their names and addresses. Bitterly, MPs labelled it the "business card bill." Dissatisfied with the scant attention paid to their concerns at the legislative committee stage, they took the unusual step of giving the bill its most searching review during third reading. The deficiencies we have noted were expanded upon and some startling examples of lobbying activity were put on record. Inevitably, their protests were ineffectual and the bill was eventually approved by the House of Commons on a vote of eighty-seven to fourteen (House of Commons, *Debates* [Daily Version], 25 July 1988: 17937) and was sent to the Senate, where it was duly passed.[11]

Despite its weaknesses, the LRA did mark an important milestone in Canadian lobby regulation. Commenting on the act in 1987, I suggested that "the most significant thing about the bill is that it exists." This was not trivial. In fact, I thought that it might be the law's most important aspect. Lobbying had become an increasingly significant part of policy-making, and the bill was "a necessary step toward ensuring that it be conducted in an open manner that encourages a high standard of ethical behaviour on the part of both lobbyists and officials" (Pross, 1991: 94). The bill's preamble reinforced this aspect when it declared lobbying to be a legitimate and necessary part of modern public policy-making, thereby not only rejecting the stigma that is widely associated with lobbying but also reminding the lobbying community that to acquire and maintain public acceptance, lobbyists would be well advised to adhere to the law and, as some lawmakers hoped, to supplement it by voluntarily establishing a code of ethics.

A second important feature of the act was its recognition that in the Canadian political system, a great part of lobbying activity takes place at the bureaucratic level. In this respect it differed significantly from American models of lobby regulation. It also differed from those models in attempting to set up simple and straightforward reporting procedures. However, it followed American precedents in seeking to avoid creating administrative barriers to participation in policy debate by individuals and/or groups with limited resources. Finally, it is important to note that in adopting the American approach to disclosure, rather than reverting to earlier tendencies to criminalize lobbying activities, the LRA not only reaffirmed lobbying's legitimacy but laid the foundation for a regulatory regime that would, over time, formally integrate lobbying into policy processes at the federal level.

Commenting on the LRA a few months after it was introduced in the House of Commons, Bill Neville of Public Affairs International, one of Ottawa's most prominent lobbyists, allowed that "if I thought we'd get a law [like this] ... I wouldn't spend any time on this issue. But I've been around this place long enough to know that incrementalism will lead to opening it up again and adding another layer on the system" (interview, 4 February 1987). His forebodings were justified. A little noticed clause in the act provided that periodically it would be referred to a parliamentary committee, which would undertake a "comprehensive review of the administration and operation" of the act and make recommendations for changes. Three reviews have been conducted since 1989. They have brought about significant refinement of the legislation in a process of innovation fostered by the review requirement of the original legislation.

Conducted by standing committees of the House of Commons, the reviews have provided opportunities for registered lobbyists, associations, and interested observers to evaluate the act and propose changes.[12] Since in all three reviews the committees were dominated by government members, the ensuing recommendations were in line with government wishes and were generally incorporated in amending legislation. Nevertheless, the review hearings did air suggestions—such as the view that the lobby registry should be administered by an official of Parliament rather than a departmental civil servant—that were later adopted. The major exception to this process of statutorily induced innovation occurred in the aftermath of the sponsorship scandal, when the Harper government entered office with a program of reform that included important changes to the act.

Although each set of amendments addressed issues affecting most parts of the act, it is possible to discern a pattern of development. The earliest changes were particularly concerned with eliminating the loopholes in coverage and refining disclosure requirements. So, for example, though successive reviews have rejected calls for disclosure of expenditures, or receipts, contingency fees became the subject first of disclosure and, most recently, have been banned. Identification of coalitions and grassroots lobbying has become mandatory. Concern over the tendency of senior officials and politicians to gravitate into lobby firms on leaving office has led to a requirement that all previous public sector employment of lobbyists be disclosed and to the gradual extensions of moratoria on such "revolving door" employment (Pross, 2006: 204, 218–220).

With experience, however, it became clear that tinkering with definitions and elaborating disclosure requirements was having little effect on compliance. Throughout the 1990s, the number of consultant lobbyists registering slowly climbed to nearly nine hundred, but registrations by corporate and association lobbyists remained well below five hundred. The attention of lawmakers accordingly focused on issues of enforcement. In 1995 there was a significant tightening of registration requirements applying to in-house lobbyists. Investigative powers were introduced and the time limit for prosecutions for violations of the act was extended. However, registrations by in-house lobbyists did not increase, and even declined. As a result, the 2003 amendments introduced a major change, explicitly placing responsibility for the registration of in-house lobbyists on the shoulders of the chief executive officers of firms and associations.[13] The result was a dramatic increase in these registrations, so that by April 2007, the Registrar of Lobbyists (ORL) was able to report the registration of 1,895 corporate lobbyists and 2,552 association lobbyists (Registrar of Lobbyists, 2007).

The broader debate over public sector ethics brought other changes. The 1995 amendments to the act provided for the development of a

Lobbyists Code of Conduct. This had significant consequences. First, it brought a senior official within the ambit of the act. Although the lobby registry itself continued to be administered by the Office of the Registrar General, the development of the code was assigned to the Ethics Counsellor, an official appointed by the Governor-in-Council who also administered the prime minister's conflict of interest code for public office-holders (Office of the Prime Minister, 16 June 1994; Ethics Counsellor, 1994). Second, in order to enforce the code, the Ethics Counsellor was assigned investigative powers, including the power to summon witnesses and compel them to give testimony under oath and the power to demand documents. Reports of investigations would be tabled by the Registrar General in the House of Commons. Third, investigations into breaches of the code of conduct would not be subject to the time limitations normally imposed on statutory instruments other than the Criminal Code (S.C., 1995, c. 12, s. 10).

These and other amendments strengthened the LRA, so that in an evaluation of its effectiveness carried out in late 2005, I concluded it did indeed provide a framework for effective registration, even regulation. However, problems remained in securing compliance, providing clear instructions to lobbyists and officials, defining an appropriate disclosure regime, investigating infractions, and ensuring the independence of the registrar. In particular, it was difficult to establish the extent of compliance (KPMG Consulting, 2001), and the investigatory powers assigned to the Ethics Counsellor were seldom applied. The principal causes were inadequate administrative support and the fact that the entire administration of the act, including the work of the Ethics Counsellor, was subject to the direction of the government of the day (Pross, 2006).

Given the history of the act, it is likely that over time these problems would have been addressed. However, as often happens in the field of lobby regulation, political scandal forced the pace of change. The revelations triggered by the sponsorship scandal brought in their wake demands for the reform of the regulatory regime surrounding public sector ethics, including demands for changes in the LRA. During the public hearings of the Gomery Commission, so many lobbyist witnesses revealed they had not registered that Justice Gomery commented wryly that he had "the impression that nobody registers as a lobbyist.... I haven't heard [of] one case so far" (Gomery Commission, 2005a: 110: 20193). One witness, Alain Renaud, explained, "I didn't do it because it was standard practice. In the communications field, most people were not registered. So I was not alone" (Gomery Commission, 2005a: 96: 17136).

Anticipating the Gomery Commission's report, the Martin government began to raise the status of the registry and to provide it with the resources necessary for the effective administration of the act. The registry staff was augmented; the power to investigate breaches of the code, which had been assigned to the Ethics Counsellor, was transferred to the ORL; and a senior official of the Department of Industry was appointed registrar. In 2006 the registrar announced he would be taking a broad view of his powers in relation to the code of conduct. This position, together with enhanced administrative resources, saw the ORL more aggressively monitor registrations and conduct investigations into complaints. By the end of 2005, these moves began to bear fruit. There was a significant increase in registrations by lobbyists, and in early 2007, four investigation reports were tabled in Parliament (Registrar of Lobbyists, 2007a–d).

Long before this, however, lobby regulation had become a minor issue in the 2006 election, which saw the Conservatives, under Stephen Harper, propose changes that were far more radical than the steps the Martin government had taken. On coming to power, the Conservatives' first important legislative initiative was the Federal Accountability Act (FAA), which introduced symbolic and material changes to the registration system. Symbolically, the title of the "Lobbyists Registration Act" was replaced; the act now became the "Lobbying Act." Much more significantly, the FAA abolished the registrar's position and replaced it with that of the Commissioner of Lobbying, who would be appointed by resolution of the two houses and would report to Parliament. The FAA also introduced a significant change in the disclosure requirements relating to contacts with senior officials. Henceforth, lobbyists would be required to report monthly on their communications with designated public office-holders,[14] and certain senior officials themselves would be required, on request, to certify the lobbyists' filings. Designated public office-holders would also be barred from undertaking lobbying activities for a period of five years after holding senior office. These changes came into force on July 2, 2008. Independently of legislative change, the ORL became a department in its own right and received a considerable increase in resources.

At the provincial level, the six provinces that have moved to regulate lobbying have followed the federal legislation in force at the time each entered the field, but they have also copied one another. Thus, Ontario's LRA, which was proclaimed in January 1999, reflected the 1995 version of the federal legislation, and the Nova Scotia act, which was introduced in May 2000 but not passed until November 2001, drew its registration provisions from the Ontario act. Nova Scotia did not follow Ontario in setting up an Integrity Commissioner, but British Columbia, which also followed the Ontario act, did attach the position of registrar to that of the Information and Privacy Commissioner.

Quebec took a more individualistic position in several important respects. It extended coverage of the act to the lobbying of municipal office-holders and to attempts to influence officials of nonprofit organizations responsible for delivering services on the part of the Quebec government. It also became the only Canadian jurisdiction to tackle the problem of assessing the financial significance of lobbying activity. Section 9 of the Lobbying, Transparency, and Ethics Act requires consultant lobbyists to disclose which of several broad bands of compensation they expect to receive.

Quebec's most significant contribution to the evolution of lobby regulation, however, was to affirm the independence of the principal official responsible for the registration of lobbyists. Under the act, the nomination of the Lobbyists Commissioner by the prime minister of Quebec must be confirmed by a two-thirds majority of the National Assembly. The commissioner then holds office for five years, being removable only for cause following the passage of a resolution supported by two-thirds of the members of the assembly. The commissioner's independence extends to acting as the principal architect of a lobbyists' code of conduct and to powers of investigation. In electing to give the commissioner this degree of independence, the National Assembly may have been influenced by the debate on the subject at the federal level, and may in turn have influenced the decision of the federal Conservative Party to propose a similar level of independence for the chief federal official regulating lobbyists.

Quebec also influenced Newfoundland, which in 2004 became the fifth province to adopt lobby legislation, largely following Quebec's act. It also appointed a commissioner with considerable independence of the government of the day. Recently, Alberta has introduced a LRA along the earlier federal and Ontario lines—that is, without an independent commissioner. The city of Toronto has also recently joined the ranks of governments regulating lobbying.

In the United States some scholars believe that innovation in lobby regulation has come primarily at the state level (Gray and Spano, 2004: 377). In Canada, with the partial exception of Quebec's approach, it has been the federal government that has led the way. What appears to have happened is that when they were asked to prepare lobby legislation, the legal draftsmen in each province consulted the measures in force elsewhere in the country, largely adopting the most recent version, with some modification for local concerns, such as, in the case of Nova Scotia, stipulating that union activities relating to collective bargaining be excluded from coverage. Quebec introduced more significant and groundbreaking changes.

The pattern of development of Canadian legislation also has been quite different from that in the United States. There, reform has generally been precipitated by scandal, though there is an ongoing debate fostered by reform-minded legislators and interest groups (Ornstein and Elder, 1978; Thomas, 2004). In Canada, except for those changes brought about through the FAA, innovation has come as a result of routine parliamentary reviews of the lobbying legislation. Proposals for change have come largely from the policy community active in this field and internally from government itself. Many of these proposals have reflected experience with the legislation, but they also have derived from observation of, and experience with, lobby regulation in other jurisdictions. Lobbyists are frequently associated with firms elsewhere, academic observers engage in comparative analysis, and officials themselves participate in meetings organized by the Council on Governmental Ethics Laws and the OECD, in which networks are formed, information is traded, and new approaches discussed. Within Canada a similar network was inaugurated in the fall of 2006 at the suggestion of the federal registrar, Michael Nelson, and the Quebec Lobbyists Commissioner Andre Cote. These networks have been particularly useful in the adoption of technologies that have assisted registries to offer online registration and data searching, services that have made it feasible to meet the disclosure demands of legislators.

In short, while Canada's regulations have been influenced by politically significant lobbying scandals, their ongoing developments have been encouraged by statutorily mandated reviews that have enabled members of the policy community, including officials, to propose and debate change.

LOBBY REGULATION IN CANADA: PRESENT CAPACITY AND FUTURE TRENDS

When the options for lobby regulation were first examined in 1985, the House of Commons Standing Committee on Elections, Privileges, and Procedure warned that "entering any new field, especially one which poses as many difficulties as this, should be done with caution" (1987: 2: 14–15). The development of lobby regulation at the federal level has certainly proceeded cautiously. It has nevertheless come a long way since the initial LRA imposed the paltry disclosure requirements that earned it the soubriquet, the "business card bill." Today, it would be foolish to claim that all of the goals of lobby regulation can be fully achieved through the Lobbying Act and the related measures in the regulatory regime, but it does provide the tools needed to carry out a realistic measure of policing, to foster sufficient transparency and openness to create useful public debate, and to assist policy-makers to discern the sources of the advice they receive. In the following paragraphs, we will look at some of the features that have contributed to this outcome and glance ahead to the future development of lobby regulation in this country.

Definitional issues are fundamental to the successful development of a new regulatory field. There must be clear and robust definition of terms and responsibilities, and there should be consistency between the stated purposes of lobby legislation and its detailed provisions and regulations. Though these were absent in the initial version of the LRA and it has taken several iterations to give the act the force and clarity needed to make it effective, we will not dwell on the refinement of definitions or on the gradual elucidation of disclosure requirements, as this process is a relatively routine part of regulatory development. Similarly, though the strengthening of the administrative capacity of the registry was difficult to achieve and vital to its success, we do not need to comment here on that process. What does require discussion are the steps taken to elaborate the powers, status, and responsibilities of the registrar, particularly those that conferred investigative capacity on the registry and ensured its independence of the government of the day.

The first move in this development was the decision by the Chrétien government to introduce a code of conduct for lobbyists. Frequently in the early development of this regulatory field, legislators have looked to lobbyists to voluntarily create and police a professional code of conduct. This was the hope of Canadian parliamentarians in 1987, the European Commission, and the British Parliament among others (Greenwood, 2003; European Commission, 2006; Pross, 2007). Implicit in this approach has been the belief that associations organized by lobbyists themselves could enhance the professional calibre of the lobbying community by fostering a culture of integrity, promoting education in the field, and developing codes of conduct that would emulate those governing the traditional professions.

Experience has been disappointing, largely because, unlike medicine, law, architecture, or engineering, lobbying is a field of endeavour that can be entered into relatively easily. It does not require a long period of formal study, there are no vetting bodies to confer credentials on new practitioners, and the public is largely unaware both of the lobbyists' organizations and their attempts to promote professional behaviour. Furthermore, no legislature has conferred on these embryo professional bodies the same legal disciplinary powers held by the senior professions. There is, in effect, no compulsion to belong to a professional body in order to practice. The fact that many lobbyists belong to the legal profession also hampers efforts to create and impose on practitioners a single professional identity. Consequently, though some associations of lobbyists have attempted to discipline wayward practitioners (United Kingdom, House of Commons, 1997–1998: 85), the open nature of the business has rendered their efforts largely ineffective. The codes, therefore, do little to constrain those lobbyists who wish to break the rules.

The 1995 amendments to the LRA made the Canadian government the first to legislate a code of conduct. The Lobbyists Code of Conduct has two elements: a statement of principles and a set of rules that flow from those principles (Canada, Lobbyists Registration Branch, 2005). The three principles call on lobbyists to conduct themselves with openness, with integrity and honesty, and in a professional manner. These are, in Wilson's terms, "goals and objectives to be obtained," while the rules set out the "standards" that the principles enjoin (Wilson, 2005: 12). Thus, the principle of openness (or transparency) invokes three standards: an obligation to identify to officials the beneficiaries of the lobbying activity and the reasons for it; a commitment to convey information accurately, taking care not to mislead those being lobbied; and a requirement to remind office-holders of the lobbyist's own obligation to adhere to the act and the code. The standards relating to integrity and honesty are confined to a commitment to respect the confidential nature of information obtained and not to use that information "to the disadvantage of their client, employer or organization." The principle of professionalism is covered by rules relating to conflict of interest, requiring lobbyists to avoid representing conflicting or competing interests and to avoid placing office-holders in positions of conflict of interest. Recently, the FAA took this approach one step further, by connecting the registration requirements to regulations that govern the behaviour, including the post-employment behaviour, of senior officials.

While these provisions are not extensive, they are susceptible to fairly broad interpretation and can be amended and strengthened. Perhaps more important, the 1995 revisions, in authorizing the code, also conferred on the registrar powers necessary to investigate suspected breaches of the code, a measure that considerably extended the registrar's ability to enforce the LRA. The registrar has limited authority to take action on findings that the act, including the code has been breached. However, the final report on any such findings must be sent to Parliament, and in the lobbying business, where reputation is an important asset, the presentation to Parliament of an authoritative adverse report, and subsequent media interest, can be a significant consequence.

Though the introduction of the code gave muscle to the LRA, it made little difference to its enforcement or effectiveness. True, it raised the status of the registry because it brought a senior official, the Ethics Counsellor, within the ambit of the act and assigned to the counsellor investigatory powers. The counsellor's reporting relationship to the prime minister, however, was widely criticized. Critics argued that the role of guarding the public's right to be informed about lobbying activity was incompatible with the role of advising the prime minister concerning the ethical conduct of ministers and officials. Others went further and argued that the Ethics Counsellor could not be an effective watchdog for the public while simultaneously serving the government of the day. Experience validated these criticisms. In fifteen years of operation prior to 2005, the Lobbyist Registration Branch published only two reports describing the registrar's findings in relation to instances of alleged failure to register. In both cases, the investigation consisted of some public records research, and interviews with the lobbyists concerned, with their clients, and with the ministers with whom the lobbyists communicated. One can imagine how vulnerable the registry officials, themselves civil servants, would have felt as they interviewed Cabinet ministers on such a subject. In both cases no fault was found.

In its 1994–1995 review of the act, the subcommittee of the House of Commons Standing Committee on Industry justified the public service status of the registry with the argument that "the duties of the Ethics Counsellor involve requirements for impartiality and good judgment [that are not] radically different from those applying to a host of duties presently conducted to the apparent satisfaction of the public, by members of the public service" (Sub-Committee on Bill C-43, 1995: 20: 57). Criticism persisted until the sponsorship scandal demonstrated most clearly the need to separate the investigatory functions of the registrar from the influence of the government of the day. Mr. Justice Gomery, following his investigation of the scandal, recommended that the registrar be an officer of Parliament (Gomery Commission, 2006: 173–174). As we have seen, his advice was accepted by the Harper government, and was incorporated in the FAA. This, in its turn, has aroused debate. The most important criticism has to do with the view that it would be better to reform and reinforce the institutions of responsible government, rather than create around Parliament a nest of independent bodies that would be difficult to administer and would be liable to develop their own proclivities to irresponsible behaviour. These concerns are important but are outweighed by the fundamental responsibilities the FAA assigns to officials such as the Commissioner of Lobbying.

A great deal of lobbying activity can be monitored by departmental and central agencies, just as treasury and departmental officials monitor accounting practices. After all, the majority of lobbyists do little more than guide their clients to the right offices and help them avoid the pitfalls lurking in forms and demands for information. However, just as peculation and graft sometimes occurring in financial management makes necessary the appointment of outside auditors, so occasional dishonest lobbying requires surveillance by an official who has the authority and status to expose it. The Gomery Commission's account of the treatment accorded to Allan Cutler, the Public Works official who drew attention to improprieties in the awarding of advertising contracts, illustrates how extremely difficult it is for departmental civil servants to challenge corruption on the part of senior officials or Cabinet ministers (Gomery Commission, 2005b: 200–203).

Even governments that are not corrupt can demonstrate a distressing lack of interest in effective administration of lobby regulation, as the history of the LRA attests. At its inception, the registry was located in the Department of Consumer and Corporate Affairs, where it was managed by a staff of four. The registrar herself was not a senior official and had very limited authority. In the periodic reviews of the legislation, it became clear that the status of the registry and the level of staffing were inadequate. The budgets accorded to the registry spoke eloquently of its low priority. As a result of the parliamentary reviews, the status of the registry was upgraded, but even so, by 2005–2006, its budget was only $737,000, a derisory amount in the context of contemporary government funding, but particularly inappropriate for an agency monitoring individuals and organizations whose billings are regularly far greater (Pross, 2006). As a result of the sponsorship scandal, the Martin government strengthened the status and capacity of the registry. Nevertheless, these steps were taken in the midst of a political crisis; over the long term the registrar would continue to be vulnerable to pressure from Cabinet ministers and senior members of the bureaucracy, and the registry itself would be subject to the threat of budget constraints.

A second area of dishonest lobbying is far more difficult for public servants to monitor. This involves the relationship between lobbying and elections. The expense of modern election campaigns has driven politicians to extremes, regardless of their inherent integrity. In the United States, the symbiotic relationship between lobbying and election funding has driven the scandals of recent years. In other countries, including Canada, mandatory state support for election campaigns and close restrictions on expenditures have somewhat offset the impact of campaign spending, but, as the sponsorship scandal demonstrated, have not eliminated it. The inexorable demands of elections take lobbying issues out of the purview of individual ministers and members of the legislature and raise the relationships between lobbyists and politicians to the broad party level. At that point, as it almost always has, the discretion and integrity of party officials gives way before the urgent need to attain, or retain, power. Equally, the courage of any official, however senior, is likely to falter at the prospect of blowing the whistle on a party in power. Only the security of bipartisan support for a fixed term of office and the guarantee of adequate administrative resources can ensure that such an official will feel able to carry out his or her duty.

In these circumstances, Parliament has to recognize that internal controls cannot always check the corrupting influence of power and that it must place lobby regulation under the supervision of Parliament itself, for while Parliament is itself susceptible to domination by the majority, it has the advantage of being an open forum. It is a centre of media attention and has an authority that cannot be gainsaid easily by agencies in the executive branch. Notwithstanding any proclivity individual members may have for secrecy or for protecting the perquisites of their party organizations, the competitive nature of the House of Commons and its underlying responsibility for the public interest will in the long run support an agency that is charged with promoting transparency and genuinely enabling "public office holders and the public ... to know who is attempting to influence government" (Pross, 2006: 218). In other words, the peculiar responsibilities of the Commissioner of Lobbying are analogous to those of the Auditor General or the Chief Electoral Officer. They make him or her, to use Hodgetts's phrase, "in a very special sense a servant of parliament" (1973: 76).

We have treated the empowerment and independence of the registry, together with the clarification of terms and the strengthening of its administrative capacity, as the most important factors in the evolution of the federal lobby regulation. This does not gainsay the value of other developments. Transparency, for example, would be virtually impossible to aspire to, much less achieve, without a strong electronic filing and reporting system. The provisions in the FAA that affect designated senior office-holders, particularly the five-year moratorium on lobbying and the monthly reporting of lobbying contacts, may be extremely important in minimizing, in future years, the opportunities for lobbyists to unduly influence senior policy-makers. These measures, however, embellish the system; they are not fundamental.

It can now be said that at the federal level, Canadians have a functioning system of lobby registration. Does that mean we have fulfilled the promise in Mulroney's 1985 "Open Letter" that we are able to "monitor lobbying activity and to control the lobbying process by providing a reliable and accurate source of information on the activities of lobbyists"?

Unfortunately, no. We can monitor lobbying activity, but monitoring lobbyists is like monitoring motorists. Most obey the law. Some break the law. Some are caught, but some are not. Again, we have a source of information on the activities of lobbyists that has become reasonably inclusive and reliable, but filing regimes are limited by the need to compress information, and informants are prone to error, if not falsification. Least of all do we have the ability to "control" lobbying.

In fact, it is largely beyond the capacity of a lobbyist registration system to "control" lobbying. A registration system permits monitoring, and therefore it can trigger policing activity and a degree of transparency, openness, and efficacy. "Control" implies the state has the power to dictate every aspect of lobbying: the means, the place, the timing. That is neither practicable nor desirable in a democratic society. On the other hand, what lobby regulation can do is limit the range of opportunities for exercising undue influence. In this context, the monitoring of lobbying activity is only a part of the protective net we referred to earlier as the "regulatory regime." Other elements include the laws regulating elections, which are critically important because they create impediments to the formation of dependent relationships between policy-makers and influence peddlers. Equally, institutional structures, such as the distribution of power within the executive or across the arms of government, can baffle or facilitate appropriate lobbying behaviour. Regulations governing procurement and codes setting out the ethical norms that should govern the behaviour of civil servants and public office-holders are even more important than the codes recently devised for lobbyists. The Criminal Code punishes the abuse and suborning of authority. Most important of all, a culture of public integrity can create unspoken barriers to corrupt lobbying.

Given the limitations on Canadian lobby regulation, it is inevitable that this regulatory regime, including laws directly aimed at lobbying, will have to evolve to address issues that have not yet caught public attention. Some of these we can foresee today. The flow of money, nearly always at the heart of illicit lobbying activity, has been especially difficult to monitor, and Canadian legislators have generally shied away from adopting disclosure requirements that purport to show how it has been used in lobbying campaigns. There will come a time, and a scandal, that compels a Canadian legislature to follow American practice and demand financial disclosure. In another context, as lobbying becomes more closely regulated, we can expect to see more legal challenges, some of which will force amendments to legislation. Included here may be the need to sort out the proper role of senior regulators as they are accorded powers both to investigate and punish noncompliance.

In conclusion, we need to remember that the adoption of lobby regulation extends the basic regulatory regime that underlies democratic government. Where once it was sufficient to denounce corruption in constitutional documents, today it is increasingly accepted that ethical issues must be dealt with through a regime of regulation that should explicitly extend to lobbying. Furthermore, these changes are taking place in a field that is extremely sensitive politically. Lobbying, as was said earlier, is the representation of interest to power, and as such, has a pervasive influence not only on the use of power but also on its attainment and retention. The rhetoric of transparency, openness, and integrity challenges entrenched power, but it is still rhetoric. Effective lobby regulation is one means of carrying that challenge forward. Consequently, lobby regulation cannot help but affect and change fundamental aspects of politics wherever it is instituted. From a reform perspective, the adoption of lobby regulation is therefore immensely significant. For political scientists and students of public administration, the adoption of lobby regulation, because it is a minor but not insignificant shaping factor in modern politics, deserves close and continuing study.

Notes

Parts of this chapter, especially the discussion and analysis on pages 152-155, draw on an earlier publication by the author. See A. Paul Pross (1991).

[1]   In 1976, for example, two major lobbying scandals caught national attention. The Skyshops affair saw a prominent Liberal accused of using his

association with the government to secure airport retail concessions from the Department of Transport, and the Canadian version of the Lockheed scandal revealed that two prominent former civil servants had advised the company in its negotiations with the Department of Defence (Newman, 1982; Shackleton, 1977). A year later, the activities of the gun lobby attracted national attention as it worked to discourage the introduction of rigorous gun control legislation (Lewis, 1977). During the next few years, other scandals appeared regularly in the news.

2   These bills frequently replicated one another. The late Walter Baker's description of his own bill fits most others: "It defines lobbying ... as the actions of any person or any group attempting to influence the course of either legislative or executive action. It establishes a register of lobbyists to be administered jointly by the Clerks of the two Chambers. Lobbyists must set down their names, the person or group on whose behalf they are acting, and the duration of any contact. This information must be supplied before any contacts are made, supplemented with any new information applicable and submitted afresh at the beginning of every year. I have included penalties for non-compliance of up to $5,000 per month and prohibition from lobbying for two years, to show that the register which is set forth in the bill is intended to be taken seriously" (House of Commons, *Debates*, 1977: 2516).

The three bills to achieve second reading were: Bill C-38, *Debates*, 1969: 5850; Bill C-214, *Debates*, 1976–1977: 2515; and Bill C-495, *Debates*, 1980: 22010. The other bills were C-176/1969 (Mather); C-131/1970 (Mather); C-121/1972 (Mather); C-89/1973 (Mather); C-115/1974 (Mather); C-248/1974 (Robinson); C-254/1974 (Reynolds, L.); C-432/1976 (Baker); C-268/1976 (Robinson); C-316/1976 (Reynolds); C-328/1977 (Robinson); C-330/1977 (Baker); C-255/1978 (Baker); C-355/1979 (Friesen, PC); C-492/1980 (Friesen); and C-248/1985 (McGrath, PC). I am grateful to David Harvey for reviewing *Hansard* in order to provide this information. The debates were surveyed from 1946 to December 1985.

3   Thus, on July 28, 1975, Perrin Beatty asked the president of the Privy Council (Hon. Mitchell Sharp) whether "the government had 'considered the registration of lobbyists and (a) if so, (i) what studies were done (ii) by and for whom were they done (iii) when were they completed (iv) what were their recommendations (v) where can copies be obtained (b) if not, for what reason?' He also asked 'what laws, if any, govern the relationship between lobbyists and government officials at the present time?'" (House of Commons, *Debates*, 28 July 1975: 7979). The questions elicited no useful information.

4   Interview with John Rodriguez, MP, New Democratic Party (NDP), Nickel Belt, Ottawa, 18 November 1986. Rodriguez estimated that no

more than "10 percent of the members are interested in the issue." The majority of MPs "don't really appreciate the seriousness of the problem.... Unless you are watching for it you don't get a sense of how influence is used in Ottawa. It's easy to slip into acceptance of the view that this is how public policy must be informed."

5   See also the remarks of Simma Holt, MP (Vancouver Kingsway), House of Commons, *Debates*, 28 January 1977: 2520–2522.

6   See, for example, the debate on the Mather bill (House of Commons, *Debates*, 1969: 5850). W. T. Stanbury states that Ron Basford as minister of consumer and corporate affairs requested draft legislation in 1970 but moved to another department before it could be introduced (Stanbury, 1986: 407–415). Michael Pitfield, Clerk of the Privy Council during the later Trudeau years, told a seminar at Dalhousie University in 1980 that senior officials had been a good deal concerned about the lobbying problem but puzzled about what could be done to control it. Policy-makers found lobbyists useful, but suspect, channels of information, finding that representatives of associations did not always clearly pursue the interests of their members and that it was sometimes difficult to ascertain who precisely they represented. Registering lobbyists was a possibility, but "what good would it do?" (personal notes, M. Pitfield, seminar on interest groups in Canadian public policy, School of Public Administration, Dalhousie University, March 1980).

Nor were the press and general public vocal. An article in the *Vancouver Sun* in January 1977 reviewed the proliferation of lobbying activity and suggested that "there is a reluctance on the part of the [Trudeau] government to concede that Ottawa has a lobby industry and that, given the influence over the operation of government by these lobbies, perhaps some effort should be made to identify them." However, such comments were rare and little was said outside Parliament about lobbying during the 1960s and 1970s. Interest picked up a little in 1981, when the Conference Board of Canada published a report on a conference during which Walter Baker's views were given some exposure (Pigott, 1981: 11). In 1982 the Canadian Bar Association issued an important report on parliamentary reform in which the lobbying issue was discussed briefly and a system of registration endorsed (Canadian Bar Association, 1982). The Task Force on Conflict of Interest did look at the issue but explicitly avoided dealing with it, saying that "uncertainty as to the commonly used meaning of the word 'lobby'" suggested it "not be used in any rules governing ethical conduct at the federal level in Canada" (Canada, Task Force on Conflict of Interest, 1984: 175).

Finally, while backbench MPs loyally supported their colleagues who promoted lobby regulation, at least one felt that other issues were more important. MP Stanley Knowles threw his considerable influence behind the view that because members of Congress "have more control of the purse strings than we do... this question of registering lobbyists may not have as important a bearing here as it has in Washington." He believed priority should be given to legislation ensuring freedom of information and respecting conflict of interest (House of Commons, *Debates*, 28 January 1977: 2519).

7   The reasons for Mulroney's announcement are unclear. A few days after the announcement, I received a telephone call from an assistant in the office of the minister of consumer and corporate affairs who explained that the reference to lobbying had caught the minister and his officials by surprise, and asked whether my previous work on interest groups could shed any light on the approach that should be taken.

Later events tarnished the image of the Conservative government and tricked us into investing the late summer and early fall of 1985 with an atmosphere that did not exist. Some problems had arisen over patronage, but at the time of the prime minister's "Open Letter" on public sector ethics, the series of scandals catalogued by Cameron and others would not begin to seize the headlines for another six months (Cameron, 1994). Among those who have speculated on the reasons for the prime minister's action, two theories prevail. The first holds that Mulroney was genuinely upset by an incident involving Government Consultants International, headed by Newfoundland's former Conservative premier, Frank Moores, and by the brother of one of the prime minister's principal advisors, who was discovered to have charged a surprisingly high fee to secure an interview between the minister of fisheries and a fisherman anxious to obtain a fishing license. This view holds that Mulroney was anxious to find a means of distancing his ministry from overeager friends, that he was driven by a desire to preserve a "squeaky clean" image for his administration and was anxious to avoid the taint of influence peddling that affected the previous Liberal regime.

The second theory harks back to the 1984 election campaign and suggests that the prime minister was personally convinced that a system of lobby registration should be introduced as part of a package of measures intended to improve public sector ethics in general. Perhaps there is some truth in both of these theories, and perhaps, too, chance was involved. MP Walter Baker had died not very long before and MP James McGrath had reintroduced his lobby registration bill only a few weeks earlier, on June 18, 1985, as a tribute to a parliamentarian who was warmly and highly regarded by his colleagues. It may have been that McGrath's gesture caught the prime minister's eye and suggested an addition to his public sector ethics package. Whatever the prime minister's motives, there is general agreement that he himself decided that the registration issue should be addressed and that, despite opposition from lobbyists, he was responsible for ensuring that it did not die on the order paper when Parliament was prorogued in the summer of 1986 (interviews with John Rodriguez, MP [NDP], 18 November 1986 and Don Boudria, MP [Liberal], Ottawa, 20 November 1986, and interviews with officials in the Lobbyists Registration Branch, 2005, and Department of Consumer and Corporate Affairs Canada, Ottawa, November 1986).

8   This, of course, was not the end of the arguments over the definition of the word. The broad view was objected to by associations representing professionals, lawyers in particular, which argued that it would constrain their members in the course of representing the legal rights of their clients. Ultimately, their concerns were addressed in s. 4 (2) (b) of the LRA, which prohibited the act's application to oral or written representations concerning the enforcement, interpretation, or application of an Act of Parliament by a public office-holder to the affairs of a client. Another perspective was presented by several organizations and corporations that argued that, since their corporate identity was known to the public and to officials, there was no point in requiring them to register whenever they brought their concerns to government. There was not much sympathy for this view. Other lobbyists and organizational representatives, as well as MPs, pointed out that if these organizations were excused from registration, a loophole would be created that would soon be found by dubious entities. A third point was raised by lobbying firms. They argued that registration should apply to direct lobbying (i.e., the direct representation of a client to officials) and "dating" (which puts clients in touch with appropriate officials and advises them on how best to present their case) but that "mapping" (the development of strategies for taking proposals through the entire decision process) should not require registration. This latter argument seemed to carry weight with the government, though not with the committee.

9   In addition, the Coalition on Acid Rain reviewed for the committee the various forms required by the US registration process, demonstrating the financial and other burdens imposed by that system, and warned the committee against creating a burdensome reporting process (House of Commons, Standing Committee on Elections, Privileges and Procedure, 1986–1987b, 12: 4–10). Bill Neville, of Public Affairs International, injected a note of political realism, pointing out that the effectiveness of a campaign does not necessarily reflect the amount of money spent on it. Some of the most expensive campaigns, he counselled, are "inept and ineffective," while some of the most successful cost very little (House of Commons, Standing Committee on Elections, Privileges and Procedure, 1986–1987b, 14: 9).

10   The registry of lobbyists was to be located in the bowels of the Department of Consumer and Corporate Affairs, in the Office of the Registrar General of Canada, where four officials were assigned to its implementation. Sanctions for violations of the act consisted of fines or imprisonment, but as the registrar had no powers of investigation or enforcement and offences were statutory—and therefore indictable only within two years—the sanctions had very little meaning.

11   The Lobbyists Registration Act (RSC, 1985, c. 44 [4th Supp.]) came into effect on September 30, 1989.

12   Initially, the act was to be reviewed every three years (as per s. 14). This was later extended to every four years and is currently set at every five years. The first review was conducted by the Standing Committee on Consumer and Corporate Affairs and Government Operations (Felix Holtmann, chair), which reported on May 27, 1993. Its report, *A Blueprint for Transparency*, was not acted upon before the election of November 1993, which saw the defeat of the Mulroney government. However, its recommendations were considered by the Chrétien government, which adopted several of them but also referred the review to the Standing Committee on Industry, which in turn assigned it to a subcommittee chaired by Paul Zed. The subcommittee, rather than reporting on the Holtmann committee's findings, conducted a second full review. Its report, *Building Trust*, was delivered in March 1995. The third review was conducted by the Standing Committee on Industry, Science, and Technology (Susan Whelan, chair), which tabled its report, *Transparency in the Information Age: The Lobbyists Registration Act in the 21st Century*, in June 2001. The amending acts can be found at SC, 1995, c. 12; SC, 2003, c. 10; and SC, 2006, c. 9. The provisions of SC, 1995, c. 12 relating to the Ethics Counsellor came into force on July 25, 1995, and other provisions on January 31, 1996. SC, 2003, c. 10 came into force in 2005. The most recent amending act, the Federal Accountability Act, SC, 2006, c. 9, was assented to on December 12, 2006, and came into force on July 2, 2008.

13   The 1995 amendments to the act (ss. 6 and 7) had required senior officers to file this information. The dramatic increase in registrations after the 2003 amendments came into effect is attributed to their explicit references to the "responsibility" of the officer filing returns (s. 7). That officer is defined as "the employee who holds the most senior office in a corporation or organization" (s. 7 [6]). Despite the apparent lack of compliance noted here, the Office of the Registrar General currently believes that "the reported number of active consultant lobbyists in the late 1990s [and until 2005] was inflated." In 2005, for technical reasons, the office terminated the majority of registrations and asked active lobbyists to reregister. "The number who actually did so was markedly fewer than had

been noted as 'active' in the registry. Our view was that over the years, many consultant lobbyists had never bothered to de-register and thus there was an ever-growing accumulation of 'phantom' registrations" (personal communication, ORL, 14 January 2008).

14   A "designated public office holder" is defined in subsection 2 (1) of the Lobbying Act to include "ministers, ministerial staff, deputy ministers and chief executives of departments and agencies, and officials in departments and agencies at the ranks of associate deputy minister and assistant deputy minister." The Governor-in-Council may add to this list. On April 17 an Order-in-Council added the Comptroller General and the Deputy Minister of Intergovernmental Affairs to the list together with senior positions in the armed forces and the Privy Council Office (*Canada Gazette*, 2008).

REFERENCES

Alberta. (2007). *Lobbyists Registration Act*. Bill 1, 3rd Session, 26th Legislature, Alberta, 56 Eliz. II.

Aucoin, Peter. (1975). "Pressure Groups and Recent Changes in the Policy-Making Process." In *Pressure Group Behaviour in Canadian Politics*, edited by A. Paul Pross, 172–193. Toronto: McGraw-Hill.

Cameron, Stevie. (1994). *On the Take: Crime, Corruption and Greed in the Mulroney Years*. Toronto: MacFarlane, Walter and Ross

Canada. (2006). *Federal Accountability Act*. S.C., c. 9.

———. (1985). *Lobbyists Registration Act*. R.S., c. 44 (4th Supp.) amended by S.C. 1995, c. 12; S.C. 2003, c. 10; the *Act to Amend the Parliament of Canada Act (Ethics Commissioner and Senate Ethics Officer) and Other Acts in Consequence*, 2004 and by the *Federal Accountability Act*.

———. (2001). *Lobbyists Registration Act*. S.B.C., c. 42.

Canada, Commission of Inquiry into the Sponsorship Program and Advertising Activities (The Gomery Commission). (2005a). *Public Hearing* (Translation), vol. 110.

———. (2005b). *Who Is Responsible: Fact-finding Report*. Ottawa: Department of Public Works.

———. (2006). *Restoring Accountability: Recommendations*. Ottawa: Department of Public Works.

Canada, Consumer and Corporate Affairs. (1985). *Lobbying and the Registration of Paid Lobbyists*. Ottawa: Supply and Services Canada.

Canada, Ethics Counsellor. (1994). *Conflict of Interest Code and Post-Employment Code for Public Office Holders*. Ottawa: Office of the Ethics Counsellor.

Canada Gazette. (2008). Part II: Official Regulations. Vol. 142, no. 9—April 30 (Order in Council 2008-770. 17 April 2008).

Canada, House of Commons. (1984–1985). Bill C-248. "An Act to Register Lobbyists." 1: 33.

Canada, House of Commons, Legislative Committee on Bill C-82. (27 April 1988). *Minutes of Proceedings and Evidence of the Legislative Committee on Bill C-82: An Act Respecting the Registration of Lobbyists.*

Canada, House of Commons, Standing Committee on Consumer and Corporate Affairs and Government Operations. (1993). *Report.*

Canada, House of Commons, Standing Committee on Elections, Privileges and Procedure. (1986–1987a). "First Report to the House." *Minutes of Proceedings and Evidence*, Issue 2. December 2, 1986–January 20, 1987. 2: 3-2: 22.

———. (1986–1987b). *Minutes of Proceedings and Evidence.*

Canada, House of Commons, Standing Committee on Industry, Sub-Committee on Bill C-43. (1995). An Act to Amend the Lobbyists Registration Act and to Make Related Amendments to Other Acts. *Building Trust.*

Canada, House of Commons, Standing Committee on Industry, Science and Technology. (2001). *Transparency in the Information Age: The Lobbyists Registration Act in the Twenty-first Century.*

Canada, Lobbyists Registration Branch. (2005). Lobbyists Code of Conduct. <http://www.orl-bdl.gc.ca>.

Canada, Office of the Prime Minister. (16 June 1994). "Press Release: Prime Minister Appoints Canada's First Ethics Counsellor, Announces Integrity Measures."

Canada, Registrar of Lobbyists. (2007a). "Investigation Report: The Lobbying Activities of Neelam J. Makhija on Behalf of TIR Systems, Ltd." Ottawa. ORL. Report No. 1. <http://www.orl-bdl.gc.ca>.

———. (2007b). "Investigation Report: The Lobbying Activities of Neelam J. Makhija on Behalf of Infowave Software Inc." Ottawa. ORL. Report No. 2. <http://www.orl-bdl.gc.ca>.

———. (2007c). "Investigation Report: The Lobbying Activities of Neelam J. Makhija on Behalf of TIR Intrinsyc Software Inc." Ottawa. ORL. Report No. 3. <http://www.orl-bdl.gc.ca>.

———. (2007d). "Investigation Report: The Lobbying Activities of Neelam J. Makhija on Behalf of Wavemakers, Inc." Ottawa. ORL. Report No. 4. <http://www.orl-bdl.gc.ca>.

Canada, Royal Commission on the Economic Union and Development Prospects for Canada (Macdonald Commission). (1982). *Report.* Ottawa: Supply and Services Canada. Vol. 3.

Canada, Task Force on Conflict of Interest. (1984). *Ethical Conduct in the Public Sector.* Ottawa: Department of Supply and Services.

Canadian Bar Association. (1982). *Report of the Canadian Bar Association's Committee on the Reform of Parliament.* Ottawa: The Association.

City of Toronto. Municipal Code, c. 140. "Lobbying." <http://www.toronto.
ca/legdocs/municode/1184_140.pdf>.

Corry, J. A. (1981). "Sovereign People or Sovereign Governments." In *Sovereign
People or Sovereign Governments*, edited by H. V. Kroeker, 3–12. Montreal:
Institute for Research on Public Policy.

Dawson, Helen Jones. (1967). "Relations between Farm Organizations
and the Civil Service in Canada and Great Britain." *Canadian Public
Administration*. 10: 4: 450–471.

Delbridge, Pat. (1984). "David vs. Goliath: Voluntary Sector Interest Groups
in Canada Today." In *Business Can Succeed! Understanding the Political
Environment*, edited by James D. Fleck and Isaiah A. Litvak, 46–64.
Toronto: Gage.

European Commission. (2006). *Green Paper: European Transparency Initiative*.
Brussels: The Commission, COM.

Franks, C. E. S. (1987). *The Parliament of Canada*. Toronto: University of
Toronto Press.

Granatstein, J. L. (1982). *The Ottawa Men: The Civil Service Mandarins, 1935–
1957*. Toronto: Oxford University Press.

Gray, Virginia, and Wy Spano. (2004). "State and Local Regulations." In
Research Guide to US and International Interest Groups, edited by Clive S.
Thomas, 377–379. Westport, CT: Praeger.

Greenwood, Justin. (2003). *Interest Representation in the European Union*.
London: Palgrave.

Greenwood, Justin, and Clive S. Thomas. (2004). "An Evaluation of Lobby
Regulation and Its Lessons: The United States and Other Liberal
Democracies." In *Research Guide to US and International Interest Groups*,
edited by Clive S. Thomas, 381–389. Westport, CT: Praeger.

Hodgetts, J. E. (1973). *The Canadian Public Service: A Physiology of Government,
1867–1970*. Toronto: University of Toronto Press.

KPMG Consulting. (14 September 2001). *Study on Compliance under the
Lobbyists Registration Act. Final Report*. Prepared for the Office of the
Ethics Counsellor, Ottawa.

Lewis, Robert. (13 June 1977). "The Hidden Persuaders: Guns Don't Make
Laws, but Gun Lobbies Damn Well Do." *MacLean's*, 40.

Litvak, Isaiah. (1984). "The Lobbying Strategies of Business Interest Groups."
In *Business Can Succeed! Understanding the Political Environment*, edited by
James D. Fleck and Isaiah A. Litvak, 65–75. Toronto: Gage.

MacNaughton, Bruce, and Allan Gregg. (June 1977). "Interest Group Influence
in the Canadian Parliament." A paper presented at the annual meeting of
the Canadian Political Science Association, Fredericton, NB.

Mahon, Rianne. (1977). "Canadian Public Policy: The Unequal Structure of
Representation." In *The Canadian State: Political Economy and Political*

Power, edited by Leo Panitch, 164–198. Toronto: University of Toronto Press.

Nelson, Michael (Registrar of Lobbyists). (8 June 2007). "Enhancing Transparency and Accountability." A presentation given to the OECD Symposium on Lobbying, Paris.

New Brunswick and Labrador. (2004). *Lobbyists Registration Act.* S.N.L., c. L-24.1.

Newman, Christina McCall. (1982). *Grits: An Intimate Portrait of the Liberal Party.* Toronto: MacMillan.

Nova Scotia. (2001). *Lobbyists Registration Act.* S.N.S., c. 34.

Ontario. (1998). *An Act to Amend the Members' Integrity Act, 1994 and to Enact the Lobbyists Registration Act, 1998.* O.S., c. 27.

Organisation for Economic Co-operation and Development (OECD). (June 7–8 2007). "OECD Symposium on Lobbying: Enhancing Transparency." Paris, France. <http://www.oecd.org/gov/ethics>.

Ornstein, Norman J., and Shirley Elder. (1978). *Interest Groups, Lobbying, and Policymaking.* Washington, DC: Congressional Quarterly Press.

Palda, Kristian S. (1985). "Does Canada's Election Act Impede Voters' Access to Information?" *Canadian Public Policy.* 11: 3: 533–542.

Paltiel, Khayyam Z. (1982). "The Changing Environment and Role of Special Interest Groups." *Canadian Public Administration.* 25: 2: 198–210.

Pigott, Jean. (1981). "A View from the Prime Minister's Office." In *Lobbying: A Right? A Necessity? A Danger?* edited by Daniel L. Bon. Ottawa: Conference Board.

Presthus, Robert. (1971). "Interest Groups and the Canadian Parliament: Activities, Interaction, Legitimacy, and Influence." *Canadian Journal of Political Science.* 4: 4: 444–460.

———. (1984). "Interest Groups and Lobbying: Canada and the United States." *Annals of the American Academy of Political and Social Science.* 413: 44–57.

Pross, A. Paul. (1992 [1986]). *Group Politics and Public Policy.* Toronto: Oxford University Press.

———. (1991). "The Rise of the Lobbying Issue in Canada: 'The Business Card Bill.'" In *Commercial Lobbyists: Politics for Profit in Britain,* edited by Grant Jordan, 76–95. Aberdeen, Scotland: University of Aberdeen Press.

———. (2006). "The Lobbyists Registration Act, Its Application and Effectiveness." Commission of Inquiry into the Sponsorship Program and Advertising Activities. *Restoring Accountability: Reseach Studies.* 2: 163–231.

———. (2007). "Lobbying: Models for Regulation." A Study Prepared for the Organization for Economic Cooperation and Development, Paris, France. Published as GOV/PGC/ETH (2007) 4.

Quebec. (2002). *Lobbying Transparency and Ethics Act.* S.Q., c. 23; R.S.Q., c. T-11.01.

Sawatsky, John. (1987). *The Insiders: Government, Business, and the Lobbyists.* Toronto: McClelland and Stewart.

Schwartz, Mildred A. (1981). *The Environment for Policy-Making in Canada and the United States.* Montreal: C. D. Howe Institute.

Shackleton, Doris. (1977). *Power Town: Democracy Discarded.* Toronto: McClelland and Stewart.

Smith, Miriam. (2005). *A Civil Society? Collective Actors in Canadian Political Life.* Toronto: Broadview.

Stanbury, W. T. (1977). *Business Interests and the Reform of Canadian Competition Policy, 1971–75.* Toronto: Methuen.

———. (1986). *Business-Government Relations in* Canada. Toronto: Methuen.

Thomas, Clive S., ed. (2004). *Research Guide to US and International Interest Groups.* Westport, CT: Praeger.

United Kingdom, House of Commons. (1997–1998). *Sixth Report of the Committee on Standards.*

Wilson, Howard. (4 January 2005). "Lobbying: Key Policy Issues." OECD Public Governance Committee.

7

FROM ADMINISTRATION TO MANAGEMENT:

Forty Years of Public Sector Education in Quebec

Caroline Dufour

In 1961 René Lévesque, a minister of the Government of Quebec, asked Roland Parenteau, professor at the École des hautes études commerciales de Montréal (HÉC), to help develop a program to train the administrators of the provincial public service. The departments of political science in the province, where Public Administration was starting to flourish, also wanted to be part of such a project. Yet, they lacked the educational resources to be involved. This is how the history of public sector education in Quebec started.

The context of these beginnings is not that different from that of the following decades. The development of public sector programs in Quebec has involved the confluence of two fields: the politico-administrative on one hand, and the university on the other. Both fields are animated by a dynamic of competition between its agents for different forms of capital, and sharing a more or less variable degree of autonomy vis-à-vis other fields, as their agents do.[1] The autonomy is the power one field has over keeping its own values and means of functioning, which depends, among other things, on its agents' characteristics. The principal agents that evolve in these fields are ministers, public servants, universities, professional schools, and departments of political science, along with their faculty. The development of public sector education is a stake over which political imperatives and university values meet and for which agents of the university field compete. These actors and their competitive relationship represent the stable dimension of this field as changes have taken place in public sector education programs in Quebec. These changes are attributable to the varying relative influence of the political and university fields and the changing relationships between the agents, both products of socio-historical conjunctures.

The objective of this chapter is to explain the fields of influence and the context behind the development of undergraduate and graduate programs of study dedicated to the public sector in francophone Quebec universities between 1960 and 2000. In order to understand these complex structures and relationships, it is necessary to reconstruct the history of public sector education in the province. This has been done through a content analysis of the numerous archives of the province's university institutions, as well as the minutes of department and committee meetings in addition to interviews.[2]

THE 1960s: TRAINING PUBLIC ADMINISTRATORS TO MODERNIZE QUEBEC

In Quebec the interest and concern for education in public administration appeared during the 1960s, when the province was entering its "Quiet Revolution." At the time, the Liberal government elected in November 1960 intended to transform both the role the state has played in Quebec society and its structures. In order to let go of its long-time position of substitute for religious groups and private organizations and become a driving force of provincial development, the state needed the means to achieve its ambitions. In other words, Quebec needed a modern and effective public administration. Right at the beginning of his term, Premier Jean Lesage undertook a major review of the province's administrative structures. Quickly, central planning, coordination, and control, which were lacking in the administration left by the Duplessis government, were implemented. Also, an important growth in terms of budget and number of ministries and employees took place, in addition to a revision of financial management and public service functioning.

All these elements of reform were aimed at the same objective: the introduction of impersonal rules as the basis of administrative activity, so Quebec's public administration could become a model of efficiency and equity. Yet, this modernization could not be completed without the presence of public administrators, a category of employees barely present among the ranks of the Quebec public service. In 1959 there were 260 of them (Bolduc, 1978: 619). Beyond their small number, administrators fulfilled the role of "technical advisor," which translated into being simply an executant of government will, rather than a modern manager. Management was in fact a restricted part of their daily activities. This was paralleled by the fact that only a tenth of these public administrators possessed any management training.

This gap led Minister René Lévesque to ask Professor Roland Parenteau of the HÉC to help find a solution to the formation of these public administrators. Founded in 1907 and an integral part of Université de Montréal (UDM) since 1957, l'École des Hautes Études commerciales (HÉC) was the first French-language institution in the province dedicated to the study of business and management. The institution remains known for its long tradition of educating French-Canadian administrators for the private sector. The Lesage government believed, because of its tradition, the school already had at its disposal the structures, the experience, and the professors necessary to train public administrators. This collaboration between HÉC and the Quebec administration was no surprise. In Canada business schools were the first to respond to the need for training in public administration, well before departments of political science (Pross and Wilson, 1976: 530–531).

An agreement was quickly reached between the government and HÉC, but soon it appeared too good to be true (Minville, Esdras, lettre à l'Honorable Jean Lesage 10 mars 1961). In November 1961, when HÉC asked the Academic Commission of UDM to change the name of its "business administration" license program to "administrative sciences," so education related to the public sector could be offered, it met with fierce resistance from the dean of the Faculty of Social, Economic, and Political Sciences (Procès-verbaux de la Commission des études de l'Université de Montréal, 30 novembre 1961). The dean, who also happened to be chair of the Department of Political Science, argued that a complete study should be undertaken so the Academic

Commission could first get a better understanding of this complex issue. Thereafter, he maintained, a decision could be made.

An analysis of the position of the Department of Political Science provides further explanation of the dean's opposition. The department was created in 1958 and by 1961 was not yet fully developed, having, among other things, few resources in public administration. At the time, the teaching of public administration was an integral component of political science (Robson, 1955). Had the department left the development of this speciality to HÉC, it would have seriously endangered its own advancement. There were then two UDM components with an interest in public administration education: one wanted to train public administrators and gain the advantages linked to it, while the other saw it as a tool for institutional development. UDM was divided between these two structures, which were in competition with one another. In the end, it got the best of what could have been the first program in the field in the province.

While the Government of Quebec was trying to set up a solution to the public administrator formation issue with HÉC, the Department of Political Science at Université Laval, in Quebec City, was also working on the development of a program in public administration. This initiative was in line with the trajectory Laval's Faculty of Social Sciences, where the Department of Political Science was located, had been following since the 1940s. For two decades, its faculty members' activities and their political involvement had constituted a contestation of the political order in the province, particularly of the legitimacy of Duplessis's Union nationale government. Consequently, the faculty did not receive many research grants and the public service's doors remained closed to its graduates (Fournier, 1973: 53). To establish their relevance, the faculty and its professors gave their support to union and cooperative movements, as well as to the Liberal Party, the official Opposition at the National Assembly. When the Liberals came to power, the party took inspiration from Laval faculty members' work and hired several of its students (Fournier, 1973: 55; Gervais, 1970). The involvement of the Department of Political Science in the development of a program in public administration was then a logical continuation.

More, as it was the case for its UDM homologue, the political science department, created in 1954, had to make public administration part of its curriculum to establish its position in the field of political science.

The development of the program in public administration progressed rapidly at Laval. As soon as 1961, the Department of Political Science had implemented a three-year undergraduate program offered during the evening and specifically designed to accommodate Quebec public servants. Forty-two students registered the first year, fifty in 1962–1963. The thirteen courses offered by the program provided evidence of a political approach to public administration, with a particular interest in institutions. The program progressed so well that the department rapidly thought about establishing a master's degree program, maybe even a school of public administration. A 1964 report studying the project received mixed reactions (Procès-verbaux du Département de science politique de l'Université Laval, 16 mars 1964). One faculty member was struck by the multidisciplinary aspect of the proposal, another was not sure if the university structures could allow such a project, while a third wanted to include more policy analysis elements.

Beyond the divergence of opinions, the development of public administration in the political science department at Laval faced opposition because it limited the autonomy of both the department and its faculty members. As a witness explained during an interview with the author, the public administration speciality was starting to take up considerable proportions within the department, introducing an unbalance in relation to the other specialities. It represented an opportunity to be involved in the modernization of the province, in addition to establishing the department in the field of political science. Yet, the specialty was also a threat to intellectual autonomy, as the field of public administration was seen as a more practical speciality in a department where not all of the professors were interested in professional studies. An actor involved at the time confirmed this when he said the Department of Political Science did not wish to get too close to the government through the creation of a new program or school. Two participants in the process said the Government of Quebec offered the Université Laval the chance to establish the program or school of public administration it wished to see developed. However, the academic institution declined the offer, because of the fear of proximity to the government. The department at Laval stopped admitting new students to its evening program in 1964 with a view to ending it. A new project for a degree in public administration, led in 1968 by the dean of the Faculty of Social Sciences and involving several departments and faculties on campus, did not meet with success. As was the case with HÉC, Laval's structures favoured compartmentalization and competition between its components. A university committee at the time confirmed this, adding this was particularly true when it came to the appropriation of resources when establishing a new field of study (Comité de développement et de la planification de l'enseignement et de la recherché, 1968: 34).

Whereas some public servants were sent to study at the French École Nationale d'Administration as a temporary solution, the minister of education formed a committee, composed of academics and senior civil servants, and charged it to find a local solution to the public sector education issue. The committee, which presented its report in January 1965, came up with a complex solution featuring the creation of a public administration training centre that would be under the control of the government but also collaborate closely with universities to develop various program curricula (Comité d'étude sur la formation des administrateurs publics, 1964). The report was rather well received in the administrative milieu, despite its main weakness: the absence of a definition of the concept of public administrator. This omission only reflected the absence of a class of "public administrators" in the Quebec public service. The principal merit of this report was to make authorities realize that without a new system of classification, it would not be possible to implement the recommendations of any report on public administrator training because the employees who should be trained could not be properly identified.

In the midst of all the small and big reforms that were taking place, it happened that in 1965 the public service job classification had to be reviewed in order to create bargaining units. A new classification system was created in collaboration with the French public service specialist Roger Grégoire and put in place starting in 1966 by the Public Service Commission. At the base of this new system was the concept of the *corps*, a homogeneous group trained roughly equivalently and appointed to similar tasks (Commission de la Fonction publique du Quebec, 1966). The corps were divided into classes, themselves fractioned into grades. Among the newly created corps were the *cadres supérieurs*, who exercised responsibilities regarding general studies, conception, and direction in organizations whose staff was part of the Quebec public service (Commission de la Fonction publique du Quebec, 1968). The *adjoints aux cadres supérieurs* fulfilled the role of collaborator and constituted an important pool of potential *cadres supérieurs*. The commission considered the creation of standards for admission to these corps to be an indication of promotion to these levels.

Soon after his election at the end of 1966, the newly elected Minister of Education, Paul Gérin-Lajoie, created a working group, formed almost exclusively of public servants, whose mandate was to study the training and improvement of public administrators and present useful suggestions for a development policy for Quebec *cadres supérieurs* (Groupe de travail chargé d'étudier les problèmes de formation et de perfectionnement des administrateurs publics, 1967: 1). In its April 1967 report, the group wrote that only the creation of a school of public administration, offering an education that had recourse to the humanities and modern management techniques, could solve the issue. Yet, the authors were conscious of the fact that their report raised a problem, as they realized the proposed school should hold university status to ensure the quality of the offered education. An administrative regime that would allow close links with the government, something the established higher education institutions of the province could not offer, had to be established.

The problem was solved when a new government creation, the Université du Quebec (UQ), was established in 1968 with the *Loi sur l'Université du Quebec*. Less than ten months after the creation of the organization, it was decided the new school of public administration would be a UQ constituent. The decision seemed sound as the new school's mission matched UQ's philosophy (i.e., a public, yet not a state, university, making room for adult education, whose mission includes both academic knowledge transmission and concrete involvement with its environment) (Ferretti, 1994: 27). At the request of UQ's governors, on June 26, 1969, the Government of Quebec sanctioned the patent letters of the École nationale d'administration publique (ÉNAP). The school had the mission of assuring the formation of public administrators, improving their development, and conducting research in disciplines related to the field. To use the Ministry of Education's words, its formula lay between an American business school and ÉNA (Ministère de l'Éducation, 1969: 66). The foundations for the development of public sector education in Quebec were established, after ten years of effort.

THE 1970s: NAVIGATING BETWEEN THE STATE AND THE UNIVERSITY

The 1970s witnessed the development of public sector education in the province, as there was now an institution devoted to it. During its beginnings, ÉNAP maintained a privileged relationship with the Government of Quebec and its administration. This translated into the presence, among others, of Quebec administration officials on different decision-making bodies of the school and the initial orientation given to the school: to adapt teaching to the real needs of the administration. (Parenteau, 1972: 465).

Even though ÉNAP had close ties with the provincial administration, it remained a separate university institution, which helps explain why the school first put in place a program leading to a master's degree. Oriented to respond to the needs of Quebec's public administration, the aim of the master's in public administration (M.P.A.) was to develop practitioners, rather than "scientific" specialists, and was addressed exclusively to professional public servants. Within a duration of sixteen months, the program was said to include a theoretical component divided into three blocks: knowledge of the environment; sociological, economic, and political analysis; and management techniques. Two internships, one in Canada and another abroad, completed the program. A content analysis indicates the program was more oriented towards policy analysis and the study of socio-economic milieu. There were two activities related to management techniques and their content sounded rather theoretical.

It was not long before the program was challenged. In 1971 UQ demanded that ÉNAP's program be complementary to those of its other components. Of these components, almost all of them offered business administration programs, notably master's degrees in business administration (M.B.A.s). Therefore, it was felt ÉNAP should develop a degree more compatible with this type of education, so the institutions could collaborate and exchange resources. To achieve these objectives, UQ's academic council expected a radical reform of the (very young) program. They felt ÉNAP should address two issues, among others. First, it should define what a professional master's degree is. Second, it should let go of the prejudice that everything is specific to public administration and be open to an M.B.A.'s contributions and exchanges (Procès-verbaux de la Commission des études de l'École nationale d'administration publique, 7 avril 1971).

Despite the fear of losing its identity and its students to the profit of business schools, in 1971 ÉNAP adopted, with reticence, new objectives for the M.P.A. In addition to the program's concern for public policy, an interest in the management of public organizations and their external relations was added (Procès-verbaux de la Commission des études de l'École nationale d'administration publique, 26 avril 1971). Still, the content of the program remained the same and the school would use its relationship with the government to protect it, along with the school's very survival (Procès-verbaux de la Commission des études de l'École nationale d'administration publique, 10 décembre 1971).

After ÉNAP had adjusted its program to satisfy UQ, there arose another less explicit challenge from the Quebec public administration. During the 1970s, there was a rationalization of the administrative apparatus characterized by the introduction of more rational administration methods, especially in financial administration. With the new Bill on Financial Administration adopted in December 1970,

Quebec's Treasury Board gained significant powers. It became the architect of the new Planning-Programming-Budgeting system, which links resources to objectives, measures results, and adjusts either the resources or the objectives. The adoption of this budgeting system meant a new role for public administrators: From now on, they had to be able to choose the most efficient means to reach organizational ends. This also meant public administrators were required to play an equivalent role from one ministry to another, because the emphasis would be on their managerial abilities rather than on their knowledge of a policy field.

In light of this managerial wave, ÉNAP had no choice but to amend its M.P.A.—again. The appointment by the government of Jean Lessard as director of the institution in July 1974 facilitated the task. Lessard was previously assistant secretary of the Treasury Board of Quebec and a member of ÉNAP's board of directors. He wished to have additional practitioners from the administration within the master's program teach more courses, in addition to the school maintaining a close relationship with the administration (Procès-verbaux de la Commission des études de l'École nationale d'administration publique, 20 février 1976). The most outstanding characteristic of Lessard's term at ÉNAP consisted of his commitment to the development of management, both in the public sector and at the school.

The M.P.A. was the main vehicle used to fulfill this objective. In 1975 the concept of management became explicit, even dominant, in the program. Its objectives came to form new and future public administrators by transmitting a set of knowledge of management and behavioural sciences and to allow them to accelerate the development of their management aptitudes and abilities. The structure of the program experienced drastic changes and management occupied far more space than it had in the past. Management was clearly the core concept behind the mandatory activities of the M.P.A., and nine of the twenty-five optional activities were centred on management. The change was also manifest in the school's discourse. In his speech to the 1976 M.P.A. graduates, Lessard (1976) referred to the new concept of "public management" to describe what was lacking in public administration and the school's intention to implement it.

As innovative as this idea of public management may have been, ÉNAP's master's program was once again the target of public administration's criticisms during the last years of the decade, translating among other things into a decrease in the number of applications for admission (Plan d'action publicitaire—MAP 1979). A working group set up to examine the criticisms of the program and the declining student demand concluded the program presented too many mandatory activities that prevented personalized progress and lacked courses related to management abilities (École nationale d'administration publique, 1993: 56). A second working group's report suggested the program's philosophy should have been clearly oriented towards management (Procès-verbaux de la Commission des études de l'École nationale administration publique, Annexe à la résolution E-65-170, 14 avril 1978). At the end of the 1970s, ÉNAP presented a program that accorded more importance to the development of practical management abilities and knowledge—the "how-to," rather than the acquisition of pure and simple knowledge. Yet, it conserved the "policy analysis" and "knowledge of the environment" dimensions present in 1970.

The creation of ÉNAP and its M.P.A. helped, in a certain way, the development of public administration education at Laval by allowing a clear definition of their respective positions. At the beginning of the 1970s, Laval tried a new incursion into public administration education. The Ministry of Education offered sixty scholarships to students who would undertake studies in public administration. For the departments welcoming them, it would have translated into faculty hiring and increased budgets. This is without counting the resources other students interested in a career in the growing Quebec public service would have brought in. Unlike its previous experience, Laval did not have to fear for its independence this time, or at least that is what the Department of Political Science believed. With the creation of ÉNAP, the government had an institution to work closely with to answer its needs in the matter of *cadres supérieurs* training. The Department of Political Science, for its part, could train specialists in public administration at the master and doctorate levels, who, besides the academia, could achieve careers in the highest spheres of the public service. With these objectives in mind, any possibility of competition with ÉNAP was pushed aside (Balthazar, Louis, lettre à Monseigneur Louis-Albert Vachon, 23 décembre 1970).

While the Universities Council (UC), the provincial organism that evaluates new university programs and their repartition among the higher education institutions, studied Laval's request to offer a public administration program, the Department of Political Science prepared a master's degree project in public administration, focusing on policy analysis (Pour un projet de maîtrise en Administration Publique, 1972). The department would offer the foundation courses of the program, while other faculties and departments would provide specialty and more practical courses. The institution from which the department faculty members received their doctoral degree is an interesting clue to understanding the shift from public administration to policy analysis emphasized by the project. Whereas Laval professors were traditionally educated in France, the situation changed at the turn of the 1970s, with eight of the eleven professors hired by the department between 1967 and 1975 owning an American graduate degree (Lemieux, 1988: 259). This meant they frequently attended a university in the United States during the 1960s. During that decade, American political science departments were trying to expel public administration from their ranks, because they considered it too practical, not involved enough in fundamental research (Ricci, 1984). In other words, public administration posed a threat to university autonomy. In its place, the study of policy analysis, which allows for reaching generalizations and theoretical conclusions more easily, developed. The department's position was not unique. By putting policy analysis at the centre of the proposed program, it followed other Canadian departments of political science in preferring policy analysis over public administration (Savoie, 1990: 395). The shift to policy analysis was made all the more prominent as the proportion of professors of public administration in the department decreased. They also tended not to stay as long within the department.

In 1972 the field of public administration was bubbling over at Université Laval as interdepartmental and faculty committees were given the responsibility of preparing detailed program projects. No matter how enthusiastic the contributors, disagreements between contributing units put an end to a number of projects. Shortly after, Laval learned the UC had refused to accredit its "public administration" axis and any program related to it. The UC was afraid of the rigorous position Laval took with respect to the government's needs and judged that the university was not accepting ÉNAP's objectives and conditions of admission. Therefore, the UC recommended that the "public administration" axis not be accepted as long as the university refused to change its position towards the government's needs and until it was able to organize its different resources linked to public administration into a single entity (Conseil des universities, 1973: 128–131).

This series of setbacks was not enough to signal the defeat of public sector education on the Laval campus. Faculty members from the Department of Political Science recognized they had lost the battle regarding public administration and they should concentrate their future energies on developing a specificity and resources that no one could contest that would allow them to integrate the department's concentrations. The "policy analysis" tag seemed to be the solution (Procès-verbaux du département de science politique, Annexe au procès-verbal, 26 juin 1973). This was not a difficult decision to make for the department members, as the content of the last proposal was already centred on policy analysis and the composition of the faculty was favourable to it. The difference was that the title of the program would no longer be public administration but policy analysis. And, fewer players would be involved.

The Department of Political Science collaborated only with the Department of Economics in its development of a master's degree program in policy analysis. Meanwhile, the economics department had been taking advantage of the growth of Quebec's public administration, as its graduates were finding jobs within it and its faculty members were collaborating with the government on research projects on planning (Thibault, 1988: 144). The UC gave its approval to the program, which bore the name master's degree in "policy analysis" to distinguish it from programs with a practical approach to public sector education that carried the name "public administration." The departments of political science and economics offered the program conjointly for the first time in 1976–1977. Its content revealed a few more courses in political science than economics, an importance accorded to quantitative methods, and the requirement of writing a thesis.[3]

It was not only near Parliament Hill that university institutions struggled to implement public administration programs in the 1970s. HÉC, which had never let go of the idea of training public servants, collaborated with several UDM faculties and departments on the concept of a master's degree in public administration. HÉC and UDM's Faculty of Law being unable to agree on the means and ends to such a program, the project quickly fell through (Comité sur l'enseignement de l'administration publique, 17 juin 1969). At UDM public administration essentially remained a field of teaching within the program of political science, even if the HÉC director believed the school should have had the right to offer a master's degree in the field. Until 1978 the school attempted to integrate public sector management into its different programs with the introduction of courses and options related to the topic. The success of this enterprise remained at best mitigated and it did not carry on after 1991. Besides the difficulty for the students of finding a job in the public sector because of the financial context, it seemed the program structure, which required students to specialize in the area of organization functions, helped to explain the overall unpopularity of the program (Séguin, Francine, mémo à Jean-Guy Desforges, 27 janvier 1987). It is also worth noting, according to a HÉC professor who was involved in the effort to introduce public sector education in the school, that the large majority of the school's faculty members did not see an important difference between public and private management, this being because the majority of them held a graduate degree in business administration. In the end, it was difficult to implement programs of study in public administration when the faculty members themselves did not have the knowledge or the interest necessary to implement them.

THE 1980s: FROM PUBLIC ADMINISTRATION TO PUBLIC MANAGEMENT EDUCATION

The revision of the means and ends of state intervention dominated administrative concerns in the 1980s, across the world as in Quebec. This took place in a context of public financial crises marked by a growing desire for political control of public administration (Gow, 1984). Early on in the decade, the political and administrative elite of the province made explicit the link between management training and administrative efficiency. In 1981 Premier René Lévesque established a clear relation between the context of budgetary restriction and the necessity of a formation focusing on administrative sciences for administrators (Lévesque, 24 novembre 1981). For the first time, the concept of management was used in Quebec political discourse when the Minister of Public Service deplored the lack of formation (training) and improved development courses in management for administrators (Leblanc-Bantey, 17 novembre 1981). It was, however, the general secretary of the government, the head of the public service, who expressed in the best words what the government expected from its cadres. For him, the government looked for administrators who had a deep understanding of their policy fields and set the priority to find the means to do more with less. To reach this objective, he suggested that a development policy aimed at administrators who were already in place should be developed and that future administrators receive training focusing on administration theory and practice (Bernard, 21 mai 1981).

Besides the search for increased productivity, political considerations incited the public administration within the province to offer more room for management. In 1979, after the presentation of the Lambert Report in Ottawa, Quebec members of Parliament realized they did not exercise enough control over public administration, which led to the adoption of a new law governing the public service in December 1983. This law favoured the development of management with the concept of accountability. With lightened central controls, the *cadres supérieurs* were to assume more responsibility for quality of service and in regard to their economy and efficiency (Gow, 1984). In addition, political control over the public administration became easier because one could identify who was responsible for what.

The Ministry of Public Service responded quickly to the wishes of the political and administrative authorities with the development of a series of policies and programs related to the training of public servants (Ministère de la Fonction publique du Quebec, Direction générale du personnel d'encadrement, 1982a; 1982b; 1983; 1984). The new initiatives all rested on one central concept—"management"—used repeatedly in the policy documents. It marked the transition from "administration," associated with a period where public order was the main concern rather than optimal resource use. Management was seen as a more modern dynamic approach to public administration, marking a clear distinction between the political and administrative spheres (Gow, 1993: 6).

This shift in the administration had repercussions at ÉNAP by contributing to the institutionalization of the managerial trend introduced to the school at the end of the 1970s. The new director of the institution, who was appointed in 1979, responded to the message as he declared his intention to centre ÉNAP's development on management and make it the public managers' school. During the first half of the 1980s, the content of the M.P.A. was resolutely oriented towards Quebec's public administration's needs as its content remained centred on the concept of management. To reflect this concern, the curriculum design adopted explicit references to the concept of management (such as *Management public* and *Le manager et son environment*). The M.P.A.'s structure remained relatively unchanged until 1992.

Unlike his predecessors, the new director as well as the program coordinator of the school wanted to reposition ÉNAP on the university scene and further exploit its higher education dimension (Brunel, 9 juin 1981). This change became necessary, as during the 1980s, UQ felt more or less formally pressured to adapt its approach to graduate studies by using a model that conformed more to the traditional university. The minister of education's concept of the university system, the institutional maturation of logic, and a new and acute concern for respectability incited UQ curriculum to move in this direction (Ferretti, 1994: 145). From 1985 influence coming from the university field became a determinant of ÉNAP's functioning. The school first announced its decision to adopt new priorities to encourage research development, including changing the norms guiding the hiring, promotion, and evaluation of its professors (Procès-verbaux de la Commission des études de l'École nationale d'administration publique, Annexe au procès-verbal, 11 décembre 1985).

Aside from the influences that applied to the whole UQ, another factor pushed ÉNAP towards the direction of the traditional university. The report of a working group formed by a commission of the National Assembly to study the evolution of UQ recognized ÉNAP as a professional school, and, for this reason, noted that its relationship with the government authorities could even be closer and that it should hire professors with both academic qualifications and practical experience within public administration (Groupe de travail sur l'évolution de l'Université du Quebec, 1987: 48). Yet, the working group did not want the university dimension of the institution to be considered of secondary importance and recommended that ÉNAP develop its teaching and research functions by concentrating on the development of its M.P.A. and eventually a doctorate program. This orientation was confirmed when the Minister of Higher Education and Science declared ÉNAP had to accentuate its university role. These pressures directed the school to start working on a "scientific" master's degree in public administration for students holding an undergraduate degree but without practical experience in public administration. In the same vein, public sector education at ÉNAP saw a new type of development beginning in the middle of the 1980s, when the school allied with other institutions of the UQ network to put in place specialized master's programs.

The development of public sector education in Quebec during the 1980s remained largely under ÉNAP's leadership. However, it did not prevent other institutions from becoming involved in some activities. At HÉC, Roland Parenteau's return between 1978 and 1987 revived the institution's interest in public sector education. It took the form of concentrations and courses at the undergraduate level, which did not meet with popularity which were not popular with students. (Plan de développement pédagogique [perspectives 1980–1985], n.d.). At Université Laval, in the policy analysis program, the course *Gestion du secteur public* replaced *Administration du secteur public*. This change of titles was not superficial. The subject of the course *Administration du secteur public* was the bureaucracy, and it covered topics that included comparative administration, budgetary process, bureaucracy theory, and a comparison between the public and private sectors. For its part, *Gestion du secteur public* concentrated on the different operations of public policy management after their adoption by political authorities. There was a clear shift towards management as a complement to policy analysis in the principal course of the program dedicated to public administration, which indicated Laval had also taken the turn to public management.

THE 1990s: CONTINUING TO FORGE AHEAD

"Stability" was the key word to understanding public sector education in Quebec during the 1990s. Yet, the programs did not remain the same. On the contrary, their expansion was considerable. It was the influence of the university and politico-administrative fields that remained stable. The university milieu seemed satisfied with what was happening because it did not express any request or remonstrance towards any institution. Within Quebec's public administration, a 1993 reform inspired by the American experience and resting on the concepts of competitiveness and productivity led to the creation of autonomous service centres the following year (Ministère du Conseil exécutif du Québec, Secrétariat à la réforme administrative et aux emplois supérieurs, 1993).

However, an important difference between the 1980s and the 1990s in the provincial administration was the interest the government paid to its administrators' qualifications. The only initiative it was concerned with during the 1990s was the creation of a collaborative commission between the government and ÉNAP on future managers' needs. The commission's report underlined traditional elements, such as the concern for productivity, as well as newer ones, such as the importance of having a strategic vision and a strong general education (École nationale d'administration publique, 1993). This administrative context constituted as fertile a ground for the growth of public management in public sector education as the university one did.

ÉNAP propelled forward in the 1990s on the tracks that were set during the 1980s. The school entered a phase of institutionalization, where it consolidated its university dimension, and, at the same time, instituted public management as the foundation of its teaching. The creation of a course called *Management des organisations publiques* played an important part in this process, as it was a mandatory course requirement in all the school's programs, including the numerous short graduate programs that had been put in place over the decade. The course was said to allow students to acquire knowledge applied to the public sector and that concepts and theories of management science constituted its core. Interestingly, the content of the course was set by the school and not the instructors, showing the importance of a certain conception of public management for the institution.

The year 1991 marked the establishment of the "scientific" master's degree in public administration at ÉNAP, four years after the first discussions on the subject took place. In setting up the degree, the school created two options in the existing M.P.A. "Option A" referred to the professional degree ÉNAP had been offering since its creation, and "option B," which included the redaction of a thesis or the realization of an internship, aimed at developing analysts, advisors, and researchers in specialized fields in public administration. Option A was intended for people who had practical experience in public administration, while option B was dedicated to traditional students. These two streams reflected both influences that had blown over ÉNAP since its creation: public administration and the university milieu.

In 1993 ÉNAP's M.P.A. saw its last transformation during the 1990s. For option A, two concentrations were created (*Management public* and *Management international*). All students were exposed to management courses, and there was also room for the more classical aspects of public administration, such as administrative law and the sociology of organizations, but these were fewer. The program's optional course requirements were shared about equally between management courses and different disciplines useful to public sector education, such as political science, economics, and law. For its part, option B presented fewer courses on management than option A did.

After the implementation of a "scientific" master's degree, ÉNAP undertook the creation of a doctoral program. The idea for such a project had cropped up a few times in the past, but each time UQ had decided ÉNAP was not ready to offer such a program, research capabilities not being fully developed within the institution (Procès-verbaux de la Commission des études de l'École nationale d'administration publique, 4 décembre 1987). In 1993 the situation was different, as more than half of the school's faculty members held a doctoral degree. After a few exchanges with the National Association of Schools of Public Affairs and Administration and the creation of a working group responsible for developing a program, ÉNAP welcomed its first Ph.D. candidates in September 1996. The program included common core courses in methodology and theory, specialized seminars and courses on more applied topics, comprehensive examinations, and the redaction of a dissertation. Students had the choice between two concentrations: *Théorie des organisations et management public* or *Analyse de politique et management.*

Public management was not ÉNAP's prerogative. In 1996 the Department of Political Science at Laval started offering a course bearing that name in the master's in policy analysis program, in addition to offering it as an optional course in the master's and doctoral programs in political science. This course replaced *Gestion publique* and focused, among other things, on the definition and nature of public management, accountability, the public sector environment, and the management of resource implementation. The introduction of this course was part of a larger movement that took place in the Department of Political Science. Indeed, the concentration, *Administration et politique publique* was renamed *Politique et management public* at the graduate level.

When interviewed, the department's faculty members gave a simple explanation for this change. In the 1990s, the department's members had almost stopped publishing research results in public administration due to the weak number of academics in this specialization. Moreover, for different reasons, the public administration professors published less often than their colleagues did. This was one part of the explanation. The other was that faculty members associated with policy analysis had become more numerous since the creation of the program in policy analysis and had published a fair amount of research. Since public management appeared in American schools of public policy as a complement to policy analysis, aiming to develop the means to reach the best results in policy implementation (Bozeman, 1993), a shift to public management in the master's program in policy analysis was natural. After ÉNAP and Laval, public management appeared at HÉC at the end of the 1990s, when the school created a short undergraduate program in public management. However, the program attracted almost no students and was rapidly abolished.

CONCLUSION

The influence of the politico-administrative field was a determining factor in the emergence of public sector education in Quebec. First, the government's need to develop and modernize public administration lit a spark to an area of study that was not yet even gestating in Quebec university institutions. In the same vein, the reform of the public service classification system was an essential element to the creation of any program. Second, it was with the establishment of UQ, a university with a different structure and mandate, established by the Government of Quebec, that the first program of study in public administration could be created. Third, because public sector education was implemented for and by government institutions, the transformations that took place in public administration, sometimes accompanied by specific demands, had a clear impact on the content of the programs, taking them from administration in the 1970s to management in the 1990s.

The university field had, for its part, a different type of influence on public sector education. One aspect of it was its blocking effect on the development of programs of study, especially during the

1960s and 1970s. A second influence rested in the push it gave to the institutionalization of a certain approach to public sector education in the university system. In the development of public sector education, the politico-administrative field more visibly influenced the content, while the university's influence was more observable in terms of format. The relative stability the programs in this area have known since the end of the 1980s indicates an equilibrium has been found between the two fields of force.

This balance shows the institutions and agents that have been involved. It also shows that the key elements to understanding the evolution of public sector education were more autonomous vis-à-vis these fields because with time a structure of relationships between their specific positions has developed. It is then no surprise that ÉNAP, an institution established by the government to answer its needs, was more susceptible to political and administrative variations, even if it is a university school. In the same logic, a traditional university like Université Laval searched to develop programs as it saw the issue, without government interference. Thus, the easiest place to develop public sector programs of study is a specialized school, and the most challenging is a traditional university department of political science.

Besides institutions, the composition of faculty should also not be neglected. Some types of education and research interests paved the way for public sector education (political science and public administration), while others were an obstacle (business administration), or reoriented it (policy analysis). This leads to the most practical conclusion of this study: Whatever the institution's will, if the trajectory of the faculty members is not compatible with the development of public sector teaching, any project related to it is likely to fail.

Are these conclusions unique to Quebec? Even if detailed information on other cases is not available, one can say it is likely not. Because of its subject matter, public sector education has operated and will continue to operate in a sphere under the influence of both the state and the university, whatever the country or the province. In the same way, university structures and the composition of faculty are elements that cannot be avoided when trying to understand this field of study. The differences between cases reside in the variable weight of each of these factors due to specific socio-political conditions.

What is most unique in the case of Quebec is the unmatched direct contribution, unmatched in any other jurisdiction in North America, of the government and public administration in the development of public sector education. They were involved over several years, demanding the first program of study, putting in place the university structures that led to its implementation, and presenting specific requests in matters of training, in addition to influencing the development of public administration through administrative changes and reforms. This significant participation, paralleled with the universities' difficulty in entering the field, explains why professional programs offered strictly to public servants remained the only form of education dedicated to the public sector for many years. It also explains why the content of the programs has bared political and administrative imprints. Of course, over the years, the study of public administration in Quebec has developed in more traditional university settings, resulting in the completion of professional degrees. Professional training and traditional teaching are not what is expected of a discipline that is neither completely a profession nor completely a science (Nadon, 1997: 34).

NOTES

[1] This theoretical framework is primarily based on Bourdieu's work (1975).

[2] In addition to the archival documents mentioned throughout the chapter, general university publications were also consulted. These include the yearbooks of the HÉC, Université de Montréal, Université Laval, and École nationale d'administration publique (ÉNAP) for information on programs, courses, and faculty members, as well as ÉNAP and ÉNAP director's annual reports. Recorded semiconducted interviews were conducted between November 15, 1998, and October 20, 1999, with seventeen professors who have been involved at one point or another with public sector education in the province.

[3] The program has witnessed important changes since 2000. It now counts a professional stream and is open to public servants.

REFERENCES

Balthazar, Louis. (23 décembre 1970). Lettre à Monseigneur Louis-Albert Vachon. Fonds de la Faculté des sciences sociales, U567/6/1, Prog.— maîtrise en administration publique, s.d., 1972–1974. Sainte-Foy: Archives de l'Université Laval.

Bernard, Louis. (21 mai 1981). "L'administrateur public des années 80, son environnement et sa formation." A speech delivered at the Formacadres annual conference, École nationale d'administration publique, Québec.

Bolduc, Roch. (1978). "Les cadres supérieurs, quinze ans après." *Canadian Public Administration*. 21: 4: 618–639.

Bourdieu, Pierre. (1975). "La spécificité du champ scientifique et les conditions sociales du progrès de la raison." *Sociologie et Sociétés*. 7: 1: 91–116.

Bozeman, Barry. (1993). "Introduction: Two Concepts of Public Management." In *Public Management. The State of the Art*, edited by B. Bozeman. San Fransisco: Jossey-Bass.

Brunel, Louis. (9 juin 1981). "L'ÉNAP: L'École du management public." A speech delivered at École nationale d'administration publique, Québec.

Comité d'étude sur la formation des administrateurs publics. (1964). *Rapport du comité*. Quebec: le Comité.

Comité de développement et de la planification de l'enseignement et de la recherché. (1968). *Un projet de réforme pour l'Université Laval*. Quebec: Université Laval.

Comité sur l'enseignement de l'administration publique. (17 juin 1969). Fonds de la Faculté des sciences sociales, E-100, D2, 37, Programme de maîtrise en administration publique. Montréal: Archives de l'Université de Montréal.

Commission de la Fonction publique du Quebec. (1966). *Rapport annuel, 1965–1966*. Quebec: la Commission.

———. (1968). *Rapport annuel, 1967–1968*. Quebec: la Commission.

Conseil des universités. (1973). *Objectifs généraux de l'enseignement supérieur et grandes orientations des établissements. Cahier III: Première et deuxième parties. Les orientations de l'enseignement supérieur dans les années '70*. Quebec: le Conseil.

École nationale d'administration publique. (1993). *L'ÉNAP au service des gestionnaires publics. Rapport de la commission concernant les besoins de la relève des gestionnaires pour la fonction publique québécoise*. Quebec: l'École.

Ferretti, Lucia. (1994). *L'université en réseau. Les 25 ans de l'Université du Quebec*. Sainte-Foy: Presses de l'Université du Quebec.

Fournier, Marcel. (1973). "L'institutionnalisation des sciences sociales au Quebec." *Sociologie et Sociétés*. 5: 1: 27–57.

Gervais, Paul. (1970). *Les diplômés en sciences sociales dans la fonction publique du Quebec.* Université de Montréal: master's thesis.

Gow, James Iain. (1984). "La réforme institutionnelle de la fonction publique de 1983: contexte, contenu et enjeux." *Politique.* 6: 53–101.

———. (1993). "Comment étudier l'administration publique?" In *Introduction à l'administration publique. Une approche politique,* edited by J. I. Gow et al. Montréal: Gaëtan Morin.

Groupe de travail chargé d'étudier les problèmes de formation et de perfectionnement des administrateurs publics. (1967). *Premier rapport (Rapport Bolduc I).* Quebec: le groupe.

Groupe de travail sur l'évolution de l'Université du Quebec. (1987). *Rapport du groupe de travail sur l'évolution de l'Université du Quebec (Rapport Després).* Quebec: le groupe.

Leblanc-Bantey, Denise. (17 novembre 1981). "Expérience et prospective de la fonction managériale au sein du gouvernement du Quebec." A speech delivered at the Association of M.B.A. of Quebec, Québec City, Québec.

Lemieux, Vincent. (1988). "Le Département de science politique." In *Cinquante ans de sciences sociales à l'Université Laval. L'histoire de la Faculté des Sciences sociales (1938–1988),* edited by A. Faucher. Sainte-Foy: Faculté des Sciences sociales de l'Université Laval.

Lessard, Jean. (1976). "Le rôle privilégié de l'ÉNAP dans le développement du Quebec." A speech delivered at the fifth ÉNAP convocation, Quebec.

Lévesque, René. (24 novembre 1981). Discours du premier ministre à l'Institut d'administration publique du canada, section régionale de Québec. A speech delivered at the Institute of Public Administration of Canada, Toronto, ON.

Ministère de l'Éducation du Quebec. (1969). "Création de l'École nationale d'administration." *Hebdo-Éducation.* 59: 66–67.

Ministère de la Fonction publique du Quebec, Direction générale du personnel d'encadrement. (1982a). *Le développement du personnel d'encadrement supérieur dans la fonction publique québécoise.* Quebec: le Ministère.

———. (1982b). *Cadre général d'intervention en matière de développement de la relève cadre.* Quebec: le Ministère.

———. (1983). *Formacadres, un programme témoin.* Quebec: le Ministère.

———. (1984). *Orientations gouvernementales de développement concernant le personnel d'encadrement et sa relève, année 1984–1985 et 1985–1986.* Quebec: le Ministère.

Ministère du Conseil exécutif du Quebec, Secrétariat à la réforme administrative et aux emplois supérieurs. (1993). *Opération réalignement de l'administration publique. Document de présentation.* Quebec: le Conseil.

Minville, Esdras. (10 mars 1961). Lettre à l'Honorable Jean Lesage. Fonds du directorat, A007, K1, Correspondance d'Esdras Minville. Montréal: Archives de l'École des Hautes Études commerciales de Montréal.

Nadon, Sylvia. (1997). *Émergence de l'administration publique comme spécialité: l'apport des universités canadiennes.* Université de Montréal: Ph.D. dissertation.

Parenteau, Roland. (1972). "Une nouvelle approche dans la formation des administrateurs publics: l'École nationale d'administration publique." *Canadian Public Administration.* 15: 3: 465–480.

Plan d'action publicitaire—MAP 1979. File number 393.01. Quebec: Archives de l'École nationale d'administration publique.

Plan de développement pédagogique (perspectives 1980–1985). (n.d.). Fonds du directorat, A007, G040008. Montréal: Archives de l'École des Hautes études commerciales de Montréal.

Pour un projet de maîtrise en Administration Publique. (1972). Fonds de la Faculté des sciences sociales, U685/6/1, Prog. de maîtrise en administration publique—Comité interdépartemental. Sainte-Foy: Archives de l'Université Laval.

Procès-verbaux de la Commission des études de l'École nationale d'administration publique. Fonds de la Commission des études. Quebec: Archives de l'École nationale d'administration publique.

Procès-verbaux de la Commission des études de l'Université de Montréal. Fonds de la Commission des études, A33. Montréal: Archives de l'Université de Montréal.

Procès-verbaux du Département de science politique. (16 mars 1964). Fonds du Département de science politique, U685/31/1. Sainte-Foy: Archives de l'Université Laval.

Pross, Paul A., and V. Seymour Wilson. (1976). "Graduate Education in Canadian Public Administration: Antecedents, Present Trends, and Portents." *Canadian Public Administration.* 19: 4: 515–541.

Ricci, David M. (1984). *The Tragedy of Political Science. Politics, Scholarship, and Democracy.* New Haven, CT: Yale University Press.

Robson, William A. (1955). *Les sciences sociales dans l'enseignement supérieur: science politique.* Paris: UNESCO.

Savoie, Donald J. (1990). "Studying Public Administration." *Canadian Public Administration.* 33: 3: 389–413.

Séguin, Francine. (27 janvier 1987). Mémo à Jean-Guy Desforges. Fonds du Service de l'enseignement du management, E17, Concentration, Bloc gestion dans le secteur public. Montréal: Archives de l'École des hautes études commerciales.

Thibault, Marc-Aurèle. (1988). "Le Département d'économique 1943–1987." In *Cinquante ans de sciences sociales à l'Université Laval. L'histoire de la Faculté des Sciences sociales (1938–1988),* edited by A. Faucher. Sainte-Foy: Faculté des Sciences sociales de l'Université Laval.

8 TRUST, LEADERSHIP, AND ACCOUNTABILITY IN CANADA'S PUBLIC SECTOR[1]

Paul G. Thomas

"Our distrust is expensive."—Ralph Waldo Emerson

INTRODUCTION

Is Canada's public sector facing a crisis of trust? On all levels within the public sector, trust seems to be in short supply. Declining and low public trust in politicians and political institutions like parties and legislatures is well known, having been documented in opinion surveys going back several decades. In its January 26, 2007, edition, a *Globe and Mail* survey ranking the trustworthiness of different occupations put firefighters and nurses at over 90 percent, while car salesmen were ranked last at 7 percent, a dismal ranking shared with only one other occupation: national politicians. Apparently, those surveyed found national politicians lacking on the crucial attributes of reliability, keeping promises, and acting with integrity, which respondents indicated were the most important factors involved when deciding whom to trust. For their part, politicians reciprocate these negative feelings by exhibiting an apparent lack of respect for, and trust in, the public, as for example when they refuse to engage in honest dialogues about policy issues or seek to cover up administrative misdeeds.

Survey data on the climate of trust within government are not so readily available as the findings on external trust. However, by their rhetoric and their actions, politicians can often be seen to express wariness, if not outright hostility, towards the bureaucracy. There is the suspicion that the public service seeks to control the policy process, that it is unresponsive to changing circumstances and new political directions, and that it is inefficient and ineffective in designing and delivering programs and services. In short, there is a negative stereotype of the public service to which many politicians subscribe to varying degrees.

For the partnership between politicians and public servants to work constructively, there must be mutual understanding, respect, and trust. There is not good empirical evidence on this crucial partnership. However, impressionistically it appears that public servants in the top and middle ranks often resent the constraints that arise from the political process. They also question the commitment of politicians to evidence-based policy-making. These frustrations are reflected in the 2005 Public Service Employee Survey within the Government of Canada, where many employees complained their work suffered from constantly changing priorities (40 percent), lack of stability in the organization (41 percent), too many approval stages (40 percent), and unreasonable deadlines (30 percent) (Public Service Human Resources Management Agency, 2005). Although these responses do not speak directly to the perceptions of public servants concerning their political masters, it is likely that many public servants would blame "politics" for impairing the policy performance and productivity of their organizations. It is also likely that they resent the growing tendency of politicians—especially ministers—to shift the blame to the public service when policies prove to be flawed or principles of sound public management are skewed by political considerations.

Within the public service, "trust ties" also do not appear to be all that they should be. Central agencies serving the prime minister and the Cabinet do not fully trust line departments and nondepartmental bodies to support the corporate policy goals and budgetary directions and requirements of government. Senior management does not entirely trust front-line personnel to do their jobs efficiently and effectively. They are also suspicious of the motives and tactics of the leaders of the public sector unions. According to the 2005 employee survey, trust in senior management to address workplace issues had declined since 2002, although at 47 percent it was still above the level in 1999 (37 percent), when the first such survey was done (Public Service Human Resources Management Agency, 2005).

Finally, the public is not entirely trusting of the public service, although here again the evidence is limited and sketchy (Kanji, 2002; and Nevitte, 2002). In past surveys, Canadians who expressed their disenchantment with government in general were asked whether they had mainly politicians or public servants in mind when expressing such sentiments. By a two to one margin they said politicians were mainly to blame for their negative feelings towards governments. In the occupational ranking surveys that are done periodically, public servants usually end up in the middle of the pack compared to politicians, who are near the bottom. In general, however, the public seems to subscribe to a negative image of the bureaucracy as too powerful, self-interested, rule bound, inefficient, unresponsive, and unaccountable.

Is the above picture of the trust relationships in Canada's public sector too negative? Are we looking at a crisis of trust in the public sector? Unfortunately, the available knowledge does not allow us to answer these questions unequivocally. When it comes to the elusive and multidimensional phenomenon of trust, there is still much we do not know. The current popularity of the topic in multiple disciplines means that the notion of trust is used to investigate and analyze interpersonal relationships, the relations between people and organizations, relationships between and among organizations, and the relationships people have with entire institutional systems within society, such as the political system. While trust has emerged as a "hot topic" in many disciplines, including political science, it has received surprisingly limited attention in the public administration field.

Given what we know at this point, labelling the current conditions in Canada's public sector as a crisis of trust would be premature and likely an exaggeration. Such a description would imply that we understand the different forms of trust that exist within society, the linkages among them, and the dynamics of their evolution over time. Unfortunately, we do not have that level of knowledge at this point and may never have it.

Applying the "crisis" label to Canada's public sector would imply there has been in recent decades a precipitous and dangerous decline in trust relations. Sound empirical time-series data to support such a drastic conclusion is simply not available.

Moreover, on a philosophical or normative level, a certain degree of mistrust towards powerful institutions and their leaders has been seen for centuries to be a healthy condition within a democracy (Hardin, 2006). Weak or conditional trust is seen as necessary to promote responsiveness and accountability on the part of institutions and their leaders. It could also be argued that, in the past, Canadians were too deferential and trusting towards political and administrative elites, who in turn took the consent and the support of the public too much for granted. Recent political scandals and administrative breakdowns could be said to justify the apparent decline of trust over the past several decades. Even today, however, we do not know precisely how shallow trust levels have become within Canada's political and administrative cultures and what minimum levels are necessary to support successful and legitimate governance.

Taking these general observations as its starting point, this chapter argues the alarm about a crisis of trust in Canada's public sector is exaggerated. Canadians do indeed tell pollsters they are less trusting of public officials than in the past. In a kind of giant "echo effect," the media interpret such poll findings so as to magnify and reinforce the climate of suspicion. Media reports seldom comment on the ambiguities of the concept of trust or the difficulties of capturing the phenomenon in a few simple questions. There has always been mistrust towards government and there have always been untrustworthy public officials. Whether there is more untrustworthy behaviour today than in the past is difficult to know for certain. Whether the preferred remedy of stronger accountability mechanisms will reduce or deepen the so-called crisis of trust is also far from clear. Rather than stem a supposed crisis of trust, more extensive and intrusive accountability mechanisms may, if things go badly, lead to a genuine crisis of trust.

Working from the above perspective, this chapter seeks to accomplish three aims. The first is to demonstrate the complicated and problematic nature of the notion of trust, which has become so fashionable that it is losing its precise meaning. Secondly, the relationships between external and internal trust in the public sector are analyzed. Leadership styles and behaviours are presented in the literature as key determinants of trust. The topic of leadership is as elusive and controversial as trust. This is especially true with public sector organizations in which leadership is shared between ministers and public servants. The distinctive nature and context of leadership in the public sector makes the achievement of appropriate levels of trust more challenging than within private sector firms, which have been the focus of far more research attention.

Thirdly, the chapter explores the complicated relationship between accountability and trust. With leadership responsibility comes accountability, which is a fundamental and much debated concept in the public sector. Recently, there has been an insistence on more and stricter accountability for public sector leaders, both elected and appointed. The Federal Accountability Act (FAA), which was given royal assent in December 2006 and will be implemented on a gradual basis, is the latest and fullest expression of the prevailing view that traditional informal relationships of trust have been found wanting and must be replaced by more formal mechanisms to restrict the discretion of politicians and public servants, to promote transparency, to provide scrutiny of behaviour, and to strengthen accountability by attaching negative consequences to misdeeds or poor performance. There could well be unforeseen unwanted consequences from the elaborate regulatory structures like those established by the FAA, including a deepening of the distrust they are supposedly intended to remedy.

The following analysis of the relationships among trust, leadership, and accountability is necessarily somewhat general and does not presume to resolve ongoing controversies that swirl around these three complicated multidimensional, elusive concepts. Rather, the more modest aim is to contribute greater understanding of the problematic nature of these three "big ideas" and to identify the dangers of unanticipated consequences arising from a simplistic one-dimensional approach to applying them.

CLARIFYING TRUST

Trust has become a widely studied and highly heralded concept. Numerous academic disciplines have contributed to the vast literature on trust, and the result has been to refine our understanding of this multifaceted phenomenon (Levi and Stoker, 2000; Rousseau et al., 1998). The diversity of academic approaches to the conceptualization and measurement of trust reflects the multiple types, dimensions, and domains in which trust has been studied. However, less positively, the conceptual confusion and divergent attempts to measure trust present obstacles to sound theory construction and provide a limited basis for practical advice. In the world of practice, management consultants and other commentators tend to assume everyone knows what trust means and move directly into glib prescriptions about how trust relationships can be improved. Clarifying the concept of trust is a prerequisite to understanding how it shapes individual and institutional behaviour.

A useful distinction in the scholarly literature is the difference between *local* and *global* trust, identified by O'Hara (2004). Local trust (also called interpersonal trust) involves trusting people we know based on our interactions with them. It also encompasses those in our personal sphere whom we trust because of presumed professional competence and standards, people such as doctors or police officers. Global trust (also called institutional trust) requires people to trust beyond their own personal sphere, not just in people they know but also in organizations, institutions, and overall systems, such as government and its various components. Global trust produces generalized expectations of behaviour and allows for inference about motives, intentions, and competence. Such generalized trust enables us to simplify a complex world and to reduce uncertainty. In fact, this concept of global trust provides much of the basis for the way individuals, groups, and organizations interact in modern society.

The link between global trust and trust in government, which has been the focus of numerous opinion polls in many countries, is highly controversial. Some scholars insist there is a generalized loss of trust within society, reflecting the fact that local and global trust as measured by opinion polls shows them both tracking downward over the past several decades (Brehm and Rohn, 1997). The nature of the linkage between the two types of trust is unclear and the subject of much debate. For example, Uslaner, in his book *The Moral Foundation of Trust* (2002), disputed the linkage between the two types of trust, insisting that there is not a strong statistical correlation at the individual level.

Scholars like Hardin (2006) insist that trusting globally, as for example trust in government, is conceptually different from trusting locally. According to Hardin, the decision to trust requires some intimate knowledge of motives and intentions based on past experience. While this exists in the interpersonal realm, it is less common in terms of relationships between most citizens and their governments. In other words, most citizens do not know enough about governments to trust them in the same way they trust family members and friends. Therefore, Hardin sees no link between interpersonal trust and trust in government, calling this presumed linkage conceptually flawed and impossible, because citizens lack sufficient knowledge of governments to make a reasoned assessment of whether they are trustworthy or not. With this in mind, Hardin concludes that "we should generally speak not of trust in government but only of confidence in it" (Hardin, 2006: 29).

Despite Hardin's exhortation not to conflate the concepts of trust and confidence, most surveys of citizen opinions combine the two notions in the same question. It is conceivable, however, that trust and confidence could operate separately. For example, citizens could "trust" the motives of public sector leaders but not have "confidence" in their capacities to design and carry out effective public policy (Council for Excellence in Government, 2004). As will be demonstrated in the analysis to follow, accepting Hardin's distinction between interpersonal (local) trust and institutional (global) trust calls into question the arguments and evidence that claim to identify a crisis of trust in Canada's public sector.

Before examining that debate somewhat more closely, additional clarification of the components of trust is needed. Depending upon the context in which it is used, the term "trust" can have many different meanings. In the academic literature, definitions abound, many of them involving subtle distinctions based on the focus of inquiry by researchers in different disciplines. Writing in the field of psychology and focusing on the interpersonal domain of trust, Rousseau et al. describe trust as "a psychological state comprising the intention to accept vulnerability based on positive expectations of the intentions or behaviour of another" (1998: 394). Researchers following other disciplinary traditions, such as political science and sociology, examine the phenomenon of trust in a general social and political context. Fukuyama, a celebrity author on the topic, defines social trust as "[t]he expectations that arise within the community that there will be regular, honest and cooperative behaviour based on commonly shared norms on the part of other members of the community" (1995: 34). Societies that fail to develop social capital based upon interactions and the development of social cohesion will be weak in terms of trust. In the field of economics, trust is often defined in terms of rational calculations based upon whether it is "worth" trusting others (Crete, Pelletier, and Couture, 2006) Soroka, Helliwell, and Johnston, 2004). Many more definitions could be offered, but the real point is that trust is a complex, variegated phenomenon that can be understood and studied from many different perspectives.

Despite the diverse nature of the research and writing on trust, there are some common themes that can be identified. First, the literature suggests there are affective (emotional), cognitive (calculative), intentional, and behavioural components to trust. These components are assumed to affect each other, and the relative significance of each is assumed to vary across trust relationships. However, disentangling the impacts of the four components through research has proven to be very difficult (Lewicki, Tomlinson, and Gillespie, 2006; Tzafir and Dolan, 2004).

Second, there is usually assumed to be a future orientation to trust. It is held to involve expectations about what will happen in the future. It also implies some degree of uncertainty and risk involved with placing trust in another individual or in an institution. Definitions typically refer to feelings of security, faith, or confidence in the trusted party. Trust can be unconditional and amount to blind faith, but usually there are degrees of trust that are not easily measured.

Trust fluctuates over time. There is a debate in the psychological literature over whether there is a baseline of zero trust from which trust builds gradually over time based upon experience in newly established relationships (Lewicki, Tomlinson, and Gillespie, 2006). Other scholars suggest "swift trust" can emerge and even be fostered when there is interdependence, a focus on a specific task, and a commitment by participants to being adaptive and cooperative (Myerson, Weick, and Kramer, 1996). Trust can increase or decrease in both strength (depth) and breadth ("bandwidth") as a function of the frequency, duration, and diversity of experiences that affirm or undermine trust in others.

Third, there is considerable debate over what factors inspire or inhibit trust. One study identified more than fifty elements that could be described as determinants of trust (Connell, Ferres, and Travaglione, 2003; Tzafir and Dolan, 2004). These included whether the people involved were generally disposed to trust, their perceptions of others' trustworthiness and competence, the characteristics of their past relationships, the characteristics of their communication and decision-making patterns, and the structural arrangements that governed their relationships. Research on feedback models of changes in trust levels based upon the outcomes of placing trust in others is just beginning.

Fourth, depending upon the focus of the study, different sources and types of trust can be identified. This is much too large an aspect of the trust literature to be explored fully here. Two examples will have to suffice to illustrate the range of thinking and research along these lines. Working mainly in the organizational psychology tradition, the editors of a 1998 symposium identified four broad types of trust:

1. Deterrence-based: The potential costs of breaching a trust relationship outweigh the short-term advantages of acting in a distrustful way.
2. Calculus-based: Positive intentions and competence on the part of the trusted party are presumed based upon reliable knowledge.
3. Relational: The type of trust that derives from repeated interactions that provide grounds for confidence.

4. Institution-based: The type of trust that derives from the existence of legal protections, behavioural norms, and social connections that promote confidence in others (Rousseau et al., 1998).

These four types of trust clearly overlap. Other writers introduce the notion of identification-based trust, which arises when the parties to a trust relationship fully internalize one another's preferences and identify with each other's interests (Hurley, 2006; Jones and George, 1998).

These academic and empirically derived categories of trust can be contrasted to the rhetorical language and even looser categorizations employed by management consultants who make confident prescriptions about how to fix trust problems within organizations. For example, an article in *Harvard Business Review* identifies three kinds of trust:

1. Strategic: The trust exhibited by employees in the vision and competence of the top leaders to set directions and allocate resources.
2. Personal: The trust employees have in their own immediate "bosses."
3. Organizational: The trust people have in the organization (Galford and Drapeau, 2003).

The writers of the article insist these three dimensions of trust are related, but precisely how they interact is not made clear. The simplicity of trust as presented by the management gurus accounts in no small measure for the current popularity of the concept.

Despite their theoretical and practical disagreements, academics and practitioners agree on the value of trust within and among organizations. Some writers are positively rhapsodic on its presumed benefits. It is seen as a magic ingredient, a bonding agent that promotes cohesion and limits unproductive conflict, and a catalyst that encourages innovation and risk-taking. In a recent business bestseller, Covey writes that "when trust goes down, speed of change will also go down and costs will go up" (Covey, 2006: 13). Mistrust within and among organizations, it is often argued, leads to greater conflict, poor morale, more stress, poor communication, more secrecy, less candour, poorer decision-making, reduced productivity, less risk-taking, and both active and passive resistance to change.

LEADERSHIP AND TRUST

A close relationship is presumed to exist between trust and the style of leadership within organizations, among organizations, and within the various types of external networks that are becoming a prominent feature of so-called joined-up government. Of course, the phenomenon of leadership is itself controversial, with multiple theories, models, and "how-to" books available. In the interest of full disclosure (and greater trust), I view leadership as a process rather than a set of personal attributes that some lucky individuals possess based upon genetic inheritance or upbringing. Rost's definition of leadership as "a group process in which individuals influence others to work towards a shared purpose" appeals to me (Rost, 1991: 33). Under this definition, the distinction between leaders and followers becomes blurred and leaders can be found at all levels within organizations, as well as across organizational boundaries. Leadership becomes not so much what individuals do but what leaders and the led do collectively. As will be discussed below, leadership in the public sector has become more dispersed and collective in nature.

In his book, *Leadership and the Culture of Trust* (1994), Fairholm explores the relationships between culture, leadership, and trust. He writes that "leadership is a process of building a trust environment within which leaders and followers feel free to participate toward the accomplishment of mutually valued goals using agreed-upon processes" (Fairholm, 1994: viii). For leaders, the requirement to build trust is both a constraint and a resource. "Without capitalizing upon trust," writes Carnevale, "prospects for leader and organizational success are reduced" (Carnevale, 1994: 162). He goes on to suggest a number of specific ways leaders can use their influence to increase trust in their relationships within organizations and across organizational boundaries:

- Increase feelings of self-efficacy
- Create a shared vision
- Concentrate on tasks and relationship
- Use power to discourage dependency
- Create a healthy learning environment
- Be consistent
- Work on culture
- Integrate practices

These are familiar themes in the vast literature on trust, organizational culture, and leadership. Translating the general ideas into practice is the real challenge.

Most, if not all, organizations contain divergent values and interests that must be accommodated. This is especially true during periods of major change, scarcity, and/or downsizing. The development of consensus, conflict management, and conflict resolution are crucial during such periods of adjustment. Ideally, leaders will use their authority and influence to channel conflict in a constructive manner.

To gain support and legitimacy for their actions, leaders must engage in high trust behaviour, which sends the message that they have the right intentions, are responsive to employee concerns and issues, and will reconcile competing interests in a fair and balanced way. High trust behaviour involves such activities as clarifying competing values, appealing to ideals and common purposes, avoiding petty disputes and personalizing disagreements, being honest, telling the truth, keeping promises, avoiding the "blame game," respecting others, demonstrating a willingness to compromise, and generally keeping the inevitable conflicts that will arise in any organization as constructive and manageable as possible.

The literature on organizational justice tells us that perceptions of the fairness or unfairness of the decisions and actions taken by leaders are not isomorphic with trust, but they clearly inform employee feelings of trust (Sanders and Thornhill, 2003). All of the above sounds like "leadership ethics 101," but the reported experience of people within organizations and other research tells us that practicing high trust leadership behaviour is easier said than done. Trust cannot be demanded by leaders; it must be earned and freely given.

Even the above rather lengthy discussion of the multiple conceptions, competing theories, and methodological disagreements over how best to study trust is far from complete. To declare that the literature on trust would benefit from a consolidation and integration is obvious. This section has demonstrated the problematic and controversial nature of the concepts of trust and leadership. The chapter now turns to an analysis of the external and internal environments of Canada's public sector.

EXTERNAL POLITICAL TRUST

Like citizens in many other established democracies, Canadians have become steadily more critical over the past four decades of their political leaders, their government institutions, and even their system of democracy. We know this mainly from public opinion surveys of various kinds, but declining turnouts in elections and reduced participation in other activities, such as membership in political parties, are also taken as indicators of disillusionment with politics and governments. Canadians regularly tell pollsters they have less trust in their politicians, identify less with political parties, have less confidence in the main institutions of government, and express less satisfaction with how democracy operates in this country, believing that government is run for the benefit of a few big interests. Despite these negative sentiments, national pride and support for the principles of Canadian democracy remain high, with two-thirds of citizens usually saying Canada has the best democracy in the world (Nevitte, 1996; 2002).

There are multiple theories, models, concepts, and measures of these complicated paradoxical relationships between public opinion and government. Controversy abounds over what is being measured and the significance of the findings. In the space available here only some of the main controversies can be identified briefly, and certainly none will be resolved to everyone's satisfaction.

The problems begin, as mentioned earlier, with the glut of definitions of trust. The definitional confusion creates problems for the measurement of trust in a valid and reliable way. The survey tradition in trust literature has been the subject of considerable criticism (Hardin, 2006). Part of the difficulty arises from the fact that trust is often used interchangeably with closely related, but somewhat separate, concepts, such as faith, confidence, satisfaction, and support. "Faith" implies unconditional trust. It is mainly a psychological notion. Trust, however, is seldom absolute and unconditional; there is usually a component of calculation involved. "Confidence" usually involves an estimation of the capacity and competence of institutions and individuals, whereas trust relates more to the motives and intentions of others. "Satisfaction" is a narrower less value-laden term than trust. Satisfaction levels tend to be more short term, related to people's most recent encounters with government. Finally, "support" is a wider concept involving how people evaluate both the characteristics of the political system (diffuse support) and the performance of particular institutions and leaders (specific support). Both conceptually and methodologically, it is difficult to differentiate the four concepts, and measuring the causal relationships among them poses even greater analytical challenges.

The preoccupation with measuring trust got its start in the United States. It was originally based on answers to questions posed in the National Election Surveys (NES). Over the years, researchers have used various labels to describe what NES questions were measuring, including political cynicism, alienation, and disaffection. Only later did researchers begin to describe NES responses as measures of trust. Reversing the interpretation of the responses to claim that trust, rather than cynicism, is being measured poses both conceptual and methodological issues (Cook and Gronke, 2005). At its most basic, the research question becomes: Is trust simply the absence of cynicism? As Levi and Stoker (2000) pointed out in their major review article, researchers in the survey tradition have assumed NES questions captured trust and have not evaluated alternative survey indicators of trust. Even when respondents are asked directly whether they trust government, the options they are given are usually: Do you trust government to do what is right "just about always," "most of the time," or "only some of the time." An answer that governments can be trusted all or most of the time might be seen from a normative perspective as too high in terms of the healthy scepticism needed for a vibrant democracy. The response "only some of the time" may be just the right amount of trust for people to maintain the appropriate vigilance for democratic accountability. In short, the typical measures of trust used in surveys in the US are fraught with both measurement and evaluation problems. The original questions posed in NES surveys are still prominent today, including in published surveys in Canada.

Another methodological complication arises from the fact that the most publicized surveys often ask respondents one question to express their degree of both trust and confidence in government. Combining the two concepts in a single question confounds the problems of interpretation. It is conceivable that citizens could have confidence in the capabilities of governments to accomplish their declared aims but still mistrust the motives and intentions of public officials, both elected politicians and appointed public servants. As noted earlier, confidence and trust are at least "conceptual cousins" and are likely associated with one another in the responses of citizens, but they are not exactly the same.

Refinements in conceptualizations and methodologies over the years have produced various labels and typologies to identify different types, domains, and levels of trust. For example, general "social trust" is often distinguished from "political trust," which refers to citizen orientations towards political objects. In the political domain, trust is said to operate with respect to a range of features: the so-called regime values, the political community, the political system characteristics, the roles of particular institutions, the process of policy-making, the reputations of incumbents in public office, and the performance dimensions of government. These different variants of trust overlap and interact in not easily measured ways. For example, lack of trust towards current leaders could transform itself into distrust of institutions, and even of the political system itself. Loss of trust in institutions and our system of government would be more serious than mistrust of leaders because the foundations of support and legitimacy could be weakened.

Most opinion surveys capture only the affective dimension of citizens' views on government. It is rare to have surveys combine questions about feelings towards government with questions intended to ascertain the knowledge of respondents about the structures, processes, actions, and outcomes of government. On the matter of political knowledge, there is serious academic research that demonstrates the majority of Canadians are poorly informed about the basic features of their political system and the activities of their government (Gidengil et al., 2004; Milner, 2001). The significance of public ignorance (or what Milner calls "civic illiteracy") to the issue of public trust in government is not entirely clear. Does knowledge increase or reduce trust in government? There appear to be inconsistent findings in different countries (Council for Excellence in Government, 2004). The contradictions partly reflect whether the surveys are focusing on political system features or the behaviour of current office-holders. In any case, widespread public ignorance of government means that Canadians responding to surveys may simply be expressing feelings and opinions based upon popular negative stereotypes obtained mainly from the media, their ideologies concerning "big" versus "minimal" government intervention, their own first-hand experiences with government, or the latest scandal. The actual overall performance of government does not seem to be a major criterion for the expression of public trust, although shifting levels of public trust in government do seem to reflect the national mood, especially when it comes to feelings of optimism or pessimism regarding the economy.

Whereas media polls tap into general feelings and perceptions, other surveys ask respondents to reflect on their service delivery experiences. Such service satisfaction surveys generally produce more positive findings (Heintzman and Marson, 2005). There is a debate in the literature over whether service encounters represent "defining moments" in which governments incrementally regain trust one transaction at a time. Given the multiple and varied types of relationships citizens have with their governments, it is difficult to prove precisely how much the quality of the service experience offsets the broader trends and developments in the political system that cause disillusionment with governments. An extensive analysis of public attitudes towards government in the US by Goodsell (1994) argued persuasively that the negative stereotype of public bureaucracies caused most Americans to dismiss their own often positive dealings with government as atypical; they were simply the lucky ones who did not get hassled by the system.

There may be an additional indication of the relative contribution of the "micro" versus the "macro" level of citizen experiences to public trust in the finding across many surveys that people blame politicians more than public servants for their negative views of government. Some of the most sophisticated research on "micro-level" trust has been done in Belgium by van de Walle and his colleagues (van de Walle and Bouckaert, 2003; Christensen and Lægrid, 2005; Kampen, van de Walle, and Bouckaert, 2006). Applying regression analysis to survey data, the researchers sought to compare the relative contribution to trust of demographic factors, satisfaction scores on dealings with government, and a series of broader political and cultural variables. Put simply, their bottom-line finding was that political/cultural variables had by far the strongest overall effect on the variation in people's trust in government. Integration and involvement with the political system tended to produce more positive orientations towards government.

These findings suggest there are both "big" and "small" trust situations. Analyzing trust towards government in general terms ignores the smaller episodes that may contribute or detract marginally from trust. Based upon an extensive review of the available research, Levi and Stoker (2000) concluded that trust and mistrust primarily reflect the political lives people live, not their social background characteristics or whether they generally have "trusting personalities" (Levi and Stoker, 2000).

The above lengthy discussion of the complications of defining and measuring trust indicates the dangers of easy generalizations. Empirical data on degrees of trust towards government involve a precision that is likely to impress, but is also likely artificial. Moreover, measures of trust do not speak for themselves; they have to be interpreted, and often they say different things to different people.

Beyond these controversies over meaning and measurement, there is the issue of why trust appears to be on the decline. Once again, multiple theories, hypotheses, and models have been presented. It is impossible to summarize the vast literature that investigates this topic without simplifying greatly. Three broad sets of explanatory factors appear to be at work.

The first involves the impact of broad economic, social, and technological changes on the core citizenship values of Canadians. According to experts like Nevitte (1996), increased wealth, higher levels of education, and new technologies have transformed the values and skills of citizens. There is said to be a new Canadian political culture in which citizens are less deferential towards elites and more insistent on engagement and empowerment. Feelings of remoteness and being voiceless in relation to government are said to have negative consequences in the form of increased dissatisfaction and mistrust. The challenge for political parties and for governments is how to harness the rising participatory instincts of Canadians. Citizens still value their political community and the main values of the political culture, but they are critical of particular institutions and even more of the people serving in public office. Most recently, the phenomena of declining turnouts in elections, reduced public participation in traditional political activities, and calls for more direct forms of democracy have been labelled a "democratic deficit."

A second broad set of explanatory factors involves the actions of political institutions and the behaviour of politicians. Trust appears to fluctuate in response to the issues on the political agenda in a given period. For example, the adoption of the Charter of Rights and Freedoms in 1982 and the rounds of failed constitutional negotiations created a stronger sense of "public ownership" of the constitution, more demands for democratic participation, and arguably less trust in the capacity of political and administrative elites to resolve divisive issues faced by the political community. Scandals like the sponsorship program, which led to the Gomery inquiry, and tragedies like the tainted blood episode are high-profile events that also drain trust and confidence in political and policy processes. Adversarial and negative approaches within Parliament contribute to a lack of trust (motives/intentions) and confidence (capabilities) in politicians and political institutions. The tendency of more competitive media to simplify, sensationalize, personalize, and magnify misdeeds or mistakes adds to public disillusionment. Freedom of information laws and more oversight bodies produce more opportunities to expose problems. An excessive focus on failures and abuses of power risks discrediting government as an institution in the minds of citizens, reducing its authority and capacity to achieve positive public purposes.

A third related set of factors that affect political trust concerns the government's performance record in terms of policy success (especially economic policy), sound management, and satisfactory service delivery. As noted above, the public is generally ill-informed about government. What the majority of citizens know is based mainly on the kaleidoscopic images conveyed by the media, especially nightly television newscasts. This leads to partial, shallow, and often negative perceptions of government. Moreover, research studies suggest the public has unrealistic expectations that governments can solve complicated problems, and their patience in terms of the time allowed for success to be demonstrated seems to have shrunk.

In summary, the apparent rise of political mistrust over the past four decades has been driven by both long-term forces and short-term events. Governments have been required to deal with more complicated, turbulent, and demanding as well as increasingly negative external environments. Mistakes, abuses, unforeseen problems, and, in general, the failure to meet elevated public expectations in terms of anticipatory, responsive, and responsible behaviour has produced an apparent loss of both public confidence and trust in governments.

THE INTERNAL TRUST CLIMATE

Governments are very open to outside influences that flow mainly through the political process and the media. This means the changing external political culture overlaps and intersects with the internal political and administrative cultures of governments, often in unpredictable and immediate ways. The growing mistrust in the external political environment has produced serious consequences for how leadership, management, and accountability are conducted within government. The main argument of this section of the chapter is that recent reforms to government structures and to the public service have been based on "managerial thinking" that has both reflected and reinforced the antipolitics and antigovernment mood of the public. Managerial approaches, structures, and procedures have been presented as "solutions" to problems that were more political than managerial in their origins, notwithstanding the fact that these two domains overlap and intersect.

Public concern about the intentions and behaviour of government elites has always been a part of the Canadian political culture, but these sentiments have become much stronger over the past several decades. Traditional informal approaches to the promotion and preservation of trust came to be seen as inadequate. Gradually, informal relationships of mutual respect and trust among different institutions and actors inside government have been replaced by an ever expanding web of rules, procedures, codes, guidelines, reporting requirements, and monitoring bodies intended to deter and deal with wrongdoing, performance shortcomings, mismanagement, poor service delivery, and a perceived lack of accountability in terms of the consequences for public officials who created these problems or at least allowed them to arise.

The replacement of a culture of trust with a framework of rules began before the Harper government took office, but its FAA represents the fullest expression of the prevailing suspicion that politicians, and, to a lesser extent, public servants cannot be trusted to do the right thing and to do it well. The main features of the FAA are outlined in the list below. The act's overall rationale seems to be as follows: If the trustworthiness of public officials can be guaranteed by prescribing, regulating, and monitoring their behaviour, and by punishing wrongdoing when it occurs, then there is less need to rely on trust. In other words, the FAA sends a powerful negative symbolic message about the motives and competence of public sector leaders. It also creates an elaborate regulatory, surveillance, and reporting apparatus that could inadvertently end up deepening the mistrust it seeks to remedy.

Main Features of the FAA
- "Accounting officer" regime for "deputy minister/heads"
- Internal auditing regime strengthened and centralized control
- More oversight of procurement
- Whistleblower protection
- Criminal indictment for financial management fraud by public servants
- More power for Auditor General to follow money for grants and contributions
- New conflict of interest and ethics and lobbying regulations and oversight
- Parliamentary budget office for independent budget analysis
- Limits on political staff entering public service through backdoor
- Requirement to commission public opinion polls
- Reviews of Liberal government's corporate-administrative rules

Ideally, trusting relationships should exist within government on a number of levels, only a few of which can be discussed here. It is widely accepted in the literature on private firms that effective leaders who promote cultures and climates of trust are key ingredients in organizational success. In contrast, leadership in building and preserving trust inside government is more complicated and difficult because of the distinctive context and additional constraints involved with public sector organizations.

Leadership at the top of the public service is shared between ministers and senior public servants, especially deputy ministers. In addition, there are government-wide political, policy, financial, and administrative concerns represented by the Prime Minister's Office and other central agencies. Decisions and actions are the targets for regular criticism in question period and other parts of the parliamentary process. Various parliamentary watchdog agencies publicize problems but spend less time recognizing achievement. Outside advocacy groups and the media focus mainly on the negative aspects of government performance, something made easier over the past twenty-five years by the availability of the Access to Information Act. New disclosure and reporting bodies under the FAA will add greatly to the "fishbowl" quality of leading and managing in the public sector. In addition to these challenges and constraints, there is a lack of widespread agreement about what constitutes "success" in government compared to private firms. In short, compared to the private sector, which inspires most of the trust literature, leadership in the public sector is more collective and less unilateral; involves the need to recognize and accommodate a wider more divergent range of interests and values; involves more rules and limits on decision-making; and entails greater requirements for transparency and accountability.

In principle, there should be a strong working partnership between ministers and senior public servants based upon mutual respect and trust. Research for this chapter uncovered no empirical surveys documenting trust levels in this key relationship, either recently or in the past. Rhetorically, prime ministers and other ministers declare their trust and confidence in the public service, but often their actions speak louder than their words.

During the 1990s, when new public management thinking was at its peak, there was much talk about the need to relax centralized controls in order to promote and allow more prudent risk-taking and encourage innovation within the bureaucracy. When something went wrong, however, the almost automatic reaction was to lay on new rules and to create new oversight bodies. There was also a growing tendency to put senior public servants "out front" to take the blame when policy blunders and administrative problems were exposed.

"Bureaucrat bashing" may not be as widespread in Canada as in other countries, but a small number of high-profile cases over the past three decades appears to have damaged the trust relationships of public servants with their elected political masters. Public servants began to question the commitment of their ministers to evidence-based policy-making, to the principles of sound public management, and to accepting responsibility/accountability when bad things happened. Trust and respect seemed to become a "fair weather" condition. When "storms" erupted, ministers were less willing to uphold the traditional norm of public service anonymity. More public servants were called before parliamentary committees to explain and answer for problems. Public attacks on public servants likely served to undermine the values, attitudes, and behaviours promoted by the public service reform initiatives of the 1990s—such qualities as viewing public service as a special calling, engaging in hard work and prudent risk-taking, and learning from mistakes. The unfavourable image of the public service that developed from the negativity of the period also created a challenge in terms of the recruitment of the next generation of public servants.

Another level of trust relationships involves the senior managers in the public service and the rank-and-file employees below them in the administrative hierarchy. Direct data on this intraorganizational type of trust does not seem to exist. The federal government employee surveys conducted in 1999, 2002, and 2005 did not ask direct questions on the topic of trust at different levels within the public service. However, there were seven or eight questions that provided proxy indicators of the trust climate. At the beginning of this chapter, several findings from the 2005 survey were noted: frustration with shifting priorities, unreasonable deadlines, lack of input into decisions, and too many approval stages.

Other findings from the same survey also seemed to speak to the trust issue: 40 percent of employees said they rarely or only sometimes received encouragement to be innovative; 29 percent stated they did not receive direction on the results they were expected to achieve; and only 31 percent said their unit periodically took time to review its performance. Views on the fairness of classification and staffing processes were lower than in the 2002 survey: 43 percent felt they were not classified fairly, and 30 percent felt the staffing process in their unit was not fair. More positive findings were that 83 percent of the respondents agreed their organizations treated them in a respectful manner, and 68 percent knew where to go if they faced an ethical dilemma or value conflict in the workplace. However, less positive was the finding that only half of the respondents felt they could initiate a formal grievance and not face reprisal (Public Service Human Resources Management Agency, 2005).

Beyond these indirect empirical measures of the elusive phenomenon of trust within the public service, some even more impressionistic observations can be offered. First, a relatively rapid turnover of ministers and deputy ministers means there is less time for solid trust relationships to develop. A common assertion in the literature is that it takes time to develop trust but that it can be lost quickly and once lost (often through a high-profile event like the sponsorship scandal), it is very difficult to restore. Second, official rhetoric about the value of the public service, and the need to trust people and grant them the freedom to innovate is seen as contradicted by downsizing and the insistence on strict compliance with more rules. Third, managers are perceived to be suspicious of the motives and tactics of the leaders of public sector unions. Finally, the changed nature of work in the public sector, the greater reliance upon so-called knowledge workers who value autonomy and variety in their work, the emergence of a generation gap between "younger" employees and "older" managers, and the development of more diverse workforces are all trends that could have potential impacts on trust within the public service. For example, the employee surveys tell us that longer serving (over ten years) employees were more jaundiced than younger employees with less experience (under three years).

Given all of the developments and conditions described above, it is not surprising that a significant number of rank-and-file employees might declare in words and in deeds a lack of trust and confidence in their elected political masters and their more immediate administrative bosses. Given the scope, variety, and dynamic nature of the public sector, it is likely that trust levels vary across organizations and within particular organizations over time. For example, given its recent high-profile problems, the RCMP in 2007 is presumably an organization with very low levels of internal trust and fallen levels of external public trust. The relationship between organizational identity and loyalty and internal trust among employees is an area where more research is needed.

The capability of leaders to generate and maintain trust is also variable. Exactly how much trust is needed to generate high performance is impossible to state precisely given our present knowledge of the complex elusive phenomenon of trust. The basis for trust within different contexts undergoing change is also an area of uncertainty. The recent insistence on stricter top-down control and accountability processes has problematic consequences for both external and internal trust in Canada's public sector—as the next section of this chapter seeks to make clear.

CONTROL, ACCOUNTABILITY, AND TRUST

Accountability is almost as controversial a concept as trust and leadership. Over time, the term has acquired multiple meanings (Thomas, 2008). In the present climate of suspicion and mistrust, the almost automatic reaction when something goes wrong is to insist on more control and stricter forms of accountability. The relationships among trust, control, and accountability are more complicated and less symbiotic than is presumed by the prevailing tendency to add new accountability requirements as the answer to declining trust levels throughout the political system.

In beginning this section, a brief clarification of the terms "control" and "accountability" is required. The term "control" has acquired mainly negative policing connotations when used to describe its purpose in the public service. Control is seen as necessary to prevent or deal with abuses of authority and problems of mismanagement. In this perspective, control and trust are seen as opposites. Through tight control, discretion and autonomy are restricted and trust is denied to people working within the administrative hierarchy. There is, however, a second more positive meaning of control that refers to the capacity of organizations and people to deal with constraints, unforeseen events, and deviations from planned developments in a way that achieves positive outcomes. To state that someone is in control means that an individual, a group, or an organization is given direction, authority, resources, autonomy, and a generally supportive environment to enable them to accomplish positive outcomes.

Ministers, central agencies, deputy ministers, and managers are constantly searching for the appropriate balance between the negative and positive approaches to control. Too much emphasis on the negative approach to control reduces discretion, diminishes the scope for judgment, creates a more risk-averse culture, and stifles innovation. Beyond a certain point, the costs of negative controls exceed the presumed benefits of reduced problems. In designing new approaches to internal and external control, more attention must be paid to how trust will be impacted by those approaches.

The term "accountability" has become a cliché and in the process has taken on multiple meanings. I favour restricting the use of the term to describe a formal relationship supported by a process. There are five components to accountability relationships:

1. the delegation or negotiation of a set of responsibilities, ideally based upon agreed expectations and standards;
2. the provision of authority, resources, and a reasonably supportive environment to allow for the fulfillment of responsibilities;
3. the obligation to answer for the performance of responsibilities, ideally based upon valid information;
4. the duty of the authorizing party to monitor performance and to take corrective action when problems arise; and
5. the bestowal of rewards of penalties based on performance. (Thomas, 2008)

There are now multiple types of accountability, each with different mechanisms of enforcement and criteria of success, operating within government. However, the essence of accountability in practice usually comes down to blaming. It is about pinpointing responsibility, setting parameters for behaviour, and making people pay a price when something goes wrong.

Reacting to parliamentary, media, and public criticisms, both Liberal and Conservative governments have added to the extensive accountability requirements that already existed in Canada's public sector. The assumption was that, if accountability is a good thing, there can never be too much of it. Accountability got a big boost from the sponsorship scandal. First, the Liberal government, in the person of Reg Alcock, president of the Treasury Board, introduced over two hundred "reforms"—mostly for greater prior control, auditing, oversight, and reporting to Parliament. A management accountability framework was introduced with a stronger emphasis on performance measurement and reporting; the Comptroller General of Canada was created; the internal audit function was strengthened; hundreds of new auditors were hired; massive investments in information and communications technologies were made; and Service Canada was created as a move towards a more service-oriented public sector.

Earlier mention was made of the FAA passed in 2006. A noteworthy feature of the FAA is its attempt to deal with perceived wrongdoing and mistakes on both the political and the administrative sides of government. As a result, the act is quite sweeping in its scope. Even though it is to be implemented on a gradual incremental basis, there is a very real chance there will be unforeseen unwanted consequences arising from specific requirements in the act, the interaction among different provisions, and the cumulative impact of the full set of new accountability mechanisms. By my count, the FAA adds eight new oversight bodies and strengthens the mandates of several others, most notably the Office of the Auditor General.

There is not the space here to review the specific provisions of the FAA. Instead, some general comments will be offered in line with the themes of this chapter. First, the act reflects and reinforces the prevailing negative public mood towards government. Second, coming on top of reforms introduced by the former Martin government, the FAA increases the centralized control, internal regulation, and extensive surveillance of both political and administrative leaders within government. Autonomy, creativity, and the scope for innovation will be reduced—something that is hardly desirable during a period of rapid change. Avoiding all mistakes, or simply unforeseen unwanted developments, will become a perverse incentive. Adherence to accountability rules will come at the cost of responsiveness to changing conditions and new public demands, and this will not do much to regain the public's trust and confidence in government.

A further ironic twist is that the spiralling of accountability requirements will force governments and Parliament to place their trust in a new "oversight bureaucracy." In a case of "who will guard the guardians," ministers and parliamentarians will have to hope that the new guardians, and the strengthened existing oversight bodies, use their authority and influence in a responsible manner. Hopefully, their reports and recommendations are well informed, balanced, and fair. The fact that "watchdog" bodies serve Parliament does not automatically mean they are responsible and accountable, as we saw with the scandal involving the Privacy Commissioner in the early 1990s (Thomas, 2003). Given the scope and complexity of the Government of Canada, there will always be uncertainty, risks, mistakes, and even misdeeds. Negative findings by oversight bodies whose mandate is to uncover such problems will be amplified and distorted in parliamentary and media processes, usually "crowding out" news about positive achievements. This dynamic could end up perpetuating and even deepening the prevailing negative views of government.

There is, of course, a more optimistic view of the impact of the FAA on trust levels, both outside and inside government. In the view of the Harper government, the elaborate regulatory, control, and accountability structures of the act will prevent misdeeds and mistakes, provide incentives for improved performance, require transparency and reporting, hold public sector leaders accountable for results, and lead over the long term to a restoration of public trust in government. Meanwhile, internally, the insistence on focus, discipline, standards, results, and accountability will restore professional commitment and pride as public organizations demonstrate they can deliver value for money. This positive scenario presumes the elaborate structural and procedural improvements of the past two decades, including the partially implemented FAA, will work as intended and have the desired consequences.

CONCLUDING THOUGHTS

Trust matters. It can be violated or exploited, but it has much to recommend it. No one would recommend absolute credulity or rampant cynicism. At present, there "appears" to be lower trust in relation to government than is desirable. "Appears" has to be used to describe the current climate of public trust in government, because the phenomenon is elusive, multifaceted, and difficult to measure precisely. Moreover, what constitutes dangerously weak trust rather than healthy skepticism is a matter on which different observers disagree.

It would be melodramatic and an exaggeration to argue that Canada's public sector is facing a crisis of trust. Clearly, voters tell pollsters they are less trusting, but these opinions appear to be ill-informed and shallow. Today, the greatest mistrust is targeted at current political actors and to a lesser extent existing political institutions. Conceivably, such negative feelings towards the most visible features of political life could spill over into a questioning of the political system and its fundamental values. This seems unlikely, however, unless there were to occur a series of scandals or disastrous policies, especially in the economic field. More likely is a persistence of low levels of trust and confidence in politicians, political institutions, and, to a more limited extent, the public service. If weak trust leads to declining political engagement by citizens (the studies are not conclusive on this point), then recent trends in public attitudes are not a trivial matter. A loss of trust, confidence, and involvement makes it more difficult for governments to mobilize support and to gain legitimacy for their actions.

. The different disciplinary traditions have produced varied conceptions of trust. The sources and types of trust are numerous and influenced by various contingencies. In the survey research tradition, many indicators of trust have been used, making it difficult to compare across studies. The variety and richness of the trust literature may reflect the complexities and subtleties of the phenomenon, but the heterogeneity of approaches poses serious problems for the formulation of practical advice for leaders who are often the key actors in establishing trust relationships.

Leadership is most popularly conceptualized in terms of individuals who possess special personal qualities that inspire trust and commitment on the part of others. This chapter has argued that leadership is better thought of in terms of process. This is particularly true in the public sector, where leadership has always been shared between ministers and senior public servants. When citizens think of what is wrong with the amorphous agglomeration called "government," they mostly blame politicians rather than public servants. They do this on the basis of very limited knowledge of how government actually works or the substance of public policies and programs.

Leadership involves responsibility, which leads to accountability. Trust and accountability exist in a relationship of tension—they can contradict and undermine each other or they can complement and reinforce one another. At the most general level, an older approach to accountability is being challenged—if not displaced—by a newer approach. The traditional approach was informal, relatively simple, qualitative, and based upon a substantial measure of trust. The still emerging, increasingly predominant approach is more formal, complicated, and quantitative, and it manifests low trust. What is too seldom noted is that political systems cannot have any form of accountability without some type of trust. The FAA and the other accountability mechanisms ask us to trust in a new set of extensive and mainly opaque processes of regulating, controlling, monitoring, auditing, and performance-reporting. In short, we must trust the new "watchdogs" who are there to ensure others are trustworthy.

Dealing with the trust deficit will not be easy for governments. Social and political conditions have been identified as the greatest contributing factors to declining trust. Those factors are traditional and long term, as well as contemporary in nature. Structural, procedural, managerial, and program-delivery reforms undertaken by the Government of Canada over the past two decades may make a marginal different to public trust and also enhance internal accountability, but they will not overcome deeper causes of discontent.

The public sector world of trust, leadership, and accountability will not become any less complicated based upon current trends towards more consultative approaches to policy-making and the use of third parties to deliver programs. Leadership will be dispersed and more networked in character. Trust relationships will have to be developed in the context of shorter term shifting alliances involving negotiation, shared power, and heightened risks. Accountability will become complicated and blurred. For the new approaches to governance to work as intended, the present negative approaches to enforcing accountability based on naming and blaming individuals will have to be replaced by a more collective approach that is more cultural than legal and procedural, and emphasizes learning more than blaming. Trust will be central to the new accountability approach.

NOTES

[1]   The author would like to thank particularly Mark Hammer for his insightful advice on the employee survey findings within the Government of Canada. Others who read the paper and deserve to be thanked for their constructive advice are Chris Adams, Frank Graves, Ralph Heintzmann, Jim McDavid, John Nethercote, Andrew Podger, Herb Robertson, David Siegel, and David Zussman.

REFERENCES

Blind, Perri K. "Government in the Twenty-First Century: A Review of Literature and Emerging Issues." Paper from UNDESA. <http://www. unpan1.un.org/intradoc/groups/publications>.

Brehm, John, and Wendy Rohn. (1997). "Individual Level Evidence for the Causes and Consequences of Social Capital." *American Journal of Political Science*. 41: 4: 999–1023.

Canada, Public Service Human Resources Management Agency of Canada. (2005). "What You Told Us—Public Service Wide Results." 2005 Employee Survey. <http://www.hmra-agrh.gc.ca/survey-sondage2005/r-publication/survey>.

Carnevale, David G. (1995). *Trustworthy Government: Leadership and Management Strategies for Building Trust and High Performance*. San Francisco: Jossey Bass.

Christensen, Tom, and Per Lægrid. (June 2005). "Trust in Government: The Relative Importance of Service Satisfaction, Political Factors and

Geography." *Public Performance and Management Review.* 28: 4: 487–511.

Connell, Julia, Natalie Ferres, and Tony Travaglione. (2003). "Engendering Trust in Manager-Subordinate Relationships: Predictors and Outcomes." *Personnel Review.* 32: 5: 569–587.

Cook, Timothy E., and Paul Gronke. (2005). "The Skeptical American: Revisiting the Meanings of Trust in Government and Confidence in Institutions." *Journal of Politics.* 67: 3: 784–803.

Council for Excellence in Government. (2004). *A Matter of Trust: Americans and Their Government: 1958–2004.* Washington, DC: Council for Excellence in Government.

Coutu, Diane L. (1998). "Trust in Virtual Terms." *Harvard Business Review.* 76: 3: 1–4.

Covey, Stephen M. R. (2006). *The Speed of Trust.* New York: Free Press.

Crete, Jean, Rejean Pelletier, and Jerome Couture. (1–4 June 2006). "Political Trust in Canada: What Matters: Politics or Economics?" A paper presented at the annual meeting of the Canadian Political Science Association, York University, Toronto, ON.

Fairholm, Gilbert. (1994). *Leadership and the Culture of Trust.* Westport, CT: Praeger.

Fukuyama, Francis. (1995). *Trust: The Social Virtues and the Creation of Prosperity.* New York: Basic Books.

Galford, Robert, and Anne Siebold Drapeau. (2003). "The Enemies of Trust." *Harvard Business Review.* 81: 1: 33–38.

Gidengil, Elizabeth, et. al. (2004). *Citizens.* Vancouver: UBC Press.

Goodsell, Charles. (1994). *The Case for Bureaucracy.* Chatham, NJ: Chatham House.

Hardin, Russell. (2006). *Trust.* Cambridge: Polity.

Heintzman, Ralph, and Brian Marson. (2005). "People, Service, and Trust: Is There a Public Sector Service Value Chain?" *International Review of Administrative Sciences.* 7: 4: 549–575.

Hudson, Bob. (2004). "Trust: Towards a Clarification." *Australian Journal of Political Science.* 39: 1: 75–87.

Hurley, Robert F. (September 2006). "The Decision to Trust." *Harvard Business Review.* 1–11.

Jones, Gareth, and Jennifer M. George. (1998). "The Experience and Evolution of Trust: Implications for Cooperation and Teamwork." *Academy of Management Review.* 23: 3: 531–546.

Kampen, Jarl K., Steven van de Walle, and Geert Bouckaert. (2006). "Assessing the Relation between Satisfaction with Public Service and Trust in Government: The Impact of the Predisposition of Citizens toward Government on Evaluation of its Performance." *Public Performance and Management Review.* 29: 4: 387–404.

Kanji, Mebs. (2002). "Political Discontent, Human Capital, and Representative Governance in Canada." In *Value Change and Governance in Canada*, edited by Neil Nevitte, 71–106. Toronto: University of Toronto Press.

Levi, M., and M. L. Stoker. (2000). "Political Trust and Trustworthiness." *Annual Review of Political Science*. 3: 1: 475–507.

Lewicki, Roy, Edward C. Tomlinson, and Nicole Gillespie. (2006). "Models of Interpersonal Trust Development: Theoretical Approaches, Empirical Evidence and Future Directions." *Journal of Management*. 32: 6: 991–1022.

Luhmann, Niklas. (1988). "Familiarity, Confidence, Trust: Problems and Alternatives." In *Trust: Making and Breaking of Cooperative Relations*, edited by D. Gambetta, 58–73. Oxford: Blackwell Press.

Milner, Henry. (2001). "Civic Literacy in a Comparative Context: Why Canadians Should Be Concerned." *Policy Matters*. 2: 2: 1–32.

Myerson, D., K. Weik, and R. M. Kramer. (1996). "Swift Trust and Temporary Groups." In *Trust in Organizations: Frontiers of Theory and Research*, edited by R. M. Kramer and T. R. Tyler, 166–195. Thousand Oaks, CA: Sage.

Nevitte, Neil. (1996). *The Decline of Deference: Canadian Value Change in a Cross-National Perspective*. Peterborough, ON: Broadview Press.

———. (2002). "Value Change and Reorientation in Citizen-State Relations." In *Value Change and Governance in Canada*, edited by Neil Nevitte, 3–35. Toronto: University of Toronto Press.

O'Hara, Kieron. (2004). *Trust: From Socrates to Spin*. Cambridge: Icon Books.

Rost, Joseph S. (1993). *Leadership for the Twenty-First Century*. Westport, CT: Praeger.

Rousseau, Denise M., et al. (1998). "Introduction to Special Topic Forum: Not so Different after All: A Cross Discipline View of Trust." *The Academy of Management Review*. 23: 3: 393–404.

Sanders, Mark N. K., and Adrian Thornhill. (2003). "Organizational Justice, Trust and the Management of Change: An Exploration." *Personnel Review*. 32: 3: 360–375.

Soroka, Stuart, John F. Helliwell, and Richard Johnston. (2004). "Measuring and Modelling Trust." In *Diversity, Social Capital, and the Welfare State*, edited by Fiona Kay and Richard Johnston. Vancouver: UBC Press.

Thomas, Paul G. (2003). "The Past, Present, and Future of Officers of Parliament." *Canadian Public Administration*. 46: 3: 287–314.

———. (2008). "The Swirling Meanings and Practices of Accountability in Canadian Government." In *Professionalism & Public Service: Essays in Honour of Kenneth Kernaghan*, edited by David Siegel and Ken Rasmussen, 34–62. Toronto: University of Toronto Press.

Tzafir, Shay S., and Simon L. Dolan. (2004). "Trust Me: A Scale for Measuring Manager-Employee Trust." *Management Research*. 2: 2: 115–132.

Uslaner, Erik M. (2002). *The Moral Foundation of Trust*. Cambridge: Cambridge University Press.

van de Walle, Steven, and Geert Bouckaert. (2003). "Public Service Performance and Trust in Government: The Problem of Causality." *International Review of Administrative Sciences*. 8: 9: 891–913.

9 PUTTING CITIZENS FIRST:
Service Delivery and Integrated Public Governance

Kenneth Kernaghan

J. E. Hodgetts, in a 1955 review of antibureaucracy writings, referred to the traditional stereotype of the lazy civil servant who, "as was once said, is like the fountains of Trafalgar Square because he plays from ten until four" (179). At that date, it was difficult to imagine that fifty years later public servants would be providing many government services twenty-four hours a day, seven days a week. Moreover, government services are now available through several delivery channels. This improvement in service delivery has been greatly facilitated by government's increased use of information technology (IT), especially the Internet. It is also the result of the creation and expansion of walk-in service centres and telephone call centres for which the Internet is the backbone of the service delivery arrangements.

As early as 1973, Hodgetts made prescient observations about the probable impact on the public service of advances in electronic technology—what he called "the new age of gadgetry." He described at one extreme a somewhat gloomy scenario

> in which the machines play havoc with the public service: suffocating it in the burden of paper products; displacing large numbers of the lower grade clerical and technical personnel; and substituting for the humanized, across-the-counter dealings with the public a species of 'numbers game' in which every citizen, equipped with coded punch cards as identification, simply feeds his card into the electronic brain

> and receives his birth or marriage or death certificates ... old age
> pension or unemployment insurance benefits ... or his passport.
> Even the venerable Post Office might become redundant as electronic
> media of communication make letter writing obsolete.

At the other extreme, Hodgetts painted a more optimistic scenario,
one in which machines will take over

> much of the less interesting and stimulating work which stultifies
> and deadens so many people performing routine operations in
> the public service; we can envisage the machines speeding up the
> processes of bureaucracy, *resulting in improved service from officials*
> vested with more authority to make decisions on the spot and yet
> held accountable by the machines' capacity to improve reporting
> procedures. (emphasis added) (1973: 30)

This paper provides evidence that key components of *both* scenarios
have since been realized or are emerging.

The main argument presented here is that substantially greater
progress towards an integrated multichannel cross-jurisdictional service
delivery system is essential for the widely heralded transformation
of service delivery in general. The chapter begins with definitions
of relevant key concepts. This is followed by a brief reference to the
evolution of service delivery during the periods of traditional public
administration (TPA) and new public management (NPM). Several
subsequent sections discuss developments in service delivery over the
past decade—a period during which the field of public administration
has been significantly influenced by a movement towards a dominant
emphasis on what is conceptualized in this chapter as integrated public
governance (IPG).[1] The final section of the chapter assesses the extent to
which government service delivery has been transformed. The chapter
deals primarily with the federal sphere of government, but reference is
also made to the provincial and municipal experience. Moreover, while
governments are concerned with service improvement for businesses,
as well as for citizens, the focus here is primarily on citizen-centred
service.

CONCEPTUAL CONSIDERATIONS[2]

The concept of IPG refers here to the following:

- the exercise of authority, power, and/or influence
- by a broad range of political actors, including citizens and groups
- that involves the joining up of policies, programs, services, structures, processes, and systems
- in arrangements that extend across departmental, governmental, and/or sectoral boundaries

IPG takes a broad perspective on governing; covers policy development, implementation, and evaluation; includes a wide variety of participants; and extends across governments and civil society. It is offered here as a collective term for the major trends and characteristics of public administration and management during the post-NPM period. The concept of IPG is similar to what has been called "holistic" governance, that is, a form of governance "centrally focused on delivering integrated policies and practices delivering genuinely desirable outcomes to meet real needs" (6 et al., 2002: 1) Integration is envisaged as extending across the key government activity areas of policy, regulation, service provision, and scrutiny (6 et al., 2002: 28–29). Perri 6 et al. predict "[t]he search for a more holistic approach to policy and management" will "be as much a hallmark of public service reform in the early twenty-first century as the changes introduced under the rubric of 'new public management' or 'reinventing government' were in the closing decades of the twentieth" (2002: 1). Other terms that have been used to capture the main features of IPG or holistic government are "collaborative governance" and "the networked state."

Among the several components of IPG is what Bourgault describes as integrated corporate management, an approach that goes beyond horizontal management to take "a relatively institutionalized form of the holistic governmental management model" proposed by Perri 6 and his colleagues (2007: 258). Bourgault argues the federal government and most of the provincial governments are using integrated corporate management, and that Canada is more committed to this approach than other Westminster countries (2007: 259).

This chapter does not examine all the integrative opportunities and challenges across government, the private sector, and civil society that are covered by the concept of IPG. It is primarily concerned with collaborative arrangements for successful policy and program implementation, with particular emphasis on service delivery. The major focus is on two key words in the definition of IPG, namely "citizens" and "services," and, more specifically, on the improvement of service to citizens through integrated service delivery (ISD).

ISD involves bringing together and, where desirable and possible, fitting together related government services so citizens can access them in a single seamless experience based on their wants and needs. ISD is an advanced form of what is commonly described as a "one-stop shop" or a "single window" for government service. It is a central component of the broader notion of IPG and will be a major determinant of its success.

IPG in general, and ISD in particular, can be fostered by cooperation, coordination, and/or collaboration among individuals, groups, and organizations. All three of these concepts involve working together to achieve such common objectives as reducing fragmentation, avoiding duplication, and removing gaps, but they should not be used interchangeably. Cooperation and coordination can be viewed as stages along a continuum leading to the collaboration that is characteristic of effective ISD arrangements.

"Cooperation" refers to informal relationships that do not involve the sharing of such elements as objective-setting, structures, planning, risks, or rewards. "Coordination" is a more formal process than cooperation in that it does or can involve the sharing of these elements, as well as the sharing of work and resources. "Collaboration" is an even more formal process that involves the sharing of authority, rather than just work or resources. Collaboration not only brings together policies, programs, services, structures, processes, and systems but is also more likely than coordination to enable political actors to fit these elements together. Moreover, since collaboration can involve the sharing of decision-making authority across departments, governments, or sectors, it raises concerns about where accountability for results lies. Coordination and collaboration are closely related to the concept of partnership. Coordination, through sharing work, is often described as an operational partnership, whereas collaboration, through sharing power, is commonly described as a collaborative or "real" partnership.

FROM TRADITIONAL PUBLIC ADMINISTRATION TO NEW PUBLIC MANAGEMENT

During the broad sweep of Canadian history, before the NPM movement began in the early 1980s, many scholarly writings and government reports were concerned with improving government service by such means as eliminating patronage, seeking efficiency and effectiveness, promoting responsiveness, and restructuring government. However, these writings and reports rarely highlighted service as the primary focus of analysis or as a major public service value. Indeed, there were few explicit references to the concepts of service and service delivery. Only over the past two decades has the call for improved service to citizens and clients become an central element of Canada's public administration dialogue.

A major exception to the low profile given to service during the TPA period was the report of the Glassco Royal Commission on Government Organization that was appointed in 1960 and charged with the responsibility of making recommendations to "promote efficiency, economy and improved service in the dispatch of public business" (Canada, 1965: vol. 1, 19). Using the term "responsiveness" in the sense of service to Canadians, the commission noted that while the values of integrity and efficiency were great, "even greater is the importance of a service responsive to public wants and expectations" (Canada, 1965: vol. 1, 27). The tone and recommendations of the commission's report foreshadowed the focus on improved service through a business-like approach that was central to the 1980s application of NPM principles to government. In a 2007 reminiscence on the role of Royal Commissions,

Hodgetts noted that "[p]erhaps the most lasting impact of the Glassco Commission was the introduction of the first wave of management consultant philosophy whereby managing government was seen to be just an enlarged version of management in the private sector" (2007: 3).

Another notable service delivery initiative during the TPA period was the creation of a task force on service to the public in 1977 and another one in 1978. The former took the form of a survey that was a precursor to the *Citizens First* surveys on Canadians' perception of service delivery that began in 1998. The latter took the form of a report that anticipated some of the service initiatives of the 1990s by suggesting such measures as a federal-provincial central telephone referral network to improve citizens' access to services and an emphasis on client service and satisfaction (Marson and Heintzman, forthcoming).

Aside from the Glassco Commission and task force reports, service improvement per se received little focused attention over the TPA period preceding the emergence of NPM. While service was not a high-profile theme of public administration during this period, it was a constant underlying objective of many public service reforms. Service became a much more central element of public administration discourse during the mid-1980s, in part as a result of NPM's widely publicized focus on improving government service.

NPM had much less influence on governments in Canada than in such countries as the United Kingdom and New Zealand, but it did foster a vigorous dialogue on improving government service by focusing on Canadians as "customers" and clients. In addition, many public organizations in Canada implemented ideas from two service improvement approaches that are often lumped under the broad banner of NPM, namely, total quality management (TQM) and service quality (SQ) (Kernaghan, Marson, and Borins, 2000: 132–140). The influence of the SQ movement, which involved such service improvement tools as customer surveys, service standards, and service quality plans, was reflected in the research studies and the final report of Public Service 2000 (Canada, 1990). This 1990 federal government white paper on public service renewal focused on improving service to the public. The report noted that service had been one of the "simple and unchanging" values of the public service since the early 1900s. It also announced the government's desire to create a client-oriented public service. This was described as "a major change since the Public Service has not been used to regarding Canadians as clients.... Members of the public have been looked upon more as recipients of service than as clients" (Canada, Public Service 2000, 1990: 51).

By the early 1990s, service had become widely viewed as a central public service value. A 1994 study showed that public organizations in Canada's federal and provincial governments considered service to be a high-priority public service value, ranking lower than only integrity, accountability/responsibility, and respect (Kernaghan, 1994: 620). In 2000 the federal government report on *Results for Canadians* (Canada, Treasury Board, 2000) committed the government to "focusing on citizens" as one of four areas of critical importance to a high-performing professional public service. More specifically, this report identified the key components of the government's service improvement plans for the early years of the new century.

> Government services must respond to the needs of citizens, be easy to find, and be available through the mail, by phone, on the Internet or—where populations warrant—at walk-in centres. Too often in the past, government services were designed from the 'inside out'; they reflected the structures of government organizations more than the needs and priorities of citizens. This is changing, and it will continue to change in the coming years.
>
> Citizens want the government to respond to their needs and provide choice: one-stop, integrated access via Internet, telephone or mail, or in person.
>
> Citizen-focused government is seamless. It is easy to deal with. Citizen-centred services are brought together in one place to facilitate client access.
>
> Information technology and electronic service are key enablers in meeting these challenges (Canada, Treasury Board, 2000: Section B).

From New Public Management to Integrated Public Governance

The periods of NPM and IPG have overlapped. The influence of NPM had waned considerably by the turn of the century, while the relative influence of IPG has increased steadily since about the mid-1990s. Certain features of NPM, notably its emphasis on service and the use of IT, are also manifest in IPG.

Canada's governments took a cautious, pragmatic, incremental approach to the implementation of NPM principles, including those related to service improvement. These governments were, however, sensitive to the public's desire for improved service and sought to satisfy this desire with an approach consisting of two major components: the use of alternative service delivery (ASD) mechanisms and a focus on citizen-centred service. ASD is widely viewed as a Canadian invention (Wilkins, 2003: 173). Among the many ASD mechanisms are special operating agencies, service agencies, public-private partnerships, contracting out for services, and ISD arrangements. The early focus of the NPM period on service to customers gradually gave way to a widespread emphasis on serving citizens. This usage reflects the realization that citizens can perform several roles in their relations with government, not only that of customer but also client, complier, captive, or claimant (Kernaghan, Marson, and Borins, 2000: 127).

During the NPM period, an international emphasis in the public sector on the theory and practice of "governance" emerged (Rhodes, 1997). The term "governance" is defined here as the institutions, structures, and processes through which power, influence, and authority are exercised, including decision-making processes, i.e., who participates and how. When applied to the public sector, it includes the notion of participation in government decision-making by a broad range of actors, both within government and in civil society. ASD and citizen-centred service are linked to the concept of governance as well as to one another. A widely cited definition of ASD is that it is "a creative and dynamic process of public sector restructuring that improves the delivery of services to clients by sharing governance functions with individuals, community groups and other government entities" (Ford and Zussman, 1997: 7).

Several developments that began in the mid-1990s fostered gradual movement toward IPG. Especially notable was the greatly increased emphasis on the horizontal dimension of government, including increased concern about the interdepartmental and intergovernmental aspects of policy development and implementation. Central to effective implementation was greatly increased emphasis on improving service delivery. A key influence here was the 1996 report of the Deputy Minister Task Force on Service Delivery Models that called for a citizen-centred approach to service delivery, for service integration, and for citizen participation in the design and delivery of services. The task force also observed that "not all 'services' delivered by government can be managed simply by borrowing best practices from the business community" (1996: 20).

Several other developments over the next five years greatly advanced the cause of improved service delivery in general and ISD in particular (Marson, 2008; Marson and Heintzman, forthcoming). The Citizen-Centred Service Network (now the Public Sector Service Delivery Council) (PSSDC), a community of practice established in 1997, collaborated with the Canadian Centre for Management Development (now the Canada School of Public Service) to carry out a research program that significantly informed service improvement decisions.[3] The PSSDC, in concert with the Public Sector Chief Information Officers' Council (PSCIOC), created in 1998, continues to champion service improvement at all levels of government.

During this period, the federal government also adopted a three-part strategy to improve service delivery through

1. the creation in 1999 of Government On-Line (GOL) with the aim of using IT to provide high-level service to citizens;[4]
2. the Service Improvement Initiative (SII), approved by the Treasury Board in 2000 for the purposes, among other things, of adopting a continuous improvement planning and implementation approach to service improvement and

client satisfaction, setting service standards for each delivery channel, and bringing about a 10 percent increase in client satisfaction with federal government services by 2005; and

3. the creation in 1999 of an early version of Service Canada in the form of a pilot project that included in-person access centres in government buildings across the country, a one-stop telephone call centre (1-800-O-CANADA), and the Canada Site Internet portal (http://www.canada.gc.ca) that had gone online in 1995.

The following brief comments on the implementation of these three initiatives illustrate the federal government's progress in improving service delivery in general and ISD in particular.

In its final report in 2006, GOL claimed several achievements, including "making the Canadian government the world's most connected country to its citizens" (Canada, Government On-Line). More specifically, GOL was reported to have allowed departments and agencies to

- accelerate the design and on-line delivery of 130 of the most commonly used services;
- fundamentally rethink how they used the e-channel to provide information and services to clients;
- collaborate to offer "no wrong door" access to government services;
- share experiences, approaches, learning, and tools while becoming more client-centric; and
- build a secure and robust electronic infrastructure capable of expanding to support steadily more sophisticated online transactions in the future. (Canada Government On-Line, 2006)

Like GOL, SII wrapped up its operations in 2006, having contributed substantially to improved service delivery and to laying a solid foundation for further improvement. Especially notable was SII's success in meeting its original objective of a 10 percent increase in client satisfaction with federal government services. The *Citizens First* surveys show the percentage of Canadians who reported satisfaction with federal government service rose by more than 10 percent between 1998 and 2005.

Service Canada was officially established in 2005. It is an extraordinarily large and ambitious single-window initiative designed to provide seamless service to Canadians through a multichannel and multijurisdictional network. To enhance service delivery, Service Canada partners not only with more than a dozen federal departments and agencies but also with other jurisdictions and nongovernmental organizations. It has encountered all the political, legal, structural, operational, managerial, and cultural barriers associated with ISD initiatives (Flumian, Coe, and Kernaghan, 2007). Among the lessons Service Canada learned early on in its development was that "creating a culture of service excellence among employees is essential to successful service transformation," that "putting services on-line is just a first step towards the goal of integrated service delivery across channels, departments and jurisdictions," and that "the objectives of ISD initiatives can go beyond increased service satisfaction or cost savings to foster greater citizen trust and confidence in government" (Flumian, Coe, and Kernaghan, 2007: 567).

The four *Citizens First* national surveys provided important learning points about service improvement and, in particular, about ISD. The 1998 survey (Erin Research Inc.) showed that nearly all Canadians expect the same or better service from the public sector than from the private sector; that citizens rate their satisfaction with public services at a very similar level to that for private sector services; and that there are five drivers (e.g., timeliness, knowledge and competence, courtesy, fairness, and outcome) that account for most of the citizen satisfaction with public sector performance. The 2000 *Citizens First 2* survey (Erin Research Inc.) confirmed these findings and noted that the drivers of citizen satisfaction differ according to the delivery channel being used. The 2003 *Citizens First 3* survey (Erin Researsch Inc.) dealt with the provision of seamless service to citizens through the use of multiple service channels and suggested a causal link between citizens' perception of the quality of service delivery and their confidence in government. The 2005 *Citizens First 4* survey (Phase 5 Consulting Group) provided additional evidence of this link and took particular note of the challenge to seamless access to government services arising from citizens' concerns about the privacy and security of their personal information.

The 2003 and 2005 *Citizens First* surveys provided empirical data for the examination, by Heintzman and Marson, of the concept of a public sector service value chain (2005). They examined the links between: (1) the engagement (satisfaction and commitment) of public employees and client satisfaction, and (2) the satisfaction of clients with the public sector and their trust and confidence in government. They cited data from country studies, including *Citizens First* data from Canada, which appear to show a causal link "between service satisfaction and citizens' trust and confidence in individual public institutions and in government generally" (2005: 567).

INTEGRATED SERVICE DELIVERY

By putting into practice much of the learning gained from the *Citizens First* surveys and other research on service improvement, the federal government has earned substantial international recognition. The annual survey of e-government maturity conducted by the consulting company Accenture ranked Canada first in the world for five consecutive years (2001–2005) and in 2005 noted that "perhaps more than any other country, Canada has the foundations of leadership in customer service in place" (Accenture, 2005: 60). Accenture was especially impressed by Canada's progress towards ISD and noted, by way of example, the initiatives of Seniors Info and BizPal. Many of the ISD initiatives in Canada, while impressive, have focused on individual governments rather than interjurisdictional arrangements. Thus, the Accenture report urged Canada to speed up its implementation of the next stage of improved service delivery—seamless multijurisdictional service (Accenture 2005: 61).

Since the nature and evolution of ISD in Canada has been examined at length elsewhere (Borins et al., 2007), only a brief summary is provided here. While the origins of ISD can be traced back as far as the creation of British Columbia's government agents in 1858, the great majority of ISD initiatives have been adopted since the mid-1990s. In keeping with the general movement towards IPG, ISD arrangements have become much more numerous and sophisticated. There has been a gradual movement from an emphasis on interdepartmental ISD during the 1990s towards interjurisdictional initiatives and, to a much smaller extent, intersectoral ones during the first decade of the new century.

ISD initiatives vary greatly in size, organizational design, and governance arrangements. In terms of size, Service Canada and such provincial service agencies as Service BC and Service Ontario exemplify the "department store" model. Service Canada has more than twenty-two thousand employees providing a broad range of related and unrelated services on behalf of fourteen federal departments, and it is partnering with other governments and nongovernmental organizations to provide seamless multichannel service. Most ISD entities, however, are based on the "boutique" model, involving the delivery of a group of related services and ranging in size from the Canada Business Service Network to such initiatives as the Nova Scotia Business Registry.

ISD entities have taken a variety of organizational forms, thereby significantly increasing the array of ASD mechanisms. The entities involve varying degrees of integration—from colocations (e.g., federal and provincial services provided in the same building) to "service utilities" that provide services on behalf of other departments and agencies. These service utilities can take such forms as a public corporation in a single government (e.g., Service New Brunswick) to a not-for-profit organization run by a board composed of public servants from the federal and provincial governments, as well as nongovernmental partners (e.g., Canadian Tourism Commission).

ISD initiatives can face, with varying degrees of intensity, a formidable range of political, structural, operational, and other challenges. Not only the governance structure but also the initial governance agreement between the partners must be carefully crafted and revised over time to help meet these challenges (Borins et al., 2007: 123–124). Note that the challenge becomes greater as integration initiatives move from intradepartmental to interdepartmental ISD and then to interjurisdictional arrangements. Among the challenges posed by the latter are harmonizing conflicting policies, rules, and standards across governments.

An issue that cuts across several of these types of challenges is that of privacy and security. The success of many ISD initiatives and the prospects for their greater integration and rationalization (e.g., bringing business-related ISD entities under one roof) depends on the sharing of personal information across departments and governments. Similarly, progress towards integration of systems and processes in the "back offices" of ISD entities, rather than just at the level of the computer screen or at the front counter, requires substantial information-sharing between ISD partners (departments, governments, sectors). Yet, *Citizens First 4* shows that Canadians have strong privacy and security concerns about dealing with governments online (Phase 5 Consulting Group, 2005). Overcoming these concerns through an effective identity management and authentication (IM&A) system is a challenge of considerable magnitude, even within a single government where departments often have different IM&A systems. The challenge is truly formidable in the interjurisdictional sphere, where a pan-Canadian system, involving all three levels of government, is required.

INTEGRATED CHANNEL DELIVERY

The provision of multiple service channels has greatly improved citizen access to government services. Most of the services that have traditionally been provided through the regular mail and through visits and telephone calls to government offices are now available through electronic mail and government websites, in-person service centres, and telephone call centres. For example, the Canada Business Service Network offers several "service delivery modes," including the telephone, the Web, e-mail, in-person, and a feature called "Talk to Us" that connects the user by voice to an employee who helps the user search the Internet for the information he or she needs.

The challenge is not simply to provide a broad range of government services through multiple channels but also to integrate the channels. Integrated channel delivery (ICD) is the result of joining up the major service delivery channels (e.g., Internet, telephone, walk-in service centres) to provide seamless service to citizens and create cost savings. The fact that one-half of Canadians already use two or more channels when seeking government services argues for channel rationalization and convergence.

While much of the focus of improved service delivery has been on exploiting the Internet channel, *Citizens First* research has shown that the telephone is both the most popular service channel and is ranked the lowest in citizen satisfaction. Governments have responded in part with one-stop telephone call centres (e.g., 1-800-O-CANADA). The 311 telephone system is especially notable. Beginning with Baltimore, Maryland, in 1996, 311 systems have been adopted in several municipalities, including Calgary, Gatineau, Halton, Ottawa, and Windsor in Canada. These municipalities have consolidated their many telephone numbers into call centres, so citizens can simply dial 311 to access nonemergency government services around the clock. Among the benefits of 311 systems are improved convenience, better quality service, the freeing up of 911 systems from nonemergency calls, and enhanced transparency and accountability. Among concerns about the 311 approach are diminished privacy, caller confusion (911 versus 311), and technological challenges (Borins et al., 2007: 144–152).

The impediments to ICD are very similar to those for service delivery in general. There are, for example, important political, managerial, and operational considerations involved in ensuring that all citizens, including the elderly, the poor, and the disabled, have equitable access to government services. Governments have to seek a balance between providing all citizens with a choice of channels and persuading them to migrate to the less costly self-help channels (Internet and telephone interactive voice response).

ON THE ROAD TO TRANSFORMATION

During the first decade of what has been described in this chapter as the IPG period in the evolution of public administration and management, governments at all levels in Canada have made considerable progress towards the integration of service delivery. The emphasis moved from intradepartmental ISD to interdepartmental ISD during the 1990s, and this has been complemented in the 2000s by the more active pursuit of integration across jurisdictions and channels. This movement has been accompanied by the development of new service delivery models, beginning with simple colocations and moving to more innovative and integrated arrangements such as not-for-profit service utilities.

Canadian achievements in ISD are at the cutting edge of what is often described as a transformation in the delivery of government services. Shown below is a framework composed of six benefits for assessing the transformative potential of information and communication technologies (ICTs) on public administration reform in general and the relations of governments with citizens and clients (Culbertson, 2004). This framework makes clear that the transformation of service delivery through ISD is tightly tied to the overall transformation of service delivery.

- Advanced networking power enabling the integration of information and data and a sharing of business processes and systems among governmental organizations—eliminating redundancies and saving resources
- The ability to reinvent organizations based on a primary focus of seamless service to the citizen—not dictated or prescribed by the organizational boundaries of the agencies responsible for these services
- More accessible and up-to-date services—the ability to provide current information instantaneously without having to incur publishing and distribution costs; the ability to serve citizens and clients at their convenience on a '24/7' basis
- The potential for simplified business processes and citizen/client self-service in e-government applications—reducing

costs and increasing efficiency of both government and client
- A quicker response time—the ability to connect instantly with a broad range of clients and solicit their input/feedback on proposed changes
- The advancement of key good governance goals, including enhanced accountability and openness, citizen/client participation, and a focus on effectiveness and responsiveness (Culbertson, 2004: 60–61)

ISD initiatives are contributing to the realization of these benefits, especially those relating to the integration of data, the provision of seamless service, improved access to services, and increased efficiency. In addition, these initiatives are helping to promote good governance in terms of the key public service values of effectiveness and responsiveness.

Governments should only pursue ISD if a careful consideration of the challenges and remedies discussed in this chapter suggests that significant benefits are likely to result. There are many instances in which joining up services and service channels is not desirable or feasible. For example, a government may reject integration of service transactions with other governments if this involves reduced control over the level of fees to be charged. And citizen-government transactions involving sensitive legal documents or requiring negotiation are better handled in government offices than through other modes of service delivery.

The state of government service delivery now, compared to the time of Hodgetts's 1955 article, will appear to many observers to constitute a transformation, especially as a result of ISD. However, ISD has not yet realized its transformative potential. E-government is often conceptualized as a multistage process of development that begins with the placing of government information online and then moves to a second stage of interactions between citizens and government (e.g., downloadable tax forms), followed by a third stage of citizen-government transactions (e.g., licence renewals), and finally moves on to the fourth and most challenging stage of providing ISD across departments, jurisdictions, sectors, and channels. While Canada's governments are operating primarily at the third stage, several of them are making progress towards the fourth stage. Success at this stage depends on much more than progress in e-government. It requires organizational restructuring and the harmonization of such factors as services, programs, and rules across departments and jurisdictions.

Fountain, in *Building the Virtual State*, notes that "web-based efforts at integration ... reveal the 'cracks' in the machinery of the bureaucratic state: the extent of fragmentation and lack of fit among programs, data measures, information, rules, and services in government" (2001: 202). In the Canadian context, attention has been drawn to the development of portals, like Seniors Canada On-Line, that expose "the fragmented, disorderly state of [governments'] policies, regulations, programs and services" and to the need "to take a more holistic approach to policy and program delivery" (Crossing Boundaries Canada 2020 Working Group, 2007: 110).

The expansion and effectiveness of ISD arrangements will depend to a large extent on governments' commitment to the integration of public governance more broadly, including integration at the level of policies and programs. To some extent, effective ISD depends on technological innovations such as the Internet telephone that promote channel convergence. As explained above, however, the most daunting challenges to ISD are not technological. They are political, legal, structural, operational, managerial, and cultural. Further movement towards the transformation of government service delivery will require sustained efforts to craft innovative solutions to these challenges.

NOTES

[1]   The briefer term, "integrated governance," has been used by the Institute of Public Administration Australia (2002).

[2]   This section is drawn in part from Kernaghan (forthcoming).

[3]   See Dinsdale and Marson (1999); Blythe and Marson (1999); Bent, Kernaghan, and Marson (1999); and Schmidt and Strickland (1999).

[4]   For a comprehensive examination of GOL, see Brown (2007).

REFERENCES

6, Perri, et al. (2002). *Towards Holistic Governance: The New Agenda in Government Reform.* Basingstoke, UK: Palgrave.

Accenture. (2005). *Leadership in Customer Service: New Expectations, New Experiences.* <http://www.accenture.com/Global/Research_and_Insights/By_Industry/Government/LeadershipExperiences.htm>.

Bent, Stephen, Kenneth Kernaghan, and D. Brian Marson. (1999). *Innovations and Good Practices in Single-Window Service.* Ottawa: Canadian Centre for Management Development.

Blythe, Marie, and D. Brian Marson. (1999). *Good Practices in Citizen-Centred Service.* Ottawa: Canadian Centre for Management Development.

Borins, Sandford. (2002). "Transformation of the Public Sector: Canada in Comparative Perspective." In *Handbook of Canadian Public Administration*, edited by Christopher Dunn. Toronto: Oxford University Press.

Borins, Sandford, et al. (2007). *Digital State at the Leading Edge.* Toronto: University of Toronto Press.

Bourgault, Jacques. (2007). "Corporate Management at Top Level of Governments: The Canadian Case." *International Review of Administrative Sciences.* 73: 2: 257–274.

Brown, David. (2007). "The Government of Canada. Government On-Line and Citizen-Centred Service." In *Digital State at the Leading Edge*, edited by Sandford Borins et al., 37–68. Toronto: University of Toronto Press.

Canada, Deputy Minister Task Force on Service Delivery Models. (1996). *Discussion Paper on Service Delivery Models.* <http://www.myschool-monecole.gc.ca/Research/publications/pdfs/srdel1.pdf>.

Canada, Government On-Line. (2006). *Government On-Line 2006: Executive Summary.* <http://www.gol-ged.gc.ca/rpt2006/rpt/rpt04_e.asp>.

Canada, Public Service 2000. (1990). *The Renewal of the Public Service of Canada.* Ottawa: Minister of Government Services.

Canada, Royal Commission on Government Organization (Glassco Commission). (1965). *Report,* vol. 1. Ottawa: Queen's Printer.

Canada, Treasury Board. (2000). *Results for Canadians: A Management Framework for the Government of Canada.* <http://www.tbs-sct.gc.ca/report/res_can/rc-PR_e.asp?printable=True>.

Crossing Boundaries Canada 2020 Working Group (Don Lenihan, Tim Barber, Graham Fox, and John Milloy). (2007). *Progressive Governance for Canadians: What You Need to Know.* <http://www.crossingboundaries.ca/files/progresssivegovernancecbnc.pdf>.

Culbertson, Stuart. (2004). "Building E-Government: Organisational and Cultural Change in Public Administration." In *E-Government Reconsidered,*

        edited by E. Lynn Oliver and Larry Sanders. Regina: Canadian Plains
        Research Centre, University of Regina.
Dinsdale, Geoff, and D. Brian Marson. (1999). *Citizen/Client Surveys: Dispelling
        Myths and Redrawing Maps*. Ottawa: Canadian Centre for Management
        Development.
Erin Research Inc. (1998). *Citizens First*. For the Citizen-Centred Network and
        the Canadian Centre for Management Development. Ottawa: Canadian
        Centre for Management Development.
————. (2000). *Citizens First 2*. For the Public Sector Service Delivery Council
        and the Institute of Public Administration of Canada. Toronto: Institute
        of Public Administration of Canada.
————. (2003). *Citizens First 3*. For the Institute for Citizen-Centred Service
        and the Institute of Public Administration of Canada. Toronto: Institute
        of Public Administration of Canada.
Flumian, Maryantonett, Amanda Coe, and Kenneth Kernaghan. (2007).
        "Transforming Service to Canadians: The Service Canada Model."
        International Review of Administrative Sciences. 73: 4: 557–568.
Ford, Robin and David Zussman, eds. (1997). *Alternative Service Delivery:
        Sharing Governance in Canada*. Toronto: KPMG Centre for Government
        Foundation and Institute of Public Administration of Canada.
Fountain, Jane. (2001). *Building the Virtual State: Information Technology and
        Institutional Change*. Washington, DC: The Brookings Institution.
Heintzman, Ralph, and Brian Marson. (2005). "People, Service, and Trust:
        Is There a Public Sector Service Value Chain? *International Review of
        Administrative Sciences*. 71: 4: 549–575.
Hodgetts, J. E. (1955). "The Liberal and the Bureaucrat: A Rose by Any Other
        Name." *Queen's Quarterly*. 62: 176–183.
————. (1973). *The Canadian Public Service: A Physiology of Government,
        1867–1970*. Toronto: University of Toronto Press.
————. (2007). "Royal Commissions and Public Service Reform: A Personal
        Memoir." *Canadian Public Administration*. 50: 4: 1–12.
Institute of Public Administration Australia. (2002). *Working Together—
        Integrated Governance*. <http://www.ipaa.org.au/_dbase_upl/national_
        research_final.pdf>.
Kernaghan, Kenneth. (1993). "Partnership and Public Administration:
        Conceptual and Practical Considerations." *Canadian Public Administration*.
        36: 1: 57–76.
————. (1994). "The Emerging Public Service Culture: Values, Ethics, and
        Reforms." *Canadian Public Administration*. 37: 4: 614–630.
————. (2008). *Integrating Service Delivery: Barriers and Benchmarks*. Toronto:
        Institute for Citizen-Centred Service.

Kernaghan, Kenneth, Brian Marson, and Sandford Borins. (2000). *The New Public Organization*. Toronto: Institute of Public Administration of Canada.

Lindquist, Evert. (2006). *A Critical Moment: Capturing and Conveying the Evolution of the Canadian Public Service*. Ottawa: Canada School of Public Service. <http://www.myschool-monecole.gc.ca/Research/publications/html/p134/3_e.html>.

Marson, Brian. (2008). "Citizen-Centred Service in Canada: From Research to Results." In *Professionalism and Public Service: Essays in Honour of Kenneth Kernaghan*, edited by David Siegel and Ken Rasmussen. Toronto: University of Toronto Press.

Marson, Brian, and Ralph Heintzman. (Forthcoming). "From Research to Results: A Decade of Results-Based Service Improvement in Canada." Toronto: Institute of Public Administration of Canada, "New Directions" Series.

Phase 5 Consulting Group for the Institute for Citizen-Centred Service and the Institute of Public Administration of Canada. (2005). *Citizens First 4*. Toronto: Institute of Public Administration of Canada.

Rhodes, R. A. W. (1997). *Understanding Governance: Policy Networks, Governance, Reflexivity and Accountability*. Buckingham, UK: Open University Press.

Schmidt, Faye, and Teresa Strickland. (1999). *Client Satisfaction Surveying: A Common Measurements Tool (CMT)*. Ottawa: Canadian Centre for Management Development.

Wilkins, John K. (2003). "Conceptual and Practical Considerations in Alternative Service Delivery." *International Review of Administrative Sciences*. 69: 2: 173–189.

III THE STATE OF THE DISCIPLINE: FUTURE CHALLENGES IN ADMINISTRATION AND GOVERNANCE

10 AMERICAN PERSPECTIVES ON CANADIAN PUBLIC ADMINISTRATION

Keith Henderson

Canadian public administration scholars have long been aware of the relevance of the American discipline and profession of public administration. Hodgetts studied in the United States—under L. D. White—and alludes to American influences on Canadian practice in his writings. In his epic *Biography of an Institution* (Hodgetts et al., 1972), for example, he discusses the 1918–1919 reforms of the Canadian Civil Service Commission in relation to scientific management as developed in the United States: "Founded on scientific management originating in the United States, these precepts became the decisive influences on Canadian ideas and practices, just at their most formative stage. Thus the moral fervour behind civil service reform was reinforced by the 'rational' and 'objective' respectability claimed for the scientific management ideas imported from across the border" (Hodgetts et al., 1972: 60).

The purpose of this chapter is to present American perspectives on Canadian public administration by showing their commonalities, interrelationships, and influences. The discussion is divided into three parts: a brief outsider's view of the Canadian study of public administration using Canadian sources; the American[1] counterpoint, emphasizing similar but earlier developments; and a simultaneous movement—mirrored in other countries—from the excesses of new public management (NPM) towards a governance paradigm (GP). Canada's special relationship with the United States—both being major trading partners astride the world's longest undefended border—and the numerous interactions involving administrative issues between the two countries makes this a useful quest. Common interests and orientations; various joint efforts in security, resource management, immigration, energy, environment, and other arenas; economic and political alliances, agreements, treaties, and understandings—including the North American Free Trade Agreement (NAFTA) and the North Atlantic Treaty Organization (NATO)—and cultural/social linkages provide a unique interrelationship between these two Western democracies. Within the broader context, the discipline/profession of public administration in both countries has addressed similar concerns about its proper role, the importance of policy analysis and generic management in contrast to traditional public administration, and its participation in the broader worldwide public administration community.

Clearly, the shorter time frame for Canadian study, the parliamentary institutional context, the difference in scale, the French tradition centred in Quebec but also evident in bilingualism, and other factors provide distinct differences with the United States. The "positive state" (welfare state) orientation in Canada—involving a proportionately more extensive public sector—is another difference between the two countries. Dwivedi and Wilson note that Canadians have been more comfortable with big government than Americans: "Thus while Americans have extensively debated the advent and nature of their administrative state, in contrast Canadians have been less concerned about their ubiquitous government" (Wilson and Dwivedi, 1981: 12).

CANADIAN ADMINISTRATIVE STUDY

Like their counterparts in the United States, concerned Canadians in the middle and late nineteenth century began to question the quality of their administrative system in its political context. The United Kingdom had taken a major step against patronage with the Northcote-Trevelyan reforms of 1854–1855, and the result was widely visible. In Canada, arguments for patronage included its necessity for building a party system and maintaining full control by ministers—the people's elected representatives—of the bureaucracy (Hodgetts et al., 1972: 14–15). However, several early Canadian government reports called attention to the need for qualified civil servants and rational delivery structures. Rasmussen (2007) mentions a report in 1869 by John Langton, Canada's first Auditor General, noting that existing conditions were discouraging young men of ability from entering the public service: "Thus the very earliest arguments favoring the reform of the public service were based on a desire to see the public service become a profession dedicated to efficient, effective, and 'businesslike' public administration" (Rasmussen 2007: 8).

Nevertheless, the academic discipline/profession of public administration did not take root until well into the twentieth century. One of Hodgetts's mentors—Robert MacGregor Dawson—had written a doctoral thesis at the London School of Economics that was supervised by the widely respected political theorist and reformer Graham Wallas. Dawson took issue with the traditional doctrine of ministerial responsibility, arguing for the "principle of official independence," and suggested that modern experience has confirmed the use of skilled officials as an essential condition of a democracy's existence (Dawson, 1922). Later, Dawson published *The Civil Service of Canada*, showing the need for the Canadian public service to be reformed following the British example (Dawson, 1929). These two works mark the beginning of the academic pursuit of public administration in Canada, and personnel administration became the cornerstone of serious study of the field.

Associated with the new attention to improving public administration was a quest for suitable staff for the reformed civil service. The United States and other Western democracies had created or were contemplating academic programs; why not Canada? Degree programs were established at Dalhousie University in 1936 and Carleton University (Carleton College) in 1946. These two institutions—with their distinctive approaches to the study—set the tone for subsequent scholarship and program development. Carleton now has a School of Public Policy and Administration (2007) and recently revised its master's degree curriculum with a common core of seven courses for all students. Today, Dalhousie defines public administration as the overarching rubric under which management and policy are subsumed and includes the not-for-profit sector(s): "Public administration is the profession of those employed in government, the not-for-profit sectors, and the academic study of these sectors. Public policy and management are the two major elements of public administration. The School believes its graduates must understand and be able to practice both elements." (Dalhousie University Faculty of Management—Graduate Programs, 2007). Dalhousie has also recently revamped its master's of public administration (M.P.A.) program.

Interestingly, Pross and Wilson noted in 1976 that the rise of academic public administration in Canada was heavily influenced by the United States. They also acknowledge British influences on Canadian administrative thought, but they find American influences pervasive. One could, of course, debate the relative significance of the United States as opposed to Britain as models. Also influential in Canada were the general administration thinkers such as Max Weber, F. W. Taylor, and Luther Gulick and Lyndall Urwick. Kernaghan and Siegel, in their book, *Public Administration in Canada*, devote their third chapter to these contributors (1995).

In Canada, as elsewhere, public administration has not been a field with high consensus among academics. Indeed, disputes continue as to whether it is a discipline, subdiscipline, or multidiscipline; its methodologies, its "practical" nature, and its relationship to policy-oriented political science. The Dalhousie definition cited above is by no means universally accepted throughout Canada.

Public administration's relationship with political science is worth exploring. In Canada, political science was dominant, as even the faculty in schools of public administration not directly affiliated with political science usually had their training in that discipline: "It is this essential political element (rooting in the political environment) which makes the policy/management approach in Canada and the so-called 'public affairs' programs in the United States somewhat similar" (Pross and Wilson, 1976: 521). Canadian interpreters of the development of Canadian public administration also recognized that in the post-war years—when critique of traditional approaches as well as behaviour science findings gained prominence—it was embracing the fields of sociology, psychology, and business administration. Those trying to bridge the gap between political science/policy and generic administration were presented with a dilemma. "This massive infusion of behaviouralism, while providing a host of insights and intellectual stimulation to students in public administration, left in its wake a number of contradictions and unexplained aspects of reality" (Pross and Wilson, 1976: 519).

Further complicating the picture was the role of political economy. Pross and Wilson believed that Canadian political scientists—of whom there were few at the time—were preoccupied with avoiding excessive influence by economics, particularly political economy. Smiley—who they quoted—had earlier suggested that Canadian public problems nearly always present themselves with both political and economic aspects and economists could therefore claim this as their terrain (Smiley, 1967). Nevertheless, political science remained dominant in the 1950s, 1960s, and 1970s.

The post-war period saw enormous contributions to the Canadian study of public administration. Hodgetts—sometimes in collaboration with others—produced a prodigious volume of research in the years from 1945 onward. His books, from 1956 to 1974, consisted of eight volumes, supplemented by forty to fifty articles and book chapters (Hodgetts, 1956; Hodgetts and Corry, 1959; Hodgetts and Corbett, 1960; 1964; 1966; Hodgetts et al., 1972; 1973; Hodgetts and Dwivedi, 1974). Kernaghan and Siegel indicate that the study of public administration really began to flourish in the late 1960s: "Indeed, the progress in the study of Canadian public administration since 1970, as measured by research, publications, teachers, and programs, has been greater than in all the preceding years combined" (1995: 11). They relate this to the growth of federal, provincial, and municipal governments, as well as to expansions in Canadian higher education, which made more resources available for teaching and research. Undoubtedly, the contributions of Hodgetts and others were influential.

A unique feature of Canadian public administration is the francophone tradition centred in the province of Quebec, where the French language, legal environment, and culture, along with some separatist sentiment colour the teaching and practice of public administration. Dufour has carefully documented forty years of public sector education in Quebec in the context of Quebec politics and political management. She indicates that concern for public administration education developed in the early 1960s as the province was entering its Quiet Revolution under a Liberal government implementing a new expanded role for the state. Premier Jean Lesage began a re-examination of administrative institutions, resulting in budgetary and organizational changes, part of which were focused on training public administrators (Dufour, 2002; 2007). In his commentary on Dufour's work, Phidd discussed the strong emphasis on public policy in the Quebec experience and noted the 1993 reform in Quebec public administration as being inspired by the American experience (Phidd, 2007).

Following the French model, the Université du Québec established its own École nationale d'administration publique (ÉNAP) but relied on American ideas as well (Dufour, 2007: 10). The Université Laval increasingly recruited faculty from the United States rather than France beginning at the turn of the 1970s, when eight of the eleven professors hired between 1967 and 1975 had American graduate degrees. ÉNAP revealed its interest in reaching out to the larger worldwide enterprise of public administration in an international conference in 1979 that brought top-level public administrationists from around the world—with French experts like Michael Crozier much in evidence—for 123 sessions that resulted in a comprehensive twelve-volume publication of the conference proceedings (ÉNAP, 1979).

In the early 1970s, an organization known as the Committee of Schools and Programs in Public Administration (CSPPA) sought to exchange ideas and information, as well as to improve ties to the federal government. Governments wanted M.P.A. graduates who had the potential to be skilled managers rather than narrow specialists; academicians wanted acceptance of the M.P.A. as an important qualification for public sector employment. The Institute of Public

Administration of Canada (IPAC) had been established as far back as 1947 to bring together public servants, academics, and others interested in public administration. CSPPA came under the aegis of IPAC in a close working relationship; along with a separate organization (Association of Graduate Programs in Public Administration), it evolved into the present Canadian Association of Programs in Public Administration (CAPPA) in 1987. Unlike its counterpart in the United States (the National Association of Schools of Public Affairs and Administration [NASPAA]), it has only recently begun an accreditation process for master's degree–level programs.

The environment for administrative study throughout Canada changed dramatically in the 1980s and 1990s:

> As a result of persistent deficits, public services throughout Canada were downsizing by means of voluntary replacement packages, occasional layoffs, and hiring freezes. This reduced the demand for public administration graduates, and called into question the raison d'etre of the professional programs. In addition, the ascendance of conservative governments reflected a public distrust of big government, bureaucracy, and public servants, and, conversely, a public glorification of the business sector. (CAPPA, 2007: 5)

As Savoie (1994) and others have pointed out, this environment was common to Canada, the United Kingdom, and the United States, although with distinctive characteristics in each location. The Thatcher, Reagan, and Mulroney era marked a paradigm shift from government as problem-solver to government as hindrance (in contrast to the much-admired private sector), because of its increasing size, procedural complexities, intrusiveness into the economy and society, and tax burden. In Canada, of course, Brian Mulroney was prime minister from 1984 to mid-1993, followed briefly by fellow Conservative Kim Campbell. They were succeeded by a Liberal government less intent on the "bureaucrat bashing" agenda. The transition from the Mulroney-Campbell period, however, continued some of the innovation and entrepreneurship within the public sector, with awareness of the "Next Steps" program in the United Kingdom, and "Reinventing Government"—under Vice President Al Gore—in the United States.

A shift in academic thinking accompanied (and sometimes aided and abetted) these "real world" developments and much of it came to be called NPM. As is well known, New Zealand and Australia were early laboratories for NPM and the news of institutional change spread to all corners of the world as Thatcher in the United Kingdom and Reagan in the United States began downsizing and privatizing with an announced negative view of the bureaucracy. As is also well known, reactions to the ideology and implications of NPM were often unfavourable in the academic community, and a large evaluative literature developed. Of primary concern was the loss of democratic values in the quest for empowerment, innovation, entrepreneurship, and customer satisfaction based on the business model.

Currently in Canada, again under a Conservative (but minority) government, there is attention paid in both the academic and practitioner communities to reform and clarify the proper role of the public sector. Enviably—from a US perspective—close relations continue between the academic community and the world of practitioners, with ongoing meetings, study groups, and miniconferences, many of them under the aegis of IPAC. The government-run Canada School of Public Service, which reports to the president of the Treasury Board through a board of governors made up of members from the public and private sectors, sponsors fellows from the academic community. It offers classroom courses, leadership development programs, publications, and language training for the acquirement of a second language. This provides a model (absent the language training) for the United States to consider as an ongoing debate concerning a federal government–sponsored public administration school continues. At present, there is only a low-profile National Academy of Public Administration.

Importantly, ten years ago, the clerk of the Privy Council, Jocelyne Bourgon, who had links to academia, created an initiative to revitalize the public service at the time she became president of the Canadian Centre for Management Development (now the above-mentioned Canada School of Public Service), and suggested a similar initiative that would revitalize the academic community. In 2003, responding to that suggestion as part of its Governance Research Program, the Canada School of Public Service authorized the study of a "Canadian model" of public administration, which was then developed by Gow and widely disseminated. Gow extensively reviewed the literature and identified the core elements and context in which the Canadian model has evolved. He pointed to the enviable reputation of Canada's public service for quality, competence, and autonomy. One hundred and forty-four references are included in his "Canadian model," providing a good overview of the literature (Gow, 2004). Canada—it might be argued—has joined in the public management revolution and moved towards a governance model based on fundamental Canadian values such as social fairness and redistribution policies, and a professional nonpartisan public service. "The 'Canadian model' seeks a balance between the virtues of traditional bureaucracy on the one hand, and entrepreneurship and innovation on the other" (Cochrane, 2004).

As for academic public administration (along with "public policy") in Canada, it is now in a growth phase. New schools have been established or will soon be established at Simon Fraser University, the University of Waterloo, York University, the University of Toronto, Ryerson University, and the University of Ottawa. Some established programs have also been revamped.

THE AMERICAN COUNTERPOINT

Preceding Canadian public administration, coexisting with it for many years, and influencing it is American public administration. The same debate has existed in the United States as to how the discipline/ profession of public administration should focus its efforts, and how it can appropriately pursue study and education for the public service, but for the early years, there are well-established landmarks. Although some American scholars reference the Federalist Papers and the Founding Fathers' reflections on the proper nature of public service, the academic enterprise is conventionally dated from Woodrow Wilson's essay "The Study of Administration" in 1887. Wilson set the stage for the "politics-administration dichotomy" discussed by Frank Goodnow in 1900 and in the first textbooks by White (1955 [1926]) and Willoughby (1927). According to White, "Defined in broadest terms, *public administration consists of all those operations having for their purpose the fulfillment or enforcement of public policy*" (White, 1955 [1926]: 1). White—it might be noted—had previously published *The Civil Service in the Modern State, A Collection of Documents*, which included a chapter on the civil service of Canada (White, 1920). Eighty-three years later, an Australian, Halligan, contributed *Civil Service Systems in Anglo-American Countries*, also with the prominent inclusion of Canada (Halligan, 2003).

The civil service and its quality became an even more important issue in political discussion, along with the expansion of the concept of merit as the best criterion for the selection of officials. However, formal education and training for the public service did not begin until an academic degree program was first established in 1924 at Syracuse University's Maxwell School, which was followed five years later in 1929 with the creation of a program at the University of Southern California. The former—then and now—was labelled "Citizenship and Public Affairs," reflecting its broad public interest mission and the latter—until recently—"Graduate School of Public Administration."

A second line of development in the United States during the 1920s and 1930s from which business administration also derived—and similarly incorporated in academic programs—was general (or generic) administration. Max Weber, Frederick W. Taylor, and Henri Fayol are prominent in this regard and, curiously, only Taylor was American. Gulick and Urwick's famous *Papers on the Science of Administration*— one of the most widely cited sources on the pre–World War II study of administration—includes a chapter by French industrialist Fayol (Gulick and Urwick, 1937).

Meanwhile, political science provided a sympathetic home to public administration in a short-lived ascendancy, which gave way to other approaches after World War II. Bureaus of municipal research were established, reform efforts were undertaken in close consultation with top administrators, and "principles of administration" were widely discussed. Prominent public administrationists, including Gulick, were included in President Franklin Roosevelt's 1937 Committee on Administrative Management, also known as the Brownlow Committee for its chairman, Louis Brownlow.

As in Canada and elsewhere, World War II marked a turning point for public administration study in the United States. The change was slow, beginning earlier with democratic leadership and voluntary cooperation as significant neglected variables, along with attention to cooperative social action. The *coup de grâce* was an assault on the principles of administration (Simon, 1947) and Waldo's convincing statements in *The Administrative State* (1948) that pre-war public administration was culture-bound and tied to unique economic, social, governmental, and ideological facts. Departure from pre-war writing was also evident in the first post-war textbook, which brought together fourteen political scientists for a "broadly political rather than merely technical study" (Marx, 1946).

The behavioural revolution, including Simon's stress on decision-making (1947) was complemented by the rejection of a politics-administration dichotomy and the focus on the politics of administration by political scientists. "Public policy" rose in prominence as "public administration" declined. A newer generation of political scientists was trained quantitatively and needed no real-world experience to gain credibility. As older faculty retired, died, or moved on, they took their place. By the 1960s, and President Lyndon Johnson's War on Poverty and Great Society programs, which required policy analysis to justify and, then, to measure success, traditional public administration emphasizing reform and problem-solving based on universal precepts and principles was largely replaced. On the behavioural side, a plethora of theories was developed—often tied to organization theory—and some empirically based studies were undertaken. Generic schools of management and administration proliferated, nearly always dominated by those interested in business.

In the years prior to the rise of NPM in the 1980s and 1990s, there were numerous specific American influences on Canadian public administration. Beginning with the studies of civil service reforms alluded to before and continuing through the post-war expansion era, administrative reforms were often undertaken in Canada with full knowledge of similar efforts in the United States. Clearly, the Westminster model was also influential, giving Canadians a double opportunity to view the debate and decision—as well as the early implementation of administrative reforms—on a variety of fronts. Hodgetts refers to the Civil Service Assembly of the United States and Canada (1906–1956) that aligned Canadian and American specialists. The assembly in the United States was closely related to the National Municipal League and the National Civil Service Reform League (Hodgetts et al., 1972: 60–62).

Post–World War II reform and reorganization in the United States reflected numerous studies and analyses, but the most conspicuous were the first and second Hoover Commission Reports (1949; 1955). These were influential for the Canadian Glassco Royal Commission appointed in 1960 to make recommendations on the public sector's efficiency, economy, and improved service delivery (Halligan, 2007: 3).

In the early 1960s, the Planning Programming Budgeting System (PPBS) was implemented in the US Defense Department and—by extension through an Executive Order in 1965—other departments. This system came to Canada in the 1970s with the introduction by the Treasury Board of the Operational Performance Measurement System (OPMS). The emergence of the management culture initiated by the Lambert Royal Commission also showed American influences.[2] Gow refers to fifteen Canadian innovations in the 1960s, 1970s, 1980s, and early 1990s, seven of which were influenced by the United States, including PPBS; zero-based budgeting (a successor to PPBS in the Carter presidency); affirmative action; the Freedom of Information Act; and others (Gow, 1994). The list might be extended for the years after 1994, with the experiences of the United States under the Government Performance and Results Act of 1993; various Reinventing Government developments; regulatory changes; and security/privacy policies added to the list. The latter, however, may arguably be given to Canadians for preferred policy direction in privacy protection (Bennett, 2003).

Indeed, there are numerous reciprocal Canadian influences on American public administration. Here is not the place to fully discuss this aspect of Canadian-American administrative relationships, but several areas are worth mentioning. Canadian health care and welfare policies continue as models for the numerous initiatives considered from time to time in the United States; integrated heath care delivery, national pharmacare, and daycare proposals are highly visible. In the United States, an active Association for Canadian Studies and various Canadian studies programs at major universities and colleges pay close attention to Canadian innovations.

In 2000 the Canadian federal government issued a report entitled *Results for Canadians*, emphasizing a citizen-focus as one critical area for a professional public service. Key components of a service improvement plan for the new century were identified (Canada, Treasury Board, 2000). This and the concurrent stress on results-oriented management—some aspects reflecting NPM thinking—are reciprocal in their influences. Service delivery systems, which sometimes seem to work better in Canada, include aspects of environmental management and conservation; transportation pricing; more uniform criminal justice practice; provincially directed regionalization and metropolitan consolidation; and other areas. Canadian innovations at both the federal and provincial levels have been examined by experts in other countries.

FROM NEW PUBLIC MANAGEMENT TO THE GOVERNANCE PARADIGM

When "bureaucrat bashing" by political leaders became the norm (in the 1980s and onward), and hiring freezes, buyout inducements, and widespread contracting out were instituted, attention in both the United States and Canada shifted to issues of downsizing, privatizing, and reordering public services. Various studies discussed "cutback management" under a slower rate of government expansion and the implications for citizens and public officials. NPM extolled business models and a culture of entrepreneurship, "reinvented" government, and relaxed civil service rules. It encouraged contracting out if not outright privatization of public programs. Light carefully documented the shift in the United States to contracted programs (Light, 1999a; 1999b), and Suleiman lamented the virtual privatization of Homeland Security (Suleiman, 2003: 2). From the standpoint of many civil servants, setbacks for civil service protection (particularly in the Homeland Security and Defense departments), morale, and due process have been characteristics of the George W. Bush presidency.

Although it is too early to tell, NPM may have exhausted its opportunities and become subordinate to GP in Western countries. Certainly, scandals in the corporate world (Enron, Worldcom, etc.) compromised the reputation of the business sector in the United States. Additionally, considerable attention since 9/11 has been given to the crucial role of government in combating terrorism. Other stakeholders have become aligned with the federal government in networks, partnerships, and cooperative arrangements. The current thrust requires a rethinking of administrative institutions, personnel, and processes, and attention to the implications for service delivery of a less hierarchical more networked pattern grounded in information technology (Agranoff, 2007; Borins, 2007). Illustrative of the GP approach in the United States, Kettl proposes ten new strategies for problem-solving (Kettl, 2002), and Salamon (2002) suggests a paradigm entitled "new governance," stressing network management. Canadian scholars, along with those in other Commonwealth countries, as well as Holland, Israel, France, Germany, Scandinavia, and elsewhere, have also made significant contributions to the understanding of governance as they have in the past to the nation-specific or overall study of administration in the public sphere.

In Canada recent contributions on governance include Restakis and Lindquist's edited volume (2001), Aucoin's "next wave" (2002), Johnson's book (2002), and Juillet and Mingus's chapter in the *Handbook of Administrative Reform* (2008). Many of the recent volumes are collaborative works by contributors from different countries including US-Canadian collaboration (Peters and Savoie, 2000; Rosenau, 2000; Henderson and Dwivedi, 1999). "Governance"—though difficult to define—follows a long tradition in the United States, Canada, and elsewhere by responding to the need for responsible, responsive, professional, and efficient administration of government, whether as the primary provider of goods, services, and regulations, or in a reduced role as a partner, coordinator, promoter, and/or overseer with business and nonprofit sectors. Governance envisions a flattened hierarchy; postprivatization cooperative functions; and networks of stakeholders, including citizens. It moves beyond NPM by addressing "good government" as democratically rooted and less influenced by citizen satisfaction than by citizen participation.

Terms other than "governance" have been used for the move away from NPM to a more diffuse delivery system. "Contractualist," "whole of government," "joined-up government," "coproduction" and "alternative service delivery" now appear in the literature (Ford and Zussman, 1997). "Alternative Service Delivery is widely viewed as a Canadian invention. Among the many ASD mechanisms were special operating agencies, and ISD [Integrated Service Delivery] arrangements" (Kernaghan, 2007: 10). Kernaghan's own preferred term is "integrated service delivery." Henderson and Dwivedi's concern is "to extend the concern with bureaucratic reform based only on New Public Management, World Bank/International Monetary Fund, and other Northern thinking stressing private sector models, to a fuller range of ideas and practices" (1999: xiii). Various combinations of NPM thinking and "governance" or "alternative service delivery" are also found, some with Canadian contributors.

One interesting prospect of GP—if, indeed, it may currently be called a paradigm—is the reintroduction of comparative and development administration. As Dwivedi and Mau carefully document in their empirical analysis of topics covered in journals, texts, and M.P.A. programs, comparative and development administration—basically concerned with other countries' administrative systems—has been neglected in recent years (Dwivedi and Mau, 2007). What they find for Canada would also be true for the United States. Public administration textbooks, graduate programs, and articles are lacking in meaningful comparative and developmental topics. In another survey, Candler contrasts Canadian content on a variety of topics and methodologies with the Australian and Brazilian cases. Through a content analysis of journal articles, he develops profiles for the three countries. Canada, for example, has fewer comparative articles than do Brazil or Australia (Candler, 2006).

GP encourages attention to other perspectives, as scholars from around the world contribute to the growing literature, and promises to reintroduce comparative study as well as broaden the outlook of practicing administrators. Along with the important institutional and professional developments mentioned before, Canada, in many respects, serves as an administrative model in the international arena. Free from some of the constraints of a single superpower, it can support administrative reform in Eastern Europe (as IPAC is doing), participate in the United Nations' efforts without appearing to dominate the field, and even edit the *International Review of Administrative Sciences* (as Kernaghan is doing) without the onus of an American agenda.

Cooperative relationships between IPAC and the American Society for Public Administration (ASPA) should continue, perhaps with a repeat of the 1995 joint regional meeting of the two organizations in Toronto. Recently, of course, IPAC has joined other countries in a network with ASPA that involves reciprocal academic and practitioner-oriented exchanges coordinated by a designated university. The University of Akron in Ohio has been so designated for Canada by ASPA. CAPPA is also now affiliated with NASPAA as an "international associate member."

Both the United States and Canada (and other Northern countries) reflect the shift over time from "nuts and bolts" administration, to public management (including the extensively discussed NPM), to the networking/partnering/collaborative enterprise often labelled "governance" or—at least—to discussions of alternatives to NPM. Confronting the twenty-first-century challenges of rapidly changing practical world demands, the discipline/profession of public administration in various countries has attempted to respond with new institutional arrangements, strategies, and ideas. In this enterprise, Canada will play a leading role.

NOTES

[1]   Following convention, I will use the words "America/American" and
      "United States" interchangeably. This is done with some reluctance since
      historians remind us that the first use of the word "America" in a document
      was the Waldseemiller map in 1507, where "America" was superimposed
      on what is now Brazil. We have also forgotten that Quebec is every bit as
      North American as Jamestown and that its exploration (if not its founding
      as a trading post by Samuel de Champlain in 1608) preceded Jamestown
      (Widmer, 2007: 42).
[2]   Information conveyed to author in e-mail from O. P. Dwivedi, 18
      December 2007.

REFERENCES

Agranoff, R. (2007). *Managing Within Networks.* Washington, DC: Georgetown
    University Press.

Aucoin, P. (2002). "Beyond the 'New' in Public Management Reform in Canada:
    Catching the Next Wave." In *Handbook of Canadian Public Administration*,
    edited by C. Dunn. Don Mills, ON: Oxford University Press.

Bennett, C. J. (2003). "The Privacy Commissioner of Canada: Multiple
    Roles, Diverse Expectations, and Structural Dilemmas." *Canadian Public
    Administration.* 46: 2.

Borins, S. (2007). *Digital State at the Leading Edge.* Toronto: University of
    Toronto Press.

Canada, Treasury Board. (2000). *Results for Canadians: A Management
    Framework for the Government of Canada.* Ottawa: Treasury Board.

Canadian Association of Programs in Public Administration (CAPPA). (2007).
    *History of CAPPA, CAPPA: Promoting Public Administration and Scholarship
    in Canada.* <http://www.cappa.ca/new.html>.

Candler, G. G. (2006). "The Comparative Evolution of Public Administration
    in Australia, Brazil and Canada." *Canadian Public Administration.* 49:
    334–349.

Cochrane, J. (2004). "Preface." In *A Canadian Model of Public Administration?*
    Edited by J. I. Gow. Ottawa: Canada School of Public Administration.

Dalhousie University Faculty of Management—Graduate Programs. (2007).
    "Public Administration." <http://dalgrad.dal.ca/programs/fact_sheets/
    puad.pdf>.

Dawson, R. MacGregor. (1922). *The Principle of Official Independence.* London:
    P. S. King and Son.

———. (1929). *The Civil Service of Canada.* London: Oxford University
    Press.

Dufour, C. (2002). "Émergence, institutionalisation et identité du Management Public en milieu universitaire au Québec." Université de Montréal: Ph.D. dissertation.

———. (21–22 September 2007). "Forty Years of Public Sector Education in Quebec." A paper presented at the conference in honour of Professor J. E. Hodgetts, Canadian Public Administration in Transition: From Administration to Management to Governance (the Hodgetts Conference), University of Guelph, Guelph, ON.

Dwivedi, O. P., ed. (1981). *The Administrative State in Canada, Essays in Honour of J. E. Hodgetts.* Toronto: University of Toronto Press.

Dwivedi, O. P., and T. Mau. (21–22 September 2007). "Comparative and Development Administration: State of the Discipline in Canada." A paper presented at the Hodgetts Conference, University of Guelph, Guelph, ON.

École nationale d'administration publique (ÉNAP). (1979). *Conference Proceedings, International Conference on the Future of Public Administration.* Quebec: ÉNAP.

Ford, R., and David Zussman, eds. (1997). *Alternative Service Delivery.* Toronto: IPAC.

Gow, James Iain. (1994). *Learning From Others: Administrative Innovations Among Canadian Governments.* Toronto: Institute of Public Administration of Canada.

———. (2004). *A Canadian Model of Public Administration?* Ottawa: Canada School of Public Administration.

Gulick, L., and L. Urwick, eds. (1937). *Papers on the Science of Administration.* New York: Institute of Public Administration.

Halligan, John. (21–22 September 2007). "A Comparative Perspective on Canadian Public Administration." A paper presented at the Hodgetts Conference, University of Guelph, Guelph, ON.

Halligan, John, ed. (2003). *Civil Service Systems in Anglo-American Countries.* Cheltenham, UK: Edward Elgar.

Henderson, K., and O. P. Dwivedi, eds. (1999). *Bureaucracy and the Alternatives in World Perspective.* London: Macmillan.

Hodgetts, J. E. (1956). *Pioneer Public Service: An Administrative History of the United Canadas, 1841–1867.* Toronto: University of Toronto Press.

———. (1964). *Administering the Atom for Peace.* New York: Atherton Press.

———. (1966). *Higher Education in a Changing Canada.* Toronto: University of Toronto Press.

———. (1973). *The Canadian Public Service: A Physiology of Government 1867–1972.* Toronto: University of Toronto Press.

Hodgetts, J. E., et al. (1972). *The Biography of an Institution: The Civil Service Commission of Canada 1908–1967.* Montreal: McGill-Queen's University Press.

Hodgetts, J. E., and J. A. Corry. (1959). *Democratic Government and Politics*, revised 3rd edition. Toronto: University of Toronto Press.

Hodgetts, J. E., and O. P. Dwivedi. (1974). *Provincial Governments as Employers: A Survey of Public Personnel Administration in Canada*. Montreal: McGill-Queen's University Press.

Hodgetts, J. E., and D. C. Corbett, eds. (1960) *Canadian Public Administration: A Book of Readings*. Toronto: Macmillan.

Johnson, D. (2002). *Thinking Government: Ideas, Policies, Institutions, and Public Sector Management in Canada*. Peterborough, ON: Broadview Press.

Juillet, L., and M. S. Mingus. (2008). "Reconsidering the History of Administrative Reforms in Canada." In *Handbook of Administrative Reform, An International Perspective*, edited by J. Killian and N. Eklund. Atlanta, GA: CRC Press.

Kernaghan, K. (21–22 September 2007). "Putting Citizens First: Service Delivery and Integrated Public Governance." A paper presented at the Hodgetts Conference, University of Guelph, Guelph, ON.

Kernaghan, K., and David Siegel. (1995). *Public Administration in Canada*. Scarborough, ON: Nelson.

Kettl, D. (2002). *The Transformation of Governance: Public Administration for the Twenty-first Century*. Baltimore, MD: Johns Hopkins University Press.

Light, P. (1999a). *The True Size of Government*. Washington, DC: Brookings.

———. (1999b). *The New Public Service*. Washington, DC: Brookings.

Marx, F. M., ed. (1946). *Elements of Public Administration*. New York: Prentice Hall.

Peters, B. G., and D. Savoie. (2000). *Governance in the Twenty-first Century: Revitalizing the Public Service*. Montreal: McGill-Queens University Press.

Phidd, R. (21–22 September 2007). "Comments on Forty Years of Public Sector Education in Quebec." Written comments following the Hodgetts Conference, University of Guelph, Guelph, ON.

Pross, A. P., and V. S. Wilson. (1976). "Graduate Education in Canadian Public Administration: Antecedents, Present Trends and Portents." *Canadian Public Administration*. 19: 515–541.

Rasmussen, K. (21–22 September 2007). "The Biography of a Concept: The Origins of Merit in Canada." A paper presented at the Hodgetts Conference, University of Guelph, Guelph, ON.

Restakis, J., and Evert Lindquist, eds. (2001). *The Cooperative Alternative: Civil Society and the Future of Public Services*. Toronto: IPAC.

Rosenau, P., ed. (2000). *Public-Private Policy Partnerships*. Cambridge, MA: MIT Press.

Salamon, L. (2002). *The Tools of Government: A Guide to the New Governance*. New York: Oxford University Press.

Savoie, D. (1994). *Thatcher, Reagan, and Mulroney: In Search of a New Bureaucracy.* Pittsburgh, PA: University of Pittsburgh Press.

Simon, H. (1947). *Administrative Behavior.* New York: Free Press.

Smiley, D. V. (1967). "Contributions to Canadian Political Science since the Second World War." *Journal of Economics and Political Science.* 33: 569–580.

Smith, Alasdair. (1996). *How American Consultants Remade the Canadian Civil Service, 1918–21.* Toronto: Institute of Public Administration of Canada.

Suleiman, E. (2003). *Dismantling Democratic States.* Princeton, NJ: Princeton University Press.

Waldo, Dwight. (1948). *The Administrative State.* New York: Holmes and Meier.

White, L. D. (1920). *The Civil Service in the Modern State, a Collection of Documents.* Chicago: University of Chicago Press.

———. (1955 [1926]). *Introduction to Public Administration*, 4th ed. New York: Macmillan.

Widmer, T. (2007). "Navigating the Age of Exploration." *American Educator.* 28: 42–46.

Willoughby, W. F. (1927). *Principles of Public Administration.* Baltimore: The Johns Hopkins University Press.

Wilson, V. S., and O. P. Dwivedi. (1981). Introduction to *The Administrative State in Canada: Essays in Honour of J. E. Hodgetts*, edited by O. P. Dwivedi. Toronto: University of Toronto Press.

Wilson, Woodrow. (1887). "The Study of Administration." *Political Science Quarterly.* 2: 197–222.

11 A COMPARATIVE PERSPECTIVE ON CANADIAN PUBLIC ADMINISTRATION WITHIN AN ANGLOPHONE TRADITION

John Halligan

This chapter examines Canadian public administration within a comparative perspective grounded in the anglophone tradition. Canadian public administration presents a set of features to the external observer that is familiar as well as elusive in some respects. Several themes explore the Canadian variant by seeking to place it in a comparative context as part of the anglophone family, as a contributor to public administration, and in terms of how it has evolved a distinct administrative style, identity, and developmental pathway. The differences turn out to be rather fewer than the similarities at a time when considerable convergence is apparent among countries, but Canada nevertheless offers an illuminating case of how to address the issues of anglophone public administration.

RELATING TO THE ANGLOPHONE FAMILY

The four anglophone countries of Australia, Canada, New Zealand, and the United Kingdom have formed a coherent group by way of a common tradition and historical and continuing close associations and interactions (Halligan, 2003a; 2003b). The "old Commonwealth"—or the "Westminster parliamentary democracies"—forms a natural group with institutional roots in the British tradition. The anglophone group of countries is regarded as reasonably homogeneous for analytical and comparative purposes. The assumption is this comparability results from a shared heritage, even though the countries are in some respects heterogeneous (Campbell, 1983).

From the outside, the commonalities look strong, but within this group substantial variations are apparent in governmental institutions, with two being federal and two being unitary systems. The combination of federalism and responsible government along Westminster lines has linked Canada and Australia, whereas unitary government has produced a special bond between Britain and New Zealand. The antipodean countries of Australia and New Zealand share a regional location and have closely linked administrative pathways, while Canadian development has reflected its proximity to the United States.

The countries have drawn on their shared and individual experience, but national factors and prevailing politics have, of course, shaped traditions historically and provided for variations in some areas. The four systems have exhibited patterns of development that are generally similar within broad historical phases: colonial administration; clarification of the roles of elected representatives and representative institutions; development of public services as systems (personnel and business efficiency); the administrative state; and contemporary reform (Halligan, 2003b). The parallels are fairly striking in terms of the developmental phases, although the timing and length of the phases vary with the time lag between the emergence and implementation of a concept in the country of origin vis-à-vis other countries (more a matter of decades for nineteenth-century reforms, or years for late-twentieth-century reforms).

The move in anglophone countries to establish a professional service in the nineteenth century was largely a reaction to the excesses of patronage and eventually led to two major outcomes (Halligan, 2003b): a career public service based on merit, and a central personnel agency for producing a standard approach across the service. Led by Britain, public service commissions emerged in anglophone countries in the second half of the nineteenth century, and the process was completed in the second decade of the twentieth century by Canada (Hodgetts et al., 1972).

1997); the level of decentralization (Koutsogeorgopoulou, 2007) and the accommodations of a plural society reflecting significant minority concentration in specific jurisdictions. The influence of francophones on public administration can be seen in bilingualism and measures for recruitment and promotion, but the full extent of this influence on mainstream public administration is not so apparent from the outside.[1] The state in Westminster systems has become more complex, but is this complexity greater in the more devolved of the two federations, Canada, which is responsive to both anglophone and francophone identities?[2]

REFORM OF PUBLIC MANAGEMENT AND GOVERNANCE

In terms of management reform, two features are well established: the innovative creative quality that has produced significant management ideas over the decades—Canada's distinctive pathway, which has sometimes seemed out of character for an anglophone country, and a lack of assurance when it comes to implementing new initiatives systematically. Insufficient political commitment and excessive political conflict are said to explain why implementation of reform has been problematic in North America (Pollitt and Bouckaert, 2004; Halligan, 2003a). This disinclination to operate at the reform frontier avoids the dysfunctional experiences arising from experimentation and risk-taking. It has also allowed public servants greater scope than elsewhere to pursue an agenda (Good, 2003: 182).

Canada was one of the first anglophone countries to explore management reform but was slow to incorporate and institutionalize it. In some respects, the public service remained unmanagerialized; yet, despite having never fully embraced managerialism, the Canadian public service came to exhibit standard management features and to experience the tensions and conflicts produced by attempts to change the administrative culture. New public management (NPM) was not introduced rapidly or through a sustained reform program at the national level. The Audit Office sometimes filled the vacuum left by a lack of sustained leadership from senior politicians and lead central agencies.

The verdict at the beginning of this decade was critical of weaknesses in the management reform process; divided responsibility for human resource management; and limited parliamentary review compared to other jurisdictions (Aucoin, 2001). By the mid-2000s, a number of questions had been attended to and recent initiatives seemed promising, if tending to be top-down from central agencies. Canada now had a developed performance management framework that was being refined as part of a set of initiatives covering roles of central agencies, a management and accountability framework, and human resource management (although the Canadian approach to integrating human resource management still required more agencies, six instead of four). A more sustained approach to implementing management reform was now apparent, but the lack of fuller information has made it difficult to form a firmer judgment of the impact on practice.

With performance management, there has also been considerable movement since the critical judgments of a few years ago on the slow progress in using information for improved results. The Office of the Auditor General continued to raise issues "about the quality of financial data, the lack of focus on outcomes, problems of coverage of performance data, and information from new forms of service delivery" (Talbot, Daunton, and Morgan, 2001: 34). In the 2000s, a sequence of initiatives produced an ambitious scheme for departments. The performance indicators have been expanding in recent years and are being reviewed with the intention of rationalizing and reducing them. Organizational performance has now been linked to deputy minister performance. There has been a developmental logic that is cumulative, but the system appears to have reached a turning point where answers are required about the public availability and quality of performance information and the appropriate roles of central and line agencies. In terms of tolerance of variance, Canada appears to be at the stage where the mandatory and centralized approach of central agencies to management improvement is unsympathetic to departmental variations.

Canada now has a developed performance management framework, which has the formal attributes of an official performance management model in keeping with other Anglo-American countries (Bouckaert and

Halligan, 2008). However, the level and efficacy of implementation is less than other anglophone countries and remains unclear at this stage. There appears to be a shortage of independent analysis, although scepticism exists about performance management and the mandatory federal agenda (Clark and Swain, 2005; Thomas, 2004).[3]

Canada remains the exception among anglophone countries insofar as the politicians have generally gone missing from the reform process (Aucoin, 2002). They have not taken up the options available under the Canadian system to lead on reform, generally leaving it to the public service leadership. The pattern for Canada is that the "public service and its political leaders have a tradition of *pragmatism and moderation* that keeps it evolving. [It has only] mildly embraced downsizing and the new public management ... and avoided over committing to one or two radical reforms" (Aucoin, 2002: 21).

With the move towards a governance approach, Canadian creativeness has again been apparent. There have been interesting experiments that have tested the potential of flexible and focused organization, such as alternative service delivery and horizontal management (Bakvis and Juillet, 2004; Zussman, 2003). Canada has become well known internationally for its early focus on citizens and emerging modes of governance, in particular integrated service delivery, e-governance, and other smart practices (Borins et al., 2007; Campbell, 2006; Kernaghan, 2004; see also World Bank Institute, 2007). Yet, questions continue to be asked about how to define the Canadian system. Reflections on its tradition and identity offer a number of insights.

ADMINISTRATIVE TRADITION

Canada has been depicted as having a tradition of pragmatism and moderation that applies to political as well as public service leaders. We need to put the Canadian case in perspective. The other anglophone countries also have a tradition of pragmatism that derives from the British legacy and is linked to the instrumental basis of the anglophone tradition. Instrumentalism is recognized at one level as part of the government tradition, and importantly provides the "significant *potential* to transform administrative structures and practices, assuming there is a government committed to do so" (Knill, 1999: 127). The identification of instrumental administration with Britain resonates with the experience of other anglophone countries.

The application of instrumentalism to the public service means that its primary role is to execute the will of the government of the day, and in return the public service is protected in certain respects from arbitrary decisions at the individual level. However, organizational change is fair game for political executives seeking to implement their policies, because they have the right to pursue a range of options through reform and other initiatives while being mindful of the boundaries of action in areas such as partisanship in appointments and the use of the public service. It should not be assumed that politicians have either availed themselves of these opportunities or do so to the same extent. The anglophone countries' administrative histories, like most others up until the 1980s, are littered with unimplemented reform initiatives. Accumulated discretionary responsibilities and the powers of public officials and agencies have historically placed brakes on meaningful change. Importantly, in this context, the politicians of one of the four anglophone countries, Canada, have not exercised this reserve power to play empowering and directive roles in reform.

A related attribute of administrative and political style is pragmatism, which features in the country's literature as characteristic practice. Anglo-American systems are identified with the "pragmatic and incremental nature of governing.... In contrast to most continental political and administrative systems, ideology plays a relatively minor role in Anglo-American politics, and perhaps even less in public administration" (Peters, 2003: 21–22). This feature is regarded as having its origins both in traditions inherited from Britain and the colonial development experience, where conditions (e.g., a lack of political parties with strong ideologies) reinforced it. For its part, the British tradition was generally accepted as atheoretical, dominated by experience, and characterized by working through problems.

Pragmatism is not, of course, exclusive to this tradition, but it has been important for how the conception of the state has evolved. What is distinctive is that pragmatism can be readily employed as part of the change agenda to serve the requirements of the government of the day, whether under conditions of reform or traditional incrementalism. A pragmatic approach supports change-oriented governments in their acceptance of the malleability of governance and allowing significant reforms to proceed. Compare New Zealand, where a decade and a half since the heyday of "rational choice instrumentalism," second-generation reforms have emerged to reduce problems from the first round and to re-establish the standing, ethos, and capability of the core public service. "The current response is pragmatically rather than theoretically driven, but it is a pragmatism that as yet remains too securely locked within the theoretical framework that shaped the changes of the 1980s" (Gregory, 2006: 157).

The Australian case saw the ascendancy of an instrumental conception of the public service in the reform era, as politicians reasserted their roles and correspondingly reduced public service discretion. However, there was also a sense in which reform and pragmatism could work in unison. A midreform era judgment observed that successes with implementing and sustaining reform derived from the Australian approach. Major reform required adherence to principles that allowed for the pursuit of the reform paradigm and permitted incremental and cumulative development of the reform's core ideas. Pragmatism produced openness to ideas and allowed for new learning and modifications as they were required. In balancing principle and pragmatism, Australia developed the habit of employing self-correcting mechanisms and being able to adjust the scope and components of reform, to expand the capacity to change over time and respond to reform excesses and conflicting objectives in the reform program (Halligan, 1996).

All anglophone countries would see pragmatism as part of their tradition, and it is not an element that has been lost during the reform era. For Canada, the pattern differs insofar as less is made of systemic instrumentalism, allowing pragmatism to play a more prominent role. The emphasis is explicit in commentary that the public service culture is "pragmatic, little driven by theory," and that public sector reform is pragmatic and evolutionary (Gow, 2004: 9; Lindquist, 2006: 61; Aucoin, 2002). This is illustrated through the case of alternative service delivery, where the approach has been pragmatic and tentative, "without necessarily separating service delivery from the responsibilities of the core public service" (Lindquist, 2006: 36). The resulting "diversity in service delivery structures ... emerged from pragmatic deliberations about ... the best governance arrangements for each program function" (Lindquist, 2006: 40).

Elements of the Canadian character may also be reflected in the use of particular instruments for public purposes. The Canadian commitment to retaining the Royal Commission as an instrument of public policy long after other anglophone systems have discarded (or relegated) it in favour of task forces and other approaches indicates something about the character of the system.[4] Similarly, Canada's attachment to an array of central agencies and officers of Parliament suggests an attachment to incrementalism, process, and oversight. While the recent Federal Accountability Act is one government's response to shortcomings evinced under the previous government of its political opponents, the flurry of recent appointments to new positions resounds of a Canadian approach: a Conflict of Interest and Ethics Commissioner, a Public Sector Integrity Commissioner, a Procurement Ombudsman, and a Public Service Disclosure Protection Tribunal.

SEARCHING FOR A CANADIAN IDENTITY AND WAY

A number of attempts have been made to identify the Canadian model. Bourgon has argued there is a distinctive Canadian model comprising continuing respect for the role of government and a public service that is not overshadowed by a hardline NPM approach that emphasizes contracts and markets. At the same time, new features have been incorporated, which could claim to being a "new public sector" that is centred on three new sets of relationships: within government, between governments and citizens, and new partnerships with external actors. "While none of its elements are uniquely Canadian, taken together they amount to an approach that is sufficiently different from all the others to warrant attention" (Canada, Clerk of the Privy Council, 1997: 8).

According to Gow (2004), the classic Canadian bureaucratic model developed during the last sixty years combines five features: (1) political control; (2) a legal framework; (3) an autonomous nonpartisan professional public service; (4) a tradition of moderation and pragmatism; and (5) a tolerance for ambiguity in some spheres. These are, of course, subject to constraints of oversight agencies and other features. A further perspective comes from Lindquist (2006), who engages in something of a meta-analysis of other formulations, which he sees as largely normative, before advancing his own framework: an "empirical model" that seeks to map the main dimensions of the public service. This exercise yields a set of features that suggests distinctiveness in the Canadian public service.

However, international patterns of change indicate Canada is less of an exception than before. As the other anglophone countries have moved well beyond NPM in the 2000s, the more radical features of that agenda have faded. The spectrum of recent reform ranges from the United Kingdom's constant reformulations of its reform agenda, at least under Tony Blair (the downside of such constant change being chronic reformism, according to Pollitt [2006]), to the cautious revisionism of New Zealand, which itself contrasts with the somewhat more adamant Australian approach. More generally, some of the features that served to differentiate countries' public management internationally are no longer so salient. The fading of NPM, or rather the rise of a more hybrid form of public management, means that Canada, in some respects, is now closer to the mainstream of anglophone countries.

COMPARATIVE PERSPECTIVES

The reform era has been remarkable for sustained transformations of public administration in countries internationally. The anglophone systems are both early- and long-term reforming countries by OECD standards that display some distinctive features of their own, as well as including "Anglo-Saxon" members that have been most identified with NPM. The products of two decades or more of activity have now become clearer: The more stark manifestations of NPM have less prominence in practice. This is not a revelation for scholars, who have been pronouncing on NPM for some time, but a more elusive matter is how to characterize its successor. Some interpretations recognize the complexities by distinguishing tiers of NPM or contending models based on traditional control and autonomy tensions. What is apparent is that a set of trends has emerged with commonalities across anglophone countries (Halligan, 2007a).

The synthesis of elements in the current generation suggests that system integration and performance are central to the prevailing approach of the mid-2000s, at least in Australia and New Zealand. This broader conception addresses mechanisms for more effectively integrating and controlling the components of the executive branch. The resulting synthesis of elements suggests integrated governance has become the prevailing approach of the mid-2000s at the national level. Where once reinventing was part of the lexicon, the indicators point now to an emergent model that can be represented in the mid-2000s as reintegrating governance. It is also apparent that such a model is an amalgam of new elements and design features derived from previous models.

In these countries there has been a rebalancing of the centre, new horizontal relationships, reform corrections, and realignments of different components. The strong reassertion of the centre reverses central agency weaknesses by giving them greater capacity for leadership and direction. The commitment to integration and whole-of-government is designed to counter the reinforcement given to vertical functionally constituted departments and agencies. The renewed interest in capacity and capability reflects in large part the limits to extensive outsourcing experienced during years of contraction. Renewal has also reflected more positive attitudes towards the public sector as expressed through public service leaders.

It is clear that new conceptions of governance address a different mix of features than those that have been prevalent during the last twenty years. The reaction to NPM features has produced similar responses in several countries (Christensen and Lægrid, 2006), and there are now a number of country-derived interpretations that reflect local conditions and their stage in the reform cycle. Among recent conceptions, Aucoin's (2006) "new public governance" is based on the political management apparent in the Canadian context: concentration of power at the centre; the growth of the role and influence of ministerial staff; personalization of appointments; and politicization of public communications. There are interesting parallels between Australian developments (Halligan, 2003b) with the political executive and those depicted by Savoie (1999) for Canada. The disconnect between politicians and public servants was apparent under Brian Mulroney, and Stephen Harper's government is regarded as not being particularly interested in using the public service for policy advice, instead preferring its own advisers from thinktanks located outside Ottawa. This is not inconsistent with the broader disposition towards the public service, characterized as disinterested.

What we now find is the coexistence of several features derived from different models. There has been a reconfirmation of the organizational components of the traditional system: the Cabinet, the central agency, and the department. The revival of features associated with traditional bureaucracy—such as risk aversion in fields with an external orientation—suggests the emergence of neo-Weberianism. However, there are a number of significantly different features from the earlier hierarchical model of integration. The public service is operating under a political executive with more instruments for securing and sustaining control and direction. There is a brace of instruments for working the system strategically and at several levels. The empowered departments have greater responsibilities than traditional arrangements, and performance is conceived differently. This adds up to a potentially formidable apparatus for control, scrutiny, and performance.

Under integrated governance, elements of NPM persist and may be central. This is especially the case with performance management, which continues to provide a cornerstone of the public management framework (even though questions remain about the quality and use of performance information) (Halligan, 2007b). In this new iteration, there has been growth in, and continuing commitment to, performance management despite the fate of NPM. Under the broader agendas of integrated governance, some aspects, such as contracts and markets, are less prominent, while others, such as outcomes and evaluation review, have come more into focus.

There has been divergence and convergence in the countries' approaches across the generations of reform. By the end of the 1980s, it was possible to depict distinctive models in three anglophone countries (Hood, 1990), but a decade later the common features were more salient. In the 2000s, there are again parallel engagements of similar public issues. The long-term consequences of reform can be seen to have in part gone full circle through the rebalancing of constituent features, yet there is also a sense of movement along new pathways. At this point, it remains unclear whether the emergent model represents a durable approach that has effectively incorporated recent experience, or whether it is transient and a bridge to an as yet indeterminate model. Governments have experimented with new forms and found them to offer a mixed bag of benefits and deficits. Consequently, the NPM model of the 1990s has now been succeeded, even though its basic ideas still underpin the new model. The main trends in the 2000s have either moderated key NPM features or represent new agendas that do not align closely with those of the immediate past.

WHITHER CANADIAN PUBLIC ADMINISTRATION

There have been several phases of change in Canada during the last two decades. First was the extended period of tentative responses to the international reform movement leading up to program review in the 1990s. A second period was marked by developments at two levels: the growing understanding of the centralization of power, particularly around the prime minister, and of the potential for innovation in delivery. Canada was now seen to be well placed internationally in several spheres, was addressing management reform, and could make stronger claims for its approaches to governance.

Moving towards the mid-2000s, the quality and identity of the public service again came under challenge. According to recent appraisals, serious questions are being asked that do not have parallels in other anglophone countries (although this is not to discount that each has its own brand of crisis). There are references to "a critical moment" for the Canadian public service, and in the preface to that study, Ruth Dantzer, president of the Canada School of Public Service, noted a "public service under stress ... emerging from controversies that have raised questions about its nature and how it functions" (Lindquist, 2006: iv). Dantzer further observed that despite decades of reform, it remains unclear how "character-shifting for the public service" the change has been (Lindquist, 2006: iv). The position is complicated by the long-term fallout from the sponsorship scandal, which has raised questions about trust and confidence but also whether enlarging the accountability requirements is a panacea.

Canada has been regarded as a major contributor to the intellectual development and application of ideas and practice internationally. These extend from the management ideas of the Glassco Commission through to the ideas of e-governance and integrated service delivery in recent years. At the same time, the state and relevance of public administration has been raised (a theme familiar to other anglophone countries),[5] with a report of "unease among Canadian public administration experts ... a feeling that the discipline has either not been asking the right questions or has not moved far enough ahead of events to be able to give a critical overview" (Dunn, 2002: ix). Furthermore, according to the Canadian Centre for Management Development, change was producing developments yet to be addressed by the public administration discipline (Dunn, 2002). More recently, it was noted there is "a lack of ready, detailed, comparative information about the practices and performance of high-performing public service institutions across different functions to determine if the Canadian public service is an exemplar" (Lindquist, 2006: 66). Public administration has also been diagnosed as being subject to "theoretical malnutrition" and the need for theoretical development (Savoie, 1999: 6).

One option is to draw more from the long tradition of comparative research among anglophone countries (Bouckhaert and Halligan, 2008; Campbell, 2006; Saint-Martin, 2004; Halligan, 2003a; Aucoin,

1995; Savoie, 1994). Insights about comparabilities and contrasts are available, particularly from Canadian-Australian comparisons in fields such as organization, political-bureaucratic relations, and patterns of reform (Lindquist, 2004; see also Aucoin, 2006). An ambitious and promising research agenda has been proposed for comprehensively mapping the main dimensions (Lindquist, 2006: 64–65). The more sustained comparative studies have a strong base to build on the earlier analysis of Campbell, Savoie, and Aucoin.

Canada has been, in some respects, an enigmatic anglophone country, with a public service system that reflects both the Westminster tradition and the influence of the United States but retains an administrative tradition and public service that are distinctively Canadian. The country's experience offers distinctive insights on how to attend to major questions of public administration. While it has been better at addressing management in the realm of ideas rather than the realm of practice, it has been prescient in recognizing governance movements by embracing features relatively early on when compared to other jurisdictions. It is also likely that elements of several models coexist in Canada, as in other anglophone systems, and that with the tendencies towards mainstreaming in those countries, the commonalities within the anglophone tradition are now greater.

NOTES

1   It is apparently unclear to many Canadian observers also. A colleague in the province of Quebec was asked, "Are you able to suggest any publications that examine the influence of the francophone (Napoleonic tradition) on Canadian federal public administration?" The response was that he was unaware of any written material.

2   Another anglophone case is the United Kingdom, with its supranational membership in the European Union, as well as internal devolution to subnations.

3   An Organisation for Economic Co-operation and Development (OECD) depiction of a Canadian lesson of learning from using performance information is that "there is no end point on results-based management—persistence over many years is required and you never get it 'right'" (Curristine, 2006).

⁴   The instigation of a Royal Commission on Renewing and Strengthening
     Our Place in Canada sounds like a distinctively Canadian approach, even
     though the focus was Labrador and Newfoundland.
⁵   There has recently been an inquiry in Australia as to how the research
     agenda of the Australian and New Zealand School of Government can be
     made more relevant to the public service.

REFERENCES

Aucoin, Peter. (1995). *The New Public Management in Canada in Comparative Perspective*. Montreal: Institute for Research in Public Policy.

———. (2001). *Comparative Perspectives on Canadian Public Service Reform in the 1990s*. Ottawa: Office of the Auditor General of Canada.

———. (2002). "Beyond the 'New' in Public Management Reform in Canada: Catching the Next Wave?" In *The Handbook of Canadian Public Administration*, edited by C. Dunn, 37–52. Don Mills, ON: Oxford University Press.

———. (March 2006). "Corporate Governance for the Public Sector: The Canadian Perspective." A paper presented at the Corporate Governance in the Public Sector—from Theory to Practice conference, Canberra, Australia.

Aucoin, Peter, and Mark D. Jarvis. (2005). *Modernizing Government Accountability: A Framework for Reform*. Ottawa: Canada School of Public Service.

Aucoin, Peter, J. Smith, and G. Dinsdale. (2004). *Responsible Government: Clarifying Essentials, Dispelling Myths, and Exploring Change*. Ottawa: Canadian Centre for Management Development.

Bakvis, H., and L. Juillet. (2004). *The Horizontal Challenge: Line Departments, Central Agencies, and Leadership*. Ottawa: Canada School of Public Service.

Borins, S., et al. (2007). *Digital State at the Leading Edge*. Toronto: University of Toronto Press.

Bouckaert, Geert, and John Halligan. (2008). *Managing Performance: International Comparisons*. London: Routledge.

Campbell, Colin. (1983). *Governments under Stress: Political Executives and Key Bureaucrats in Washington*. Toronto: University of Toronto Press.

Campbell, Colin, ed. (2006). *Comparative Trends in Public Management: Smart Practices toward Blending Policy and Administration*. Ottawa: Canada School of Public Service.

Canada, Clerk of the Privy Council. (1997). *Fifth Annual Report to the Prime Minister on the Public Service of Canada*. Ottawa: Privy Council Office.

Christensen, Tom, and Per Lægrid, eds. (2006). *Autonomy and Regulation: Coping with Agencies in the Modern State*. Cheltenham, UK: Edward Elgar.

Clark, I. D., and H. Swain. (2005). "Distinguishing the Real from the Surreal in Management Reform: Suggestions for Beleaguered Administrators in the Government of Canada." *Canadian Public Administration*. 48: 4: 453–477.

Curristine, Teresa. (5 June 2006). "Experiences of Using Performance Information in the Budget Process." A presentation to the Twenty-seventh Annual Meeting of Senior Budget Officials, Sydney, Australia.

Dunn, Christopher. (2002). *The Handbook of Canadian Public Administration*. Don Mills, ON: Oxford University Press.

Dwivedi, O. P., and J. I. Gow. (1999). *From Bureaucracy to Public Management: The Administrative Culture of the Government of Canada*. Toronto: Broadview Press.

Dwivedi, O. P., and J. Halligan. (2003). "The Canadian Public Service: Balancing Values and Management." In *Civil Service Systems in Anglo-American Countries*, edited by J. Halligan, 148–173. Cheltenham, UK: Edward Elgar.

Franks, C. E. S. (1987). *The Parliament of Canada*. Toronto: University of Toronto Press.

Good, David. (2003). *The Politics of Public Management*. Toronto: University of Toronto Press.

Gow, J. I. (1994). *Learning from Others: Administrative Innovations among Canadian Governments*. Toronto: Institute of Public Administration of Canada.

———. (2004). *A Canadian Model of Public Administration?* Ottawa: Canada School of Public Service.

Gregory, Robert. (2006). "Theoretical Faith and Practical Works." In *Autonomy and Regulation: Coping with Agencies in the Modern State*, edited by Tom Christensen and Per Lægrid, 137–161. Cheltenham, UK: Edward Elgar.

Halligan, John. (1996). "Learning from Experience in Australian Reform: Balancing Principle and Pragmatism." In *Learning from Reform*, edited by J. P. Olsen and B. G. Peters. Oslo, Norway: Scandinavia University Press.

Halligan, John, ed. (2003a). *Civil Service Systems in Anglo-American Countries*. Cheltenham, UK: Edward Elgar.

Halligan, John. (2003b). "Anglo-American Civil Service Systems: Comparative Perspectives." In *Civil Service Systems in Anglo-American Countries*, edited by John Halligan, 195–216. Cheltenham, UK: Edward Elgar.

———. (2007a). "Reintegrating Government in Third Generation Reforms of Australia and New Zealand." *Public Policy and Administration*. 22: 2: 217–238.

———. (2007b). "Reform Design and Performance in Australia and New Zealand." In *Transcending New Public Management*, edited by Tom Christensen and Per Lægrid, 86–124. Aldershot, UK: Ashgate.

Heintzman, Ralph. (1997). "Canada and Public Administration." In *Public Administration and Public Management Experiences in Canada*, edited by J. Bourgault, M. Demers, and C. Williams. Quebec: Les Publications du Québec.

Hodgetts, J. E. (1983). "Implicit Values in the Administration of Public Affairs." In *Canadian Public Administration: Administration and Profession*, edited by K. Kernaghan. Toronto: Butterworths.

Hodgetts, J. E., et al. (1972). *The Biography of an Institution: The Civil Service Commission of Canada 1908–1967*. Montreal: McGill-Queen's University Press.

Hood, Christopher. (1990). "De-Sir Humphreyfying the Westminster Model of Bureaucracy: A New Style of Governance?" *Governance*. 3: 2: 205–214.

Kernaghan, K. (1997). "Values, Ethics and Public Service." In *Public Administration and Public Management: Experiences in Canada*, edited by J. Bourgault, M. Demers, and C. Williams. Quebec: Les Publications du Québec.

———. (2002). "East Block and Westminster: Conventions, Values and Public Service." In *A Handbook of Canadian Public Administration*, edited by Christopher Dunn. Don Mills, ON: Oxford University Press.

———. (2004). "Moving toward the Virtual State: Integrating Services and Service Channels for Citizen-Centred Service Delivery." *International Review of Administrative Sciences*. 17: 1: 119–131.

Knill, C. (1999). "Explaining Cross-National Variance in Administrative Reform: Autonomous versus Instrumental Bureaucracies." *Journal of Public Policy*. 19: 2: 113–139.

Koutsogeorgopoulou, Vassiliki. (2007). *Fiscal Relations across Levels of Government in Australia*. Paris: OECD Economic Department Working Papers No. 541.

Lindquist, E. (2004). "Strategy, Capacity, and Horizontal Governance: Perspectives from Australia and Canada." *Optimum*. 34: 4.

———. (2006). *A Critical Moment: Capturing and Conveying the Evolution of the Canadian Public Service*. Ottawa: Canada School of Public Service.

Peters, B. G. (2003). "Administrative Traditions and the Anglo-American Democracies." In *Civil Service Systems in Anglo-American Countries*, edited by J. Halligan, 10–26. Cheltenham, UK: Edward Elgar.

Pollitt, Christopher. (24 October 2006). "Blair's Re-Disorganization: Hyper-Modernism and the Costs of Reform—A Cautionary Tale." A paper presented at the University of Canberra, Canberra, Australia.

Pollitt, Christopher, and Geert Bouckaert. (2004). *Public Management Reform: A Comparative Analysis*. Oxford: Oxford University Press.

Roberts, A. (1996). *So-called Experts: How American Consultants Remade the Canadian Civil Service, 1918–21*. Toronto: Institute of Public Administration of Canada.

Saint-Martin, D. (2004). *Building the New Managerialist State: Consultants and the Politics of Public Sector Reform in Comparative Perspective*. Oxford: Oxford University Press.

Savoie, Donald J. (1994). *Thatcher, Reagan, and Mulroney: In Search of a New Bureaucracy*. Pittsburgh, PA: University of Pittsburgh Press.

———. (1999). *Governing from the Centre: The Concentration of Power in Canadian Politics*. Toronto: University of Toronto Press.

———. (2003). *Breaking the Bargain: Public Servants, Ministers, and Parliament*. Toronto: University of Toronto Press.

Talbot, C., L. Daunton, and C. Morgan. (2001). *Measuring Performance of Government Departments—International Developments*. Monmouthshire, UK: Public Futures Ltd.

Thomas, Paul G. (1998). "The Changing Nature of Accountability." In *Taking Stock: Assessing Public Sector Reform*, edited by B. G. Peters and D. J. Savoie. Montreal: McGill-Queen's University Press.

———. (2002). "Parliament and the Public Service." In *A Handbook of Canadian Public Administration*, edited by C. Dunn, 341–368. Don Mills, ON: Oxford University Press.

Thomas, Paul. (2004). *Performance Measurement, Reporting and Accountability: Recent Trends and Future Directions*. Regina: The Saskatchewan Institute of Public Policy, Public Policy Paper 23.

World Bank Institute. (2007). *Topical Briefs for Leaders*. Washington, DC: World Bank.

Zussman, David. (2003). "Alternative Service Delivery." In *The Handbook of Canadian Public Administration*, edited by C. Dunn, 53–76. Don Mills, ON: Oxford University Press.

12 COMPARATIVE AND DEVELOPMENT ADMINISTRATION IN CANADA:

A Preliminary Assessment and Call to Action

O. P. Dwivedi and Tim A. Mau[1]

INTRODUCTION

While public administration is a relative "newcomer" to academic circles, given the proliferation of bureaucracies throughout the world over the past forty years it has nonetheless gained academic prominence. However, while the scholarly importance of public administration may not be in dispute, there is no consensus as to whether it should be conceived of as a subdiscipline of either political science or administrative science, or as a distinct discipline in its own right (Raadschelders, 1999; Gray and Jenkins, 1995). In Canada this ambiguity is reflected in the current organization of the various university programs in public policy and administration: There are programs of public administration that are offered principally through departments of political science; a second, rather limited, group of institutions where these programs are offered through schools or faculties of business; and finally, an increasingly common trend to offer such programs through autonomous schools of public policy and administration (Geva-May and Maslove, 2006; Gow and Sutherland, 2004).

It is not the intention of the chapter to contribute to this particular debate, but in the interest of ensuring conceptual clarity we will categorize public administration as a subdiscipline of political science. In doing so, we endorse the position advanced by Kernaghan and Siegel (1999 [1991]: 12) in their seminal textbook on public administration:

> The study of public administration is commonly described as
> a discipline, but it is not a discipline in the restrictive sense of an
> intellectual endeavour with a body of coherent and accepted theory.
> Even if the term discipline is defined less rigorously as a field of study
> with a nucleus of unifying beliefs, public administration has not yet
> achieved agreement on what those beliefs are.

This reflects the fact that the intellectual ties between public administration and political science are well established and continue to remain relevant. For example, Candler (2006: 338) discovered that roughly 38 percent of the articles published in *Canadian Public Administration* (*CPA*) between 1990 and 2002 were published by academics whose appointments were in departments of political science.

As a subdiscipline of political science, public administration can be further divided into various fields, including comparative public administration and development administration, or what is now widely referred to as development management. Comparative administration refers to the study of several administrative systems in an attempt to compare or contrast approaches, while development management focuses on "theory and practice that concentrates upon organizational and managerial problems, issues and practices in developing countries of Africa, Asia, Latin America, and in the transitional economies of Eastern Europe and the former Soviet Union" (Brinkerhoff and Coston, 1999: 346). Herein resides the focus of the chapter: to provide a preliminary assessment regarding the extent to which the fields of comparative and development administration are adequately addressed in the subdiscipline of public administration. Given the impact of globalization on public administration, which would seemingly lead to common challenges in the theory and practice of public administration across countries, and the fact that a number of leading authorities in this subdiscipline have made the argument that public administration "could be better studied from a comparative perspective than from a narrow, national one" (Peters, 1988: 181),[2] it was expected that comparative and development administration would be well integrated into the mainstream of public administration. However, as this chapter will demonstrate, the reality is that public administration remains largely focused inward.[3]

The unfortunate reality is that most scholars have developed a very ethnocentric approach to the study of public administration. As Heady (2001) stated in the Donald C. Stone Lecture, "As we enter this new century and new millennium, parochialism continues to be the dominant perspective." He further noted that "we need to be less parochial in our focus and place more stress on understanding government and public administration outside the limited boundaries of American experience. In other words, we should give more attention to comparative and international administration" (392).

Although he was writing explicitly about the American experience, a similar lament could be articulated with respect to Canadian contributions to the subdiscipline. As a whole, Canadian public administration scholars have tended to focus on domestic public administration concerns and have virtually neglected its comparative and development dimensions. Both our flagship public administration journal, *CPA*, and the various scholarly textbooks devoted to this topic have largely ignored the comparative and development fields of the subdiscipline, creating a noticeable gap in the literature. Moreover, both comparative and development administration are not very prominently reflected in either the undergraduate or graduate curricula of the political science and public administration programs in this country. It is our argument that this paucity of scholarly focus on comparative and development administration, and the fact that these fields are not better integrated into the larger subdiscipline, is a very serious limitation of Canadian public administration scholarship and that to understand the development of bureaucracies the world over, a more outward vision of public administration is essential.

The chapter is divided into three main sections: First, after outlining the key methodological considerations of this study, it begins by providing a broad overview of the state of comparative and development administration worldwide; second, it offers a preliminary assessment of the extent to which Canadian scholars and academic programs at the undergraduate and graduate levels have been sufficiently grounded in the study—research, publishing, and teaching—of comparative and development administration; and finally, it concludes by offering our view of the future challenges facing public administration.

METHODOLOGY

While Canadian public administration scholars are undoubtedly contributing articles to more specialized academic journals that have comparative and development administration as a more central focus, such as *International Review of Administrative Sciences* or *International Journal of Public Administration*, we wanted to gauge the extent to which our flagship public administration journal, *CPA*, has been contributing to the growth of scholarship in these important fields of the subdiscipline. This approach, it should be noted, is not without precedent. Our study is modelled after similar analyses regarding the status of public administration in the United States and the United Kingdom, in terms of both the approach adopted, that is to say a content analysis of the leading journals, and our choice of journals (Candler, 2006; Rhodes et al., 1995; Van Wart and Cayer, 1990).

By examining the focus of the articles published in *CPA*, we can assess the extent to which both comparative and development administration have been integrated into the mainstream of the subdiscipline of public administration in this country. Our objective, therefore, is not to provide a comprehensive picture of the extent to which Canadian scholars are contributing to the fields of comparative and development public administration, but rather to ascertain whether they have been effectively integrated into the subdiscipline. This is not a trivial undertaking. As Jreisat (2005: 231) noted in his examination of the public administration in the United States, "Comparative public administration has practically evolved as a distinct topic of study rather than an integrated component." This was deemed to be a serious shortcoming that needs to be addressed.

In order to ascertain whether this observation would similarly apply to Canada, we have conducted a content analysis of the articles published in the journal during the past twenty-five years (1982–2006). Each contribution was classified according to its primary focus, be it country specific (Canada, United States, United Kingdom, Western Europe, Eastern Europe, Middle East, Australia, New Zealand, Africa, Asia, or Latin America/Caribbean, of which the latter two categories were further subdivided according to whether the country in question is categorized as being high, medium, or low on the United Nations Human Development Index [UNHDI]);[4] theoretical; or comparative (between industrialized countries, industrialized and developing countries, two or more developing countries, or international, which broadly addresses a multitude of countries).

It should be noted that an article referring to public administration in a country other than the country of the publication was not deemed to be comparative work; only those articles that specifically provided a comparison of two or more countries or administrative jurisdictions (for example, a comparison of some aspect of federal and provincial administration or between different provinces) were classified as such. In our own effort to be comparative, we conducted a similar content analysis of the leading public administration journals in both the United Kingdom (*Public Administration* [*PA*]) and the United States (*Public Administration Review* [*PAR*]). This data will allow us to comment on whether the Canadian experience is anomalous or follows a more common pattern of neglect of comparative and development administration in developed Western countries.

Given the broad classification of scholarly contributions that have been published in these three journals, from traditional articles, to notes and surveys, to commentary, to communications, with their varying lengths and academic rigour, codifying the content of each issue of the three journals over the period in question proved to be a challenge. While our principal concern was to determine the absolute and relative number of traditional scholarly articles that have been devoted to comparative and development administration, it was often difficult to ascertain what constituted the "main" articles of the journal. Moreover, we recognized these various other types of scholarly contributions often comprise a significant proportion of each journal, make an important contribution to its content, and, in most instances, resemble a journal article, albeit usually a much shorter one. Therefore, most contributions in each journal were coded in one of two tables—one for traditional journal articles, some of which were quite short in length, and the other for what we have called "other scholarly contributions." In this latter category were written works identified in the journals as "National Seminars," "Notes," "Special Reports," "Symposium,"[5] "Research Notes," "Commentary," "Professional Stream," "Public Management Forum," "European Forum," "Notes and Surveys," "Currents," "Comparative and International Administration," and "Public Management." Excluded from the data were those contributions identified within each journal as "Book Reviews," "Reply," "Comments," "Reviews," or "Communications" related to any previously published article; "Review Article"; "Review Essays"; "Editor's Note"; "Correspondence"; "Those Other Publications (TOPS)"; "Leaders in the Field"; and "The Reflective Practitioner."

With respect to the section of the chapter that examines the state of teaching public administration in Canada, we have chosen to examine a representative, rather than universal, sample of political science and public administration programs at twelve leading universities across the country to determine, firstly, whether comparative and development administration are being taught at both the graduate and undergraduate levels, and secondly, if so, whether the course(s) are electives or core to the program. This information was gathered by consulting the departmental websites of each of the universities in question. It should be noted that, in many cases, some of the public administration and policy courses that were listed are not available to students every year. This data is supplemented with the results of a recently published study on Canadian master's programs in public administration, public management, and public policy (Gow and Sutherland, 2004). The analysis offered in the chapter also includes a review of the seven different textbooks that have been used to teach public administration since the early 1980s in order to determine the treatment given to this subject matter in mainstream Canadian public administration.

THE GENESIS OF COMPARATIVE AND DEVELOPMENT ADMINISTRATION

The study of public administration is hardly new. One can trace the contributions of Kautilya in India, Herodotus and Aristotle in Greece, Machiavelli in Italy, and Ibn Khaldun in the Middle East, while most of the world scriptures have also outlined duties and obligations of rulers and their officials/servants (Raadschelders, 1998). The field of comparative public administration traces its origins to post–World War II, when a new field came into being as part of the subdiscipline of public administration. North American scholars and practitioners in the field of comparative administration set out to achieve greater understanding of the administrative culture and style, institutions, and structures and functions of the other nations with whom their countries became involved during World War II. However, their primary concern was to concentrate on the countries of Western Europe. Interaction with Europeans not only enabled these scholars to compare their own domestic systems, but later it also encouraged them to broaden their horizons to include countries within Asia, Latin America, and Africa when programs for foreign aid first got started.

By the early 1960s, when several Asian and African nations gained independence, North American (and later Western European) scholars were impelled by curiosity, and a need by newly independent nations for consultants and aid management, to shift their attention from the industrialized world (or the First World) to the emerging Third World. It is during that process that these academics created a new field: development administration. Further, spurred on by the American Ford Foundation's desire to develop new paradigms and funding, scholarly focus shifted to the administration of developing countries with a great fervour and missionary zeal to transplant Western administrative technologies. While the number of Western academics researching and consulting in developing countries increased by leaps and bounds (resulting in a rich variety of studies, theories, paradigms, and models), comparative public administration studies involving Western countries also continued. By the 1970s, two separate fields became distinct:

comparative public administration[6] (with its emphasis on similarities and differences), and development administration[7] (concerned with nation-building and social change processes in the Third World). In the latter instance, Jreisat (2005: 233) has argued that "the knowledge of administrative problems of developing countries is one of the most important achievements of comparative administration in the post-World War II era." International administration, although studied as part of comparative public administration, did not gain the same status as development administration.

Two major epistemological developments at the beginning of the twentieth century shaped the subdiscipline of public administration. One was the emphasis Woodrow Wilson and Frank Goodnow placed on the separation of administration from politics as the single most essential public administration reform in achieving efficiency and removing the objectionable and immoral practices of spoils and patronage from the democratic system. While Wilson expounded his politics versus administration dichotomy in 1887, by the 1950s, the "proverb" was assumed to be both a self-evident truth and a desirable goal. Administration was perceived as a self-contained world of its own, with its own separate values, rules, and methods, which were universalistic in nature. Thus, public administration came to be known as the universe of "facts," enshrined in a value-free environment, ready to be applied anywhere in the world, and nurtured by new positivist logic.

The second related development was the rise of scienticism in the discipline. While the roots of scientific analysis in social science disciplines can be traced back to the Enlightenment, the two core elements of the scientific method only slowly started to influence philosophy and human sciences. These core elements are rational objectivity and quantification. The main purpose of these scientific elements was, and still is, to remove biases and fallacies of human thought by searching for "hard" data, which can be measured and then presented in an objective and rational manner. In this context, academics and practitioners of public administration were considered to be applied scientists who remained dispassionately aloof from the subjective (and therefore irrational) realm of culture, values, and ethical issues. Furthermore, the American scientific management specialists thought the science of administration was an end itself, worthy of systematic study and improvement. For them, government administration was a machine to be driven by scientific management theories such as the planning, organizing, staffing, directing, coordinating, reporting, and budgeting (POSDCORB) principles, Planning Programming Budgeting System (PPBS), Management by Objectives (MBO), and, most recently, new public management (NPM). It was also thought the scientific study of administration led to the discovery of principles of administration analogous to the principles—or laws—of the physical sciences. And finally, it was assumed the principles of administration determined the way in which specific administrative values, such as efficiency and economy, could be realized. In such a scientific environment, the use of the merit principle became the main ingredient sustaining the operation of government administration.

Thus, public administration was thought by many as being a scientific endeavour in which individuality was emphasized, since the individual was the fundamental rational unit of measurement in relation to output, efficiency, and accountability. A philosophy of individual achievement was the foundation for the entrenchment of the merit principle. Only much later, in the 1980s, did a different philosophy of administration emerge. It contended that public administration could not be reduced to behaviourist experiments alone, since the latter tended to ignore factors such as spirituality, ethics, and morality.

COMPARATIVE PUBLIC ADMINISTRATION[8]

During the pre–World War II period, the focus of comparative public administration was largely on comparing the civil services (and their reforms) of selected European countries with those of the United States. With White's book, *Civil Service Abroad* (1964 [1935]), and a few books on British, French, and German bureaucracies, an interest emerged in some American universities to understand and compare the administrative style and operations of different civil services. Meanwhile,

British scholars, such as Herman Finer and William MacKenzie, had already started showing sustained interest not only in nations across the English Channel but also in the United States. Of course, students coming to British universities from dominions and colonies were encouraged to conduct research on their homeland.

World War II, the emergence of United Nations Organizations, and the post-war era of reconstruction in Europe suddenly propelled a great amount of interest towards comparative public administration. In the United States, scholars such as Dwight Waldo, Lynton Caldwell, Fred Riggs, Ferrel Heady, W. J. Siffin, and F. M. Marx, to name but a few, started teaching and writing about comparative administration beyond what White had initiated in the 1930s. But the main spurt of scholarly activity came in the late 1950s and early 1960s when the Ford, Carnegie, and Rockefeller foundations gave generous grants to American universities to support research on the problems of administration—not only in the industrialized West but also among the newly independent developing nations. At the same time, the International Institute of Administrative Sciences at Brussels was taking the lead in Europe to encourage research and publications in comparative administrative science.

However, the field was able to take a quantum leap in 1962 when a Ford Foundation grant to the American Society for Public Administration enabled its Comparative Administration Group (CAG) to organize regular seminars and conferences, and to encourage research and publications. A flood of scholarly activities engulfed the field (Henderson, 1971; Raphaeli, 1967; Caldwell, 1965; Waldo, 1953; Heady and Stokes, 1962; Riggs, 1961; Siffin, 1957). This was further supplemented by the contributions made by scholars from across the Atlantic and in interaction with developing countries' researchers. Among scholars, it was the innovative leadership of Riggs that provided the necessary theoretical underpinnings to the field (Jones and Klingner, 2007; Riggs, 1998).

Riggs (1961) discerned three trends in comparative public administration: (1) a movement from normative to more empirical approaches; (2) a movement from ideographic to nomothetic approaches; and (3) a shift from a nonecological to an ecological form of study. These trends stressed the need for empirical description and explanation, a distinction between unique case studies as opposed to those aimed at testing general propositions, and a shift from the isolated study of administrative institutions to placing them in a larger context or societal framework. From this, Riggs suggested that, ideally, the work of CAG should be generally empirical, nomothetic, and ecological. However, such a paradigm was more appropriate in the context of the West, where empiricism and theory-testing were considered a routine matter rather than a concerted effort or anthropological venture. Nevertheless, Western public administration experts continued working on developing nations, trying to make sense of the unfathomable and unpredictable situations in those countries. Undaunted, the "experts in public administration, not only from the United States but from several European countries as well, were scattered around the world, engaged in similar projects to export administrative technology, largely drawn from American experience, to a multitude of developing countries" (Heady, 1979: 17). They were all enthused with translating the dream of the "American way" into a reality by changing, transplanting, and replicating the administrative system they knew best.

The 1950s and 1960s were actually the days of great vision and hope that the whole world might eventually speak the same administrative language. However, within a decade, and certainly by the early 1970s, a serious crisis emerged in the field partly due to the decline in funding by American foundations, which constrained research, and partly to the failure of the American dream materializing in the transfer of administrative technology to developing nations. Not only did CAG go out of existence in 1973, but even its flagship, the *Journal of Comparative Administration*, ceased publication in 1974, after only five years of existence (Heady, 1979: 23). Henderson (1971), writing for the "new public administration" (the Minnowbrook Conference), predicted that the future of comparative public administration might be relegated to insignificance, partly because of the funding shift to research on the problems of cities and local government, and partly due to rejection of CAG thinking by the public administration establishment. From then on until the mid-1980s, the field suffered a period of disillusionment, confusion, identity crisis, and retrospection. Only by the late 1980s did interest in comparative public administration slowly start to resurface due to the efforts of some scholars, in both developed and developing nations, who came to recognize the usefulness of multicultural and multidimensional approaches to administration. Thus, a new emphasis emerged, along with the new name, "development administration," generally involving the globalization of paradigms.

DEVELOPMENT ADMINISTRATION

Despite the problems in the evolution of comparative public administration noted above, remarkably, development administration had seen the light of the day and made its mark already, principally with reference to countries of the Middle East, East and South Asia, Africa, and Latin America emerging from the process of decolonization and seeking to secure the benefits of aid under either bilateral or multilateral programs of economic and social development. Soon, development became an intellectual concern in American social sciences. During the late 1950s, when Rostow's *The Stages of Economic Growth: A Non-Communist Manifesto* (1960) was published, the political development literature tried hard to identify the noneconomic conditions for an accelerated—and orderly—economic growth. Development administration was perceived as an institution contributing mainly to stability and systems maintenance, along with its bureaucracy as a functional condition for stability and legitimacy in the political development of newer states. It was through development administration that an institutional framework was to be operative by converting inputs of objectives, capital, and know-how into developmental outputs.

This characterization of development administration emphasized the formal and technical aspects of government machinery. Developmental goals were assumed to be self-evident and, therefore, broadly agreed upon by the local and Westernized elites. Their names were "nation-building" and "socio-economic development" (Esman, 1966). Swerdlow (1975) identified two interrelated tasks in the development process: institution-building and planning. Other authors outlined a number of other development-oriented activities, such as the management of change, establishing an interface between the "inner" environment and the larger intra- and extrasocietal context, and the mobilization of human and physical capital for development objectives and related political action.

The 1950s and 1960s were decades of hope and prosperity. It was confidently expected that, armed with modern technology, the administrative state would overcome the challenges of poverty and backwardness. The rapid reconstruction of Europe and Japan reinforced this strong conviction. Almost throughout the world, the approach was technocratic. The assumption was that problems, whatever their nature, lay *with* and *at* the periphery; by contrast, the solution was always locked in the centre. In a way, the prevalent attitude was that developing countries not only had the problem but really were the problem. Conversely, the West postulated both to have and to be the solution. It was tacitly taken for granted that traditional societies had to be saved, both from the appeal of Communism and from themselves (Nef and Dwivedi, 1981).

A developmental creed soon emerged, which posited that in order to attain development, a country's administrative structure ought to be overhauled in order to conform to the standards of the most advanced industrial societies. The issue, thus, consisted in the reorganization of the existing traditional machinery into a new entity. This needed to be accomplished through administrative development: the modernization of the public service machinery through exogenous inducement, and the transfer of technology and training of local staff by so-called foreign experts. For this task, there was already a neat prescriptive model to be found in Western traditions. This was based on the dichotomy between politics and administration, a system that exemplified a pyramidal hierarchy, along with unity of command, political neutrality, recruitment and promotion based on the merit principle, public service accountability, objectivity, and integrity. In reality, these principles coexisted in most places with local traditional methods. Thus, a parallel value system gained currency in those parts of the world where Western models were set up, but it operated concurrently with traditional economies and black markets. Rarely were the principles of development administration, as recommended by the "experts," seriously questioned in theory; they were generally accepted at face value by the indigenous elites, especially in those countries where a relatively smooth transition to nationhood had taken place.

The post-independence political and bureaucratic elites rapidly moved to replace colonial administrators in developing countries. A Western education was widely perceived to be the vehicle both for personal advancement and for acceptance into the global community of Western-trained professionals. Thus, it is not surprising to find that the administrative machinery that progressively took shape was incapable of implementing developmental goals, particularly when dealing with poverty and scarcity. In spite of modern rhetoric, administrative systems in developing countries continued to be imitative and ritualistic. Practices, styles, and structures of administration generally unrelated to local traditions, needs, and realities succeeded in reproducing the symbolism, but not the substance, of a British, French, or American administrative system. Even where a relatively large contingent of trained functionaries existed, as was the case in India, Pakistan, Sri Lanka, Kenya, Nigeria, or Ghana, the perpetuation of the colonial administrative culture prevailed. For most of the local elites, technical solutions appeared more palatable than the substantive political options needed to bring about real socio-economic change. Reorganization and rationalization soon became ends in themselves, far more than the means of development or development administration.

FROM HOPE TO GROWING DOUBTS

Not surprisingly, euphoria in the 1950s and the 1960s gave way to a rude awakening during the 1970s. With the energy and debt crises bringing two decades of prosperity to a rather abrupt close, the very foundations of development administration were badly shaken. Not only was its usefulness to the Third World suddenly called into question but an intellectual crisis also spread among the students of development administration in Western countries. The gap between the centre and the periphery was widening rather than narrowing, both in relative and absolute terms. Instead of development and nation-building, turmoil and fragmentation proliferated throughout Africa, Asia, the Middle East, and Latin America. Urban crises, the drastic cessation of growth and resulting unemployment, breakdowns of public institutions, and the decline of civic morality dashed earlier hopes that First-World administrative technology and science would solve all the globe's problems.

During the fourth development decade, the New International Economic Order (NIEO) became an important new symbol in the development arena. Its demand for a basic realignment of the world economy through changes in trade, aid, and technological transfers received lip service but was generally ignored by the richer donor nations. In fact, there was no consensus concerning NIEO objectives, and some commentators felt that it might even harm certain countries. While the World Bank and the International Labour Organisation symbolically endorsed this approach, the monumental changes demanded by NIEO did not occur. In the absence of shared strategies, NIEO soon went the way of earlier concepts. By the end of the 1980s, another major event badly shook the existing order: the withering away of the USSR and the related entry of these former Communist states into the ambit of the Third World. Soon, attention was diverted and a share of aid resources were channelled towards these countries, which were now denoted as "transitional"; for how long that would be the case, no one ventured to say.

Cataclysmic events in the East coincided with an impressive revival of ultraconservative ideologies in the West. First, the rise of Margaret Thatcher, and later, Ronald Reagan, added a powerful impetus to the NPM paradigm. NPM dominated the scene during the 1980s and into the 1990s. Its recipes emphasized drastic reforms predicated on a number of standard prescriptions: (1) an accent on results, both in the planning and in the evaluation of programs and people; (2) the treatment of the public and citizens as customers; (3) the delegation of authority as close to the action level as possible; (4) the empowerment of "clients" (devolution); (5) paying greater attention to cost through comprehensive auditing, contracting out (outsourcing), and the introduction of competitive practices into the public sphere; and (6) the introduction of private sector techniques calculated to motivate employees, such as merit/performance pay, mission statements, and quality circles (Dwivedi and Gow, 1999: 130; Aucoin, 1995). Other key operational "principles" included budget restraint and "downsizing" bureaucracy. NPM also introduced the notions of corporate management, corporate culture, and market-driven rhetoric. The NPM paradigm was based on the premise that by reducing bureaucracy and monopolistic practices, corruption in government would decline, and that by narrowing down the scope of government activities, an efficient, transparent, and accountable system of governance would necessarily emerge. It was thought that with less government there would be fewer bureaucratic problems.

In retrospect, we know this did not happen. However, in the 1980s and well into the 1990s, NPM became a fixation in the Anglo-Saxon world, as well as in some important financial institutions. Its advocates did not realize that their precepts would soon prove to be a "recipe for disasters by advocating measures that encourage information distortion and public risk-taking, stifling voices of caution, experience and independence" (Hood and Jackson, 1994: 478). For many theoreticians and practitioners, the greatest charge against the type of managerialism promoted by NPM was its reductionism and lack of imagination. It tried to encapsulate a complex prismatic phenomenon into a single model drawn from an idealized version of the private sector, which, in reality, existed in only a limited number of capitalist countries. It turned the public servant from being a steward of the state to being an entrepreneur, for whom the moral constraints of public accountability were formalistic irritants. Carried to their extreme, NPM techniques created an ethical vacuum and an amoral state. It can be asserted that NPM produced a sort of "McDonaldization" of development, with multinational corporations joining forces with international agencies to demand similar laws, access to state apparatus, less rules and regulations, and outsourcing and privatization, all in the name of freedom and debureaucratization (Argyriades, Dwivedi, and Jabbra, 2007: xx–xxxvii).

As a prescriptive model to solve the problems of government and open the road to development, NPM left no scope for diversity. During the 1980s and well into the 1990s, it underpinned the programs of structural adjustments with which development agencies sought to address the needs of countries in the Third World. Presently better known as "one size fits all" solutions, NPM recipes seldom availed the countries for which they were intended. Rather, they have contributed to a legacy that earned the 1980s the name, "the lost decade."

The golden age of the 1960s turned into an age of pessimism during the 1980s and early 1990s. Developing nations were disillusioned when they found that instead of being treated truly as recipient countries, they were compelled to make net transfers of their meager resources to the West. In order to service their debt, several countries came very close to bankruptcy. Restrictive trade practices prohibited poor nations from exporting their products. The problem was further compounded at the beginning of the 1990s, when commodity prices fell to their lowest level in fifty years, while the prices of manufactured goods from rich countries kept rising. It is no wonder that poverty, inequality, oppression, and despair have continued to rise in the South. Nevertheless, there were new rays of hope from the worldwide awareness displayed at the Earth Summit in 1992 and the September 2000 Millennium Summit at the United Nations in New York. Both of these events affirmed the need for greater solidarity worldwide, as well as shared responsibility in meeting and addressing the challenges confronting all countries and all peoples in the twenty-first century.

CANADIAN CONTRIBUTIONS TO THE FIELDS OF COMPARATIVE AND DEVELOPMENT ADMINISTRATION

Now that the chapter has broadly surveyed the genesis and evolution of both comparative and development administration, it will consider some of the specific contributions of Canadian public administration scholars to this body of knowledge, since, as Jreisat (2005: 236) noted,

Table 12.1 Selected university courses in public administration and public policy, 2008

	Number of courses in public administration/public policy		Number of courses in comparative/development administration			
			Undergraduate		Graduate	
University	Undergraduate	Graduate	Elective	Core	Elective	Core
Alberta	12	2	0	0	0	0
Brock	21	5	0	0	0	0
Carleton	41	65	2ª	0	9ᵇ	0
Dalhousie	16	26	1	0	0	1ᶜ
École nationale d'administration publique (ÉNAP)	N/A	44(M.P.A.) 9(Ph.D.)	N/A	N/A	1(M.P.A.) 0(Ph.D.)	0(M.P.A.) 0(Ph.D.)
Guelph	17	15(Guelph-McMaster)	1(B.A.) 1(B.Comm. PMGT)	0(B.A.) 1(B.Comm. PMGT)	1(Guelph-McMaster)	0(Guelph-McMaster)
Queen's	6	50	0	0	0ᵈ	0
Regina	7	9(M.A.) 52(M.P.A./Ph.D.)	0	0	0(M.A.) 1(M.P.A./Ph.D.)	0(M.A.) 0(M.P.A./Ph.D.)
Ryerson	33	17	1ª	0	1	0

Toronto	17	5(M.A.) 12(M.P.P.)	0	0	0	0(M.A.) 0(M.P.P.)	0(M.A.) 0(M.P.P.)
Victoria	9	1(M.A.—Poli Sci) 1(Ph.D.—Poli Sci) 23(M.P.A.) 7(Ph.D.–ADMN)	0	0	1e(M.A.—Poli Sci) 1e(Ph.D.—Poli Sci) 0(M.P.A.) 1e(Ph.D.—ADMN)	0(M.A.—Poli Sci) 0(Ph.D.—Poli Sci) 0(M.P.A.) 0(Ph.D.—ADMN)
Waterloo	18	14	1[a]	0	1	0

[a] There are one or more additional courses that focus on various aspects of comparative public policy.

[b] Those enrolled in an M.A. in public administration with an international and development concentration must take 2.0 credits from this group of courses, which focus on administration, policy, civil society, and evaluation in the context of developing countries.

[c] One of the core courses is "Management without Borders," which appears to have an international focus.

[d] Queen's does, however, offer two courses that focus on policy issues and economic reform in China, but these are taught at Fudan University in China as part of the School of Policy Studies-Fudan Interchange Program.

[e] This is a course on comparative public policy and governance.

"a realistic assessment of where we are and where we want to be is necessary for comparative public administration to reach its potential." First, the chapter considers the extent to which Canadian scholars are teaching comparative and development administration in both their undergraduate and graduate programs in political science and public administration. It then considers the textbooks that have been available to teach students public administration to determine whether the fields of comparative and development administration have been given due consideration. Finally, the chapter examines *CPA* and two foreign journals to assess the extent to which they have embraced this subject matter.

THE STATE OF PUBLIC ADMINISTRATION EDUCATION IN CANADA

Public administration as a field of study in Canada really only got started in the 1950s, although Dalhousie University did start offering degrees in public administration in 1936 and Carleton University—formerly Carleton College—followed suit in 1946 (Inwood, 2004 [1999]: 5). Thus, it is not surprising that two of public administration's fields, comparative and development administration, had an even later start. During the period of the 1950s and early 1960s, Carleton University was perhaps the first and one of only a few institutions where comparative public administration was taught on a regular basis, and even then this was only done at the graduate level.[9] Another exception was the Department of Political Economy at the University of Toronto, where such a course was on the books but not offered on a regular basis. In those days, the field of comparative public administration was so underdeveloped that Canadian academics were forced to rely largely on American materials in their course curricula.

When a new wave of academics joined Canadian universities in the mid-1960s, some of them were able to introduce undergraduate and/or graduate courses in comparative public administration in their political science departments. However, these "exotic" courses became an easy victim of Canadian nationalism in the early 1970s. As demonstrated in Table 12.1, our survey of selected Canadian departments of political science and schools of public administration and public policy reveals that the situation has not appreciably improved since that time. Comparative and development administration generally continue to languish in the curricula of both undergraduate and graduate programs of political science and public administration at Canadian universities. A similar situation exists in the United States. Jreisat (2005: 231) wrote, "In most master of public administration programs in the US, the extent of curriculum commitment to the comparative approach is either a stand-alone elective course or none at all."

Only five of the eleven undergraduate programs surveyed offered a course in either comparative or development administration, although a few of them (Carleton, Ryerson, and Waterloo) had one or more additional courses on various comparative public policy topics. The University of Guelph was unique among all of the institutions in terms of requiring a course in comparative or development administration. As part of its degree, students enrolled in the B.Comm. public management program at Guelph must complete a third-year course in comparative public policy and administration.

At the graduate level, the results were marginally better, with seven out of twelve of the universities examined offering a single course on comparative or development administration. Perhaps not surprising given its early leadership role in this field, Carleton University actually offers nine different graduate courses out of a complement of sixty-five that focus on administration, policy, civil society, and evaluation in the context of developing countries. Students specializing in the international and development concentration in the M.A. in public administration must complete 2.0 credits from this group of nine courses. The sole core course among the graduate programs was a course entitled, "Management without Borders" at Dalhousie, which, while perhaps not explicitly comparative, appears to have an international focus.

Gow and Sutherland (2004) recently conducted a review of sixteen Canadian master's degree programs in public administration, public policy, and public management. They discovered a great deal of variation across the programs and were able to identify seventeen different core courses, including, among others, micro- and macro-economics, governance, theories of public administration and public policy, research methods, public finance, and human resources. Conspicuously absent from the list were courses in the fields of comparative and development administration. Based on their evaluation of these programs, Gow and Sutherland classified them into four distinct clusters: those with a management orientation (Dalhousie, ÉNAP, and Regina); those with a public policy orientation (Carleton, Concordia, Laval, Queen's, Regina, and Simon Fraser); those with a political science orientation (Concordia, Guelph-McMaster, and Manitoba-Winnipeg); and those that combined management and policy (Dalhousie, Victoria, and York). One of the conclusions stemming from their research was that, when compared with the curriculum standards established by the National Association of Schools and Programs of Public Administration (NASPAA) in the United States, most Canadian programs focus too much on policy to the detriment of management.

In light of this fact, it is not at all surprising that comparative and development administration have not figured prominently in the course curricula in Canadian universities. Even when an undergraduate or graduate program offered a course on comparative or development administration, in virtually all cases the course was an elective for the program, which means that students can and do sidestep these courses at their discretion. Heady (2001: 393) lamented this was the case with respect to graduate programs in public administration in the United States, suggesting that other countries did a better job in terms of "exposing students preparing for careers in the public service to at least rudimentary instruction about comparative experience." Our research, however, indicates that Canadian institutions are likely no better in this regard.

TEXTBOOK TREATMENTS OF COMPARATIVE AND DEVELOPMENT ADMINISTRATION

Textbooks used to teach public administration have also remained inward in their approach. Throughout most of the 1980s and 1990s, most academics who taught courses in public administration relied primarily on one of two books, both of which were revised several times: *Public Administration in Canada* by Kernaghan and Siegel (1999 [1991]) and *Canadian Public Administration* by Adie and Thomas (1990 [1982]). Neither of these books, at over seven hundred and six hundred pages in length, respectively, had a chapter dealing with comparative or development administration. The only mention of comparative material in the Adie and Thomas book was found in the third chapter in a seven-page section entitled, "Britain and the US: Similar Impetus but Different Paths to Merit," and in an additional six pages in the fifth chapter under the heading, "Alternative Approaches to Bureaucratic Accountability: Valuable Lessons from Abroad," which again drew upon material from the United Kingdom and the United States. Nothing in the Kernaghan and Siegel text is overtly comparative, although the influence of American public administration scholars is palpable.[10] The same can be said for Wilson's book, *Canadian Public Policy and Administration* (1981).

By 2006 three new Canadian public administration textbooks had been introduced into the marketplace. The first edition of Inwood's book, *Understanding Canadian Public Administration* (2004), was published in 1999, while *Thinking Government* by Johnson (2006) was initially introduced in 2002. The third contribution was an edited book on Canadian public administration by Dunn (2002). Upon reviewing the content of these books, however, it is readily apparent that they continued to ignore comparative and development administration. Dunn's edited book is the most comparative of the three but like the other two has nothing to say about development administration. Two of the twenty-nine chapters place elements of Canadian public administration in a comparative context. The first chapter, by Borins, examines changes in the public sector by comparing developments in the United Kingdom, New Zealand, and the United States with those in Canada, while in the sixth chapter Kernaghan offers a modicum of comparison when discussing political conventions, values, and public service in Canada by placing them in the context of other Westminster-style democracies.

Inwood's book is a good exemplar of the problem of comparative and development administration evolving separately from the broader subdiscipline of public administration. In the preface to his book, Inwood (2004 [1999]: xv) suggests that "it is meant to be used as the primary text for courses in public administration," noting further that the purpose of his work is to "foster an understanding of basic elements of public administration, leaving detailed analysis of specific sub-fields to more specialized sources." The book, therefore, like Johnson's *Thinking Government*, covers the usual terrain of public administration— organization theory, the machinery of government, evaluation, public sector human resources and financial management, ethics, accountability and the relationship between public administration and both the law and public policy—and it devotes no attention to comparative and development administration.

The problem, of course, is that most students do not necessarily gain exposure to comparative and development administration in these more specialized courses, either because they are not offered or students make a conscious choice not to enroll in them. Furthermore, given the fact that comparative and development administration have not been adequately incorporated into the curricula (both in terms of the types of more specialized courses offered and the public administration textbooks used to teach the discipline more generically) at Canadian universities, it becomes a formidable challenge to break the cycle of neglect. Successive generations of scholars have not had much, if any, exposure to comparative and development administration and therefore are ill-equipped to teach and conduct research in these areas once they join the professoriate.

Another consequence of the prevailing situation is that both our practitioners and academics are not adequately prepared to deal with other foreign administrations. Since the end of the Cold War, global integration has become the trend. Therefore, Canada's public administration body will have to understand and work with other foreign governments and their bureaucracies. Cooperative tasks might include trade initiatives under the auspices of the World Trade Organization, environmentally sound and sustainable development (Kyoto, for example), or dealing with the ever-present threat of global terrorism in the post-9/11 environment. Furthermore, it is unimaginable how

Canada's foreign aid policy-makers can formulate aid policy without a thorough background in comparative and development administration. They can plan all kinds of development projects, but if they do not take into account the administrative structure of the country where the project is to be implemented, the project is likely to fail (Caiden and Caiden, 1990: 385).

Therefore, if we are going to be able to rectify this deficiency, at a minimum, comparative and development administration chapters must be included in Canadian public administration textbooks. This would provide all students of public administration with at least some exposure to comparative and development administration. Departments also need to offer more course options on these topics. Enhancing the number of elective courses in comparative and development administration, however, is a necessary but not sufficient means of addressing the problem, since many students would not choose to enroll in such courses of their own volition. A more progressive step would be for departments to actually recognize the value of the fields of comparative and development administration to the subdiscipline of public administration and ultimately stipulate that courses in these areas must be completed as part of the requirements for a degree program.

JOURNAL PUBLICATIONS

Having considered some important pedagogical issues pertaining to comparative and development administration, the chapter now turns to an examination of the focus of articles and other scholarly contributions to *CPA*, which is the main journal in this country that caters to the exchange of scholarly work by the public administration community— both practitioner and academic. Given the stature of this journal, it is informative to examine how the fields of comparative and development administration have fared on its pages over the years, both through the articles published and the editorial policies set by the various editors. The importance of this latter point should not be underestimated. After all, one of the key determinants of the types of articles that are published in journals is the policy direction provided by the editor. While noting that it is difficult to ascertain exactly the extent to which editors can shape the content of the journal, because they are dependent on both the types of articles that are submitted and the assessment of the referees, Carroll and Kpessa (2007: 488) nonetheless recently acknowledged, "They do, however, have the scope of determining what is of interest to the readers and encouraging, or commissioning, articles in certain areas."

Five editors have provided leadership for *CPA* since 1980, namely Kenneth Kernaghan (1980–1987), V. Seymour Wilson (1987–1992), Paul Thomas (1993–1997), Allan Tupper (1998–2004), and Barbara Carroll (2004–present), with each one providing a statement of his or her editorial intent. It is a practice that first began when Donald Smiley was editor of the journal between 1974 and 1979. Smiley (1974: 365, 366) stated, "There are several important areas of public policy about which the journal has published very little and I intend some general promotional activity here," and noted further that "although it is inevitable that a journal such as this will come to reflect the biases and priorities of its editor, I have no immediate plans to effect radical changes in *Canadian Public Administration*." Despite this disclaimer, it is difficult to say that he and subsequent editors have not influenced, directly or indirectly, the flow and content of the journal.

Kernaghan succeeded Smiley in 1979 and his editorial statement appeared in 1980. He said that his appointment "as editor of *Canadian Public Administration* prompted me to reflect on the progress, problems and prospects of the study and practice of public administration in this country" (Kernaghan, 1980: 1). As such, his statement carried information about the number of manuscripts received, published, rejected, and withdrawn. He set the editorial direction of the journal by very explicitly stating that "the journal will continue to focus primarily on Canadian concerns," although he did mention he would welcome manuscripts "if they compare Canadian institutions and developments with those in other countries or if they examine matters in foreign states or international organizations that are of particular relevance to public administration in Canada" (Kernaghan, 1980: 4). Nevertheless, the number of articles dealing with comparative and development administration remained negligible.

Wilson took over from Kernaghan in 1987. During his first term, Wilson did not expound on his editorial policy, so it is likely safe to assume that he continued the policy of his predecessor. However, there was a change in the air. Carroll and Kpessa (2007: 486), for example, noted a palpable increase in the number of articles on personnel management and human resources management under his editorship. In our own survey of the journal, we found that a number of articles dealing with issues such as multicultural policy and race relations, development administration, and administrative reforms in China were published. More specifically, six articles dealing with the administrative systems of foreign governments were published in 1989 and 1990. However, Wilson (1990: 469) was quick to admit in a second editorial statement (the first such acknowledgment by an editor of *CPA*) that "given our mandate, we have not been particularly successful in attracting high-quality comparative and international administration manuscripts." He went on to say that he hoped "to begin rectifying this lacuna over the next three years" (469).

The next editor was Thomas. It was during his tenure that a readership survey was conducted to help shape the future direction of the journal. In his first editorial statement, Thomas (1994a: 3) wrote: "To what extent should the journal publish articles on the substance of public policy, on the general political process, and on comparative public administration?" Implicit in this question is the recognition that the journal had not devoted enough attention to public administration concerns from a comparative perspective. As the results of the readership survey revealed, it was a concern shared by the membership. When asked which topics should receive more coverage in the journal, the two more frequently cited categories were, firstly, municipal government, and, secondly, comparative public administration. Thomas (1994b: 539), however, noted the journal "cannot be all things to all readers," and reaffirmed that "the primary purpose of the Journal will remain to promote and to publish research findings which add to the knowledge base of the theory and practice of public administration in a Canadian context." However, in response to some concern that had been expressed that the journal "might be unreceptive to non-Canadian material," the editorial board made a decision to reaffirm "its policy of welcoming submissions in the field of comparative public administration when they have relevance to Canadian readers" (540).

Tupper began his stint as editor in 1998. He, too, provided a statement regarding the editorial policies and priorities of the journal, and, as might be expected, it had much in common with earlier statements. Tupper was hoping to see more controversial topics covered in the journal, as well as major review articles and policy analysis related to the public sector in the broadest sense. An emphasis on Canada, in particular the "administrative systems and practices of the federal, provincial and municipal governments," continued to be the primary focus of the journal (Tupper, 1999: 149). However, Tupper, like those before him, acknowledged that

> the Journal, while particularly interested in Canada, must reflect and understand major developments in other countries and parts of the world. We therefore invite essays on relevant topics in non-Canadian settings. Essays that examine the experiences of countries other than Canada need not hold direct lessons for Canadian readers. Explicitly comparative essays are welcome and necessary in an era of change. (1999: 149–150)

The current editor of *CPA* is Carroll, who assumed the position in 2004. Her identified goal is to continue to maintain the overall quality of the journal "while reflecting the changing interests and priorities of public administration." She went on to say, "To reflect the changing interests of some researchers, I would welcome more articles that are quantitative in nature and more articles that are comparative in analysis" (Carroll, 2005: 1–2).

It is one thing to identify editorial preferences and intentions, but it is quite another to exactly determine the focus of the articles that were published during one's editorship. As noted previously, aside from the editorial policies and preferences of the journal's editor, this is obviously determined in large part by what the scholars and practitioners themselves are researching and writing about, and, in turn, which journals they are submitting their work to for peer review. For example, in 1982, the first year of our study, *CPA* published a twenty-fifth anniversary issue that consisted of fifteen articles ranging from the state of the discipline, to the future of public administration in Canada, to organization theory, administration in provincial and municipal governments, public enterprise, administrative law, and personnel management in Canada. However, there was not a single article on comparative and development administration. The editor explained the purpose of this special number: "The essays in this volume traverse the field of Canadian public administration to see how far we have traveled, the directions in which we are moving and the barriers still standing in the way of our progress" (Kernaghan, 1982: 444). In that same statement, Kernaghan provided a statistical distribution of the articles published in the journal from 1968 to 1981; notably, neither comparative nor development administration were listed as subject matter worthy of mention among fourteen topics.

In the same anniversary issue, Laframboise (1982: 507), writing on the future of public administration in Canada, admonished,

> It is my view that a failure by the discipline and the profession to keep up to date on the evolving real world, both externally … and internally as reflected in the way we manage our public service, is the underlying reason why the discipline of public administration, as a body of knowledge, suffers from diminishing relevance.

It is the field of comparative and development administration that reflects the "evolving real world" externally, which makes such a glaring gap in the field at the time so troubling.

While development administration is a topic that does not appear to have registered at all in the consciousness of successive journal editors, clearly, as noted in the editorial statements above, there has been both a persistent identification of the need to be more comparative in the journal and an editorial receptivity to publishing such articles. Yet, the important question to address is whether this has resulted in any real progress over the last twenty-five years in terms of the number of comparative public administration articles published in the journal. Unfortunately, our research suggests that has not been the case. Almost a decade after the Laframboise piece was published, Savoie (1990) wrote an article that examined the discipline of public administration as practiced by academics in Canada. However, in his "call to action," the fields of comparative and development administration were not included.

Since academics and their programs were commented upon by Savoie, Pross (1990) took the challenge and wrote a rebuttal published in the next issue of *CPA*. He, too, did not mention the comparative and development administration fields in his article, although he did state that "financial constraints severely hamper attempts to diversify the field" (1990: 624). Ironically, in Candler's recent survey of the evolution of public administration in Australia, Brazil, and Canada, he noted that the public administration journals examined in his study have paid scant attention to diversity (race, gender, social class, and indigenous peoples) as a "locus of research" and lamented "the slowness with which these journals have adapted to new trends in the field" (2006: 344). Yet, he himself chose to adopt a categorization of issue focus that ignores the fields of comparative and development administration (Candler, 2006: 342). This, too, was the case in Carroll and Kpessa's fifty-year survey of the trends in *CPA*, whose "dominant areas of interest have been administrative theory, and political and legal institutions" (2007: 484).

Our own content analysis of the various contributions to *CPA* over the past twenty-five years confirms the troubling state of the field. Tables 12.2 and 12.3 summarize the results, not only for this journal but also for *PAR* and *PA*, the flagship public administration journals in the United States and United Kingdom, respectively, since we wanted to determine whether our neglect is anomalous or more symptomatic of a deep-seated problem of public administration in the Western world. Table 12.2 clearly shows that for each five-year interval, 80 to 90 percent of the main articles published in *CPA* since 1982 have focused on public administration issues in a Canadian context. A total of 398 out of the 461 main articles (86 percent) have been dedicated to Canadian topics. An equally large percentage of the "other scholarly contributions" (see table 12.3) in this journal has similarly been devoted

Table 12.2 Focus of main articles in CPA, PAR, and PA, 1982–2006

Focus	1982–1986 CPA N (%)	1982–1986 PAR N (%)	1982–1986 PA N (%)	1987–1991 CPA N (%)	1987–1991 PAR N (%)	1987–1991 PA N (%)	1992–1996 CPA N (%)	1992–1996 PAR N (%)	1992–1996 PA N (%)	1997–2001 CPA N (%)	1997–2001 PAR N (%)	1997–2001 PA N (%)	2002–2006 CPA N (%)	2002–2006 PAR N (%)	2002–2006 PA N (%)
Canada	80 (89)	2 (0.8)	0	76 (84)	0	0	90 (87)	1 (0.4)	0	77 (92)	0	0	75 (81.5)	4 (1)	1 (1)
United States	0	207 (87)	4 (4)	0	208 (90)	0	0	201 (81)	1 (1)	0	176 (85)	1 (.9)	0	206 (77)	2 (2)
United Kingdom	0	0	72 (79)	0	0	77 (83)	0	2 (0.8)	77 (83)	0	1 (0.5)	95 (83)	0	3 (1)	80 (75)
Western Europe	0	1 (0.4)	0	0	0	4 (4)	0	5 (2)	2 (2)	0	1 (0.5)	2 (2)	0	9 (3)	5 (4.5)
Eastern Europe	0	0	0	0	0	1 (1)	0	1 (0.4)	0	0	1 (0.5)	0	0	2 (0.7)	0
Middle East	0	0	0	0	2 (0.8)	0	0	0	0	0	1 (0.5)	0	0	0	0
Australia	0	1 (0.4)	1 (1)	0	0	0	0	0	0	0	0	1 (0.9)	0	2 (0.7)	1 (1)
New Zealand	0	0	0	0	0	1 (1)	0	0	0	0	1 (0.5)	2 (2)	0	0	1 (1)
Asia High UNHDI	0	0	1 (1)	0	2 (0.8)	0	0	5 (2)	0	0	0	0	0	5 (2)	0

Med UNHDI	0	1 (0.4)	0	0	0	0	0	0	0	0	0	0	0	0	0
Low UNHDI	0	1 (0.4)	0	0	0	0	0	0	0	0	0	0	0	0	0
Africa	0	1 (0.4)	0	0	0	0	0	0	0	0	0	0	0	2 (0.7)	0
Latin America Caribbean High UNHDI	0	0	0	0	0	0	0	0	0	0	0	0	0	2 (0.7)	0
Med UNHDI	0	1 (0.4)	0	0	0	0	0	0	0	0				2 (0.7)	
Low UNHDI	0	0	0	0	0	0	0	0	0	0				0	
Theory	1 (1)	16 (7)	1 (1)	3 (3)	14 (6)	3 (3)	0	21 (8)	1 (1)	0	10 (5)	3 (2.5)	2 (2)	17 (6)	4 (4)
Comparative industrialized	9 (10)	3 (1)	11 (12)	9 (10)	5 (2)	6 (6)	13 (12.5)	4 (1.5)	11 (12)	5 (6)	6 (3)	9 (8)	13 (14)	9 (3)	11 (10)
Comparative industrialized-developing	0	0	0	2 (2)	0	1 (1)	0	1 (0.4)	0	1 (1)	2 (1)	0	1 (1)	1 (0.4)	0
Comparative developing-developing	0	0	0	0	0	0	0	1 (0.4)	0	0	1 (0.5)	0	0	1 (0.4)	0
International	0	4 (2)	1 (1)	1 (1)	0	0	1 (0.9)	6 (2)	1 (1)	1 (1)	6 (3)	2 (2)	1 (1)	3 (1)	2 (2)
TOTAL	**90**	**238**	**91**	**91**	**231**	**93**	**104**	**248**	**93**	**84**	**206**	**115**	**92**	**268**	**10**

Table 12.3 Focus of other scholarly contributions in *CPA*, *PAR*, and *PA*, 1982–2006

Focus	1982–1986			1987–1991			1992–1996			1997–2001			2002–2006		
	CPA N (%)	PAR N (%)	PA N (%)	CPA N (%)	PAR N (%)	PA N (%)	CPA N (%)	PAR N (%)	PA N (%)	CPA N (%)	PAR N (%)	PA N (%)	CPA N (%)	PAR N (%)	PA N (%)
Canada	77 (92)	0	0	64 (89)	0	0	27 (90)	0	0	14 (82)	0	0	3 (75)		0
United States	0	113 (84)	2 (3.5)	0	15 (79)	0	0	45 (90)	1 (1)	0	20 (83)	5 (5)	0	10 (77)	4 (4)
United Kingdom	0	0	43 (75)	0	0	25 (74)	0	0	18 (25)	0	0	28 (27)	0	0	20 (20)
Western Europe	0	0	5 (9)	0	1 (5)	1 (3)	0	0	13 (18)	0	0	32 (31)	0	1 (8)	57 (57.5)
Eastern Europe	0	0	0	0	0	0	0	0	14 (19)	0	0	22 (21)	0	0	1 (1)
Middle East	0	0	0	0	0	0	0	0	1 (1)	0	0	2 (2)	0	0	0
Australia	0	0	2 (3.5)	0	0	0	0	0	4 (5.5)	0	0	2 (2)	0	0	0
New Zealand	0	0	1 (2)	0	0	0	0	0	1 (1)	0	0	2 (2)	0	0	0

Asia	0	0	0	0	0	0	0	0	0	0	1 (4)	0	0	0	1 (1)
Africa	0	0	0	0	0	1 (3)	0	0	2 (3)	0	0	0	0	0	0
Latin America/Caribbean	0	2 (1.5)	0	0	0	0	0	0	0	0	0	0	0	0	0
Theory	5 (6)	16 (12)	2 (3.5)	2 (3)	2 (10.5)	0	1 (3)	5 (10)	2 (3)	1 (6)	0	1 (1)	0	1 (8)	3 (3)
Comparative industrialized-industrialized	2 (2)	1 (0.7)	2 (3.5)	2 (3)	0	5 (15)	2 (7)	0	14 (19)	2 (12)	3 (12.5)	9 (8.5)	1 (25)	0	12 (12)
Comparative industrialized-developing	0	1 (0.7)	0	1 (1)	0	0	0	0	0	0	0	0	0	0	0
Comparative developing-developing	0	0	0	0	0	0	0	0	0	0	0	0	0	0	0
International	0	2 (1.5)	0	3 (4)	1 (5)	2 (6)	0	0	2 (3)	0	0	1 (1)	0	1 (8)	1 (1)
TOTAL	84	135	57	72	19	34	30	50	72	17	24	104	4	13	99

to Canada. Therefore, one can easily see why successive editors of *CPA* have aspired to enhance the comparative content of the journal.

About 12.5 percent of the main articles published in *CPA* between 1982 and 2006 have been comparative in nature, but the vast majority of those contributions have compared advanced industrialized countries. There have been only a handful of papers (four) that have provided a structured comparison of some aspect of public administration between either an industrialized and developing country or between two or more developing countries. Furthermore, not one main article or "other scholarly contribution" during the past quarter-century has actually been written as a stand-alone case of a developing country in Asia, Africa, Latin American, and the Caribbean or the transitional economies of Eastern Europe. The reality, therefore, is that development administration and comparative public administration have been completely marginalized on the pages of *CPA*.

Yet, as these same tables reveal, this lamentable situation is not confined to Canada. A similar degree of ethnocentrism is discernable in both *PAR* and *PA*. In their study of the state of comparative public administration by reviewing a wide range of journals in the early 1980s, Van Wart and Cayer (1990) discovered *PA* published more comparative material than did *PAR*,[11] but in neither case were the numbers of such comparative works very significant. For example, our research revealed that 87 percent of the main articles published in *PAR* between 1982 and 1986 focused on the United States and 79 percent of the articles in *PA* pertained to the United Kingdom. The corresponding figures for the "other scholarly contributions" to these two journals were 84 and 75 percent, respectively.

As is evident from table 12.2, the skewed focus of the main articles in *PAR* and *PA* remained fairly consistent across the twenty-five-year time frame in question. As far as the main journal articles are concerned, both journals tended to publish material about administrative problems related to their respective countries. When comparative material was included, it overwhelmingly involved comparisons between two or more industrialized countries, as was the case with *CPA*. *PAR* published a total of three main articles in twenty-five years that compared developing countries and four that offered a comparison between one or more industrialized and developing countries, while *PA* did not publish any at all in the former category and only one article in the latter.

Where there was a noticeable shift was with respect to the types of "other scholarly contributions" that were published in these journals. *PAR* was still dominated by US-oriented contributions, but *PA* clearly became more comparative in orientation, particularly with respect to material devoted to Western and Eastern Europe. This is directly attributable to a policy change at the journal beginning with the spring 1992 volume, which saw the introduction of a new section called "Comparative and International Administration." With the deepening of European integration under the auspices of the European Union, this new emphasis represented a natural evolution within the journal.

CHALLENGES FACING THE WORLD OF PUBLIC ADMINISTRATION: CONCLUDING OBSERVATIONS

Weighing in on the state of public administration in the United States at the turn of the millennium, Heady (2001: 391) stated, "I must confess that I am an optimist, convinced that progress has been made in our study and understanding of the administrative process, with different investigators using different methods, but with the overall result that we are better off now than when I was starting out several decades ago." There is no disputing this fact: public administration scholars have greatly expanded our knowledge of the dynamics of organizational change in government, administrative reform, financial management and accountability, performance management, public sector values and ethics, and governance, to name but a few areas of scholarly inquiry. However, as Heady himself recognized, there nonetheless exist certain shortcomings in the state of the subdiscipline.

One such limitation is that public administration scholars have not sufficiently devoted their attention to researching and writing about comparative and development administration for the flagship public administration journals. Our research has clearly demonstrated that the articles published in *CPA*, as well as *PAR* and *PA*, overwhelmingly focus on domestic public administration concerns and lack a strong outward vision. Articles that did touch on other regions of the world were only scattered throughout the journals in question, and when they did include comparative research, the articles were invariably devoted to drawing comparisons between industrialized countries. There were scarcely any articles comparing a public administration issue in an industrialized country with a developing country or examining a relevant topic in the context of two or more developing countries. Moreover, we discovered not much is being taught in the way of comparative and development administration at our Canadian universities, and our generic textbooks in public administration do not consider this material at all.

Where, then, does this leave us? Comparative and development administration, we would argue, remains trapped in a prolonged "age of pessimism." This is problematic in and of itself, but when viewed in the context of globalization in the twenty-first century the situation becomes increasingly dire. The reality is that while the antecedents of globalization can actually be traced back several centuries, it has proceeded apace in the past three decades with far-reaching implications—not only economic but also, and perhaps more importantly, social, cultural, and political/administrative. This gives rise to a number of important propositions.

A. ONE SIZE DOESN'T FIT ALL

The fact is there has emerged a dominant culture, namely the Americanization of our global village, through food chains (such as McDonald's, Burger King, and KFC), Hollywood films, music, Levi's jeans, corporate America, information technology, and dominant scientific research and discoveries. Despite such overwhelming acculturation, the diversity of ideas and cultures, languages and customs, values and beliefs, and the style of doing things differently ought to be preserved and enhanced because, in the final analysis, cultural homogeneity, unlike economic integration, is not a progressive development. Henderson (1995: 17) made a similar point when he argued, "Indigenous models of study and application in public administration should be incorporated along with Western thinking."

Simply stated, when people lose their culture, they lose their identity and heritage. Protecting cultural diversity, sharing wealth, and taking care of the destitute beyond their immediate borders will be a normal and moral expectation for Canada, the United States, and other Western nations. And, particularly with respect to the globalization of public administration theories and practices, it is absolutely crucial that "if one does not take into account such factors as culture and style of governance, local traditions and beliefs, politics and style of doing things, social and demographic plurality, law and order situation, civil society and responsible and ethical governance, the new century may not be much different than what we have gone through within the last 50 years" (Dwivedi, 2002: 47). As Dwivedi noted further,

> For years, scholars have been unable to include the alternatives in the form of non-Western contributions to developmental studies. Ignorance in the West has continued to overshadow the need to appreciate the importance of indigenous culture, traditions and style of governance, their administrative styles, which reflect the distinctiveness and complexity of their various national identities, as well as realities and cultural diversities. (2002: 48)

These factors ought to be taken into consideration when administrative reforms and aid-related conditions are imposed on developing countries. Would it not be better if the West could use ideas of governance from the South to enrich its own prescriptive model by including sensitivity to the Third World's local customs, indigenous culture, as well as the value of spirituality? Canada, known worldwide for its leadership in international issues, still lacks collaborative and cooperative administrative research and an acceptance of the exchange of ideas between the North and South. Without bridging the existing gap, inequality in thoughts and actions will not disappear in our multicultural and multireligious world.

B. PUBLIC ADMINISTRATION AND CHALLENGES OF THE TWENTY-FIRST CENTURY

During the twentieth century, developing nations were impelled by the West to regulate their free market and commercial interests, to take care of their poor, unemployed, and socially disadvantaged, and to provide health care and social security. The results were not satisfactory. Instead, the twenty-first century will probably require active collaboration at the international level to accomplish several objectives: offset the adverse effects of unregulated international business practices (including the managerial failings of some mega-commercial concerns); control the behaviour of rogue states; monitor unprincipled nongovernmental organizations; ensure the implementation of international treaties and conventions; prevent regional wars and conflicts and maintain peace; prosecute the perpetration of crimes against humanity; advance economic stability and sustainable development by building national capabilities; minimize religious persecution and racial prejudice; enforce human rights; guarantee a food and water supply for all; improve public health and sanitation; ensure public safety and crime prevention, both within national borders and beyond; and safeguard the victims of natural and man-made disasters. To implement these objectives, public administration will be crucial. The challenge before Canadians and others from the West is how to ensure other countries have effective systems of governance and administration in order that they may deliver public services in the most efficient and least corrupt ways. This is the vanguard role for Canada in this borderless world.

C. USEFULNESS OF COMPARATIVE PUBLIC ADMINISTRATION

Caldwell (1965: 244) stated that the "ultimate test of the value of comparative studies of administration in and beyond the comparative public administration movement will be their effect upon administrative practice.... The ultimate value of comparative public administration will therefore be in stimulating some development which had nowhere before existed in precisely the same form or manner." Thus, the real test of comparative public administration is in its usefulness in ensuring that development administration becomes stronger and more effective, instead of merely regularly exchanging ideas and models among like-minded fellow nations. Ultimately, comparative public administration, as an area of academic study along with its sister, development administration, can assist both academics and practitioners by providing information and insights not otherwise available. In short, Canadian—and for that matter, American and British—public administration scholars can only improve their understanding of domestic problems if they are viewed within a world perspective. Similarly, the study of North American public administration by scholars in other parts of the world will help them to understand their own indigenous problems relating to public administration.

In the final analysis, we must face the greatest dilemma before humanity: Why is it that a small minority of people keep on accumulating all the wealth, savour all the privileges, and have the temerity to impose their brand of ideas on the rest of the world while the majority remains impoverished? This is the challenge before our community of public policy and administration specialists, who know what governance and administration mean and how poor nations can be helped if we respond quickly and effectively with a shared vision and sensitivity towards the well-being of all. The alternative is dark and nasty.

Although these propositions suggest there is a critical and enhanced role for comparative and development administration, our research on the state of the discipline in Canada at this juncture does not offer cause for a great deal of optimism. There are simply no strong signals that the existing gap in the teaching of, and research in, comparative and development administration in this country will be rectified any time soon. However, it is our hope this study can help to spur renewal by alerting the community of Canadian scholars to the narrowness of the scope of public administration as it is currently expressed in teaching and via the main conduit for public administration research in this country—*CPA*. More importantly, our intent is that it will serve as a call to action for future research agendas and curriculum development.

NOTES

1   The authors would like to acknowledge and thank Karla Lambe, a former M.A. student in the Department of Political Science at the University of Guelph, for her invaluable research assistance.

2   This view was even expressed in Wilson's (1887) classic article calling for the science of administration. He wrote, "We can never learn either our own weaknesses or our own virtues by comparing ourselves with ourselves" (219).

3   Page (1995) has offered a much more liberal interpretation of what can be appropriately classified as comparative public administration and is, therefore, much more optimistic about the contributions of British scholars to this field.

4   See United Nations Development Program (2006) for the HDI ranking of 177 countries. This distinction is important because obviously an article written about an Asian country like Japan, which ranks high on the HDI, would not constitute part of the development literature.

5   In the journal *Public Administration* prior to 1990, "Symposium" contributions were categorized as main articles since they appeared as such in the journal at that time. After 1990, however, these symposia were listed under a separate category heading within the journal itself and therefore were classified in the "other scholarly contributions" category in our tables.

6   A number of scholars such as Lynton Caldwell, Fred W. Riggs, Milton Esman, Ferrel Heady, Keith Henderson, Warren F. Ilchman, Nimord Raphaeli, and Dwight Waldo (including two Canadians, R. S. Milne and Robert Jackson) contributed to the growth of the field of comparative public administration.

7   A beginning was made by Riggs (1964), when he published *Administration in Developing Countries—The Theory of Prismatic Society*. In addition, Princeton University Press published a series of books on topics dealing with developing countries, including the book by LaPalombara (1963). Within a few years, a spate of books appeared on the same subject (Riggs, 1970; Briabanti, 1966; 1969; Montgomery and Siffin, 1966).

8   This section draws from Dwivedi and Henderson (1990: 10–12).

9   Donald Rowat used to teach comparative public administration at Carleton beginning in the 1950s, but since there were no textbooks written on the subject from a Canadian perspective, he would use his own edited book, *Basic Issues in Public Administration* (1961).

10 An updated and abbreviated version of this classic text has been published, but it does not stray from the framework provided by Kernaghan and Siegel. See Barker (2008).

11   It should be noted that Van Wart and Cayer classified something as
      comparative as long as it focused on the administration of a country other
      than the country that published the journal, or if more than two countries
      were compared.

REFERENCES

Adie, Robert, and Paul Thomas. (1990 [1982]). *Canadian Public Administration:
    Problematical Perspectives*. Scarborough, ON: Prentice Hall.

Argyriades, Dimitri, O. P. Dwivedi, and Joseph G. Jabbra, eds. (2007). *Public
    Administration in Transition: Introduction*. London: Vallentine Mitchell.

Aucoin, Peter. (1995). *The New Public Management: Canada in Comparative
    Perspective*. Montreal: Institute for Research on Public Policy.

Barker, Paul. (2008). *Public Administration in Canada: Brief Edition*.
    Scarborough, ON: Thomson Nelson.

Bertucci, Guido, and Adriana Alberti. (2005). "The United Nations Programme
    in Public Administration: Reinventing Itself to Help Reinvent Public
    Administration." *International Review of Administrative Sciences*. 71: 2:
    337–353.

Briabanti, Ralph, ed. (1966). *Asian Bureaucratic Systems Emergent from the
    British Imperial Tradition*. Durham, NC: Duke University Press.

———. (1969). *Political and Administrative Development*. Durham, NC: Duke
    University Press.

Brinkerhoff, Derick W., and Jennifer M. Coston. (1999). "International
    Development Management in a Globalized World." *Public Administration
    Review*. 59: 4: 346–361.

Caiden, Gerald E., and Naomi Caiden. (1990). "Towards the Future of
    Comparative Public Administration." In *Public Administration in World
    Perspective*, edited by O. P. Dwivedi and Keith M. Henderson, 363–399.
    Ames, IA: Iowa State University Press.

Caldwell, Lynton K. (1965). "Conjectures on Comparative Public
    Administration." In *Public Administration and Democracy: Essays in Honor
    of Paul H. Appleby*, edited by Roscoe Martin. Syracuse, NY: Syracuse
    University Press.

Candler, Gaylord George. (2006). "The Comparative Evolution of Public
    Administration in Australia, Brazil and Canada." *Canadian Public
    Administration*. 49: 3: 334–349.

Carroll, Barbara Wake. (2005). "Editor's Note." *Canadian Public Administration*.
    48: 1: 1–3.

Carroll, Barbara Wake, and Michael Whyte Kpessa. (2007). "Enduring,
    Ephemeral and Emerging Issues in Public Administration in Canada:

Trends in *Canadian Public Administration* over Fifty Years (1958–2007)." *Canadian Public Administration.* 50: 4: 477–491.

Dunn, Christopher, ed. (2002). *The Handbook of Canadian Public Administration.* Toronto: Oxford University Press.

Dwivedi, O. P. (2002). "Challenges in Public Administration in Developing Nations." In *The Turning World: Globalization and Governance at the Start of the Twenty-first Century,* edited by Guido Bertucci and Michael Dugget, 47–54. Amsterdam: IOS Press.

Dwivedi, O. P., and James Iain Gow. (1999). *From Bureaucracy to New Public Management: The Administrative Culture of the Government of Canada.* Peterborough, ON: Broadview Press.

Dwivedi, O. P., and Jorge Nef. (1982). "Crises and Continuities in Development Theory and Administration: First and Third World Perspectives." *Public Administration and Development.* 2: 59–77.

———. (2004). "From Development Administration to New Public Management: The Quest for Effectiveness, Democratic Governance, Governability, and Public Morality." In *Democracy, Governance, and Globalization,* edited by P. L. Sanjeev Reddy, Jaideep Singh, and R. K. Tiwari, 71–91. New Delhi: Indian Institute of Public Administration.

Dwivedi, O. P. and Keith M. Henderson, eds. (1990). *Public Administration in World Perspective.* Ames, Iowa: Iowa State University Press.

Esman, Milton D. (1966). "The Politics of Development Administration." In *Approaches to Development: Politics, Administration, and Change,* edited by John D. Montgomery and W. J. Siffin. New York: McGraw-Hill.

Geva-May, Iris, and Allan Maslove. (2006). "Canadian Public Policy Analysis and Public Policy Programs: A Comparative Perspective." *Journal of Public Affairs Education.* 12: 4: 413–438.

Gow, James Iain, and Sharon Sutherland. (2004). "Comparison of Canadian Master's Programs in Public Administration, Public Management, and Public Policy." *Canadian Public Administration.* 47: 3: 379–405.

Gray, Andrew, and Bill Jenkins. (1995). "From Public Administration to Public Management: Reassessing a Revolution?" *Public Administration.* 73: 75–99.

Heady, Ferrel. (1979). *Public Administration: A Comparative Perspective.* New Jersey: Prentice Hall.

———. (2001). "Donald C. Stone Lecture: Priorities for 2001 and Beyond." *Public Administration Review.* 61: 4: 390–395.

Heady, Ferrel, and Sybil L. Stokes. (1962). *Papers in Comparative Public Administration.* Ann Arbor, MI: Institute of Public Administration.

Henderson, Keith M. (1971). "A New Comparative Public Administration." In *Towards a New Public Administration,* edited by Frank Marini. New Jersey: Chandler Publishing.

————. (1995). "Reinventing Comparative Public Administration: Indigenous Models of Study and Application." *International Journal of Public Sector Management*. 8: 4: 17–25.

Hood, Christopher, and Michael Jackson. (1994). "Keys for Locks in Administrative Argument." *Administration & Society*. 25: 4: 467–488.

Inwood, Gregory J. (2004 [1999]). *Understanding Canadian Public Administration: An Introduction to Theory and Practice*. Toronto: Pearson.

Johnson, David. (2006 [2002]). *Thinking Government: Public Sector Management in Canada*. Peterborough, ON: Broadview Press.

Jones, L. R., and Donald E. Klingner. (2007). "The Consummate Comparative Public Administrationist: A Tribute to Ferrel Heady, 1916–2006." *Public Administration Review*. 67: 2: 188–196.

Jreisat, Jamil E. (2005). "Comparative Public Administration Is Back In, Prudently." *Public Administration Review*. 65: 2: 231–242.

Kernaghan, Kenneth. (1980). "Editorial Statement." *Canadian Public Administration*. 23: 1: 1–5.

————. (1982). "Canadian Public Administration: Progress and Prospects." *Canadian Public Administration*. 25: 4: 444–456.

Kernaghan, Kenneth, and David Siegel. (1999 [1991]). *Public Administration in Canada: A Text*. Scarborough, ON: ITP Nelson.

Laframboise, H. L. (1982). "The Future of Public Administration in Canada." *Canadian Public Administration*. 25: 4: 507–519.

LaPalombara, Joseph, ed. (1963). *Bureaucracy and Political Development*. New Jersey: Princeton University Press.

Montgomery, John D., and William J. Siffin, eds. (1966). *Approaches to Development Politics, Administration and Change*. New York: McGraw-Hill.

Nef, Jorge, and O. P. Dwivedi. (1981). "Development Theory and Administration: A Fence Around an Empty Lot?" *Indian Journal of Public Administration*. 27: 1: 42–66.

Page, Edward C. (1995). "Comparative Administration in Britain." *Public Administration*. 73: 123–141.

Peters, B. Guy. (1988). *Comparing Public Bureaucracies: Problems of Theory and Method*. Tuscaloosa: The University of Alabama Press.

Pross, Paul. (1990). "Assessing Public Administration Education in Canada." *Canadian Public Administration*. 33: 4: 618–632.

Raadschelders, Jos C. N. (1998). *Handbook of Administrative History*. New Jersey: Transaction Publishers.

————. (1999). "A Coherent Framework for the Study of Public Administration." *Journal of Public Administration Research and Theory*. 9: 2: 281–303.

Raphaeli, Nimrod, ed. (1967). *Readings in Comparative Public Administration*. Boston: Allyn and Bacon.

Rhodes, R. A. W., et al. (1995). "The State of Public Administration: A Professional History, 1970–1995." *Public Administration*. 73: 1–15.

Riggs, Fred W. (1961). *The Ecology of Public Administration*. New Delhi: Asia Publishing House.

———. (1964). *Administration in Developing Countries—The Theory of Prismatic Society*. Boston: Houghton Mifflin.

———. (1998). "Public Administration in America: Why Our Uniqueness Is Exceptional and Important." *Public Administration Review*. 58: 1: 22–31.

Riggs, Fred W., ed. (1970). *Frontiers of Development Administration*. Durham, NC: Duke University Press.

Rostow, Walt Whitman. (1960). *The Stages of Economic Growth: A Non-Communist Manifesto*. Cambridge, UK: Cambridge University Press.

Rowat, Donald C., ed. (1961). *Basic Issues in Public Administration*. New York: Macmillan.

Savoie, Donald. (1990). "Studying Public Administration." *Canadian Public Administration*. 33: 3: 389–413.

Schaffer, Bernard. (1973). *The Administrative Factor*. London: Frank Cass.

Siffin, W. J. (1957). *Towards the Comparative Study of Public Administration*. Bloomington: Indiana University Press.

Smiley, Donald V. (1974). "Editor's Note." *Canadian Public Administration*. 17: 3: 365–366.

Swerdlow, Irving. (1975). *The Public Administration of Economic Development*. New York: Praeger.

Thomas, Paul G. (1994a). "Editor's Statement." *Canadian Public Administration*. 37: 1: 1–3.

———. (1994b). "Editorial Note." *Canadian Public Administration*. 37: 4: 537–541.

Tupper, Allan. (1999). "Editor's Note." *Canadian Public Administration*. 42: 2: 147–152.

United Nations Development Program. (2006). *Human Development Report 2006: Beyond Scarcity—Power, Poverty and the Global Water Crisis*. New York: United Nations. <http://hdr.undp.org/hdr2006/pdfs/report/HDR06-complete.pdf>.

Van Wart, Montgomery, and N. Joseph Cayer. (1990). "Comparative Public Administration: Defunct, Dispersed, or Redefined?" *Public Administration Review*. 50: 2: 238–248.

Waldo, Dwight. (1953). *Comparative Public Administration: Prologue, Problems, and Promise*. Chicago: American Society for Public Administration.

White, L. D. (1964 [1935]). *Civil Service Abroad*. New York: McGraw-Hill.

Wilson, V. Seymour. (1981). *Canadian Public Policy and Administration: Theory and Environment*. Toronto: McGraw-Hill Ryerson Ltd.

———. (1990). "Editorial Statement." *Canadian Public Administration*. 33: 4: 465–472.

Wilson, Woodrow. (1887). "The Study of Administration." *Political Science Quarterly*. 2: 2: 197–222.

World Bank. (2002). *Civil Service Reform: Strengthening World Bank and IMF Collaboration*. Washington, DC: The World Bank.

13 ADMINISTRATIVE LAW AND PUBLIC GOVERNANCE:

An Overlooked Dimension of Governance

Byron Sheldrick

The study of public administration in Canada has generally not addressed the significance of administrative law. Standard texts in the area pay scant attention to the subject (Kernaghan and Siegel, 1999; Inwood, 2004). Undoubtedly, there has been a growing interest in public law, particularly the impact of the Charter of Rights and Freedoms on policy-making and state structures (Morton and Knopff, 2000; Kelly, 2005; Hiebert, 1996; 2002). Consequently, judicial review has largely been understood at the macro-level of broad court oversight of constitutional standards. There has been less attention paid to the importance of administrative boards and tribunals.[1] These entities operate within a sphere that crosses both judicial and administrative boundaries. Moreover, courts have developed a rich and detailed history of judicial review of these bodies. While administrative law and administrative judicial review have been important fields of study within the legal academy, it has tended to emphasize doctrinal matters, with less regard for the administrative context in which the judicial review of administrative decision-making takes place. There is a need to assess the role of courts in overseeing administrative decision-making and to situate both courts and structures of quasi-judicial decision-making (boards and tribunals) within a broader context. Some, particularly the work of Sossin, have recognized the need to contextualize administrative law within a broader political and administrative context (Sossin and Flood, 2007; Sossin and Houle, 2006; Sossin and Pottie, 2005). There is a need to continue this work and to rethink these institutions and their operation within a governance framework, rather than simply as either administrative or legal decision-making bodies.

One of the difficulties of integrating administrative boards into a broad framework of administration is the diversity of form and function that characterizes these institutions. Regulatory boards and tribunals are created in order to bring specialized expertise to complex regulatory decisions. In this respect, they are considered superior to courts and judges, who have a more generalist background and lack specific policy expertise. Nevertheless, administrative boards are a diverse bunch, ranging from very small entities, with part-time members and little to no staff that meet intermittently, to regulatory boards that have a large full-time membership and staff that include policy and research experts and a full hearing schedule.

They also perform a large range of functions. Some administrative boards may operate within a fairly limited and narrow policy framework. They may hear applications on a particular issue or for a particular program, or hear appeals against administrative decisions. Their range of discretion, and the policy implications of their decisions, may be small. Other administrative boards have been given a large degree of policy responsibility and autonomy. Significant portions of the policy field of labour relations, for example, have largely been delegated to labour relations boards. Similarly, telecommunications policy has become the purview of the Canadian Radio and Telecommunications Commission (CRTC), while policy development about pensions—an increasingly important topic—requires consideration by provincial pension boards. While the standards and principles applied by the boards may be defined in their enabling legislation, the boards themselves are also involved in a significant policy development function. Moreover, the scope and range of that policy function is not always captured by the statutory language of the enabling legislation.

To borrow from Hodgetts, these administrative boards are truly structural heretics. They do not really fit within the structure of the administrative state (Hodgetts, 1971). They stand apart, operate at arm's length from line departments, and perform a wide array of functions. More telling, though, is that their structure and function are, themselves, highly variable. This is one of the reasons why any discussion of administrative boards often becomes focused on judicial review. It is the courts, through the administrative principles articulated through judicial review, that have imposed some degree of order and consistency on the multiplicity of forms and processes that characterize administrative boards. This intervention by the courts can be viewed in a negative or positive fashion. As Leyland and Woods have argued, courts can take a "red light" approach to administrative boards, where essentially their decisions seek to constrain and limit the operation of these boards, or a "green light" approach, in which the courts view their role as facilitative (Leyland and Woods, 1997). In this context, the courts articulate principles of good administrative and establish broad standards without seeking to insert themselves into the substantive decisions of the boards themselves.

In some respects, administrative boards operate as a hub within a governance structure. They play an important role in the policy process and also serve as a vehicle for the representation of both state and nonstate interests. They provide an opportunity for those affected by both policy formulation and implementation decisions to make submissions and representations. They also provide an opportunity for state actors involved in the development and administration of those policies to articulate the principles underpinning those policies. In this way, they serve as a forum in which the networks of governance between state and nonstate actors come together. The fact that this forum is quasi-judicial in its operation, and subject to oversight by the courts, adds to the complexity of the situation.

This chapter is a preliminary attempt to consider the relationship between judicial review and public administration, which stands at the nexus of administrative boards. It will attempt to "map" the institutions and principles of judicial review onto the basic contours of both "old" and "new" administration models. In this way, we can begin to situate judicial review within the context of current administrative practices and consider the implications of the restructuring of public administration for the future of judicial review. The chapter is divided into two parts.

The first section examines the grounds of judicial review and argues there exists a close congruence between principles of judicial review and the traditional Weberian model of bureaucracy and administration.

The second section of the chapter outlines the challenges posed to judicial review by the emergence of new public management (NPM) and new forms of governance. This section looks at the possible directions judicial review might take in order to adapt to the changed landscape of public administration. It argues that judicial review has shown remarkable adaptability and flexibility in the past, and will likely continue to do so. Despite this, however, the courts have not developed a sufficiently flexible and contextual approach to understanding the policy context in which administrative decision-makers operate. It may be, however, that unless the courts are able to develop the conceptual tools to integrate a broader understanding of networks of governance that the disconnect between the values of the court and the values of the administrative state will continue. If this is the case, a more radical overhaul of the relationship between judicial review and administrative decision-making may be required.

THE GROUNDS OF JUDICIAL REVIEW: DICEY AND WEBER

The modern principles of judicial review emerged in the late nineteenth century and were shaped primarily by A. V. Dicey, the British constitutional scholar. Although Dicey's writings have been widely criticized as failing to reflect the realities of the modern administrative state (indeed, they may have even failed to accurately reflect the realities of the British state about which he was writing), nevertheless, they continue to have an overwhelming impact on the thinking of lawyers and judges about the nature of the state (Dicey, 1902; for a commentary on Dicey's influence on administrative law, see Arthurs, 1989).

Dicey was writing within a classical liberal framework. The late nineteenth century witnessed an expansion of the state's administrative capacity as it began to assume responsibility for such matters as basic public health, sewage, and the regulation of occupational health and safety. For Dicey, this reflected an unwarranted adoption of what he called "collectivist principles" and a threat to individual freedom. The expansion of the administrative state brought with it the possibility of increased discretion, which in a classical liberal framework threatened the autonomy of the individual and raised the spectre of an arbitrary and potentially capricious state.

Dicey's solution to this conundrum was to insist on the primacy of the rule of law. The basic formulation of the principle insists that all actions are permissible unless prohibited by law, and that state agents have no special privileges or powers beyond those of any citizen. This represents an assertion of the limited nature of state authority through the requirement that all state actions be sanctioned and approved by a specific piece of parliamentary legislation. In short, state authority is both founded in and constrained by the law. For Dicey, the courts were the logical vehicle for safeguarding the "rights" of individuals from the dangers of arbitrary discretion. The courts had long been the guardians of what Dicey called the "ordinary" law. The common law, with its emphasis on individual private property rights, was well suited to resist the incursion and growth of a state that Dicey saw as fundamentally flawed and potentially dangerous to the interests of individuals.

These assumptions underpin the foundations of modern administrative law and the principles of judicial review. Although administrative law doctrine has become much more flexible and accommodating of administrative practices than Dicey would have liked, nevertheless, it continues to operate in an extremely Diceyan framework. This is clearly evidenced through a consideration of the three basic grounds of judicial review: procedural error, error of law, and jurisdictional error. Failure to adhere to the judicial standards established by these grounds of review may result in an administrative decision being quashed and invalidated by the courts. These are the core principles of "good administration" that the courts are prepared to impose on administrative bodies. These principles are fairly broad in nature, and centre around concepts of due process and reasonableness.

Review for procedural errors attempts to ensure administrators follow sound decision-making processes. Historically, the courts interpreted this to require a full oral hearing if an individual's rights were adversely affected by a state's decision. The hearing itself was to look as much like a judicial process as possible. In effect, the courts imposed on administrative decision-makers a process that was modelled on themselves as the most appropriate mechanism for adjudicating rights. This was termed "natural justice." This resulted in many administrative boards developing an increasingly formalized and "quasi-judicial" model of decision-making. Procedural protection, under this model, was an all-or-nothing affair. Either a full hearing was ordered, or the individual received no protection whatsoever.

Over time, the courts have become more flexible and developed a more contextual approach to procedures. The doctrine of procedural fairness now requires that basic procedural protections be available in virtually any decision-making context. However, on the question of what procedures will be considered appropriate, the courts are now willing to defer to the expertise of administrators and permit a broader range of procedural options, depending on the nature of the decision and its significance to the parties concerned. The basic requirement is that the process must permit the individual to "know" the case against them (the basis for the administrative decision) and have an opportunity to "respond" (to put their side forward to the decision-maker) (*Nicholson v. Haldimand-Norfolk Police Commrs. Bd.*, [1979] 1 S.C.R. 311). The more significant the decision being made by the administrative board (i.e., the more serious the context), the greater the expectation on the part of the court that the board will extend greater procedural protections. As the seriousness of the decision increases— often involving questions of livelihood (hearings held by professional societies regarding the right to practise of lawyers or doctors); issues of liberty (mental health assessments); or financial matters (Securities Commission hearings, CRTC hearings, labour board hearings, municipal board hearings)—the greater the likelihood the procedural requirements will look increasingly court-like.

Review for errors of law and review for jurisdictional errors are interlinked in that both raise the issue of to what extent administrators should be permitted to interpret the statutory provisions that define their legal mandate. Consequently, in applying these grounds of review, judges need to determine the extent to which they will defer to the expertise of administrators or privilege their own statutory interpretations. In each case, the courts have moved from a position of strictly applying these grounds of review to a position that respects the autonomy and expertise of administrators.

Error of law requires that administrative decision-makers interpret and apply both their own mandating statute and other laws to an acceptable judicial standard. In other words, the courts have asserted the right to oversee administrative decisions to ensure the interpretation of statutes and the common law has been done "correctly." In effect, the primacy of judicial interpretation over administrative application underpins "error of law" as a ground of judicial review. This ground, more than any other, invites judges to substitute their understanding of what constitutes an appropriate outcome for that of the administrative decision-maker. It also, in the Diceyan framework, tries to ensure the primacy of law over discretion. It is not for the administrator to interpret the statute that authorizes and empowers her to act. Rather, this is a job for which the courts have an exclusive and privileged role.

Jurisdiction as a ground of review requires that administrative decision-makers stay within their legal/statutory mandate. As already discussed, Dicey's understanding of the state required that administrative decision-makers be constrained by the limits of their authority as defined by law (a "red light" approach). In effect, enabling statutes can be understood to create a box in which the administrator is free to act, with the courts exercising vigilance to ensure that decisions do not stray outside the framework established by the box. Of course, deciding just where the lines of the box are to be drawn is not always a simple or straightforward task. Statutes are frequently imprecise and ambiguous. This raises the question of to what extent courts will defer to the expertise of administrators, who, in exercising their authority, must frequently interpret the scope of their mandate.

Both the doctrines of error of law and jurisdiction have undergone significant evolution during the twentieth century. Undoubtedly, this evolution reflects the development of the modern administrative state and the increase in the complexity and range of administrative decision-making. Quite simply, Dicey's understanding of the capacity of the courts to oversee and constrain administrative decisions became seriously compromised once the state went beyond the administration of rudimentary programs and became involved in a range of complex regulatory activities.

With the expansion of regulatory programs, the state tried to limit the capacity of the courts to overturn administrative decisions on the grounds of error of law through the use of privative clauses. Privative clauses are inserted in legislation and operate to insulate the decisions of administrative boards and tribunals from judicial review. In effect, they instruct the courts not to review for error of law. Courts were initially resistant and hostile to what they viewed as an attempt to deny individuals recourse to the courts and a departure from the principles of the rule of law. They frequently evaded the effect of privative clauses by simply holding that errors in legal interpretation amounted to jurisdictional errors (*Anisminic Ltd. v. Foreign Compensation Commission*, [1969] 2 A.C. 147 (H.L.) is a classic statement of this approach). The privative clause, the courts argued, could only insulate a decision-maker from errors made within its jurisdiction, but not prevent review for errors that went to the question of jurisdiction itself.

Over time, the courts developed (as in the case of procedural review) what appeared to be a more flexible and contextual approach to review for error of law and jurisdiction. The approach of the courts, however, has tended to swing back and forth from extending great degrees of deference to the decisions of administrative decision-makers to periods of greater scrutiny. As will be discussed below, the courts have had difficulty in developing a coherent framework for understanding the role and context of administrative decision-making.

This brief review of some of the broad parameters of judicial review doctrine should demonstrate two things. First, the doctrine has evolved over time in response to the growth of the administrative state. While retaining the core of the Diceyan principles that underpin it, the doctrine has moved beyond a fundamentally hostile position vis-à-vis administration, to a more functional approach that recognizes the importance of administration in the modern state. Second, one can fairly easily see the basic congruence between judicial review doctrine and traditional understandings of the nature of bureaucracy and administration. Shields and Evans (1998) have summarized many of the features of the traditional model of administration as derived from Weber, Wilson, and others. They argue the traditional model is characterized by the primacy of written rules and procedures, a conception of legal rights and entitlements, and a hierarchical organizational structure in which jurisdictional mandates and responsibilities are clearly defined.

The doctrine of judicial review fits nicely into this picture. Error of law and jurisdictional review complement Weber's notion that the modern bureaucracy should be premised on the importance of written rules and decisions made in accordance with due process and law. In effect, judicial review oversees and safeguards the legal-rational core of the administrative state. Procedural review, for example, operates to ensure consistency of treatment for those who come into contact with the state. To the extent that modern administrative principles originated in response to the excesses of an administrative state that was rife with patronage and graft, its processes and underpinnings share Dicey's concern with constraining and limiting discretion. While Woodrow Wilson conceptualized the elimination of these problems in terms of the development of a "science of administration," Dicey saw it in terms of the assertion of the primacy of law (Dicey, 1902; Wilson, 1887). For both the traditional model of administration and judicial review, rules and law occupy a central position. In this context, judicial review operates to establish and enforce principles of "good administration" within a fairly orthodox administrative framework (Oliver, 1987).

Judicial review's concern with establishing a set of administrative principles centred on the importance of rules can be seen in the approach of the courts to the question of remedies. It is one thing to say that individuals or groups who feel aggrieved by the state can seek recourse to the courts, but without some remedy this is fairly meaningless. In this regard, judicial review differs considerably from most common law doctrines in that its concern is not with the individual claimant but rather with the process and structure of state decision-making. If you were to successfully sue for compensation in a breach of contract case, you would be awarded damages designed to put you in a position as if the contract had been honoured. In judicial review cases, on the other hand, the typical remedy is for the decision to be quashed and remitted to the original decision-maker for a new hearing. There is no prohibition on the subsequent decision being exactly the same as the first, so long as the deficiencies in process, or errors in interpretation, have been remedied. The individual claimant may actually receive nothing for their trouble save the knowledge that the state's administrative processes have been improved. This may have greater implications in future cases than it will in the case that prompted the litigation. In this sense, judicial review produces collective remedies in that the improved or remedied administrative processes are of benefit to us all. The outcomes of a judicial review case are not reserved for the individual claimant as are damage awards in the context of private law.

NPM AND GOVERNANCE: CHALLENGES FOR ADMINISTRATION AND JUDICIAL REVIEW

The restructuring of public administration and the apparent ascendancy of NPM as a new orthodoxy has challenged both traditional administrative models and the role of judicial review. NPM displaces the centrality of rules and an emphasis on process in favour of the private sector values of flexibility, entrepreneurism, and risk-taking. Much has been made of the apparent shift from conceptions of citizenship embedded in concepts of rights and law to a notion of customers and consumers that has its roots in principles of contractualism. A full discussion of the significance of that shift is beyond the scope of this chapter but is discussed in other chapters in this volume, and it has been the subject of much academic literature (Osborne and Gaebler, 1992; Dwivedi and Gow, 1999).

The independence of the judiciary, however, means that judicial review doctrines are largely beyond the restructuring of the state. In this sense, judicial review, rooted in a more traditional model of administration, may also pose challenges and obstacles to NPM. The shift to governance further complicates matters by envisioning administration as a network of relations involving both state and nonstate actors. In a governance framework, the significance of government and administration is replaced by "governmentality" and networks of decision-making that cross between state and civil society. The clarity of role definition and jurisdictional authority assumed by traditional administrative models is replaced by more fluid networks of state and nonstate actors. This is not a framework Dicey could ever have imagined.

Judicial review challenges newer governance models in several ways. First, recourse to the courts opens decisions of administrators up to review. This may inhibit the flexibility and "entrepreneurial" approach that characterizes NPM decision-making. Risk-taking and an emphasis on "getting results" may be undermined if those who are dissatisfied with the results seek judicial review. As McCann and Silverstein have argued, judicial institutions provide the opportunity for those excluded from process to leverage access to the state (1993; Sheldrick, 2004). In this context, a judicial review action, even if not ultimately successful, may result in significant delays and costs to both state and nonstate actors, thereby providing a basis for negotiation with state officials.

At the heart of judicial review and traditional models of bureaucracy is a particular conception of due process: that the rules should be followed and applied consistently. This is critical to the whole judicial review approach. The insistence on consistency, on constraining discretion, and on administrative processes that give fair representation to all stakeholders may run counter to NPM ideals. Much of what NPM advocates might denigrate as "red tape" would be viewed as critical when due process is the lens through which the adequacy of administrative practices is judged.

While judicial review clearly poses challenges to NPM and governance, the reverse is also true. Both judicial review and traditional public administration are based on a fairly conventional understanding of state structure. Hierarchical arrangements based on the Westminster model of parliamentary accountability are at the heart of both systems. NPM and governance turn this on its head. Attenuated models of ministerial responsibility, privatization and contracting out, public-private partnerships, and alternative service delivery mechanisms all blur the line between the public and the private. This poses difficulties for courts in terms of assessing the applicability of judicial principles to these new institutional and organizational structures. While it may be clear that judicial review and the public law remedies that go along with it are available in prison discipline cases, for example, can the same be said if the prison has been privatized and is no longer under the direct supervision of the Ministry of Corrections? Similar questions arise in a whole host of deregulated, privatized, and/or power-sharing contexts (Mullan, 1997).

This is not to say that judicial review has become irrelevant with the restructuring of the state. It is, however, probably true that there has developed a greater disconnect between the values of judicial review and the underlying premises of administration. This certainly is not the first time this has happened. Indeed, much of the history of judicial review has been characterized by periods when the courts were at odds with the administrative state and/or attempting to develop an approach that would allow a greater complementarity between judicial review and administration. It is likely, therefore, that judicial review will continue to evolve as it has before. As discussed above, judicial review has demonstrated a remarkable flexibility in responding to the growth of the administrative state. The real question is not whether judicial review will adapt but rather in what direction it will move.

This brings us back to the question of standards of review that was briefly discussed earlier. As public sector decision-making becomes more complex and takes on a broader range of different forms, the degree to which the courts will be involved in a judicial oversight function, or will defer to governance structures that may not resemble traditional public administrative forms, becomes important. As indicated above, the courts have responded to the growth of the administrative state by developing more flexible and functional approaches that better appreciate the complex nature of administration and regulation. Despite this, however, the courts arguably have not developed a set of tools to enable them to analyze the significance of administrative decision-making in a governance context.

Judicial adaptations have taken place largely around the questions of standards of review and the degree to which courts should defer to the expertise of administrators or intervene and substitute their own decisions. Initially, the courts developed the position that there is a range of standards of review from "correctness" at one end to "patently unreasonable" at the other (*Pezim v. British Columbia (Superintendant of Brokers)*, [1994] 2 S.C.R. 557). At the one end of the spectrum, the courts insisted the administrative decision-maker make a "correct" decision in the sense of coming to a decision the courts agreed with. At the other end of the spectrum, the courts would defer to the expertise of the decision-maker and permit a decision to stand even if the judge would not have come to the same decision. Intervention in this instance would be limited to those cases where the court viewed the decision as being so unreasonable that no "reasonable decision-maker" could possibly have reached it. Although the standard clearly involved a tautology, it nevertheless provided a workable framework for judges to think about whether intervention was warranted. Moreover, it tended to operate in favour of preserving the integrity of administrative decisions by establishing a relatively high standard for intervention.

This dichotomy, however, eventually became more rigid in its application. The correct standard of review became reduced to whether there was a statutory right of appeal from board decisions (correctness) or whether the board's decisions were protected by a privative clause (patently unreasonable). In part, this tendency towards dichotomous options resulted from the fact that the courts really did not have the tools to assess the context in which administrative boards operated with any degree of sophistication.

The courts attempted to analyze context by developing what was called a "pragmatic and functional approach" (*U.E.S., Local 298 v. Bibeault*, [1988] 2 S.C.R. 1048). This involved assessing four factors: the wording of the statute, and particularly whether or not a privative clause or a statutory right to appeal existed; the expertise of the decision-maker relative to the court; the purpose of the provision and the statue as a whole; and finally, the nature of the problem. In assessing the final factor, the court was particularly concerned with whether or not the problem being addressed was a question of fact, law, or one of mixed fact and law (Sossin and Flood, 2007: 586).

There were obvious problems with this categorization in terms of the court's capacity to operationalize the analysis. The first two factors rely on a reading and interpretation of statutory language. This was certainly true of the first factor—an assessment of the significance of a privative clause versus a statutory right of appeal. The difficulty here, however, was this factor simply took the court back to the very clear dichotomous option: deference if there was a privative clause, or no deference if there was a statutory right of appeal. A consideration of the purpose of the provision and the statute as a whole also depended on a reading of the statute. In assessing this, the court took into account such factors as whether or not the administrative body seemed to have a policy role or had been given a policy mandate. The difficulty, however, was that these sorts of questions are not always purposefully included in the drafting of a statute. When one looks at the range of administrative boards and tribunals, and their range of functions, it appears to a certain extent random as to whether or not the legislative drafters have sought fit to include language of this sort or not. Indeed, it would be difficult to derive any logical framework to explain even the presence or absence of privative clauses versus statutory rights of appeal.

The difficulty with relying on a statute is that enabling legislation is written before the administrative board is in operation. As such, it provides a poor guide to understanding the nature of the policy role that the board has developed over time. Governance structures develop as policy stakeholders, including both state and nonstate actors, appear before the board over time. It is through this process that the board itself becomes integrated into a broader policy community and its networks of policy formulation and implementation. Governance networks develop; they are not simply created by statutory decree. Consequently, many administrative boards have developed important and clearly defined policy roles that cannot be captured through an analysis of statutory language.

Given this, the court's need to rely on the language of the statute really precludes it from actually conducting an analysis of the governance structure in which the tribunal operates. It would be through this sort of analysis that the court could really begin to make an assessment of the policy significance of the board and the implications of its decisions within its broader policy community. If the question of an appropriate standard of review is really about how much deference the courts should show to administrative decision-makers, then this is the sort of analysis that is necessary and one that cannot be deduced from the language of the enabling legislation.

The other two factors are just as problematic. In some ways they take us back to the Diceyan notion that there should be a clear distinction between law and policy/politics. The second factor, the expertise of the decision-maker versus the court, clearly fits into that framework. Dicey's concerns were largely that administrative decision-making not stray too far into the traditional role of the courts. Hence, the "red light" approach to constraining administrative decision-making. The courts have often operationalized this factor—the relative expertise of the administrative board—by asking whether the administrative question is one the courts are just as capable of addressing as the administrative board. Put another way, does the administrative board have some special expertise that makes it better placed to deal with the issue?

Of course, this is simply another way of restating the deference question without really developing any better analytical tools for answering it. The fact remains that, whether the administrative tribunal has any special expertise or not, the legislature opted to remove the question from the ordinary courts. More broadly, however, I would argue that assessing the expertise of the board of a tribunal is not as simple as the courts would have us believe. Indeed, if one understands the administrative board as operating within a broader governance network, its expertise and capacity is rooted within that network. Even when it is addressing questions that might be similar to those addressed by courts, it will be doing so within a particular policy context that the courts simply may not have the expertise to assess. Judicial intervention, even if the court has expertise, may have significant, and possibly negative, implications for the stability of the governance framework.

The final factor assessed by the courts in the "pragmatic and functional" approach is the nature of the problem and whether it involves a question of fact, of law, or of mixed fact and law. This takes us into a rather arcane area of legal jurisprudence. Suffice it to say, appellate principles are largely based on the notion that issues of fact are best determined by the decision-maker who hears the evidence, while questions of law and legal interpretation can just as easily be determined by an appellate court. Presumably, then, courts will be more likely to defer to administrative boards on factual questions than on legal questions.

In a way, though, this is a restatement of the original error of law question. Again, it really does not help us grapple with the question of when the courts should defer to administrative decision-makers. What is missing from the court's assessment of "the nature of the question" is a consideration of the complexity of policy. The courts seem to think that questions can be characterized in a dichotomous fashion as either law or fact. In truth, policy questions of the sorts that many administrative boards deal with involve a complex of factual, legal, discretionary, and political/policy questions. An assessment of how these various questions interrelate to each other in order to understand "the nature of the question" is beyond the capacity of the courts. Indeed, it is not really the "question" that needs to be assessed in the narrow sense of the particular issue the board is dealing with at any given moment, but rather the broader decision-making and administrative context of which that "question" is a part.

The concept of patently unreasonableness has caused some conceptual difficulty. There might be a situation where a decision might be considered "unreasonable," but not so unreasonable as to meet the standard of review. As already discussed, despite the attempt to develop a contextual approach, the courts ended up with dichotomous options around the issue of whether to defer or intervene. The result was an abandonment of contextualism in favour of a new formalism (Sossin and Flood, 2007: 591). The courts have tried to make the standard of review more workable by adopting a third category of review: "reasonableness simpliciteur," a middle ground between correctness and patent unreasonability (*Canada (Director of Investigation and Research) v. Southam Inc.*, [1997] 1 S.C.R. 748). More recently, the Supreme Court of Canada has taken a further step in trying to clarify the standard by collapsing the two standards of reasonableness into a single standard of review based on the reasonableness of a decision (*Dunsmuir v. New Brunswick*, [2008] S.C.R. 9).

It remains to be seen how this clarification of standards of review will alter the approach of the courts in reviewing administrative decision-making. The single standard of "reasonableness" could open up administrative boards to greater judicial scrutiny, or the courts might consider there to be a range of "reasonable decisions" and allow administrative decision-makers the latitude to determine the best outcome given their understanding of administrative and policy needs. The difficulty for the courts is that the simplification of the standards of review has not been accompanied by the development of better judicial tools for assessing when deference should be extended. The courts remain trapped by their own formalisms.

Sossin and Flood (2007) have argued that the courts need to return to a truly contextual approach, and in general, I would agree with this. Sossin and Flood suggest a new standard of review that would not be based on "fixed categories of review into which all decisions must fit" (Sossin and Flood, 2007: 599). Instead, they argue that the number of factors to be considered needs to be expanded to include the "impact on the individual, opening up the possibility of a floating spectrum of review, and the application of much greater judicial energy to articulating the factors that speak for and against greater degrees of deference to different kinds of decision-makers and different kinds of decisions" (Sossin and Flood, 2007: 599). They further suggest that instead of categories of judicial review based on reasonableness, the emphasis should conceptually be on fairness. They argue that a more contextual approach to standards of review would consider a wide range of factors, including the need for deference, and centre on needs for minimum, medium, and high degrees of fairness.

While the need to return to a greater contextual approach is warranted, I am doubtful that a categorization based on fairness will achieve much different results than a categorization based on reasonableness. Presumably, a reasonable decision will in most instances be fair, and a fair decision should be capable of being justified as reasonable. It would also be hard to explain to potential parties to administrative decisions why they are only entitled to "minimal fairness," while others are legally entitled to high degrees of fairness. Conceptualizing "fairness" as a variable standard is highly problematic. The hallmark of public decision-making in a democracy is that those decisions can be justified on criteria of both fairness and reasonableness.

More broadly, though, it could be argued the "fairness" approach narrows the scope of contextualization to the impact of decisions on the individual. Although such an interpretation is not necessarily the case, I suspect courts would interpret fairness as "fairness to the parties" directly affected by a decision. Reasonableness has the potential for taking into account the nature of the rationale for a decision in the broader context of state policy considerations. While this could be built into a fairness consideration, it is not clear to me that the courts would follow this path. Arguably, one of the difficulties the courts have faced in making the standards of review work is precisely that they have not had a sufficiently broad understanding of the governance structure in which administrative boards operate when considering standards of review. Replacing reasonableness with fairness will not address this more fundamental difficulty. Indeed, it may be interpreted by some courts as an invitation to impose further judicial standards and judicial understandings of reasonableness, rather than defer to administrative expertise.

Conclusion

Administrative decision-making takes a wide range of forms. It can include everything from discretionary decisions to those that are highly constrained by legislative and regulatory requirements. Administrative boards and tribunals play an important role in overseeing state decision-making but also in shaping and framing policy outcomes themselves. In this context, they often stand at the hub of a complex array of governance structures, providing a representative context in which both state and nonstate actors articulate their interests. At the same time, the administrative board itself is a state actor, although outside the usual hierarchical structure of line departments.

The decisions of administrative boards represent a juridical approach to decision-making but also an administrative approach. They straddle the judicial and the administrative worlds. They are also subject to oversight by the courts. To a certain extent, there has always been an uncomfortable relationship between administrative boards and the courts. This reflects the Diceyan framework that underpins the administrative law of judicial review. Administrative boards may have been structural heretics within the state, but they were also juridical heretics from the point of view of the courts. Over time, courts have come to appreciate the presence of administrative boards and have developed more flexible and contextual approaches to judicial review. This has been particularly evident in the area of procedure, where the courts have successfully developed frameworks that, while establishing a baseline for good administrative practice, have left administrative decision-makers a great deal of flexibility to determine what processes are appropriate in particular contexts.

In the area of standards of review, however, the courts have been less successful. Here, they have come up against their own limitations in that they lack the conceptual tools to understand the changing governance structure of the state and integrate an understanding of the policy significance of administrative boards into their decisions. As a result, while the courts have attempted to develop a more functional approach, they have tended to resort to old approaches rooted in traditional understandings of the state, administration, and the role of the courts. Consequently, the courts seem particularly ill-equipped to facilitate administrative reform. It is very likely, therefore, that the courts will continue to develop standards of review on a relatively ad hoc basis. While there may be halting moves towards contextualism, these will likely prove to be inadequate and incomplete.

This raises the question of what is to be done. There are three possible options. The first would be for the courts to continue to operate as they have. This has involved a gradual and halting movement towards contextualism. Yet, this process is incomplete and partial at best, and is frequently subject to pendulum swings between greater and lesser deference to administrative boards. This, in my view, is the least desirable option. Second, the courts could develop the contextual skills necessary to better understand the policy and governance context in which administrative boards and tribunals operate. This, however, in my view, cannot be accomplished within a jurisprudential context or through a reliance on the language of enabling legislation. This approach is too narrow and fails to take into account the real nature of governance structures. Nor can it take into account the changing political and policy context in which administrative boards operate. It is, however, doubtful in my opinion, that the courts have either the conceptual tools or the capacity to analyze governance structures. It would likely require expert social scientific testimony and the ability to map administrative structures and assess the policy impact of decisions.

The final option might be to rethink the very nature of judicial review in administrative contexts. If the rationale for creating administrative boards and tribunals was to remove certain types of questions from the courts, then perhaps it is time to apply the same reasoning to the oversight and review of those boards and tribunals. The creation of divisional courts was an attempt to accomplish this by having judges with an interest and background in administrative law hear judicial review cases separate and apart from private law disputes. This logic could be extended by creating specialized "administrative courts." These administrative courts might include judges and lawyers but could also include those with experience in the operation of administrative tribunals. They would operate outside the judicial structure and would not be "courts" as such. They would be free of many of the jurisprudential limits of the courts and better placed to understand and appreciate the administrative and governance context in which boards operate.

Just how these administrative appeal courts would operate and be structured requires careful consideration. This is a direction that administrative law scholarship, both within law schools and schools of public administration, should be oriented towards. Dicey was opposed to the expansion of administrative boards because they seemed to usurp the courts. Perhaps we can be less sceptical and somewhat bolder. Within the context of the review of administrative boards and tribunals, perhaps it is time to seriously consider whether there is a better structure than the courts.

NOTES

[1]   "Boards" and "tribunals" are generic terms that are used to refer to administrative regulatory agencies that operate in a quasi-judicial manner. In addition to their regulatory and policy functions, they also exercise a judicial/adjudicative function. "Tribunal" is a slightly more specific term and usually refers to a board that has a tripartite (i.e., three panel members) decision-making structure.

REFERENCES

Arthurs, Harry. (1989). "Rethinking Administrative Law: A Slightly Dicey Business." *Osgoode Hall Law Journal.* 17: 1–45.

Dicey, A. V. (1902). *An Introduction to the Study of the Law of the Constitution.* London: MacMillan.

Dwivedi, O. P., and J. I. Gow. (1999). *From Bureaucracy to Public Management: The Administrative Culture of the Government of Canada.* Peterborough, ON: Broadview Press.

Hiebert, Janet. (1996). *Limiting Rights: The Dilemma of Judicial Review.* Montreal: McGill-Queen's University Press.

———. (2002). *Charter Conflicts: What Is Parliament's Role?* Montreal: McGill-Queen's University Press.

Hodgetts, J. E. (1971). *The Canadian Public Service, 1867–1970.* Toronto: University of Toronto Press.

Inwood, Greg. (2004). *Understanding Canadian Public Administration: An Introduction to Theory and Practice.* Toronto: Prentice-Hall.

Kelly, James. (2005). *Governing with the Charter: Legislative and Judicial Activism and the Framers' Intent.* Vancouver: UBC Press.

Kernaghan, Kenneth, and David Siegel. (1999). *Public Administration in Canada.* Toronto: ITP Nelson.

Leyland, Peter, and Terry Woods. (1997). *Administrative Law*. London: Blackstone Press.

McCann, Michael, and Helena Silverstein. (1993). "Social Movements and the American State: Legal Moblization as a Strategy for Democratization." In *A Different Kind of State? Popular Power and Democratic Administration*, edited by Greg Albo, David Langille, and Leo Panitch, 131–143. Toronto: Oxford University Press.

Morton F. L., and R. Knopff. (2000). *The Charter Revolution and the Court Party*. Peterborough, ON: Broadview Press.

Mullan, David. (1997). "Administrative Law at the Margins." In *The Province of Administrative Law*, edited by M. Taggart. Oxford: Hart Publishing.

Oliver, Dawn. (1987). "Is the Ultra Vires Rule the Basis of Judicial Review?" *Public Law*. 543–569.

Osborne, David, and Ted Gaebler. (1992). *Reinventing Government: How the Entrepreneurial Spirit Is Transforming the Public Sector*. Reading, MA: Addison-Wesley.

Sheldrick, Byron. (2004). *Perils and Possibilities: Social Activism and the Law*. Halifax, NS: Fernwood Press.

Shields, John, and Mitchell B. Evans. (1998). *Shrinking the State: Globalization and Public Administration "Reform."* Halifax, NS: Fernwood Press.

Sossin, Lorne, and Colleen Flood. (2007). "The Contextual Turn: Iacobuccci's Legacy and the Standard of Review in Administrative Law." *University of Toronto Law Journal*. 57: 581–606.

Sossin, Lorne, and France Houle. (2006). "Tribunals and Guidelines: Exploring the Relationship between Fairness and Legitimacy in Administrative Decision-Making." *Canadian Public Administration*. 46: 283–307.

Sossin, Lorne, and Laura Pottie. (2005). "Demystifying the Boundaries of Public Law: Policy, Discretion, and Social Welfare." *University of British Columbia Law Review*. 147–187.

Wilson, Woodrow. (1887). "The Study of Administration." *Political Studies Quarterly*. 2: 197–222.

ABOUT THE CONTRIBUTORS

Peter Aucoin is the Eric Dennis Memorial Professor of Government and Political Science and a professor of public administration at Dalhousie University.

Caroline Dufour is an assistant professor in the School of Public Policy and Administration at York University.

O. P. Dwivedi is a professor emeritus in the Department of Political Science at the University of Guelph.

C. E. S. Franks is a professor emeritus in the Department of Political Studies and School of Physical and Health Education at Queen's University.

James Iain Gow is a professor emeritus in the Department of Political Science at l'Université de Montréal.

John Halligan is a research professor of government and public administration in the Faculty of Business and Government at the University of Canberra, Australia.

Keith Henderson is a professor of political science and chairperson pro tem in the Department of Political Science at the State University of New York, College at Buffalo.

J. E. Hodgetts is a professor emeritus in the Department of Political Science at the University of Toronto.

Kenneth Kernaghan is a professor emeritus in the Department of Political Science at Brock University.

Luc Juillet is the director of the Graduate School of Public and International Affairs at the University of Ottawa.

Evert Lindquist is a professor and the director of the School of Public Administration at the University of Victoria.

Tim A. Mau is an assistant professor in the Department of Political Science at the University of Guelph.

John Meisel is the Sir Edward Peacock Professor of Political Science Emeritus at Queen's University.

A. Paul Pross is a professor emeritus in the School of Public Administration at Dalhousie University.

Ken Rasmussen is the director of the Johnson-Shoyama Graduate School of Public Policy at the University of Regina.

Donald J. Savoie is a Canada Research Chair in public administration and governance at the Université de Moncton.

Byron Sheldrick is the chair of the Department of Political Science at the University of Guelph.

Paul G. Thomas is the Duff Roblin Professor of Government at the University of Manitoba.

INDEX

10. Emmanuel Brunet-Jailly (ed.) 2007
    Borderlands – Comparing Border Security in North America and Europe

9. Christian Rouillard, E. Montpetit, I. Fortier, and A.G. Gagnon 2006
   Reengineering the State – Toward an Impoverishment of Quebec Governance

8. Jeffrey Roy 2006
   E-Government in Canada

7. Gilles Paquet 2005
   The New Geo-Governance – A Baroque Approach

6. C. Andrew, M. Gattinger, M.S. Jeannotte, and W. Straw (eds) 2005
   Accounting for Culture – Thinking Through Cultural Citizenship

5. P .Boyer, L. Cardinal, and D. Headon (eds) 2004
   From Subjects to Citizens – A Hundred Years of Citizenship in Australia and Canada

4. Linda Cardinal and D. Headon (eds.) 2002
   Shaping Nations – Constitutionalism and Society in Australia and Canada

3. Linda Cardinal et Caroline Andrew (dir.) 2001
   La démocratie à l'épreuve de la gouvernance

2. Gilles Paquet 1999
   Governance Through Social Learning

1. David McInnes 1999, 2005
   Taking It to the Hill – The Complete Guide to Appearing Before Parliamentary Committees

Composed by Brad Horning in Adobe Garamond Pro 9.5 on 12.5

The paper used in this publication is
Rolland Opaque Bright White 50lb

Printed and bound in Canada

Marquis Book Printing Inc.

Québec, Canada
2009